Praise for the hardback

'Many new books with a sporting theme are tumbling onto the shelves but I doubt any will be superior to the illuminating and comprehensive biography of Sir Matt Busby by the irrepressible football sage Patrick Barclay. The events and emotions are recounted with haunting eloquence by Barclay: a master of his craft.'
— **Jim Holden**, *Sunday Express*

'Must-buy is over-used – but not here. Patrick Barclay has elegantly written a magisterial, exhaustively researched book, with an irresistible emotional pull ... A magnificent tribute to the creator of a footballing superpower.'
— *Sunday Mirror*

'The research is prodigious and the result is totally enthralling ... a flood of fresh insights and anecdotes ... Barclay's handling of the disaster is exhaustive, sensitive and deeply moving.'
— **Patrick Collins**

'Magnificent.'
— **Alan Pattullo**, *Scotland on Sunday*

'A wholly elegant account of the pivotal figure in Manchester United's history.'
— **Giles Smith**, **Sports Books of the Year**, *The Times*

'The eye is met with authenticity on every page.'
— **John Roberts, author of** *The Team That Wouldn't Die*

'An outstanding book.'
— **Phil Shaw**, *Backpass*

ABOUT THE AUTHOR

Patrick Barclay began his career in football writing with the *Guardian* in Manchester in the mid-1970s. Barclay became one of Sir Matt's many acquaintances in the newspaper world and in 1994, having moved to the *Observer* by way of the *Independent*, attended the unforgettable match against Everton at Old Trafford that swiftly followed the great man's death. In that year Barclay was voted Britain's leading sports writer.

Barclay later worked for the *Sunday Telegraph*, *The Times* and the *Evening Standard* in London before retiring from regular journalism at the end of his tenth European Championship in 2016. He covered nine World Cups. Barclay has written acclaimed biographies of Sir Alex Ferguson and José Mourinho and is also the author of *The Life and Times of Herbert Chapman*.

ALSO BY PATRICK BARCLAY

Football – Bloody Hell!: the biography of Alex Ferguson

Mourinho: Further anatomy of a winner

The Life & Times of Herbert Chapman: The story of one of football's most influential figures

Sir MATT BUSBY

THE MAN WHO MADE
A FOOTBALL CLUB

PATRICK BARCLAY

EBURY
PRESS

3 5 7 9 10 8 6 4

Ebury Press, an imprint of Ebury Publishing
20 Vauxhall Bridge Road
London SW1V 2SA

Ebury Press is part of the Penguin Random House group of companies
whose addresses can be found at global.penguinrandomhouse.com

Penguin
Random House
UK

First published by Ebury Press in 2017
This edition published in 2018

www.penguin.co.uk

A CIP catalogue record for this book is available from the British Library

ISBN 9781785032080

Typeset in India by Integra Software Services Pvt. Ltd, Pondicherry

Printed and bound in Great Britain by Clays Ltd, Elcograf S.p.A.

*This book is dedicated to the Association of Former
Manchester United Players, especially Alan Wardle,
Arthur Albiston, John Aston, Sir Bobby Charlton,
Paddy Crerand, Barry Fry, John Giles, Alan Gowling,
Harry Gregg, Denis Law, Wilf McGuinness,
Sammy McIlroy, Jimmy Ryan, David Sadler,
Alex Stepney, Ian Storey-Moore and Jeff Whitefoot;
to the Busby family, especially Alison and
Irene Busby and Mike Bones; to Barry Hayes
and everyone at the Circus Tavern;
and to the Pussycat.*

CONTENTS

CHAPTER ONE

THE IMMORTAL MANAGER

THE AURA

In 1993, the 84th year of Sir Matt Busby's life, the eminent sports writer Patrick Collins was allotted an enviable task. At the behest of a television company he was to accompany Busby and members of his 1968 Manchester United team, the first representatives of English football to become champions of Europe, on a sentimental journey marking the 25th anniversary of their achievement, memorably completed with a 4–1 triumph over Benfica after extra time at Wembley.

United, now managed by Alex Ferguson with Busby a largely ceremonial club president, had made the team bus available. With Bobby Charlton, Pat Crerand, Alex Stepney and the rest aboard, and Sir Matt reinstalled in the manager's seat at the front, it set off from Old Trafford for London (the 1968 team had travelled by train, but this was no time for pedantry). Collins fondly recalled Busby 'puffing his pipe and watching the motorway slide past' while 'discreetly, without show or fuss, his old boys would take turns to keep him company, reminding him of shared deeds and familiar jokes'.

When the bus arrived at their hotel near Wembley, there was a queue at the reception desk. Denis Law, whom injury had denied a part in the sweat-soaked satisfaction of the final – the Scot's place had been taken by Brian Kidd – marched Busby straight to the front. 'Key for Sir Matt Busby, please,' Law cheerfully demanded, and it was produced. Bobby Charlton guided Busby to his room and half an hour later Collins encountered him in a corridor, his arm resting lightly on the shoulder of Crerand. 'Our bloody luck,' said Crerand, who revered Sir Matt like a father. 'The Boss's room is on the same floor! We won't be getting out tonight.' And Sir Matt smiled at the memory. 'Ah, Paddy,' he said. 'All that was years ago, eh? Years ago.'

Early in the next year, Busby died and Collins's tribute in the *Mail on Sunday* concluded with another memory of the outing:

> I last saw him walking off the Wembley pitch. In the company of George Best, the pair of them moving slowly, deep in conversation. At the mouth of the tunnel a couple of Irish construction workers spotted Best and shouted a raucous greeting. Then they saw his companion, and they straightened their backs and removed their hard hats.

Sir Alex Ferguson was another eloquent witness to the awe Busby inspired: an awe that, when he died, would slip into immortality. Busby had accompanied Ferguson's team to the 1991 final of the Cup Winners' Cup against Barcelona in Rotterdam and Ferguson remembered that, as the bus approached the Feyenoord Stadium, a warming sight was that of the old man's smiling face, 'glowing with pride'. When the bus stopped,

> our supporters were in a frenzy, battering the windows and sides of the bus, urging us with clenched fists ... But as the door swung open and Sir Matt led us out, the clamour ceased instantly and in its place there was polite clapping, which he acknowledged with a dignified wave. There could hardly have been more reverence for the Pope in St Peter's Square.

The analogy resonated with the former United player Alan Gowling. 'Papal,' he said. 'That's the word.' He was speaking in 2016, more than half a century after he had joined United, and Gowling could think of only one comparably charismatic figure at the club in all that time. 'It was at the unveiling of Sir Alex

Ferguson's statue. We were all having a bite to eat when a sudden silence fell over the room. And everyone looked at the door. And Eric Cantona had just walked in. You had to be there to experience it. And that's how it was with Sir Matt.'

Even those with no interest in football were liable to find Busby compelling. The acclaimed Irish novelist John McGahern once saw him walk into the Russell Hotel in Dublin: 'He was an extraordinary presence, like a great politician or theatrical figure. Who is that, we all wondered?'

He was, of course, one of the greatest British football managers ever. He had masterminded, over a quarter of a century, the creation of Britain's biggest and most glamorous football club. He had nearly died in the process, and lost some of his most beloved players in a crashed aircraft at Munich, and yet within a decade made European football history. Amid painfully conflicting emotions, he had given football a new dimension.

Busby had also written the textbook that, consciously or otherwise, Ferguson would use in rebuilding the glory lost after Busby's retirement. Busby's son Sandy, who died in 2014, had an apt way of putting it. 'My dad was the foundation,' he would say, 'and Sir Alex the resurrection.' The coincidence of their methods and principles was extraordinary. A desire to form teams from home-grown youths was only part of it. So was attacking with wingers. And rotating a squad to cope with a heavy workload. All these and many other supposedly Ferguson characteristics – most fundamentally, an insistence that the manager must be the most powerful man at a club – were Busby's.

Nor would Ferguson have been likely to arrive at Old Trafford but for the Busby legacy. 'Without Matt Busby,' wrote David Meek, a perennially respected chronicler of Old Trafford affairs, 'Manchester United might be just another football club.' Prior to leaving Aberdeen in 1986, Ferguson had told his chairman, Dick Donald, that United were one of only two clubs who could tempt him away. That he could mention them in the same breath as Barcelona was due to Busby, whose European champions had emphasised the club's potential by setting an English record average League attendance of nearly 58,000.

Before him, United had never been the best-supported club in England. Even when he had won his first title in 1951/52, they had trailed Tottenham Hotspur, Arsenal and Newcastle United by nearly 10,000. But they overtook everyone in a hurry and just before Munich, with huge numbers clamouring to see European ties, had announced plans to accommodate 100,000. Under Ferguson the upward trend was to recur and, having enlarged and modernised Old Trafford, the club became accustomed to disappointing aspirants to its 76,000 seats. And twice United had ruled Europe again; the resurrection was complete.

Although in terms of trophies Ferguson was the more successful, simple comparison of his statistics with Busby's would be misleading. Busby led United to five English titles, Ferguson thirteen. But seldom in Busby's time, which began with post-war austerity and saw the promise of power perish amid the wreckage of an underinsured airliner, were United able to beat all domestic rivals in the transfer market; even in the euphoric aftermath of the European Cup triumph, they could not prevent the Fulham striker Allan Clarke from joining Leicester City instead. Ferguson, though obliged to use all his skills in resisting challenges from Roman Abramovich's *nouveau riche* Chelsea and an Abu Dhabi-funded Manchester City, was backed by the strongest economy in English football for more than half of his stewardship and used it, often threatening or breaking transfer records in the engagement of such key players as Roy Keane and Rio Ferdinand (while also picking up his share of bargains like Eric Cantona and Peter Schmeichel).

Busby made a profit on transfers while building the team he unhesitatingly considered his greatest – the side destroyed at Munich – and, despite the ravages of the crash, he spent only a net £12,000 per year on the reconstruction that culminated in the European title.

Also, in Busby's time, the game was more egalitarian, deliberately so in terms of the distribution of revenue. Ascendancy would change hands more often than in the era of Ferguson, whose privilege was to arrive at Old Trafford just as League rules changed to allow clubs to keep all their gate receipts. Thus, as soon as Ferguson had restored United's attendances to Busby levels, he acquired a muscle in the market that Busby never had.

Busby guided United to the European title once, Ferguson twice. But Busby had only five seasons in the competition known as the European Cup; Ferguson had nineteen in its successor, the Champions League. Busby never failed to reach the semi-finals and it is hard to believe that his Babes, had everyone survived, would not have been leading contenders for the crown Real Madrid ultimately surrendered to Benfica in 1961.

The recovery from Munich enhanced Busby's air of greatness. No football manager – not even his contemporaries Bill Shankly and Jock Stein – could hold a wider audience than this unpretentious and devoutly Roman Catholic wielder of influence, who took to management so naturally that he hardly had to raise his voice and never swore, according to Crerand, 'even though, where he came from [Lanarkshire mining country, not far from Crerand's Glasgow or Ferguson's Govan], swearing was a second language'.

If Busby had been an actor – and how well he would have been suited to that profession with his elegant bearing and dress sense, strong but gently expressive features and firmly mellifluous brogue – he might have played a statesman or a magnate, a cardinal or even messiah. Anyone to whom strangers were supposed to be drawn by sheer presence. Anyone except a mere football manager. Certainly not a football manager of the kind portrayed as Busby in a piece of 'faction' televised by the BBC after his death which, in making him look more like Arthur Daley than a football man of rare dignity, upset his son Sandy. The noted Shakespearean Brian Cox made a better fist in the 2013 feature film *Believe*, but that was such hokum about how in retirement Busby was supposed to have coached a five-a-side team to success after one of the players stole his wallet ('Cringeworthy' – *Guardian*).

The only story ever worth telling about Sir Matt Busby would be the true story. Except that, among the young or uninitiated, few would believe it.

It would go thus: a boy loses his father in the First World War and, having left school to work down a coal-mine, becomes a professional footballer, only for his career to be curtailed by the Second World War, towards the end of which, despite having no experience of management, he is offered the post at Manchester United; although the club's stadium has been bombed out of use by the Luftwaffe, he quickly organises the players into one of the best teams in the country; they win an acclaimed FA Cup final, then become League champions three times but, just as they are beginning to convince an enthralled following they can become champions of all Europe, a terrible tragedy all but destroys what Busby has built, and threatens the life of Busby himself; and yet he is nursed back to health and ten years later ...

In enacting all that and more, Busby elevated the status of the football manager. It was not so much that football became more popular – although that process did occur, and was hastened in the land of Busby's employment by English triumph in the World Cup of 1966, just two years before he made his own indelible mark on the same Wembley soil – but that his character, his beguiling exercise of a renascent power, seemed to enrich even those who cared little for the game or the fortunes of Manchester United. Alf Ramsey, who had guided England through the 1966 campaign, was also knighted. But eyes did not follow him as they followed Sir Matt.

Various walks of life produced magnetic figures in the 1950s and 1960s: in popular music Elvis Presley, in politics John F. Kennedy and the latter-day Winston Churchill, in sport Muhammad Ali (né Cassius Clay) and Pelé. Busby was football management's contribution to this generation of giants.

When television in Britain had only two channels, some programmes commanded huge audiences, appearing to bring the country together. One was *This Is Your Life*, in which famous personalities were confronted with family and friends, some from the distant past, and their stories told. Busby was the first to be featured twice. Yet, for all his star quality and way with clothes – when he showed cuff, it was the right amount, and his autumn colours subtly blended – he was a man of little ostentation who lived with his wife Jean through the glory years in a modest three-bedroom house of red brick a couple of miles from United's stadium and whose nightlife ideal would be a sing-song with friends and a glass of his favourite Scotch whisky, Black Label. After Sunday breakfast and Mass with the family, he loved to chat with the priest. Then he would drive to Old Trafford to check on the condition of his players, all of whom had to report to the ground on the morning after Saturday matches.

During his time at United, the club's support multiplied both in England and across the world. And no wonder; the unwanted emotional mountain of Munich apart, his next outstanding collection had featured three European Footballers of the Year – and two runners-up – in the space of five seasons. He had built the institution Alex Ferguson would crave.

A triumvirate of great Scottish managers – Busby, Shankly, Stein – had flourished while Ferguson remained a player in

Scotland. Ferguson had then himself blossomed in management at Aberdeen, where his twinkling confidant Donald often talked of United as 'the biggest challenge in football'. Ferguson saw the argument: it was long after the lustre of the Busby era had gone, during the apparently interminable years when Liverpool had replaced United at the pinnacle of the English game, and there was a wonderful work of restoration to be completed, a towering reputation to be claimed.

THE BEQUEST TO FERGUSON

In the 2007 edition of his superb book *A Strange Kind of Glory*, Eamon Dunphy described Busby as both 'the first great football man' and 'the last great football man' and, while admirers of Herbert Chapman might gently query the former contention, the latter would stridently demand revision in the light of Ferguson.

It could nevertheless be said that Ferguson's greatest achievement was so faithfully to have reproduced the work of Busby: to have taken the legacy and brought it back to life. Busby lived just long enough to see this footballing miracle. Having enjoyed the FA Cup win in 1990 that lifted some of the pressure of history from Ferguson, then the Rotterdam victory a year later, he was at Old Trafford, memorably elated, when in 1993 they celebrated a first League title since his time.

He was dead before they retained it a year later. He knew the future was safe, though; when friends had lost faith in Ferguson between his appointment in 1986 and the 1990 midwinter of Mark Robins and the Cup run, Busby had calmly insisted it would all come right because his fellow Scot knew no other way: 'He'll do the business, mark my words.'

In 2016 – three years after Ferguson had retired – he spoke at a dinner held by the Association of Former Manchester United Players in honour of Sir Bobby Charlton, to whom he directly addressed the declaration: 'I owe my life at Manchester United to you.' This was gracious in the extreme, and true in the senses that Charlton had both advocated Ferguson's appointment and supported him when things appeared to be going wrong. But there was also quite a debt to Busby, of whose management Charlton had been a child – even if Charlton always insisted it was Busby's assistant, Jimmy

Murphy, who had done most to form his greatness as a player. Busby's latter years around the club were of unquestioned comfort during Ferguson's days of doubt.

When Ferguson entered Old Trafford and caught a whiff of the old man's pipe smoke, he knew words of wisdom and reassurance were just around the corner and up a flight of stairs. 'That,' said Crerand, 'was the great thing about Alex [compared with some of the preceding managers who had failed to escape the shadow of Busby] – *he spoke to Matt*. And Matt would have loved it.'

One difference between the Busby and Ferguson reigns was that, while Busby was blessed with the indispensable assistance of just one right-hand man in Murphy, a variety from Archie Knox and the former Busby Babes Brian Kidd and Jimmy Ryan to Carlos Queiroz (twice) and René Meulensteen served Ferguson, most of them, including Steve McClaren, leaving as soon as an irresistible managerial challenge arose. It was to Murphy's credit as well as Busby's that United did not fall into such a lasting depression as Torino after the Superga crash which, in 1949, claimed the Italian club's entire squad. Having won five consecutive *Serie A* titles, Torino had to wait until 1976 for the only one obtained since and seemed perpetually overshadowed by their local rivals, Juventus.

The question of whether Busby gave enough weight to Murphy's part in United's rise and rise again caused many to withhold the status of a paragon. The dramatist Keith Dewhurst, who, like David Meek, covered United for a newspaper in the aftermath of Munich, later wrote:

> If David Lloyd George was the most charismatic person I have ever laid eyes on ... Matt Busby was the most charismatic I have known ... Yet he was never my hero, because I knew how ruthless he had been in the creation of his myth and power base. My hero was ... Jimmy Murphy.

Others wondered if sometimes Busby deemed a veneer of respectability more important than what lay beneath. Some thought him mean with the club's money. The European Cup winner David Sadler, as kindly and charitable an ex-player as any in the Old Trafford hall that was packed for the Charlton tribute, remembered feeling let down over a testimonial. But by and large, for cloaking a powerful ego in warm humanity, Busby was revered. More so than

Ferguson. They came from different times, though: Busby from a harder but more respectful age in which authority could be exerted with a smile. If you had it.

By the time Ferguson went to primary school, the Second World War was over. Busby had served through it. By comparison, people of Ferguson's generation enjoyed a stress-free life in which, leaving war aside, even being a passenger in an aircraft came to be safe: a life of relative trivia in which Western humanity had to devise its own dramas, such as the soap opera of football to which Ferguson lent, along with perennially entertaining team play, touchline rants and provocative abuse of mainly, but not exclusively, referees.

Perhaps Ferguson, had his lifetime coincided with rather than overlapped Busby's, would have desisted from calling Jimmy Hill a 'prat' for highlighting a nasty foul by Eric Cantona at Norwich in 1994. This was at a time, as the writer, broadcaster and United fan Michael Crick noted, when the Ferguson team of Cantona, Paul Ince and Mark Hughes were losing the public popularity built by Busby's Law, Best and Charlton.

It might fairly have been added that Law, at least, and Crerand, had been involved in enough trouble on the field during Busby's time. At any rate, Ferguson wrote Jimmy Hill a prompt and disarming apology and in 1995, after Cantona had launched a flying kick at an annoying member of the Crystal Palace crowd, he was again sensitive enough inwardly to question the degree of his support for the Frenchman. He discussed it with his friend Hugh McIlvanney and at one stage told the venerable sports writer of his wife Cathy's advice. She had said: 'You'd better let everybody out there know you have values that rise above results, that you have the same concern with the standards of Manchester United as Sir Matt Busby had.' Ferguson proceeded to steer a diplomatic course and, after Cantona had served a long suspension, got a wiser player back.

In the context of the industrial west of Scotland, from which both Busby and Ferguson came – Busby's father was a Lanarkshire miner and Ferguson's worked in a Govan shipyard – it was an interesting coincidence that both should choose partners from across the denominational divide. Busby fell for Jean Menzies, from a staunchly Protestant family (although she chose to convert during their engagement), and Ferguson, a Protestant by upbringing, for the Catholic Cathy Holding.

Both Busby and Ferguson had respectable playing careers but it was as managerial personalities that their characteristics most uncannily converged. Each extended his influence by remembering names, for example. Ferguson noted this in Jock Stein but might as well have picked it up from Busby. A classic case involved the football writer Frank McGhee. When young and obscure, he had done a single stint as a match reporter for the *Manchester Evening News*, travelling with United to Charlton Athletic. Otherwise, he had never been in Busby's company. Four years later, standing outside Hampden Park on the day of a Scotland v. England match, he felt a tap on the shoulder. 'Hello, Frank,' said Busby. 'Nice to see you again.'

Busby would infrequently have seen Arnold Howe, because he was the *Daily Express*'s man in the north-east. In the late 1960s, United were playing there and Howe, arriving late at the post-match press conference, found himself on the edge of a huddle of questioners. A little man, he could hardly see Busby or hear anything and was beginning to feel insecure, as journalists do when they might miss a spicy 'quote'. Busby spotted him. 'Hello, Arnold,' he said. A path cleared and Howe felt ten feet tall.

Occasionally, said the former United reserve Alan Wardle, he would need a little help with a name. 'Say you were at a function. Matt might ask, "Who's that?" and you'd say, "Fred Smith." Later Fred might be using the next urinal and Matt would turn and say, "All right, Fred?" Many have peed down their trousers because of that.'

Although neither Busby nor many managers of his time could be bothered much with mind games, he did know how to lift a team's head from defeat. When his United Babes were denied a place in the 1957 European final by Real Madrid, he went into the press conference and made sure the next day's papers stressed their youth; it would be different in the future. There was another Ferguson moment that night, when Busby walked on to the Old Trafford pitch and tapped his watch, as if to tell the French referee he should have allowed United's strong finish more time.

Squad rotation? Ferguson might have been the modern master, but Busby had done it almost as soon as he took United into Europe – against the League's wishes but with the prior connivance of Sir Stanley Rous at the Football Association – in 1956/57, when they were chasing the Treble a Ferguson side completed in 1999. Because of the quality and quantity of youngsters being produced by Busby and Murphy, there was a big squad and this was also a way of keeping everyone as happy as possible.

Youth development? In the mid-1950s Don Revie was injured at Manchester City and took the opportunity to watch a reserve derby. He immediately proclaimed that United were equipped to dominate the game for the next ten years, and in style, for the passing football of Busby's young second string reminded him of the famous Hungarians who had just thrashed England twice. A few years after Ferguson had gone to Old Trafford, the Luton manager David Pleat made a similar declaration about the United youth team featuring Paul Scholes, David Beckham, Nicky Butt and the Neville brothers.

In the ensuing ten years, Ferguson's United won seven League titles. Busby's United had won two out of two in 1958 and the question of how many more was to remain poignantly unanswerable.

Wingers? Ferguson, with Andrei Kanchelskis and Lee Sharpe, David Beckham (a winger of a sort) and Ryan Giggs, not to mention Cristiano Ronaldo, the winger who grew into Superman, always attacked on a broad front. To Busby, wingers were so fundamental that, in the days before substitutes, he would often use injured players at centre-forward rather than on the wings, where they were normally sent. 'Full power must be maintained on the wings,' he said, 'because football is won and lost on the wings.' Wingers were also, Crerand pointed out, his first line of defence. 'The opposition had to get past them before they could have a go at the full-backs. That was how we played nearly all the time.'

As for general footballing philosophy, Busby was the nearer to the purism that became associated with Pep Guardiola when in charge of Barcelona between 2008 and 2012; Busby yearned simply to field 11 ball-players and see how they got on and once fantasised about it in print, suggesting the England manager try it. He became accustomed to criticism for the firmness of his belief in possession.

After Ray Wood had been badly injured in the 1957 FA Cup final, he argued that goalkeepers should be exempt from physical challenge so that, having got the ball, they could restart play with care; even half a century later, that might have been regarded in England as over protective. Ferguson, though invariably practical, understood that the legacy included an obligation to entertain and excite as Busby's teams had. That was part of the reason why, like

Busby, he proved so difficult to replace. His teams, too, were as stylish as substantial.

'Matt Busby's attitude to football was so simple it was frightening,' said John Doherty, a talented Mancunian midfield player of the 1950s generally restricted to the fringes at Old Trafford due to knee problems. He quoted the astonishment of Noel Cantwell, who had come from Ron Greenwood's academic hothouse at West Ham, at hearing 'the Boss's credo that, if he had to tell his players how to play, then he wouldn't have signed them in the first place'.

Although his last words to his sides were indeed usually 'Go out and play', or 'Go out and entertain' or 'Go out and enjoy yourselves', Busby hotly denied that they performed 'off the cuff'. He wrote that, throughout the club, they worked on a pattern so they became 'thought-readers'. If this pattern, which had been 'torn to shreds at Munich and created again', represented playing off the cuff, 'then my critics know more about the game than I do'. But the football writer and broadcaster Donny Davies had wisely written after a title triumph in 1952 that Busby was 'a believer in the certainty of good football's eventual rewards' and, in that sense, he influenced Bob Paisley, whom he first met when a player at Liverpool before the Second World War – and who was certainly to share his aversion to tactical mumbo-jumbo.

Truly great teams? Busby and Ferguson could be said to have produced three each over reigns of roughly a quarter-century's duration. Patience? Busby, like Ferguson, took six full seasons to win the League, having bought time with an FA Cup. Artful flexibility? Busby knew better than to ruffle the centre-forward of his first great team, the prickly Jack Rowley, instead quietly sympathising with him over the poor service others were providing to the front. Ferguson took care never to upset Eric Cantona, even ignoring a breach of specifically issued dress rules when the Frenchman turned up for a civic reception in a tracksuit.

Persuasiveness in negotiation? Busby saw his men one by one and, having had the club's position outlined, they usually signed. And thanked him on the way out. And then wondered how to explain such submissiveness to the others. Ferguson was equally skilful, as Mark McGhee remembered from Aberdeen: 'I almost signed the contract without seeing it. While I was listening to him, he slipped the pen into my hand. He was in total control.'

Then there was the succession. Busby didn't ask Wilf McGuinness to take over in 1969; he told him. Ferguson acted likewise with David Moyes in 2013, even though Moyes was employed by Everton at the time.

Keeping nepotism in the family? The only differences between Jimmy Mathie, Busby's scout in Scotland, and Martin Ferguson, who checked on talent for Alex Ferguson from a base north of the border, were that Martin Ferguson travelled more widely and Jimmy Mathie was, strictly speaking, only a half-brother.

Managerial omnipotence? Busby, after the Wembley triumph of 1948, got rid of one of his finest players, Johnny Morris, for being 'very disinclined' to have a spell in the reserves. 'There could be only one boss,' Busby reflected.

> Otherwise we should possibly have twelve bosses and the gifted individuals I had striven to mould into a team might disintegrate into eleven individuals again … much as I admire individual, spontaneous brilliance, the greatest orchestras need a conductor.

When Wayne Rooney issued a press statement challenging Ferguson on transfer policy in 2010, Ferguson's thoughts were:

> This is a club which bases all its history and tradition on the loyalty and trust between managers and players and the club. That goes back to the days of Sir Matt Busby. That's what it's founded on.

But perhaps the most bizarre similarity between the United lives of Busby and Ferguson is that both, through friendships with rich men which they believed would enhance their own power bases, inadvertently caused the club to fall into profiteering hands. Busby encouraged Louis Edwards to become United's chairman but, after Edwards had fully understood how wealthy his family could become through club share dealings, a promise that Busby's son Sandy would follow his own son Martin on to the board was repeatedly broken. When Louis Edwards died, Martin could have put matters right from the Busbys' point of view but, believing that, while Sandy had his father's affability and absence of airs and graces, he lacked quite the same tact or sophistication, he never got around to it during an immensely lucrative chairmanship that ended in 2002. Sandy remained a popular figure around the club, occupying his father's seat in the directors' box at matches between 1994 and his own death in 2014, never saying a public word against the Edwards family.

It was in the afterglow of the 1999 Treble triumph under Ferguson that John Magnier and J.P. McManus began to build up a 29 per cent holding in United. Magnier, one of the world's leading racehorse breeders, and his fellow Irishman, a big-time gambler, had befriended Ferguson. In due course, Magnier made Ferguson a present (as Ferguson understood it) of the stallion Rock of Gibraltar, which became so successful that, when it retired in November 2002, its stud rights were estimated to be worth £50 million.

Ferguson, subsequently hearing little from Magnier, got in touch with the stud registrars and discovered that his name was not entered next to the Rock's. Magnier made Ferguson several offers to drop his claim to the rights, the most generous being £7 million, but Ferguson refused and engaged lawyers, who posted a writ and even argued that the horse's value had been enhanced by association with the United manager's name. This was enough for Magnier to take off the gloves. He sent the Old Trafford board 99 questions about, among other things, 'conflicts of interest' in transfer business – and the list found its way into the *Daily Mail*. It was fortunate that such a dispute did not take place during the fastidious Busby's lifetime.

An out-of-court settlement brought Ferguson a mere £2.5 million, even though the Rock's earnings were now said to exceed £100 million, but more significantly the battle had disaffected Magnier from United, where supporters' pro-Ferguson chants had told him where to stick his 99 questions. In May 2005, he and McManus sold out to the Glazer family, filling the support with even greater dismay because the Americans not only took United back into private ownership but left the club, traditionally a model of footballing prudence, with a £650 million debt, interest on which had to be paid to the financiers of the takeover. Ferguson, ever the pragmatist, defended the Glazers at every opportunity, and continued to do so until his retirement in 2013. And, because the supporters were so grateful for United's achievements in his time, there was hardly a whisper of his brush with the law of unwanted consequences.

Busby might have sympathised too. Had he been around, it would certainly have brought back a few memories.

As would Ferguson's last match in charge of United. A 5–5 draw away to West Bromwich Albion, with the squandering of a three-goal lead: Busby's Babes had done that in each of their last two matches before Munich, each away from home. First, they had beaten Arsenal 5–4 in a classic at Highbury and then they had hung on for a 3–3 draw with Red Star in Belgrade to reach the European Cup semi-finals on a 5–4 aggregate. Those who could remember Busby's heydays identified them with high-scoring matches: the 1948 FA Cup final, in which Blackpool were beaten 4–2; the wonderful if ill-starred abandon of that 1958 midwinter; the 5–1 victory of what would become known as the 1968 team away to Benfica with George Best outshining Eusébio and the historic 4–1 win over the same club at Wembley.

Although the game had changed and defences tightened by the time Ferguson arrived at Old Trafford, he too entertained richly, his 1999 team twice sharing six goals with Barcelona on their path to a European final whose unforgettable culmination in stoppage time was redolent of the Busby tradition as well as his own natural defiance. All through Ferguson's reign, and after, the slopes of Old Trafford rang to songs and chants in praise of Busby – even the calypso introduced in honour of the Babes and their 'football taught by Matt Bus-bee' – as if to confirm his immortality.

GRACE UNDER PRESSURE

When Ferguson stepped down, he was justifiably hailed as the greatest of managers. But great men are judged, wrote Michael Crick, at least partly by 'the lasting differences they make to the world'. Busby, though not a highbrow – in *Who's Who* he listed his interests as 'golf, football' – was a visionary. In pursuit of his concept of an Old Trafford fit for European champions, he had helped to make the club an aggregate profit, from his arrival to the summer before Munich, of £300,000, the present value of which would be best calculated as ten times the amount United had paid for their most expensive player at that time, Tommy Taylor.

He was also, by the testimony of his friend Father Patrick McMahon, a living example of courage by Ernest Hemingway's definition: grace under pressure. Among the many who agreed with that was Bernard Halford, for 39 years the club secretary at Manchester City. 'You would never see Matt's temper,' said Halford. 'He knew what he wanted and how to get it without a fuss. He built a great team after coming off his deathbed. And still kept his even temperament. And didn't think he was owed anything in life.' His faith, Halford added, was 'a wonderful thing'. It did much to shape a man regarded by many as the best they ever met.

Busby was also a creature of his environment. Of his mother, his beloved 'Maw'. Of his warm-hearted grandfather Jimmy Greer, who created a fondness for rascals in the Runyonesque image of Busby's great friend Paddy McGrath, characters who, as Eamon Dunphy so elegantly put it, had spirits freer than his own. Of the mining community in which he grew up, which instilled in him senses of comradeship, interdependence and proportion, and demanded physical and mental courage; mining communities had produced Herbert Chapman and others and, after Busby, would raise Stein, Shankly and Bob Paisley.

Busby was a creature of the football to which his father just had time to introduce him. 'I saw magic in those early days,' Busby was to recall, 'the magic of two of the greatest footballers in the game's history in one small village.' Their names were Alex James and Hughie Gallacher. As Busby took his first steps, the land of his birth was so rich in football that, had there been FIFA rankings, Scotland would have been top. The English could beat anyone. Except, more often than not, Scotland. And the relative subtlety of the Scottish style was fundamental, as Busby developed, to his own.

But truly the main influence in Busby's life was his mother. She gave him such goodness that he could resist the corrosive effects of envy or bad luck. Something of his Orbiston upbringing went with him to Munich and, when eventually he died, it was with the same dignity as he had learned to live.

CHAPTER TWO

ORBISTON ORIGINS

A FOOTBALLER HAS COME

A couple of dark hours before the dawn of 26 May 1909, as the bronchial King Edward VII slept in his palace bed, perhaps enjoying a dreamy premonition of his horse Minoru's victory in the Derby that afternoon, an event of infinitely greater significance in the history of sport took place in a coal-miner's cottage some 400 miles to the north. A son was born to the 17-year-old Helen Busby, known as Nellie, and her husband Alexander, aged 20. The boy would be called Matthew.

'A footballer has come into this house today.'

The doctor said it and the proud father Alex, who loved his football, was there to hear it. There was time before the men of the day shift would hurtle in whirring, clanking cage-loads to the depths of the Orbiston mine and get to work with picks and shovels. The doctor washed his hands and packed his instruments and went for breakfast, leaving the Busbys' humble home to welcome the Wednesday light.

The King's horse duly won by a short head at Epsom, amid rejoicing because Edward, reformed-playboy son of the late Queen Victoria and Prince Albert, was a popular monarch. He did not live to see the next Derby. Several weeks before it was run, upon hearing that another of his horses, Witch of the Air, had won at Kempton Park, he had uttered the words – 'I am very glad' – that proved his last. Minoru, meanwhile, had retired to stud and been sent to Russia, only to disappear in the Revolution of 1917. Matt Busby was to be visited by tragedy in that year. But for now all that mattered was the blessing of his health.

'A footballer has come into this house today.'

Next to Orbiston in Scotland's Black Country was Mossend, where eight years earlier, under the smoking chimneys of the steel works, Alexander Wilson James had entered the world. Eighteen months after that, across the coal-trolley tracks and stony fields in Bellshill, the main town of this Lanarkshire expanse, Hugh Kilpatrick Gallacher had emerged and already these diminutive exponents of the game were being noticed. Alex James and Hughie Gallacher were learning to harness the energy of the rubber ball, to make light of the aggressive strength of heavier opponents by seeing spaces they could not see, developing skills that were to confound eminent Englishmen under the twin towers of the imperial symbol known as Wembley.

Boys would compete with men in Orbiston and Mossend – it was all part of the street education available on Cannibal Island, as the area was nicknamed with a degree of affection that depended on whether you inhabited it or were foolhardy enough to have crossed its borders for a game of inter-village football – and one of the men was Alex Busby. To his son, football became almost as natural as walking and in time Matt would have the honour of laying out kit for Alex James and the other members of the Orbiston Celtic team who performed in the shadow of the spoil tip on Saturdays.

Matt just played with his pals, or in any-age games on which only darkness could blow the final whistle. He proudly watched his father as the miners obtained their release from the toil, tension and foul air of the underground, where two weeks after Matt's birth James McHarg had been operating a vehicle that gained speed on a slope and crushed his head; aged 26 and a keen supporter of Bellshill Athletic, he left a wife and four children.

Idealists had envisaged kinder lives. Sixteen miles from Orbiston lay New Lanark, a village founded in 1786 by David Dale, a Glasgow gentleman who, in partnership with the inventor and entrepreneur Sir Richard Arkwright, built cotton mills with workers' homes by the Clyde. Dale sold the community to his son-in-law, the social reformer Robert Owen, whose utopian vision New Lanark came to embody.

At Orbiston, too, were men who believed old money could drive noble new ideas. Archibald James Hamilton, the 12th laird, had served with the Scots Greys at Waterloo but was far from stereotypical; he believed in cooperative production and, lending several hundred acres of his estate, instituted with Owen's advice the Practical Society, to be the economic engine of a community in which 'the poor and working classes provide themselves ... with the necessities and comforts of life'. Weavers made cloth; gardeners grew vegetables for the market; and so on. The ensuing prosperity would be shared among the 120 members.

There was a school. And a moral obligation: no alcohol, tobacco or swearing. But to one member socialism, like charity, began at home and unfortunately he was in charge of the society shop, with whose funds he disappeared. Discipline slipped. There were tales of drinking and debauching on the Sabbath and the inhabitants became known as 'Babylonians', after the fabled crucible of Mesopotamian depravity. Although the experiment collapsed, its role in local gossip survived and the Orbiston Viaduct, built to carry the Caledonian Railway past the levelled land where the buildings had stood, became known as 'Babylon Bridge'.

Archibald James Hamilton had died leaving one son who, after Eton, joined the Life Guards. John Hamilton became a Liberal Member of Parliament and by 1886, when elevated to the peerage as the 1st Baron Hamilton of Dalzell, was extremely rich. The sale of land to mining companies enabled him to extend and remodel the family's ancestral home, Dalzell House, on the outskirts of Motherwell.

This process also changed the lives of Matt Busby's forebears, because both the paternal and maternal sides had come from Ireland in search of work and gravitated to the Hamiltons' land.

First to cross the sea was George Busby. He came during the Great Famine, caused by a potato blight affecting much of Europe but striking Ireland with especial force due to the island's agricultural and dietary imbalance; the population fell by two million over seven years. George Busby went to Glasgow, where his son Alexander married Mary Munday, also from Ireland. They in turn had a son, Matthew, and it was his marriage to Catherine McPake in the Lanarkshire mining village of Law in 1887 that produced Alex Busby. Alex was born in Orbiston.

Nellie's side, the Greers, came a little later. Her grandfather, James Greer, had lived through the famine. It was less severe in the northern counties and they, although Roman Catholics like the Busbys, were from the Protestant stronghold of Antrim. There, James had married Rose McStay. A son, also James, was born before the family joined a second Irish influx, one whose effects on the unity of the Scottish mining workforce were exacerbated by the arrival of fellow Catholics from Lithuania and Poland; the Protestants from Ireland were more easily accepted.

The younger James – Jimmy – married Bridget Cryne in 1882 and Nellie was their daughter. They, too, came to Orbiston. Jimmy dug alongside young Alex Busby while Nellie worked at the pithead. The families were also neighbours in the Old Orbiston rows. And that is how Alex met Nellie; they could hardly have avoided each other. Their union was swiftly fertile and the marriage almost as promptly arranged – it would take place at the Holy Family church in Mossend – in order to allow a decent interval before Matt's arrival five months later.

The house and its surroundings were a far cry from Dalzell, with its rolling lawns and immaculately tonsured shrubs. Two rows of back-to-back cottages had been built by the owners of the Orbiston and Hattonrigg mines, the Summerlee Iron Company, to whom the families paid rent. The Old Orbiston rows were of 16 one-room houses at five pounds and six shillings a year (roughly three weeks' wages at the time of Matt's birth) and 16 of two rooms; one of these cost Alex and Nellie seven pounds and seven shillings.

It was of brick with interior plaster that, because of damp, tended to crumble. The brick floors of the kitchens were often in poor condition. Other floors were of wood. There were no inside taps or sinks, with water being taken from standpipes and discarded into open gutters. A visit to the lavatory also entailed an expedition; families had to use one of two 'privies' at the end of each row.

Not that Alex and Nellie complained or considered their conditions – of which she and the other inhabitants of No.28 made the most through diligent housework – unusual. This was all they knew. Two million Scots, or half the population, lived in one or two rooms with more than two people to a room and few were aware that in England life tended, even for the working classes, to be just a little more spacious.

Within a few years there would be not only Alex and Nellie and her father and mother but Matt and three little sisters. It was close but cosy enough. There would be plenty of hot water for grimy bodies and blackened clothes at the end of each shift. Baths could be taken in the galvanised-tin tub in front of the fire, for which there was always coal.

So the grimy haze hovering over the rows was seldom penetrated by howls of protest or of envy of the stone houses of professional people and merchants, with their garrets in which servant girls slept and their neatly tended flower beds, observed on strolls around Bellshill. Let alone the luxurious bathrooms and other features said to be harboured within such residences for the extremely wealthy as that of Gavin Hamilton. The 2nd Baron Hamilton had succeeded to the title and ownership of Dalzell and followed in paternal footsteps by becoming a House of Lords whip for a Liberal government, in his case that of H.H. Asquith.

For Asquith, the land from which the Busbys and Greers had come was but an underlying issue; the Irish question was not one he or many other Westminster politicians cared to confront. 'Home Rule', or the devolution of power from London to the parts of the then United Kingdom across the Irish Sea, hardly consumed public attention in England, Scotland or Wales. Not yet.

The Prime Minister did, however, address the question of integration by speaking in support of the second reading before the House of Commons of the Roman Catholic Disabilities Removal, Etc., Bill. This lifted a restriction on Catholics from holding certain high offices – not that the Busbys or Greers were likely to apply to become Lord Chancellor of England or Lord Lieutenant of Ireland – and removed from the monarch's Coronation Oath the renunciation of the Catholic faith.

In the west of Scotland, far more than, say, Liverpool, where many Irish people had settled, sectarianism could be down-to-earth, even tangible. Not least around Bellshill on a Saturday night. And especially in nearby Motherwell, where the Protestant phobia about not only the immigrant majority's religion but their ways of life, including physical, mental and moral laziness – drink and fornicate, for tomorrow there is always the confessional – often spilled into violence.

There were grievances on both sides. Yes, the newcomers were perceived as undercutters, ready to accept lower wages than the indigenous manual workers, as well as bearers of depravity. But the Great Famine had been hideously cruel and those Irish people who took the extreme view of the London government's part in the reduction of the island's population would, if the word 'genocide' had been invented then, have surely used it in advocating the republican cause.

Although there were sectarian-themed fights in Bellshill from time to time, usually fuelled by drink, the environment in which Matt was to grow up owed more to the respectful give-and-take of the mining community, in which petty prejudice tended to be put in proportion by true danger and constant rigour and the obligation to look out for one another. Alex and Nellie were among those who, though practising Catholics, considered their religion a private matter, and that was how the children would be brought up.

On a good day, you could see the charm of Bellshill, enjoy a sense of community evident in the nicknames of local characters such as 'Reekie Willie' McDonald, a pipe-smoking pillar of the Free Church, and 'Bawbee Jamie' Munroe, manager of the Hattonrigg pit. Life could be hard but it could be happy and one fine spring evening in 1914 the community lined the streets when Bellshill Athletic came home from Douglas Park, Hamilton, with the Lanarkshire Junior Cup.

Soon an even bigger celebration greeted Empire Day, when homes and business premises were decked with red-white-and-blue bunting and children marched to the football club's Brandon Park for races watched by a crowd of 5,000. The report in the *Bellshill Speaker* appeared near an advertisement offering voyages from Glasgow to New York for five pounds and ten shillings. One way, of course. Third class. Two years before, the *Titanic* had sunk with a disproportionate loss of third-class passengers. But unemployment was rising and the lure of the New World powerful.

When Matt came along, Nellie had to stop working, but Alex and her father brought money in. Even if Jimmy Greer also took a fair bit out. Nellie had mixed feelings about her father, whose wife, Bridget, had become painfully accustomed to hours waiting for him to return from drinking bouts in one or more of the 40 pubs in the Bellshill area (one for every 200 men, women and children, though family-friendliness was hardly prominent among the working man's definitions of a good hostelry).

Nellie was embarrassed. Here, it seemed, was the incarnation of the Protestant myth. In her own house. She was Scottish, starting a Scottish family, and encumbered by this Irish throwback. But he was her father. And her first-born was to need him.

For the same tragic reason, Nellie was to be by far the more significant of Matt's parents. This might always have been so, for, while both Alex and Nellie were similarly amiable, she was the more assertive and opinionated. And one of her beliefs was in education. It chimed with the times and Liberal intentions; school meals and medical inspections had just been introduced to Scotland.

A year after the birth of the boy she lovingly called 'Mattha', Nellie became pregnant again and he acquired a sister, Bedelia Ann Cryne Greer Busby. Because Jimmy's wife, Bridget, was known as 'Bedelia', the newcomer grew up as 'Delia'. Liberal use of nicknames was necessary. 'Mattha' distinguished the boy from Alex's father, Matthew Snr, who was now widowed but remained at No.8 with his daughter Agnes and her husband, James Gilmour, yet another miner.

As more pits were sunk, Bellshill's population boomed. But any ideas that wealth might be shared on the old utopian model were, of course, fanciful. For most young men, a cigarette was the nearest they habitually got to luxury – a packet of 20 was more affordable than in health-conscious times to come – and the cinema that opened on Main Street offered a rare treat.

Playing football was free. It also offered the exceptionally talented the prospect of a living above ground. Or a bit of extra cash in the hand; that's what Alex James and Hughie Gallacher were to get in the Juvenile game (youths, mainly, though the qualifications varied from region to region) and the Juniors (semi-professional, as in Bellshill Athletic), before they went south and reached the top of the profession.

Alex and Nellie had moved from the rows to Crofthead Cottage when, two days before Matt's fourth birthday in 1913, his mother presented another sister: Catherine McPake Busby. A week later the Treaty of London was signed. This was nearly six months after the end of the First Balkan War, and it failed to prevent the outbreak of the Second Balkan War just 17 days later, and a lasting peace was not to be agreed until the Treaty of Bucharest in August.

Lasting? This was 1913 and the potential for danger in the Balkans had hardly been removed. The great powers, including Britain and Germany, had spent fortunes on their armies and navies. Kaiser Wilhelm II especially. His blundering belligerence had wound the clock. It had less than a year to tick.

ALL OVER BY CHRISTMAS

Little Matt heard nothing of the countdown to war. His head was full of football, his wildest dreams featuring Glasgow and the famous Celtic, allegiance to whose green and white hoops he had received from his father.

Watching had become as important in working-class life as playing. The Saturday half-holiday was established. The railway companies ran 'football specials' and nowhere did the game take off as a spectator sport as dramatically as in Glasgow, where the growing passion – men would somehow find money for the fitba' – came to reflect the sectarian divide.

Celtic had been founded in 1887 by an educator known as Brother Walfrid. He had taken the idea from Hibernian, formed in Edinburgh two years earlier, of using football's popularity to raise money for the Catholic poor. The first match against Rangers was a friendly in name and spirit but in 1892 Celtic had won the Scottish Cup final, beating the hitherto supreme Queen's Park, and from then the Scottish game had become an increasingly bitter duopoly.

It drew huge crowds; although Celtic had a stadium that would dwarf most in England, it was only the third biggest in Glasgow, after Hampden Park, which had broken its own world record attendance with 127,307 for a Scotland v. England match, and Rangers' Ibrox.

The trains from Bellshill station, with its twin wooden units of ticket office and waiting room linked by an elevated footbridge, would steam merrily to Glasgow in half an hour or less. But any appearance of normality was an illusion. The countdown had begun in earnest and on 28 June 1914, after Celtic had thrilled the Busbys by completing a League-and-Cup Double and the customary hordes descended on Hampden to see Scotland beat England 3–1, the assassination of Archduke Franz Ferdinand in Sarajevo lent it a terrible stridency. On 4 August, Great Britain was at war with Germany.

'It will all be over by Christmas.'

Up and down the kingdom, that was the saying. In Orbiston there had been a reminder of perils closer to home when roof falls killed a Mossend miner, Patrick Gallacher, and injured the Busbys' neighbour William Duffy. But war? Much of Great Britain's might was built in the factories and shipyards of Glasgow and surrounding towns; if Britannia ruled the waves, it was Clydeside that provided her orb, sceptre and sword. How could she not swiftly prevail?

Against this background, Matt started school. By now it was clear his father would leave Orbiston to fight. Although miners had an occupation so crucial to the war effort that many were discouraged from enlisting, and although Alex had another reason to hesitate in that he was married with children, on 7 September he made the short journey to Uddingston and signed up with the Royal Irish Regiment.

A week later, he arrived in Clonmel, County Tipperary, to begin training. But Alex's initial attempt at serving his country – and this enlistment left no doubt as to where the family's allegiance lay – was to last a mere 61 days. By November he was back at Crofthead Cottage and working down the pit. He had been discharged as 'physically unfit for war service' due to varicose veins. At least Alex's love life – whatever frustration may have been caused by the limited privacy of the curtained 'box bed' in the corner of the living room – seemed healthily to survive and in 1915 Nellie gave birth to one more girl: Margaret Greer Busby. The family moved again – 'flitted', as families often did when their leases ran out – back into the rows, to No.15.

Matt went to St Bride's School in Bothwell; it was a little farther than the Bellshill schools, but Nellie wanted him to have the best possible Catholic education. He was usually home in time for a kickabout, except when the dark fell earliest. As at Christmas. Which had, of course, come and gone without the war being all over. A source of anxiety for his mother, whose brother William Greer left Bellshill to fight with the Queen's Own Cameron Highlanders.

Bellshill's little County Hospital, known as the 'Fever Hospital' because it had been built in the 1870s for the nursing of patients with typhoid and other fevers, was already being used to treat soldiers brought back with infectious diseases. So no one was in much doubt as to the scale of losses; almost as soon as Christmas had passed, the government had ordered the conscription of all single males between 18 and 40, and as little as three months later married men of the same age range became eligible to face a range of horrors.

Nellie lost a brother, and Matt his Uncle Willie, when Private Greer died in action. It was during the early weeks of the Somme offensive, a four-month battle that had begun with the loss of 57,000 British soldiers in a day. Replacements were needed and no one worried about varicose veins any more. Alex Busby was welcome to join his late brother-in-law's regiment and travelled to France with the Cameron Highlanders' 7th Battalion, which moved out of Arras to the front line during the night of 22–3 April 1917, and joined a force under Edmund Allenby that was, over the next 36 hours, to capture the village of Guémappe.

Very heavy casualties were sustained. Due to frequent rotation as units became exhausted, there had been pauses during which the Germans brought up reinforcements, stationing machine-gun units in the many barns and other outbuildings on Guémappe's fringes. The morning advance offered this firepower a host of easy targets and among those mown down was Private Alex Busby.

The notice of his death that Nellie received was typed, due to a shortage of paper, on the back of a used document whose original contents had been scored through with a single diagonal line of red crayon.

The family thought Alex had been a victim of sniper fire. But Army records stated only that he had gone missing between 23 and 28 April, the latter date being that on which the 7th Battalion was relieved, so it seemed more likely he had fallen in one of the earlier fusillades, his body remaining for five days in a position too dangerous to permit recovery. His effects were listed as the sum of two pounds, four shillings and two pence, which was duly returned to Nellie.

Back in France was Jimmy Speirs. A Glaswegian and a professional footballer of such calibre Herbert Chapman had made him captain of Leeds City, Speirs had volunteered to join the Cameron Highlanders. He had arrived in France with Alex Busby's 7th Battalion. Wounded, he had recovered and, surviving where Alex fell, displayed such courage that he received the Military Medal. Speirs was then to enjoy a period of leave in Glasgow and Yorkshire. Only to perish, within a month or two, amid the fury of Passchendaele.

Mrs Speirs and Mrs Busby, strangers separated by a few miles, were united in grief. But Nellie had little time to dwell on her loss before getting back to work. Aged 25, a single mother of four, she'd had much to arrange. And there was to be further bad news from the war.

At least the family had been receiving a government allowance while Alex was away, and now there were widow-and-orphans pensions. Nellie needed more. She returned to the pithead. And those housewifely duties she could no longer perform fell, at least in part, to the most unlikely double act: her old rascal of a father and eight-year-old Matt.

'It will all be over by Christmas.'

Six days before the Christmas of 1917, Corporal Thomas Greer, of 189th Company, Machine Gun Corps, died of wounds on the Western Front. He died with such gallantry that, like Jimmy Speirs, he was awarded the Military Medal. Unlike Jimmy Speirs, however, he never got to find out about it. 'First Uncle Willie, then my father, then Uncle Tommy,' Matt was to reflect. 'Every man was a miner, and they all left widows.'

But somehow he survived emotionally, as many did when there was scant choice. What Matt was experiencing, at such a sensitive age, was extreme by any standard but not unusual for the time and place; you did not have to look far to see tears and mourning during the Great War and there was some small comfort in the number of names about to be inscribed on the memorial at Bellshill.

Towards the end of the summer it became clear that German resistance on the Western Front had begun to collapse and by November the Kaiser's removal from power had paved the way to armistice. On the 11th hour of the 11th day of the 11th month, the church bells pealed in the communities that had sacrificed Matt's father and uncles, as in every corner of the kingdom.

The little boys in their flat cloth caps – sometimes only knee-length trousers distinguished their dress from the menfolk's – ran to and fro. The Bellshill bunting came out and there was a parade by injured soldiers accommodated at Dalzell House. From Hamilton Barracks, which more than four years earlier had been besieged by hopeful recruits, some full of a sense of duty and others with empty stomachs, emerged brass and pipe bands playing patriotic airs.

In Glasgow, the *Herald* reported a 'spontaneous outpouring of jubilation on the part of all classes', followed by a night of revelry in Sauchiehall Street in which 'the happy discord was increased by the clanging of the tramway cars as they were driven through the surging crowds'.

And then life got back to as near normal as could be. But the advertisements in the *Herald* carried a different tone to those in the *Bellshill Speaker* a decade earlier. A department store proud of the 'courtesy that pervades the establishment' promised new customers they 'cannot be otherwise than favourably impressed' by such beautiful goods as an 'Afternoon Gown of Nigger Brown Georgette over Silk Pleated Gown and Bodice'.

Nellie could not have afforded one. Not in any colour. Although reduced by one guinea (a pound and a shilling, the currency of the discerning), it would cost far more than she scraped together in a month. But the prosperous remained so and even for those with relatively humble jobs there would be rising standards over the next two years as heavy industry pounded on – the shipyards had to replace all those vessels sunk by submarines – and the rest of the economy accepted its share.

The dancehalls thrived and the peckish flocked to the ice-cream parlours and fish-and-chip shops of second-generation Italians such as Antonio 'Tony' Coia, whose ice-cream cart became familiar on the Bellshill streets. There was a new bridge over the Calder to cater for motor vehicles and even a tree-fringed golf club where, in a few years, Matt Busby would be among the schoolboys who earned tips from caddying.

But real money was not trickling through to Nellie, who appreciated such easing of her struggle as a second marriage provided. She had not let much grass grow. Twenty months had passed since Alex's death when she became Mrs Harry Mathie at the Catholic Chapel in Bothwell two days after Christmas 1918. She was 27 and Harry a few years younger. They had met at the pit, where Harry worked underground.

A RIGHT DECENT GIRL

Matt viewed Harry Mathie with limited approval. Matt had become the young man of the household and taken to the role with a responsibility beyond his years. Although men and boys were unaccustomed to a substantial share of the chores, Matt mucked in. He had a precocious sense of gratitude for his mother's sacrifices.

He also had, in her father, his own father figure of a sort. Jimmy had little or no interest in football but an infectious gaiety. He had a nickname for Matt – 'Brian Boru', after the Irish king – and would sing to him such music-hall hits as 'I Belong to Glasgow', which became Matt's party-piece too (and was to remain prominent in a wider vocal repertoire). At least once Jimmy took his grandson to the famous Glasgow Empire. Jimmy's favourite, Harry Lauder, was Matt's too and they were pleased to hear he had been knighted in 1919 for energetic fundraising during the war.

Frequent brushes with the magic of Alex James also lifted Matt. He was his first hero and when, one Saturday at Orbiston Celtic, the 17-year-old James could not find his boots, Matt knew what to do. Aware that James had tiny feet, he raced home and got his own pair. Matt made sure everyone got to know about it. But first he had to hand out the jerseys, shorts and socks. Afterwards he took them to the woman who did the washing. What a job. What a life. Weekend after weekend. And what riches for a poor boy to be known by name – as Matt was – to Alex James.

In London and Glasgow there might have been the grandeur of the theatre and the glitter of the music hall. But Matt had his own theatre, its stage the pitches of Orbiston and Bellshill, its backcloth the towering spoil tips of the collieries and its stars in James and Hughie Gallacher.

They were pals. James was a steel-works clerk. Gallacher had gone down the Hattonrigg pit at 15. He was even smaller than the 5' 5" James, and a natural goalscorer. Matt may have thought every community in Scotland could boast entertainers like James and Gallacher; he was to come to appreciate his luck and to say: 'My football thinking has been influenced by close contact with great men from my boyhood.'

His mother's union with Harry Mathie lost little time in providing a half-brother, Jimmy, and half-sister, Helen ('Nellie' being taken, she became 'Nelsha'). Another boy, Henry after his father, died a toddler. Whether there was a conscious effort to extend the family or not, birth control was universally frowned upon by church authorities and, for Catholics especially, the choice was between 11th-hour withdrawal and abstinence.

Just as Matt idolised Alex James, little Jimmy seemed to worship Matt. There could have been worse models for the younger boy. Frank Rodgers, for example. Frank had been Matt's best pal since the early days at St Bride's. He was a big lad, rough and ready in equally liberal measure with, even in adolescence, a sectarian edge that Matt tried to discourage.

Matt and Frank were, like James and Gallacher, partners in footballing progress. But Matt remained a diligent pupil and, when he was 12, the teachers at St Bride's told his mother he would benefit from secondary education at an establishment in Motherwell providing, under the new Education (Scotland) Act, high-quality schooling for Catholics at local-authority expense; hitherto this had been the responsibility of Catholic institutions. Nellie realised it would place further strain on the family budget, for books and uniform were needed, but had no doubt; he would go.

So every morning Matt rose before seven to walk the three miles to Motherwell and late every afternoon little Jimmy would be waiting to share the last few hundred yards home. Matt's school performance had coped so comfortably with the step up that the Motherwell headmaster, George Bennett, would recommend he stay on until 18 and train to be a teacher; Nellie was heartened, for Matt would stay above ground, and be clean, and respectable.

But Matt had ambitions of his own. He did not bother his mother with them.

As his 16th birthday approached, Nellie and Harry Mathie began to think seriously about emigrating to North America. Some of the family had gone to Pittsburgh after Matt's aunts had been widowed and reports were encouraging. Nellie came to a new decision. After she and Harry had applied for visas for themselves and their children, she went to Motherwell to see George Bennett and told him Matt's name was on the forms. Bennett implored her to reconsider. In vain.

Nellie seemed to have become defeatist about Matt's teaching career. One day, she put a kindly arm around him. 'Look here, Mattha,' she said. 'If we stay in Orbiston there's nothing but the pit staring you in the face. I don't want you to be a miner.' Perhaps she envisaged teacher training across the Atlantic.

Anyway, Matt agreed to join the voyage of discovery. He went to the emigration office to complete his forms. And was told to expect six months on the waiting list.

That was his signal. There seemed no point now in staying at school and so, on his 16th birthday, he left and went down the mine, reasoning with his mother that the family would need money to settle in America.

The year was 1925. Demand for coal had flattened and, as unemployment increased, so did the exodus. Summerlee closed the

Orbiston pit. Nellie was found a job at the company's steel works, while Matt moved to another of the nearby collieries, Parkhead. To him, one was as detestable as the other. And dangerous; in Orbiston's final year, Thomas Stewart, happy in the knowledge that the ending of his shift would bring release into a late-spring afternoon, had reached for his coat only to be buried by a series of roof falls.

When at length news came that the US visas were on their way, a family conference was convened and Matt, by now inwardly set on a career in football, persuaded his mother to postpone the trip. It turned out later that, Nellie apart, few had been truly ready to go. Matt had got his way. He would have to wield his pick and shovel a little longer. But at weekends he could pursue his footballing dream: he and Frank Rodgers were established as the lads likeliest to follow James and Gallacher, each of whose fame was spreading throughout the British Isles.

James had gone to Raith Rovers and then, for £3,000, Preston North End. In October 1925, he made his first appearance for Scotland, alongside Gallacher in a 3–0 victory over Wales. Gallacher's career had ignited at Airdrie, with whom he had won the Scottish Cup. For Scotland, who won all three home internationals that season, he scored twice against Wales, once against Ireland (still a team from both sides of the border, despite the formation of the Irish Free State) and twice again against England. When he left for Newcastle United, the fee of £6,500 was only £50 short of the world record Sunderland had paid Burnley for Bob Kelly.

The sum that took James to England, although remarkable for the Second Division club Preston had become, underlined that he was the slower burner. But the offside law had recently changed and in the ensuing decade no player in Britain was more significantly to benefit than Alex James.

Also in the team who beat England was Jimmy McMullan. He had spent many years lending craft to Partick Thistle and was now at Manchester City but kept in touch with the Junior club of his home town, Denny, some 20 miles north of Orbiston. Which turned out to be fortunate for Matt. And Frank Rodgers.

Frank's reputation was growing. Not just in a scary way – although he was said to have responded to the unscheduled appearance of a horse outside his family's house by punching it on the nose so hard the poor beast sank to its knees. With Frank as a companion, Matt could hardly have avoided the odd scrap. But both were doing well enough in village football to be asked to join the best youth team in the area, Alpine Villa.

It was a welcome boost to Matt's morale, for on a May midnight in 1926 the General Strike began. Britain's workers were angry. Miners especially. Homes fit for heroes? Conditions were still poor. The coal industry was suffering from overseas competition and, when the men were offered longer hours for less pay, it proved the last straw. The Trades Union Congress called the strike and counter-claimed for greater safety down the mines. Other workers pledged support, but troops and volunteers maintained services and after nine days the TUC conceded defeat. The miners stayed out for months, until hunger drove them back underground.

Matt was one of them. He never forgot the experience. Small wonder he had developed a form of socialism. So had many other British people, notably Scots. The Labour Party was on the rise.

At least for Matt and Frank Rodgers the bitter taste of defeat was washed away. They played leading roles as Alpine Villa won the Scottish Cup for under-18 teams. The celebrations took place at the Bellshill miners' club. And there Matt met Jean Menzies.

The attraction was mutual as they exchanged the stories of their young lives. Matt had but briefly known his natural father; Jean's was a mystery. Menzies was not her original name. She had been born in Hamilton, eight months before Matt, and given the same name, Jeanie Macvie, as her mother, who was single and put her up for fostering. Mr and Mrs Menzies were staunch Protestants and from a part of Bellshill that countenanced little else. So Jean had one label and Matt the other. Not that they cared. Not between themselves. But as the weeks passed Matt's friends noticed an unusual nervousness about him. He was going to invite his girl home for tea and, for all the live-and-let-live philosophy his mother had always followed, it seemed a step into the unknown.

Reassurance came. Nellie poured for Jean and, when she had gone, pronounced her a 'right decent girl'. Matt and this girl were going to be together for the rest of their lives, and beyond.

Jean would gently mock, as sometimes people did, Matt's notion of being paid for playing football. But Alpine Villa's exploits had been noticed. Frank Rodgers was first to get the call from Denny Hibernian. Soon after he had signed as a semi-professional, the Denny secretary Alex McNeill contacted his old friend Jimmy

McMullan at Manchester City and it was arranged for Frank to travel south. Next, McNeill beckoned Busby – and again he had played only a handful of matches before the line to Manchester was humming.

City's Scottish manager, Peter Hodge, offered him a trial and it took place at Turf Moor, Burnley, where he played for the City reserves and did enough to persuade Hodge to get the train to Glasgow. There, Busby told Hodge he was supposed to be emigrating. He recalled: 'The reply was that I could go to America afterwards and meanwhile I might as well have the pleasure of playing the game – I had a lot of promise.' So the terms of a professional contract were agreed: Matt would receive £5 a week (£1 less in the close season) for a year, after which the position would be reviewed.

He was thrilled to be swapping the pit for the pitch, but inevitably had mixed feelings concerning Jean – yes, he had proved he could make money out of football after all, and considerably more than a miner would ever bring in, but he would have to be parted from her, if only temporarily. Matt went back to Orbiston and told his mother. She did not dance a fling but sighed. This meant the end of the American adventure before it had begun. 'But I suppose you know what's good for you. I hope you've made the right choice.'

And she mused: 'Well, Mattha – you'll be the first of my children to leave home.' He might not have needed to take the road south, for he had been for a trial with Rangers, who rejected him when they found out he was a Catholic. The interest of his beloved Celtic then cooled when they discovered he had been to Rangers. There was talk that Celtic were to think again. If it ever did materialise – and his half-brother later claimed to have found Matt in tears as he reflected on the irrevocability of his commitment to City instead – the people at Parkhead were too late.

Not that they seemed to have missed a great deal. Not in the early stages of his professional career. It began so unhappily that he might have left Manchester without kicking a first-team ball.

CHAPTER THREE

MANCHESTER CITY AND LIVERPOOL

THE BLUES

As the train steamed towards Manchester, entering the last hour of its journey from Glasgow, Matt Busby peered at a familiar industrial scene. He knew a bit of Lancashire from his trial at Burnley and its brooding mills and billowing factory chimneys offered a landscape not too dissimilar from Lanarkshire's. But Manchester would take some getting used to.

It was a proud and pioneering city: passenger railways had begun here in 'Cottonopolis', bustling to and from Liverpool; the Manchester Ship Canal had bypassed Liverpool, creating an inland port and facilitating the new concept of an industrial estate at Trafford Park, near the United Football Ground (as the home of the other Manchester club was then called); a majestic town hall and numerous theatres created the air of a provincial capital. But the Manchester that Matt Busby saw, when he went from the station to an address in Moss Side, seemed awfully crowded and impersonal to one three months short of his 19th birthday and cast adrift for the first time.

He was nevertheless ready for his adventure and, after reporting to the gigantic Maine Road headquarters of Manchester City, settled into club accommodation nearby. He was to share rooms with Phil McCloy, a full-back from Uddingston (where Busby's father had volunteered). This, and the knowledge that Jimmy McMullan would be another clubmate, comforted Busby as he surveyed row after row of red-brick terraced homes, endless Coronation Streets for the working masses, many with Irish origins amid the first of several waves of immigration that would wash over Moss Side and adjacent neighbourhoods.

Maine Road had been built with a capacity exceeding 80,000 five years earlier, when the club was accustomed to frequenting the upper half of the First Division. Their new home, however, witnessed relegation at the end of one of those seasons that were to establish City as an institution of bizarre extremes, their supporters all too easily identifiable by the shaking of bewildered heads: the club had combined their descent with a run to the Cup final at Wembley, where they lost to Bolton.

Under the wavy-haired Hodge, who had done brilliant work at Leicester, immediate promotion depended on the final match. Although his team beat Bradford City 8–0, a late goal that gave Portsmouth a 5–1 victory over Preston denied City by the tiniest of margins on goal average (the later criterion of goal difference would have seen them up). Busby's arrival found them again there or thereabouts, mischievous supporters relishing the thought that the place they might regain in the First Division would be that of Manchester United, who were at the perilous end of the table.

In the event, United stayed up. But they were to be City's distinct inferiors during Busby's playing years in Manchester, mostly a division below and, at one stage, almost plummeting into the third tier.

On his first appearance for the reserves at Preston, he hardly got a kick as the home side won, but cheered up when Alex James came into the dressing room for a chat afterwards. 'Good luck, young Matt,' said the erstwhile Orbison Celtic star, 'and, if you play football as well as you looked after the skip, you'll not do so bad.' That was how Busby remembered it.

James soon joined up with Gallacher in the McMullan-captained Scotland team to be dubbed the Wembley Wizards after a 5–1 triumph over England. James, although generally more a maker than taker of goals, scored two in a display that emphasised how far he remained below his station in the Second Division.

Gallacher, meanwhile, was the toast of Tyneside. He had begun by scoring 36 goals in 38 matches as Newcastle took the League title. He was already married but found love in the shape of Hannah Anderson, teenage daughter of the landlord of one of his favoured pubs – much to the ire of her family. Hannah loved him, too. But, of all the things in Gallacher's life, only the beating of goalkeepers ever lacked complication.

To Busby, even first-team football seemed a forlorn hope. In the reserves, he was moved from inside-left to the right wing – and did worse. Neither inside-right nor centre-forward suited him. Nor did it raise his morale when, between his debut for the reserves and the first team's clinching of the Second Division title, City engaged an entire forward line of new players: Alf Horne, Bobby Marshall, Tommy Tait, Fred Tilson and Eric Brook. The club were tooling up for the higher grade and, as Busby took the train home for the summer, word from Hodge that he would be retained for another season failed to dispel a sense of impending failure.

A few weeks among family and true friends helped. Loneliness had beset him at City, especially after Frank Rodgers had been released, returning to Scotland by way of a spell at Preston. Busby found few of the senior players welcoming. Perhaps the annual renewal of contracts conspired in an atmosphere of insecurity; perhaps they were just an uncaring lot, with precious exceptions such as McMullan, who took Busby into his family home for a while, and McCloy.

Mostly the aspirant was ignored and he never forgot the sadness it caused him, and resolved never to be so negligent of juniors if ever he became a senior. How unlike the camaraderie of the miners, it also struck him, when he was back home for the summer break, amid silent pitheads testifying to the recession of their industry.

It was a minority Labour government under Ramsay MacDonald that wrestled with the United Kingdom's problems. But after the general election that summer Scotland had a Labour majority; Busby's country had become a Labour country.

All too soon the close season was over and Busby's train steamed into Manchester. He had warmed a little to the city, come to appreciate the virtues of a place where strangers called you 'love'; that might not always have been taken cheerfully on Cannibal Island.

Among his fellow professionals, the friendly few included Tommy Johnson, a striker with a powerful left foot who led the way in demonstrating that City were equipped for the First Division by scoring five in a 6–2 win on the ground of the champions, Everton. Johnson went on to total 38 goals in 39 appearances, a club record for a League season that was seldom to be challenged.

A lot of scoring records were set as defences strove to adjust to the law change providing that an attacker was free of offside if two opponents, rather than three, were between him and the goal-line. The number of goals had immediately increased by one-third. In 1926/27, George Camsell had struck 59 times for Middlesbrough in the Second Division. That was a record. Yet in 1927/28 it had been beaten by Dixie Dean's 60 for Everton in the First. In 1928/29, even Johnson's 38 paled by comparison with Dave Halliday's 43 for Sunderland. Jack Allen got 33 as the Wednesday won the first of consecutive championships (the second was to be under their new name of Sheffield Wednesday), while City finished a more than respectable eighth.

Busby made his debut in the ensuing season. Johnson and the winger Brook were chosen to represent the Football League against the Scottish League in November 1929, the fixture coinciding with Middlesbrough's visit to Maine Road, and Busby took Johnson's place at inside-left. He performed quite well as City won. But, of course, Johnson had to return.

It was during the pre-Christmas weeks that the 20-year-old Busby suffered so badly from homesickness and disillusion with his career (exacerbated by a bout of pneumonia) that, in a letter to Jean, he wrote: 'I feel I am out of my sphere in football.' He even threw his clothes into his suitcase and was about to leave Moss Side for the station when Phil McCloy stopped him. Busby said he didn't want to seem a quitter but felt so terrible that the first train home seemed the best way out. 'It really was agony,' he stressed later, and in another time it might have been seen as depression. McCloy was kindly. 'Give it a little longer,' he said. 'You can still make it.' He kept cajoling until, after midnight, Busby began to unpack.

Jimmy McMullan helped with assiduous coaching, which Busby often felt he had absorbed – until he went into the next reserve match and flopped. Peter Hodge noted his fine displays in practice matches behind closed doors; he would call him in and gently suggest that, while the other players were impressed by his skills, it might be nice to let the odd paying customer have a peek at them.

An opportunity came when Fred Tilson was injured in a Cup draw at Tottenham. Busby, brought in for the replay, scored twice as City won 4–1. He stayed in at Bolton but played poorly and returned to the reserves. Although he made a handful of further appearances, he was relieved as much as excited when Hodge again retained him, allowing him to enjoy the Scottish summer in Jean's company without having to consider alternative employment above or below ground: perhaps just as well, with the Great Depression starting to bite viciously.

His feeling of good fortune was short-lived. In the autumn, far from spending more time in the first team, he could not get into the reserves. He later discovered Hodge had all but given up on him. The City manager had been approached by Louis Rocca, who recruited for Manchester United. Yes, said Hodge, United could have Busby – for £150. Rocca replied that United couldn't afford 150 shillings (£7.50). Busby resolved to see out the 1930/31 season on the assumption it would be his last in England. At least his agony had eased. He had done his best. He was philosophical.

And then it happened. Without warning.

Matches in the Northern Midweek League seldom commanded much interest at Maine Road. A typical spectator would be a parent of one of the trialists who were blended with reserves and senior professionals recovering fitness. One afternoon towards the end of November 1930, a trialist failed to turn up and 20 minutes before kick-off the trainer, Alex Bell, a Scot who had spent most of his playing career with Manchester United, told Busby he was needed in the dressing room. With his boots.

As he changed, Busby reflected on an addition to his list of positions occupied. It would be his first time at right-half. He trotted out with no inkling that it would be the first of hundreds.

He began the match confidently – as if it were a practice match – and never faltered, tackling soundly, passing with consistent accuracy. He enjoyed it so much that, when word came afterwards that Hodge wanted to speak to him, he hoped the boss had been watching from the vast, echoing grandstand. His wish was granted. 'That was a right good game you played,' said Hodge, beaming. And at right-half he would remain in the reserves on Saturday. And fate bestowed Busby another favour when the first-teamer Matt Barrass was ruled out of a match at

Huddersfield. What was Barrass's position? Right-half. He was never to wrest it back from Busby.

At 21, Matt had come of age. McMullan's work had paid off. McCloy's midnight coaxing too. An Orbiston dream had come true. Jean's future husband could play professional football. Nellie's misgivings about the abandonment of a new life in America could be set aside. 'Oor Mattha' was famous.

Not only that; he now played in the same League, trod the same turf, as the great Alex James. The proud chuckles could be imagined: what would that League do without the products of an Orbiston footballing education? Not to mention young Gallacher from Hattonrigg.

CREATIVE EVOLUTION

Within five weeks of Busby's promotion, he found himself up against Alex James. Herbert Chapman had brought James to Arsenal – for £8,750 – because he needed the last piece of a jigsaw. He had created such a picture at Huddersfield, who, never having been champions, took three titles in as many seasons. But at Arsenal, although the potential was greater, he had to find the best way of operating within the new offside law and it took time.

Chapman's first signing, Charlie Buchan, was helpful in identifying the necessity of a third back. Football until then had been discussed in 2–3–5 terms, but Chapman at Huddersfield had sometimes placed his centre-half between the full-backs – and won a Cup final with Tommy Wilson there – so he saw the sense of Buchan's argument. Eventually Chapman was to find his specialist 'stopper' in Herbie Roberts.

But the filling of the midfield hole left by the centre-half's move back was more problematic. While the new shape came to be called 'WM' – 3–2–2–3 – it more closely resembled 3–3–4 when Chapman found his pivotal figure in James. At first James became a butt of the crowd but what Chapman wanted was passing that could turn defence into attack with unprecedented speed; of all Chapman's big ideas, counterattack was the biggest. And the little man with the baggy shorts could enact it like no other. Those who watched Arsenal in 1930/31, the season in which James reached his peak, spoke of diagonal balls he would suddenly spin and hit into space that the flying wingers, Joe Hulme and Cliff Bastin, would occupy as if by magic.

When Busby was afforded a Christmas Day close-up of the new playmaking, the maestro turned on the style in a 4–1 victory. In advance, the Maine Road groundsmen had told Matt and his fellow wing-half Jackie Bray of a cunning plan to neutralise James: when, before kick-off, he went to the lavatory and slipped down those baggy shorts, they would lock him in for 90 minutes. If only.

On the way to London for the Boxing Day return, reassured to have been kept in the team, Busby was approached by a club director, Bob Smith. 'Well, Matt,' he said, 'I am glad to see you making a good shape at wing-half – because as a forward you were a complete washout.' As morale-boosters go, it needed a bit of work, but Busby could smile because his insecurity was receding. At Highbury it was 3–1 to Arsenal and there was no shame because Chapman's men had become irresistible. They had achieved a near-perfect balance. In the season they scored 127 goals, by far their highest total under Chapman, while conceding a mere 59.

Jack Lambert, the centre-forward, got 38 and David Jack, the inside-forward who acted as second striker, 31. So Chapman fielded a front four, not a front three. Wing-halves, meanwhile, had been released from their old responsibility to mark wingers, so at least one could fashion ammunition for the attack – and that, now, was how Matt saw his duty.

He would never have been fast or direct enough to score like David Jack. But, given more time and space in the middle three, he could attempt to emulate James's creativity. James, at Arsenal, averaged less than one goal every ten matches. Busby's career ratio would be similar. The game had gone through a Chapman-led change and, although Busby was notionally a wing-half and James an inside-forward, there was little difference in the playmaking obligations they fulfilled.

Like James, he could see the game and direct attacks. The ball didn't come from such difficult angles and in such a hurry. How lucky he had been to get that call from Alex Bell. In football's rearranged midfield, his moderate pace would matter less than the acuteness of his brain and accuracy of his feet, and snowballing confidence would do the rest.

As if this were not enough, Jean became Mrs Busby. After a Cup defeat at Burnley on 10 January 1931, Matt travelled home to stay with his family and two days later came the wedding at St Bride's, Bothwell, next to the school where he had received his primary education. The witnesses were Frank Rodgers, now living in Bellshill, and Matt's eldest sister Delia. Jean, while working in domestic service, had been preparing for her new life by converting to Catholicism. 'She did it herself,' Busby was to recall. 'She went to St Bride's convent – and her parents accepted it!' Now she was coming with him to Manchester. This time, he would not be taking the train south alone. Loneliness had become a memory.

The 1930/31 season brought reunions with not only James but Gallacher, whom Newcastle had sold to Chelsea. Arsenal, of course, were champions; Chapman had broken new ground by bringing League supremacy to the south of England. City, who slipped from third place to eighth, would change their manager before the next season was out, Hodge returning to Leicester and Wilf Wild, the club secretary, becoming manager as well. But the change made no difference to Busby, whose promptings helped City finally to reach Wembley in 1933.

His trademark ploy was to come inside from the right, gliding past opponents, and suddenly use his favoured left foot to switch the ball back towards the right corner flag. Ernie Toseland would already be into his stride and, from the winger's crosses and cutbacks, chances often came. Meanwhile, Arsenal would rely on James, as described by Donny Davies in the *Manchester Guardian*:

> The long ball driven to the remote right wing and with a capacious swerve on it to elude the opposing back. Followed by a flash of Hulme's heels, a swift low cross … and there would be the ice-cool Bastin leisurely picking his spot.

Hardly dissimilar: for Joe Hulme read Toseland, for Cliff Bastin read Manchester City's own goalscoring left-winger, Eric Brook.

While no team could match Arsenal in the League, the third round of the Cup featured one of the great shocks when Chapman threw in a few reserves for a visit to Walsall of the Third Division (North) and lost 2–0. Busby's City were held at equally humble Gateshead but won the replay 9–0 and put Walsall in their place with a 2–0 win at Maine Road before triumphing over Bolton, Burnley and, in the semi-finals, Derby.

At Wembley they faced an old friend in Tommy Johnson. The striker had been sold to a relegation-bound Everton in March 1930 and vindicated the protests of City fans by joining Dixie Dean in an attack that helped to win the championships of the Second and First Divisions in consecutive seasons. Now only City stood between Everton and the Cup. And City stood nervously. Busby looked as anxious as any in the line of players waiting to meet the Duke of York. He stared stonily ahead, chewing gum, before bowing deeply when introduced to the guest of honour by the City captain, Sam Cowan.

He had been upset by his club's decision to travel to Wembley from their Hertfordshire base before the bulk of the crowd. The bus arrived at 1.15 – an hour and three-quarters before kick-off. The players endeavoured to fill the time with a stroll on the pitch. They went back into the dressing room and tried to chat casually but found themselves bickering. By 2.15 they were changed and ready. Small wonder that by 2.50, when the community singing stopped and the presentations were made, Busby's stomach was knotted, and neither he nor others were to do themselves justice in a one-sided match.

On Busby's back was the number 19, the FA having taken up an idea first enacted on the opening day of the 1928/29 season, when Herbert Chapman and his Chelsea counterpart David Calderhead sent out their teams numbered 1–11 as an aid to identification. The League reacted by banning the practice but the FA could see its merits and, for the 1933 final, had Everton wearing 1–11 and City 12–22 in reverse order.

The numbers that mattered most, however, were three and nil.

Everton took the lead when Len Langford made a hash of a cross and Jimmy Stein scored. They increased their advantage when the hapless goalkeeper misdirected another high ball to the feet of Dean and Jimmy Dunn rounded matters off.

Within months, Wild began to bed in a giant keeper from the Lancashire coast called Frank Swift. Although nothing could ever dim Busby's affection for Langford, who, with his wife Tilly, had been friends in need at the birth of Matt and Jean's daughter Sheena earlier in the year, he was also fond of Swift. And it was Swift's good fortune that Busby had become the responsible footballer of his own silent vows. Just as, while some fled from autograph-hunters, Busby waited to sign with a modest smile, he always found time for a younger player.

While initially deputising for an injured Langford, the 20-year-old Swift had made mistakes but Wild kept faith as Blackburn, Hull, Wednesday and Stoke were knocked out of the Cup in the early months of 1934. Busby was advising Swift on dietary and training habits and would stay on to help him practise, just as McMullan had done with Busby himself. But Swift had still to convince a team bent on settling a score with Wembley. He did that in the semi-final against Aston Villa at Huddersfield; City won 6–1 and, although Tilson scored four, everyone knew Swift's early saves had been as influential. He would play in the final against Portsmouth.

City spent a night in Essex before arriving just an hour before kick-off. The players changed with lighter hearts. Except for Swift. Alex Bell could see it in how he sat, as if weighed down by expectations among the gathering crowd outside. The trainer hauled Swift to his feet and marched him to the bathroom, where he slapped his face and made him down a tot of whisky. Maybe the measure was too generous, for, after Busby had helpfully passed back to give Swift a calming early touch, a far from formidable shot from Septimus Rutherford slipped under his body and into the net.

Swift recovered to perform defiantly and, after Portsmouth had lost the defender Jimmy Allen to injury, City equalised, the influential Busby's throw being moved by Brook to Tilson, who shot across Jock Gilfillan. Tilson struck again, with emphatic glee, and at the other end Swift knew there were three minutes left because, behind him, a press photographer had been conducting a countdown. When Stanley Rous blew the final whistle, Swift fainted. He was brought round and helped up the Wembley steps to receive his medal from George V. As the King, having checked his wellbeing, complimented him, Swift's mother watched proudly – and then she fainted as well.

THE FINEST RIGHT-HALF

Busby had become an international in 1933/34, taking part in Scotland's 3–2 defeat by Wales in Cardiff alongside Jimmy McLuckie, a fellow wing-half who had just begun a 15-month spell at Maine Road. Busby would have received a second cap at Wembley in April, a fortnight before the Cup final, but for the League's response to a Scottish request for three players from

City: it was resolved that none should be released. So Busby, along with Alex Herd and the unlucky McLuckie, who also never earned a second cap, missed out on a chance to play alongside Hughie Gallacher in what turned out to be a 3–0 defeat.

The *Manchester Guardian* reckoned that, while Busby's 'crouching style' might not be easy on the eye, at his best he had no superior as an attacking wing-half:

> It is Busby's bewildering footcraft that most delights the crowds ... the control is perfect, the effect akin to conjuring. His dribble is a thing of swerves, feints and deceptions; few opponents are not hoodwinked by his phantom pass. Even the real one is nearly always masked: it skids off to the right when one could swear it was destined for the centre, and often when the right wing is the obvious way to attack, off goes the ball like a rocket to the left. Busby scorns the obvious.

If he had flaws they were in defence: squeamish critics would cringe at adventures close to his own goal. But like James he was an entertainer. And he had a hand on the Cup. A vast throng saw City bear it through Manchester in an open-top bus, Busby standing near the front and gently smiling as he inhaled deeply on a cigarette concealed within a cupped hand.

In 1934/35 he encountered a new opponent, a fellow Scot. Willie Shankly came from the small mining community of Glenbuck, some 25 miles south of Orbiston, and had left school at 14 to work underground. The pit closed but Shankly was engaged by Carlisle United of the Third Division (North) and from there moved, for £500, to Preston, where the tough, industrious right-half play of Bill Shankly, as he was now known, helped North End to be promoted in 1934. The friendly rivalry between Busby and Shankly had begun.

Back home, where Matt's sisters Delia and Maggie had married Bellshill men, the Orbiston rows had been demolished. The Summerlee company had closed Hattonrigg and soon the iron and steel works at Mossend would go the same way; all the places where the Busbys had worked were falling victim to the Depression.

Yet there were signs of what people called progress. The cinema was no longer silent and Bellshill had experienced the first 'talkie', Al Jolson's *The Jazz Singer*. Cars and vans motored past the horse-drawn carts of the bakers and milkmen, and there were semi-detached houses with gardens behind hedges. Occasionally a radio could be heard. Men wore the ubiquitous flat 'bunnets' as they smoked and gossiped and wondered what the future held. Busby had brought the FA Cup to them, placing it on the counter of the Angus Bar in Bellshill and having it filled with wine. He still loved to go back, even if Manchester now felt like home to him and Jean, as it always would.

The Depression had hit Manchester, especially the key industry of textile manufacturing, but football thrived and, with admission prices set reasonably at around an hour's wages for the average worker, City drew record crowds.

With the stylish full-back Sam Barkas added to the likes of Brook, Herd, Tilson, Toseland and Busby, they were seen as the team most likely to challenge Arsenal, now under the former director George Allison but with the late Chapman's excellent assistants, Tom Whittaker and Joe Shaw, doing most to keep up the old standard. Nearly 80,000 greeted them at Maine Road where, despite the absence of an injured James, the champions came away with a 1–1 draw, and they remained unbeaten until a hat-trick of titles had been completed.

City finished fourth and hopes were high as they contemplated 1935/36. The names tripped off the tongue: Swift; Dale, Barkas; Busby, Cowan, Bray (centre-backs were still listed as if they were centre-halves, and would be for several decades to come); Toseland, Heale, Tilson, Herd, Brook.

Swift – *what was he like?* Big and dominant between the posts, with an infectious grin and a boyish eccentricity that made training more fun. There were roars of laughter when someone struck the perfect rising volley – 'like a bullet from a gun,' said Busby – and, while others looked to see the net bulge, Swift threw up his hands, not only stopped but held the ball and, tucking it under an arm while he walked off the goal-line, clapped his hands and shouted: 'Well saved, Frank!'

The 1935/36 season ended with ninth place. And Busby gone: a victim of time and tide at 26. He found himself plagued by a leg injury and often supplanted by the 22-year-old Jack Percival, a solid player from County Durham. Meanwhile there were small but irritating disputes within the club. And Jean suffered from poor health. The two aspects were far from unconnected.

In 1933 she had endured Sheena's complicated birth. It turned out to be more than worthwhile, for their daughter's survival followed no fewer than four deaths at birth, all of boys, but Sheena was born a 'blue baby' – an imperfect blood flow caused the hands and feet to acquire a blue tinge – and the couple might have lost her but for the neighbourly presence of Tilly Langford, who had been a nurse.

Many years later the family's gratitude was expressed by Irene Busby, the widow of Matt and Jean's second child, Sandy, who said: 'The miscarriages were because she was tiny and they were all twelve-pounders and their lungs didn't expand. When Sheena was born, she had pneumonia and it was Auntie Tilly who kept dipping her in a hot tub and then a cold tub, over and over again, and she survived.'

In the light of the Busbys' terrible difficulties in starting a family, Matt's breakthrough at City could be seen as all the more creditable. But he felt he had deserved greater support. In fairness to City, their directors' attitude to private problems was hardly unusual – and Busby was a special football man, thinking ahead of his time.

He and Jean bore their sadness together. And in private – except for once, when she was talking to a journalist. Eyes filling with tears, she suddenly mentioned the four lost boys and, alluding to the subsequent emergence in vigorous health of Sandy, mused: 'We could have had a forward line.' It was a brave but hopeless joke.

Because Busby was so restless at City – 'I was dwelling morbidly on a run of bad luck' – he had all but resolved to leave when the club made a big signing. The British transfer record remained the £10,890 Chapman had paid for David Jack and City handed over only £890 less to bring Peter Doherty from Blackpool. The 22-year-old Northern Irishman was a lean and energetic inside-left with an unreadable body-swerve, a compendium of tricks and a shot that flashed. A transfer request from Busby was accepted and City, who received £8,000 from Liverpool in March 1936, could claim, when Doherty fully flowered, to have got him for a net £2,000.

Busby was happy to make the short journey to Liverpool with his wife and two children – Sandy had arrived a few weeks earlier – even though the Anfield club were threatened with relegation. He needed a new challenge and even then appreciated that, for footballers, a change can be as good as a rest.

LEARNING FROM KAY

Busby became less injury-prone at Liverpool. Starting at the same time as an energetic manager, George Kay, he instantly felt at home. 'Often misunderstood,' he said of Kay,

> because he could never control his feelings during a match, George was a familiar figure on the trainers' bench, shouting, beseeching, wringing his hands, holding his head in apparent anguish, and making an excellent attempt to kick and head every ball ... but a fanatical enthusiasm for his job ... should never be condemned. He was a very fine man and manager.

Busby had not been enamoured of everything when he arrived: the age structure, for instance. The full-backs were two of the best, but Tom Cooper was 32 and Ernie Blenkinsop 34. In the middle of defence was Tom 'Tiny' Bradshaw, a rare big man among the Wembley Wizards, now 32. As was another Scot, the wing-half Jimmy McDougall. But results improved under Kay and, with Busby's help, relegation was avoided.

He enjoyed a mind-broadening end-of-season tour of Czechoslovakia, Yugoslavia and Romania, for a different kind of football was associated with the banks of the Danube and its short, intricate passing hardly clashed with his own culture: it could be traced back, by way of Jimmy Hogan and like minds among the continental pioneers, to the Victorian amateurs of Queen's Park.

England had lost in Budapest and Prague two summers earlier. Notions of British superiority, amply supported by one-sided encounters with the French, Dutch or Germans before the First World War, were being challenged. Both of England's opponents in 1934 had travelled on to Italy for a World Cup overshadowed by the showmanship and meddling of Benito Mussolini. The dictator was said even to have intervened in the choice of referees – 'FIFA are not organising this tournament,' Jules Rimet declared, 'he is' – and yet the Czechoslovaks had taken Italy to extra time in the final before Mussolini got his way.

The British associations had declined, as usual, to take part. But Busby knew a trick was being missed. His old team-mate Fred

Tilson had, after all, scored in those friendlies against Hungary and Czechoslovakia; they would have found their way into the conversation at Maine Road. Now Busby himself could experience the mid-European game. Although in Zagreb he absorbed the lessons of a 5–1 beating, Liverpool's results were generally positive, with four wins and two losses.

He rested over the summer – the trip to Scotland now involved plenty of golf, to which he had become addicted when playing at the Northenden club during his City days – and returned to training under Kay at Anfield.

Kay was a Mancunian, dark, with kind eyes and a dimpled chin. He had been captain of West Ham when they lost to Bolton in the first Wembley final in 1923 and blossomed in management at Southampton, a Second Division club so short of money he had to concentrate on developing young players. One, Ted Drake, was now burgeoning at Arsenal. Busby could learn a lot about team-building from Kay, who set about rejuvenating Anfield with the likes of Phil Taylor – signed around the same time as Busby – Willie Fagan and the 17-year-old Bill Jones.

Busby's interest in the increasingly recognised art of football management was acute. He had seen how Chapman built Arsenal and, while the idea that the great man cared little for youth development was fallacious – he died of pneumonia after travelling to Guildford to watch the youth team in bitter cold – it was true that Chapman placed much reliance in the transfer market.

But Busby had also seen the leading manager of the post-Chapman period, Frank Buckley, and he preferred to raise his own; Wolverhampton Wanderers were heading for the top with a squad unashamedly based on local youngsters.

There were like minds in Manchester and Louis Rocca was one. It had been Rocca who tried to sign Busby at his lowest ebb. Busby had become involved with the Manchester Catholic community during his City years and got to know Rocca well. He knew United were concentrating on youth development.

But management could wait. Busby was only 28 and receiving rave reviews in his first full season at Anfield. Even if the threat of relegation had returned.

At Easter came a reunion with Busby's old City pals. They, with Peter Doherty, had been on an unbeaten run. At Anfield they won 5–0 by virtue of what the leading football writer Ivan Sharpe called 'the most artistic display I ever saw in the Football League'. They won the return fixture 5–1 and on each occasion Busby chased familiar shadows. At the end of the season, City were champions.

So might City indeed be the new Arsenal? Not quite. While Arsenal regained their title the following season, City were relegated. Somehow, despite Doherty's enduring brilliance. They scored more goals than any other club. And still went down. And Busby stayed up. Indeed he did much to raise Liverpool from 18th to 11th. There were triumphs home and away over City, Doherty and all, to savour.

He kept in touch with Alex Herd at City and they golfed together in Scotland during the summer of 1938. One day Herd failed to appear. Busby was told he had gone with the Hamilton Academical manager, Willie McAndrew, to watch an outstanding 16-year-old with the Junior team Lochgelly Violet. Herd confirmed this but added that Billy Liddell's parents wanted to be sure of his future in football before they let him turn professional. Busby wasted no time in telephoning George Kay, and Liverpool, armed with knowledge of the parents' reservations, were persuasive. One Saturday night Liddell came home from a youth-club dance to find his father and mother waiting. He feared a telling-off for being late but instead was asked: 'Willie, how would you like to live in Liverpool?' A fee of £200 was paid to Lochgelly.

On returning to Anfield to discover Alf Hanson had been transferred to Chelsea – the winger, son of a Norwegian seaman, was about to have even more reason for concealing his true forename of Adolf – Busby took over his departed colleague's responsibility as collector for the Players' Union.

There was a mood of militancy among members, the maximum wage having stayed at £8 a week for a decade. But pressure for action was to be eased by developments beyond any footballer's control.

SLEEP QUIETLY IN YOUR BEDS

Shortly before the 1938 World Cup took place in France, Nazi Germany had swallowed Austria, whose excellent players were instructed to follow their new allegiance. The united team failed to knit and the supposedly strengthened Germans went out after the first round. Italy retained the title. But Adolf Hitler was interested less in football results than further territory and a few weeks into the next season, with Britain seriously concerned about war over Czechoslovakia, the Prime Minister, the conciliatory Neville Chamberlain, took a particularly belligerent speech at Hitler's annual Nuremberg rally as his signal to make a third visit to the Führer and see what could be negotiated.

He returned from Munich at the end of September and, having struggled through a vast crowd, declared: 'I believe it is peace for our time … go home, and sleep quietly in your beds.'

The people awoke to a Football League weekend of which the highlight, certainly in Busby's part of the world, was a Merseyside derby that Everton won 2–1. Some 60,000 at Goodison Park belted out the National Anthem. All over the country the 'peace' was celebrated. Car ownership was increasing and suburbs becoming 'bungalow belts', embodying a feelgood factor caused by emergence from the Depression, even if it had been partly due to rearmament; people were reluctant to believe that the First World War, with all its prolonged horrors, could be followed by a Second. By and large they hailed Chamberlain. Dissenters, such as Winston Churchill, were few.

Liverpool in 1938/39 were the definitive mid-table team with 14 wins, 14 draws and 14 defeats. In the Cup, they were knocked out by Frank Buckley's young and hungry Wolves, whose captain, Stan Cullis, was only 22. Buckley was in the line of game-changers started by Chapman, a visionary. As manager of Blackpool, he had changed their shirts to tangerine. At Wolves, he had adopted old gold and black and turned a squad of local lads into Second Division champions. The achievement of his intensively coached 'Buckley Boys' in finishing second in consecutive seasons lodged in Busby's mind.

Buckley even sent out a pair of 16-year-old wingers, Jimmy Mullen and Alan Steen, against Manchester United. Wolves won 3–0 and Steen scored. If they were good enough, they were old enough. It was to become a Busby mantra.

Alex James had retired but Hughie Gallacher still scored goals. After finally obtaining a divorce he had married Hannah but continued to encounter difficulties with money and alcohol. Signing-on fees seemed to help. He had been with Derby, Notts County and Grimsby Town and was now in the Third Division (North) at Gateshead, whose crowds had swollen to 20,000.

The game still had a distinct Scottish flavour, both in terms of the crowds north of the border – the Scotland v. England record at Hampden had risen to nearly 150,000 – and the apparently inexhaustible number of players sent south. In 1938, the FA Cup final had featured seven Scots, including Shankly, on the victorious Preston side alone.

Even without the departed Bradshaw and ageing McDougall, Liverpool had four. Busby noted how the club had looked after McDougall, paying him top wages long after he had lost his place. Their handling of a stalwart's decline made a big impression; it seemed right to Busby that loyalty should work both ways in a football club, that employees should be 'treated with kindness, consideration and understanding'.

At the end of the season, a man at the opposite end of his career travelled from County Durham to Merseyside. The 20-year-old Bob Paisley was a tenacious little competitor – he wouldn't have minded being compared with the Preston dynamo Shankly – whom Kay had allowed to stay with Bishop Auckland while they completed an outstanding season by winning the FA Amateur Cup. He arrived at Anfield to find Busby had been appointed captain in succession to Tom Cooper.

Busby, remembering the indifference he had met at Manchester City, was quick to welcome Paisley, who thought him a fine man as well as one of the most cultured midfielders around, one who had helped Kay to change the Liverpool style from unceremonious to precise and thoughtful in his own image.

Busby's appetite remained keen; he was only 30. But it was never going to be a normal approach to a season. Younger players were undergoing military training. On the eve of footballing hostilities, there had been appeals for fit men to join the Territorial Army and, upon the League's suggestion that players set an example, Liverpool's were among those who responded, Busby included even though, by his own rueful admission, he was 'not a born soldier'.

The England team had played in Mussolini's Italy, just as they had visited Hitler's Germany the summer before (and been induced to offer a pre-match Nazi salute, to the especial ire of Stan Cullis) but what, it might have been asked, was the future of international football when the erstwhile opposition kept disappearing? Austria had gone, and now all Czechoslovakia, and Lithuania, and Albania, and in late August Hitler's troops were massing on the Polish border that Britain had pledged to protect.

On 1 September 1939 the line was crossed – fortunately for Alex James, who had been coaching in Poland at the request of friends, he had returned a couple of weeks earlier – and on 3 September war was declared.

CHAPTER FOUR

WAR, PEACE AND MANCHESTER UNITED

THE COMMON TOUCH

Liverpool had played three matches in the First Division. They had lost to Sheffield United and beaten Middlesbrough and Chelsea, and so Busby, who had appeared each time (at last with the No.4 on his back under new League regulations), was an ever-present in a meaningless season.

As conscription began straight away, the League was replaced by a regional system with guesting so players could represent the club nearest their unit. On New Year's Day, Billy Liddell made his debut in a 7–3 victory over Crewe Alexandra at Anfield and Busby scored a rare goal. He had joined the Territorials thinking it reasonable to donate the odd evening to the war effort. But he had been a part-time soldier for only a few weeks when the call came to join the 9th Battalion of the King's Regiment (Liverpool) – and now he was a part-time footballer.

In uniform, he became oddly defeatist. He tried to make a joke of how, while spit and polish made other men's boots come up like gleaming patent in which they could see their smiles, his obstinately retained the blank look of basic leather. When drilling, he felt victimised. Until the privilege of his profession was restored

and, in common with other leading footballers nominated by the
FA secretary Stanley Rous – the referee when Busby's City had won
at Wembley in 1934 – he accepted an offer to go to Aldershot and
learn to be a physical training instructor.

He had the stripes of a company sergeant-major and the pleasure
of familiar faces – Frank Swift, Joe Mercer and Cliff Britton from
Everton, Stan Cullis – and things got even better when Rous made
him player/manager of an all-star team whose role was to raise
morale by playing exhibition matches at home and abroad. He was
to be assisted by the erstwhile Tottenham defender Arthur Rowe.

Busby was to acknowledge his luck in being chosen by Rous, for
in the Army he could develop 'the involved technique of handling
men'. He played for Liverpool when possible but also guested for
Hibernian, Chelsea, Reading and Middlesbrough among others.
Unlike most of the Army team, he never made an appearance for
Aldershot. Much to his colleagues' amusement, he once turned up
only to be told Britton would play instead. But he did sign the
scroll of guest players and was therefore erroneously believed to
have trodden the Recreation Ground turf in borrowed colours.

His clubmate Paisley did not initially stray far from Anfield.
Released to play in his first derby, he cycled the 30 miles from a
camp in Cheshire to the Mersey Tunnel and hitched a lift to the
ground. On the return journey, he had time to reflect on Everton's
victory. But soon there was another derby which Liverpool won,
Paisley and Liddell benefiting from Busby's craft.

Early in 1940, during the 'Phoney War' in which Hitler
desisted from bombing Britain and France remained free, Company
Sergeant-Major Instructor Busby's team played the French Army
in Paris. Given that the team included such Aldershot buddies as
Mercer and Cullis, the prospect should have pleased him, but it
entailed a sea crossing that, while relatively short, tormented his
stomach; he was always a reluctant sailor.

A sense of mild paranoia returned, then, as fate decreed he
should become a regular on the flotillas to North Africa by way
of the Cape of Good Hope. These journeys took ten weeks and,
while Busby's ships were never hit by a torpedo or mine, the first
Windsor Castle, following directly behind, was sunk by a missile
fired from an aircraft off Tunisia. Fortunately, she took 13 hours to
go down and only one man – a crew member – died while nearly
3,000 were rescued by destroyers. On more tranquil days, Busby

would conduct PT sessions for bored and sometimes anxious men being transported to theatres of desert conflict.

Bob Paisley, meanwhile, had made just one journey round the Cape. He had arrived in Egypt and, shortly after Christmas 1941, received a postcard from George Kay asking if he would be available for Liverpool's first match of the season; it had taken place four months earlier.

Manning anti-tank guns, Paisley took part in the relief of Tobruk. He served under General Bernard Montgomery at El Alamein and in the final defeat of the Afrika Korps in May 1943, after which Montgomery's army moved triumphantly on to Italy, starting with Sicily and spreading up from the toe to the nation's heart.

Spared the worst of the North Africa campaigns – though the Aldershot group were naturally moved by what they saw during exhibition matches for the blitzed communities of Britain – Busby now had the pleasure of frequent trips home to play for the Army, the United Services or Scotland's unofficial sides. He was honoured to be Scotland's captain, introducing team-mates such as Shankly to royalty and other notables, including Montgomery.

The hugely popular 'Monty' liked football. He had returned from Italy to help to plot the invasion of Normandy and in February 1944 was in Wembley's royal box, seated next to the future Queen Elizabeth II in his trademark bulky greatcoat, to see England beat the Scots 6–2. When he had met the players, he surprised Busby by confessing he had never been to Scotland. 'Shame on you, sir,' said Busby, 'you've missed the grandest country in the world.' Resisting any temptation to ask why, if that were so, Busby had forsaken his homeland for its neighbour to the south, Montgomery smiled and moved on. A couple of months later, the countries met in Glasgow and, with 133,000 emitting the Hampden Roar prior to a more modest defeat – only 3–2 – Montgomery came out to be presented to the teams. Busby welcomed him and the smile returned to the general's face as he said: 'You see, Sergeant-Major – I have managed to get to Scotland.'

Busby cherished the memory. He also absorbed Montgomery's common touch; such disarming attention to human detail would be a constant companion on his journey in football management. Just as Busby could take pride in a familiarity with Montgomery, many a soul in or around the game would come to believe that somehow he had caught the eye of Busby.

But where, Busby wondered, would fate take him when the war ended, so he could use the ideas with which his head was filling? By June, when the American-led Allies liberated Rome, and Bob Paisley, among many others, rode into the city on a tank, Busby had options. One was back at Liverpool: he could become George Kay's assistant on a five-year contract, starting at £10 a week.

When Busby told the Anfield directors he preferred to be a manager in his own right, there were hints that the timescale might permit it. The notion of waiting for the 53-year-old Kay, whom he so admired, to retire, leave or be sacked did not appeal. But he accepted the offer verbally. He was still a registered player with Liverpool, and the club envisaged he would remain so, but nearing the end of his career.

And then, just before Christmas 1944, Busby received the letter that would decide his future.

Addressed to him care of his unit, it came from Louis Rocca's home at 37 Craigwell Road, Prestwich. It reached him while he was instructing at Sandhurst and it read:

Dear Matt,
    No doubt you will be surprised to get this letter from your old pal Louis. Well Matt I have been trying for the past month to find you and not having your reg. address I could not trust a letter going to Liverpool, as what I have to say is so important. I don't know if you have considered about what you are going to do when war is over, but I have a great job for you if you are willing to take it on. Will you get in touch with me at the above address and when you do I can explain things to you better, when I know there will be no danger of interception. Now Matt I hope this is plain to you. You see I have not forgotten my old friend either in my prayers or in your future welfare. I hope your good wife and family are all well and please God you will soon be home to join their happy circle.
    Wishing you a very Happy Xmas and a lucky New Year.
    With all God's Blessings in you and yours
    Your Old Pal
    Louis Rocca

Busby might have guessed what the job was. He could not have known he had been under consideration since 1942, when the United chairman, James Gibson, had visited an old friend in Dorset who was the officer in charge of sport for the Southern Command. The chairman was grateful for the work Rocca and the club secretary, Walter Crickmer, were doing as caretakers but wanted a younger man to continue the United project after the war. Prominent among those mentioned by his friend, Captain Bill Williams, had been Busby.

Gibson asked Williams to keep an eye on him. But it was Rocca's keen ear that discovered Liverpool's intention to groom Busby. Hence the letter. Busby replied and, upon hearing Gibson did indeed want to interview him, promised to travel to Manchester on his next spell of leave.

He spoke to Jean. Until then, he had planned to learn management through a sort of apprenticeship at a club with potential outside the First Division. But did they not know of footballers who had gone straight into a big job and survived? Bob McGrory had made the transition at Stoke and done well; Bill Murray, another Scot, looked set to follow a similar path at Sunderland; Jimmy Seed, twice a champion with Sheffield Wednesday, was the extremely successful manager of Charlton Athletic. And did the prospect of staying in north-west England, where the Busbys were so happily settled with their children, now aged eleven and eight, not make Manchester United doubly attractive? Yes, he would listen to their chairman and, if the conditions were right, give it a go.

He headed north, initially to Birmingham, where he played in yet another international. Thereafter he was supposed to be spending time off in Scotland, and he eventually did, after a stop in Manchester. There, at the premises of one of Gibson's companies – Cornbrook Cold Storage at 14 Hadfield Street, an address with which Busby would become familiar – he and the chairman reached a bold and momentous agreement. Busby would stop playing football and, at Old Trafford, start a revolution.

He would have absolute control over coaching appointments and player recruitment and indeed anything he regarded as crucial to the playing side of the club. Even the great Herbert Chapman had needed to win a power struggle with his first Arsenal chairman, Sir Henry Norris, to achieve that. But something about Busby and the harmonic chiming of their ideas convinced Gibson.

When he suggested a term of three years, Busby demanded five, the span Chapman had famously secured from Arsenal in 1925, and said that, for his part, he would be careful with such money as the club made available, that prudence would be fundamental to his methods. Gibson replied that, if he wanted five years, he could have them, dating from one month after his demobilisation.

MAW, I'M 36 YEARS OLD

Financial terms were also drawn up at Busby's meeting with James Gibson in early February: he would start on £15 a week and have a club-owned house in Chorlton-cum-Hardy, roughly equidistant from Old Trafford and Maine Road. Clad in khaki, he signed the contract but it was resolved that nothing would be made public until the other United directors had been informed and Busby become disengaged from Liverpool.

The latter requirement proved fraught. Liverpool suspected he might continue playing, despite assurances to the contrary, and hinted at a transfer fee. Busby insisted he would retire and was promised his release. Having asked Kay if he might be allowed a farewell appearance at Anfield, he continued his journey to Scotland.

He was excited and in a mood to celebrate. One day he brought a few pals home with a bottle of whisky. When his mother came in, it became clear that Nellie, now in her mid-fifties, retained her distaste for alcohol. She eyed her son and the glass he held.

'What's that in your hand?'

'Whisky, Maw.'

'You shouldn't be drinking that stuff.'

'But Maw, I'm 36 years old.'

The United board were to meet on 15 February. The day before found Busby speaking to the *Daily Record*, waffling, giving an impression that he saw his future as a manager in Scotland. This was duly made public. Nothing to the contrary emerged from Manchester. On the 17th, however, he attended a Queen's Park match at Hampden Park and fell into conversation with a man from the *Sunday Mail*, which, the next day, carried a Busby exclusive:

About two weeks ago he received a grand offer of the managership of Manchester United. As it happened, he had a verbal understanding with his own club, Liverpool, concerning the job of player/coach. Nothing binding of course, but Matt thought it only right that he should formally ask for his release from his promise … the Liverpool club held a board meeting to discuss the matter and decided to agree to his release. The press had … presumed his journey to Scotland was linked with a job north of the border.

Whether Busby intended the truth to be published or not, only one more day had passed when United ended their silence and made the formal announcement.

The Liverpool board refused Busby his Anfield farewell but he would play a few more times for the forces team, and for Scotland; in a 6–1 England victory at Hampden he failed from the penalty spot when Swift, with whom he had spent many hours helpfully practising penalties at Manchester City, won a guessing game. And then the all-stars gathered at the Great Western Hotel in Paddington for dinner and a night's sleep before transferring to Wiltshire for an RAF flight to Naples.

Busby and his pals were to tour Italy and Greece, entertaining troops. Hearts had been lightened by the German surrender in Italy and the imminence of victory in Europe. The defeated Mussolini had tried to escape to Italy's northern lakes but had been captured by partisans and shot dead. Hitler had killed himself as the Soviets moved on Berlin and unconditional surrender would follow in a matter of days. Britain's bunting was being prepared.

Although not quite a holiday for Busby – pockets of resistance were evident from the occasional burst of distant gunfire – the tour was enjoyable, none the worse for nights under canvas or bumpy rides in the back of the team's truck as it negotiated dusty roads; they posed happily for the photographs, Busby with his hair slightly thinning now, the dark Tommy Lawton with his off-centre parting, the wonkily smiling Joe Mercer with his bow legs and the genial giant Swift. Each player had his responsibility, allocated by Busby. He reasoned that Mercer, whose wife's family were in the grocery business, would know a little about the procurement of food, so he became 'messing officer' in charge of scrounging from villagers, while the tee-total technician Cliff Britton took charge of the truck. Swift, who had forgotten to bring his boots, might have seemed a surprising selection as baggage man.

Jack Rowley was invalided out of the squad with dysentery but the young tank driver Tom Finney joined up, with relief, after all the fierce conflict he had experienced; no Desert Rat deserved the taunts of 'dodgers' aimed by some in the crowds.

After Lawton and Swift had borrowed the truck to see Pompeii, the players made a sombre visit to the ruined monastery of Monte Cassino, where men had died in tens of thousands. There was a match in Rome, where the party were granted an audience with Pope Pius XII – the highlight for a good Catholic like Busby – and then it was off to Florence, to the ports of Ancona and Bari and across the Adriatic to Greece.

In Athens, there was a delightful illustration of why Rous had chosen Busby to lead the players. They faced a Greek team and a dispute arose over a free-kick the referee had awarded to Busby's side. As the Greek protests became increasingly vehement, Busby seized the ball and, before anyone could react, took the free-kick, pretending to aim it at goal but making sure it sailed harmlessly wide. He then ran to collect it and placed it for a goal-kick which, upon his beckoning, the Greek keeper took. Such diplomacy.

It was on that tour, at the port city of Bari, that Busby came across Jimmy Murphy.

Although this meeting was later to be portrayed as, for Busby, something of a Pauline revelation, in fact they went back a while. When Busby had played his only official international in Cardiff in 1933, Murphy had been among the victorious Welsh. They had faced each other in the First Division, for Murphy had spent a decade with West Bromwich Albion. He was a wing-half of the gritty kind. Before a match at Anfield in 1938, Busby had been chatting to him in a corridor when Tom Cooper walked past on his way to the dressing room. Nodding in Murphy's direction, Busby told his team-mate: 'You always need two pairs of shin-pads when you play against this fellow.'

But now, in the heat of an Adriatic afternoon, Murphy was doing the talking and Busby listened. Surrounding Murphy were young soldiers. Murphy was a Desert Rat, a sergeant in the Royal Artillery, and had seen a lot of action. He had earned some respite and been told to take over from Stan Cullis as chief instructor at a sports centre for lads resting and recovering from the rigours of war. He was talking to them about football and such was the force of his eloquence that Busby became transfixed.

Although Busby had come across countless characters, Murphy was one of a special few, a serious football man who could deliver a message with unforgettable clarity and, more important, fervently wanted to do so. Sergeant Murphy had experienced things even more harrowing than the congregation of pathetically debilitated and dysentery-ravaged German prisoners whose plight had moved Busby on one of his voyages back from Africa. And yet he still cared enough about helping young men with their football that relaxation could wait.

Busby would need such a man.

He spent plenty of time with Murphy in Bari and promised that, when he started at Manchester United, he would call Murphy to be his assistant. And he outlined the task. It would not be easy, for Old Trafford could not host First Division fixtures in the foreseeable future. In addition, United were so deep in debt there would be little or no buying of players. Busby and Murphy would have to improve those already at the club – and bring on youngsters, which would be the bulk of Murphy's role. Murphy didn't mind the sound of that. Not at all; as Busby had noticed, it was his passion.

And Murphy needed a job. He was approaching his mid-thirties and, after relegation with West Bromwich, had dropped down another division to Swindon just before the war. It was time to start coaching in earnest. Busby had known what he wanted to do and, after his experience of handling top-class players, was more confident than ever. And now Murphy knew.

THE ROCCA LEGACY

Although prejudice against Germans had been exacerbated by the second war – there were to be widespread protests when, in 1949, Manchester City signed the former prisoner-of-war Bernhard 'Bert' Trautmann to replace Frank Swift in goal – by and large Manchester took pride in its pockets of diversity. There was a song in the pubs. It alluded to the Cup finals held in cosmopolitan London and, although the words altered from time to time, went along these lines:

Why do you wanna go to Wembley?
Worra you wanna go to Wembley for?
Take a walk down Ancoats Lane

And you're in Italy so grand
Take a walk up Oldham Road
And you're in I-re-land
China and Japan in Upper Brook Street
Africa's in Moss Side, so they say ...

The largely Irish area where Busby lived in his first City days had indeed housed some Africans, mainly seamen and their families, since the 1920s ...

And if you wanna go further still
Palestine's in Cheetham Hill

Busby was to make friends among the Jewish community spreading out from Cheetham Hill to the more verdant likes of Prestwich as prosperity grew, as well as the predominantly Catholic descendants of Irish and Italians. Of Irish stock himself, he was familiar with Italian immigrants from his Lanarkshire youth. They were well enough liked, the Italians in Scotland, because they had come bearing affordable luxuries such as the ice-cream Tony Coia purveyed from his cart in Bellshill; rather than competing for the locals' jobs, they had brightened their lives.

It was much the same in Manchester. From the late nineteenth century, Ancoats had been the city's 'Little Italy', splashing colour on a grimy expanse of mills, foundries, glassworks and terraced houses. The arias of Enrico Caruso drifted from wind-up gramophones through open windows and the barrel organs of hurdy-gurdy men played 'O Sole Mio' or 'Torna a Surriento' as pedestrians enjoyed their ice-cream. There were even shops selling ham and cheese, oil and wine. And then had come the Second World War. When Mussolini threw in Italy's lot with Hitler, many men between 17 and 60 were interned at Worth Mill, Bury. The Manchester Italian Catholic Society, formed in 1888, helped to console their womenfolk and keep the community together.

Now Louis Rocca was in his late fifties: second generation, a pillar of Catholic society and of Manchester United. His real name was Luigi, the same as his father's. Luigi Rocca Sr had been brought up in Borzonasca, a village in prettily wooded hills east of Genoa where life was harder than it looked. At 27 he left and Ancoats, for all its rain and fug, was where he stopped. He married an Italian girl from Sheffield and from the cellar of their home ran an ice-cream business. Just as men called Pietro usually preferred to be known as Peter, and Giuseppe to be Joseph or Joe, he was Louis. He had several children and little Louis was football mad.

By the age of 12, little Louis had become a tea-boy at the Bank Street ground of the Second Division club Newton Heath and, while still in his teens, he had attended a famous 1902 meeting chaired by a much-needed benefactor, the brewer and philanthropist John Henry Davies.

Having ordered a change of colours to red with white shorts (Newton Heath had begun as a railway workers' club wearing green and gold and later switched to white and blue), Davies decided to supervise a more democratic change of name and Manchester United got the vote after objections to Manchester Celtic (too redolent of another club's history) and Manchester Central (liable to be confused with the railway station, presumably). In between, Rocca had been acting as kit man, part-time groundsman and scout, all unpaid.

The word most frequently used to describe his role over the next quarter century was 'fixer' – what United needed, he would arrange through his contacts. With the excellent Ernest Mangnall in charge of a team featuring the great Billy Meredith, the League was won twice and the FA Cup once. A guide to Rocca's contribution was that, when Meredith and his team-mates returned from Crystal Palace with the Cup in 1909, an umbrella sheltering them as they waved to the crowds from a horse-drawn coach bore the slogan 'Rocca's Brigade'.

The following year United moved to Old Trafford. By 1912, when Mangnall rather spoiled things by leaving for City, Rocca had taken over the family business. What with that and helping his wife to raise nine children, he did well to find time for the club.

After the death of Davies in 1927, United sought a new benefactor with increasing urgency until in 1931 the local sports journalist Stacey Lintott, brother of the former England defender and posthumous war hero Evelyn Lintott, suggested James Gibson. Crickmer and Rocca did the rest.

Gibson was in textiles. He had become rich making uniforms during the First World War and, when it ended, come up with a Plan B, which was to persuade the transport authorities that their drivers and conductors ought to wear uniforms too.

He was secured in the nick of time. United had been relegated under Herbert Bamlett and, with a debt of £30,000, their very existence was under threat. And not for the first time. But Stacey Lintott, who lunched regularly with a group including Gibson, said:

> I knew he had a reputation for taking over failing business and restoring them. Here was his big chance. He had no interest in football but he had a love of Manchester and would deeply regret the collapse of such a famous local institution.

A few months later, Crickmer had gone to the bank for the players' wages and been politely rebuffed. They got their money in the end but not, this year, the customary turkey for Christmas. Gibson, having put Crickmer in temporary charge with Rocca as his assistant, went to the press demanding evidence that United were worth saving. On Christmas Day more than 33,000, four times the average attendance, saw Wolves beaten 3–2.

Although such support reassured Gibson, he had resolved not merely to throw money at the club. The minutes of his first board meeting at the end of 1931 mentioned the starting of a 'colts' or 'nursery' team the next season 'so that a common idea and technique shall unite the junior with the senior members of the playing staff'. It could have been Frank Buckley talking – indeed, with Lintott's prompting, Gibson had made an unsuccessful approach to the Wolves manager, a Mancunian who had made a few appearances for United under Mangnall – but there was certainly no conflict with the aspirations of Rocca and Crickmer.

Without delay Rocca had formed a network of scouts from people he knew through the Manchester Catholic Sportsman's Club. United duly started an 'A' team of under-18s selected from schools and youth clubs. The first team endured travails under the new management of Scott Duncan but, by the time they had avoided the Third Division and settled for something between the First and Second, youngsters of true quality were being engaged and integrated. In the years leading to the war these included Johnny Carey, Allenby Chilton, John Aston, Stan Pearson, John Anderson, Charlie Mitten and Johnny Morris. A great deal more was to be heard of them, and others.

Rocca had gladly handed £250 to the League of Ireland club St James's Gate for Carey, whom he had been implored to watch by his man in Dublin, the former United reserve goalkeeper Billy Behan. Young Carey, who had been with St James's Gate for only a couple of months, could hardly believe the newspaper billboard that greeted him on arrival in Manchester: 'United Make Big Signing!' He eagerly bought the evening papers only to find that their excitement concerned the £4,500 arrival of Ernie Thompson, a bustling centre-forward from Blackburn.

Carey was 17. So was Jack Rowley, for whom £3,000 was paid to Bournemouth on the insistence of the chairman. Within a fortnight, Scott Duncan had resigned. Crickmer and Rocca went on to supervise a successful promotion campaign.

The club were, of course, lucky to have found the wealthy and visionary Gibson. But they were also blessed with Crickmer, a small and spare man of boundless energy, still only in his mid-forties but with more than 20 years' experience as secretary and well schooled in the United culture of prudence. Before the war, Charlie Mitten had been persuaded by Crickmer to re-sign for £20 – half to be paid immediately and half when he returned safe and sound. 'That was typical of Walter,' said Mitten, 'always looking after the cash.'

United were also very fortunate to have such a practised organiser of talent-spotting. Long before the phrase became institutional, Rocca established football in the community – and the community responded. The Manchester United Junior Athletic Club, to be known as the MUJACs, had been founded in 1938/39 with a brief to feed the 'A' and reserve teams with local boys. It was based at The Cliff, the former home of the Broughton Rangers rugby-league club, on which Gibson had taken a lease so it could become United's training ground.

At the end of that season, Crickmer and Rocca's first team having finished 14th, the reserves had won the Central League, the 'A' team composed of under-18s were champions of the open-age Manchester League and the MUJACs had finished top of a suburban league. A machine was functioning to the extent that Gibson declared: 'We have no intention of buying any more mediocrities. In years to come we will have a Manchester United composed of Manchester players.'

Upon the outbreak of war, The Cliff became a base for barrage balloons. Part of Old Trafford had been requisitioned for military use, but the munitions factories of Trafford Park and adjacent docks and rail yards were almost certainly the main targets when, late in 1940, the stadium and nearby Lancashire cricket ground were hit. Nearly a thousand people died in Manchester and Salford.

Although the damage was enough to cause the switching of a Christmas fixture against Stockport County to Edgeley Park, regional football continued at Old Trafford until March 1941, when, as sirens shrieked and searchlights frantically scanned the sky, stray bombs from enemy squadrons mounting a further three-hour assault on the industrial estate wrecked much of the stadium. When James Gibson heard, he cried, and it was the only time his son Alan ever saw him do that.

Patrolling nearby was Walter Crickmer. A special constable by night, he was buried under rubble but escaped with minor injuries. Johnny Carey was cycling to work at the Metro Vickers aircraft factory when he saw a 'huge ball of fire' over the stadium. It had sustained severe damage to the main stand, now roofless, offices and dressing rooms. Matches were henceforth to be played at Maine Road by arrangement with City, and the United headquarters became a single room at Gibson's premises.

When, eventually, Charlie Mitten reported back, he saw Crickmer and, having been re-engaged, asked for the second half of his £20 signing-on fee. 'He looked at me and said, "Bloody hell, I thought you'd have forgotten all about that." And I said, "Do you know, Walter, it's the only thing that's kept me alive."'

Mitten was one of hundreds who had lost six years in the game. Some had lost more. Three from United had died: the highly rated full-back Hubert Redwood from tuberculosis and younger aspirants Ben Carpenter and George Curless in action. Allenby Chilton had been twice wounded in France, Johnny Hanlon captured by Italians in Crete and sent to a POW camp in Germany.

Busby's old team-mate Tom Cooper had served with the Military Police as a dispatch rider and died in 1940 when his motorcycle collided with a bus in Suffolk. Cooper was the only Liverpool player killed in the war. Bob Paisley had travelled far and wide and yet suffered injury only once through temporary blindness – bad enough until it was treated – from desert sand splashed in his face by Luftwaffe gunfire. For him and the rest of the Liverpool squad George Kay had assembled, there were good times ahead.

THE TRACKSUIT MANAGER

One by one the footballers came back from the war and in the autumn of 1945 it was Matt Busby who arrived at Manchester Victoria station, went to the club house in Chorlton-cum-Hardy where he had installed Jean and the children, eased himself out of khaki for the last time, and began work as a manager. Having no car, he caught a bus to Gibson's premises. When he went to The Cliff, he had to take two buses, changing in the city centre for Lower Broughton, and the journey took an hour.

He had to make do without Murphy, yet to be demobbed, but was hardly bereft of staff. Busby instantly recognised Tom Curry as a football man of value. Since 1934, the first team had been trained by Curry, a former Newcastle wing-half who at Carlisle had earned the devotion of a knowledge-hungry Bill Shankly. The reserves received the benefit of Bill Inglis, a Scot and former United reserve full-back. Inglis, too, was kept on.

Already on the books were 10 of the 11 players destined for an afternoon of glory at Wembley. But only Carey, Rowley, the wartime signing Henry Cockburn and goalkeeper Jack Crompton were in the team who took part in Busby's first match. It was in the League North – the Football League would not resume until the following season – and Carey scored one of United's goals in a 2–1 win over Bolton Wanderers at Maine Road.

Busby had established a different style of management. On the very day he had introduced himself to the players – he knew only Carey, whom he had met when representing the British Army against Ireland in Belfast and found instantly impressive – a statement had been silently made. The players were dressed as all teams did for training then. They wore woollen jumpers with roll necks and baggy cotton shorts. Normally the manager would turn up in a suit and hat and shoes unsuited to the mud. Not Busby. He was kitted out as a player, down to the boots with studs. This was revolutionary.

Far from being a remote figure, he supervised training closely. He would even join in the practice matches and teach by example; he remained fit and more than accomplished enough. When the game was over, he would slip back into his tracksuit and continue teaching. He became known as the first 'tracksuit manager' and, in that sense, was to change the face of management even more radically than Herbert Chapman.

From then on, practice was intended to make perfect. Training would no longer be mere exercise. Its link with the entertainment offered to the crowd on Saturday was established. Chapman had done it with Arsenal in the late 1920s and early 1930s, while Busby was making his way with City, and, although Busby's footballing philosophy differed from Chapman's, he was essentially after the same thing. He wanted football to be a matter of educated instinct. That he did not expect it overnight was evident from the length of contract he had demanded from Gibson. All he underestimated, perhaps, was the quality of the men coming home from the war.

His training sessions began with the traditional lapping of the track and trotting up and down the damaged Old Trafford terraces. Then there would be ball work – more than players had been accustomed to – on the Manchester Ship Canal Company's ground or the rough and cinder-strewn ground behind the ruined stand: 'round the back' it was called, this humble centre of excellence. And then a match in which Busby would play, occasionally pausing to offer a tip. As the match went on, he could be seen explaining his points. The recipients listened. Busby could read the game like a child's book and land the ball on the proverbial sixpence. He didn't need to ask for respect. Or to shout. Or to pull his new-found rank. Like Chapman, he encouraged the players to debate in the dressing room and didn't mind strong characters such as the Normandy veteran Chilton if he felt the team – the family – would benefit.

On the morning of his first match as a manager, United had lain 16th in a table of 22. They had won one of 11 matches. But there was quite a Busby bounce and, despite a chastening Christmas in which they lost twice to the best team in the division, Sheffield United, they achieved some impressive results, including a 5–0 win on Busby's return to Liverpool, finishing fourth.

The FA Cup had returned, with matches up to and including the quarter-finals being played over two legs, and although United, after removing Accrington Stanley, lost 3–2 on aggregate to Preston, the home match drew an encouraging 36,237 to their temporarily adopted home.

Sadly, a more memorable event took place at nearby Bolton, where a quarter-final against Stoke attracted an estimated 85,000 and, in the ensuing crush, 33 were killed and hundreds injured. After the casualties were removed from Burnden Park, the match proceeded to a scoreless conclusion. Bolton, who prevailed 2–0 on aggregate – Stanley Matthews was only one of the participants dismayed to be told to play on – were beaten in the semi-finals and the Cup went to Derby.

And in the summer Murphy joined Busby.

The Welshman went home to the Midlands first and was introduced to his fourth child. James Murphy Junior was aged three. Then it was off to Manchester.

Although United's was not the only stadium hit during the war – Arsenal's Highbury also required repair – Old Trafford had suffered badly. There had been grants for the dismantling of what was left of the stand roof and seating and basic tidying-up, but the extra £17,500 promised by the War Damage Commission for rebuilding could not be used for at least a couple of years because the government had made an understandable priority of bombed housing. The team were to be long-term lodgers. Rent now had to be paid to City: £5,000 a year in addition to the previous 10 per cent of turnstile takings. Busby would have to keep his promise to be careful with money.

At Old Trafford, a wooden hut served as a gymnasium; the original, along with the players' recreation room and the boardroom, lay in idle disrepair. Only one of the dressing rooms had been patched up, for the reserve teams of both United and City. The pitch had been carefully cleared of shattered glass and stones by an army of volunteers. They included an 11-year-old schoolboy of artistic bent, Harold Riley. At the end of a day's work, Riley recalled, 'Matt came strolling across to thank us personally. He didn't need to, but that was his way.'

The air of austerity was hardly dispelled by cramped conditions at Cornbrook where Crickmer worked with a young assistant, Les Olive, and a typist borrowed from the chairman's company. And, of course, Busby, when a manager's administrative duties called.

But things weren't as bad as they looked. Not if football was about players; on Rocca's watch a rare collection had been assembled. Not if it was about getting the best out of them; Busby had his ideas about that. Not if it was about forming, with Murphy, younger ones brought up in the same way, to challenge them. How he needed James Patrick Murphy.

Busby was from a mining community in Scotland, Murphy one in Wales; the Maindy colliery in Ton Pentre was a sort of Orbiston of the Rhondda. Both were practising Catholics with Irish hinterland. Jimmy's father, William, had come from Kilkenny. Jimmy was above average at school and his mother wanted him to avoid the pit by becoming a teacher. Like Busby, Murphy chose football instead. Unlike Busby, he managed to dodge the pit altogether, for he was such a terrier of a wing-half that West Bromwich took him straight from school.

Murphy was as foul-mouthed as Busby was fastidious. While Busby would advise players to take retribution with cunning and apologise as if for an accident, Murphy would tell them to get their retaliation in early. But Murphy loved his football as much as Busby, and was every bit as keen to teach, and even better at it, which was why Busby had taken him aside by the Adriatic.

They were to share day-to-day work with the first team but Murphy would bring through replenishments by looking after the reserves and, on Tuesday and Thursday evenings, heading to The Cliff to coach the kids. Even in the winter, eventually, for Gibson envisaged floodlights. Murphy would also scout wherever tips sent him and was to prove brilliant at it, instantly gaining Busby's trust.

His relish was infectious, not least in the matches that rounded off training. Murphy would play on one side, Busby the other. As in most families, there were mutterings. The cocky Mitten was one who didn't think Murphy or Busby were teaching him things he didn't know. At the other extreme was Carey, quiet and studious, Busby's choice as captain, a leader who reflected Busby's ways. Carey, like Busby, never swore. He didn't smoke or drink and was considered a tightwad by the Mitten fraternity.

In the interests of bonding, Busby gave every player a club blazer and flannels, took them on outings to the seaside at Blackpool, where their hotel was the prestigious Norbreck Hydro, organised visits to shows at the Manchester theatres and presented them with free passes to the cinema. There were golfing Mondays at the lovely Davyhulme Park with its art deco clubhouse, rounded off with a communal evening meal of mixed grill, and, if any of the players found any of this a little paternalistic, they were hopelessly ahead of their time.

This was how to enjoy being a footballer in the era of the maximum wage. Busby had the knack of managing men; even Mitten understood that. There was a good feeling about the club.

Busby made another key off-the-field appointment in Bert Whalley, who had joined United from nearby Stalybridge Celtic before the war but never really established himself as a first-teamer. Whalley was well into his thirties when Busby gave him a more important role assisting Murphy with the youngsters. There were not too many around when Murphy and Whalley started – the reserves reflected the youth policy's natural decay during the war – but it was quite a first team Busby picked when Manchester United made their Football League comeback on the last day of August 1946. Only three would not have their names etched in club history as members of 'the 1948 team'.

CHAPTER FIVE

THE 1948 TEAM: ROCKY ROAD TO WEMBLEY

FIT AS BUTCHERS' DOGS

When the League resumed, Busby had paid just one transfer fee: £4,000 for Jimmy Delaney from Celtic. The deal had raised eyebrows because, although Delaney was a Scotland winger of acknowledged class, he had taken two years to get over a broken arm and was suspected of 'brittle bones'. Also, he was 31; how much service could he give United?

The question was to be magnificently answered.

In addition, Busby had good men out of khaki and back in red. Some survivors from 1938/39 who had gained First Division experience at a tender age: Johnny Carey and Stan Pearson were now 28, Jack Rowley 26. To them could be added Allenby Chilton, 28, Charlie Mitten, 26, Henry Cockburn, John Aston and the goalkeeper Jack Crompton, each 25, Johnny Morris, 23, and Joe Walton, just 21 yet rated highly enough to have played with Mitten in an unofficial England side that drew with Scotland at Maine Road in aid of the Burnden Park dependants. Jack Warner, who had played before the war, was still going strong at nearly 35.

Busby had seen enough in practice matches at The Firs – the grounds of Manchester University at Fallowfield, near Maine

Road – to convince him a decent season lay ahead. New training kit was bought with clothing coupons, some collected by Tom Curry in a dressing-room whip-round, others donated by fans in response to an appeal by Busby. Neither post-war austerity nor a stormy late August deterred nearly a million from flocking to England's football grounds, with more than 41,000 at Maine Road to see United beat Grimsby 2–1.

Those who read Busby's programme notes were asked to bear in mind, when a player had an 'off day', that he was human and 'not a mechanical engine which, when you press a button, goes through its work'. This might have been intended to help Chilton, who had a tendency to attract blame for goals; though a formidable man, a leader by nature and Normandy veteran, he was, as Busby said, only human. Busby had put the former wing-half between the full-backs. Behind him was Crompton, despite well-founded rumours that Busby wanted to lure Swift from United's landlords, who had another season to serve in the Second Division.

The wing-halves were Warner and the very bright little Cockburn. Like Walton, who continued to work as a plumber, Cockburn was a local boy with a full-time job away from football. He was an engineer's fitter at an Oldham cotton mill. But his football career had taken off after Busby, watching a reserve match, switched him from inside-forward to wing-half. It was the move that had made Busby's own playing career and, in Cockburn's case, the effect of being allowed to face the play was even more spectacular. Within weeks he was making his England debut.

Cockburn tackled with such ferocious relish that journalists portrayed him as a terrier. The players could see his feline side: they called him 'Mouser'. Either way, he had Jimmy Murphy's love of chasing, catching and killing an attack. And then he'd start one of his own. He could pass precisely, and see the game. And, for a man of 5' 4", he was extraordinary in the air. But he had only average pace and that was probably why Busby had moved him back.

In Cockburn's second League match, a 3–0 win at rainy Chelsea, he impressed Walter Winterbottom, who had just been appointed England's first manager (and director of coaching) by Stanley Rous. A youthful member of the crowd was John Moynihan, later to write the classic *Soccer Syndrome*. He noticed that despite rationing, the United players looked 'fit as butchers' dogs, as if the Busby effect was already at work'.

Winterbottom, a United defender before the war, had gone to watch his old club with one of the FA selectors; the England team was still picked by committee and, after Grimsby's Arthur Drewry had seen United's opening match, the manager was accompanied at Stamford Bridge by Arthur Oakley of Wolves. This was in early September. By the end of the month Cockburn had dazzled in a 7–2 triumph over Ireland in Belfast. On the Monday, he went back to the mill and on the Tuesday, after finishing his shift, he trained.

At Liverpool, Bob Paisley was making his way. In their third match George Kay's team conceded four to Chelsea at Anfield, but it hardly mattered because the goals were flying in even more frequently at the other end, Billy Liddell scoring two of Liverpool's seven. And then they visited United and, finding Busby's forwards in irresistible form, conceded five without reply. Stan Pearson, Paisley's direct opponent, completed a hat-trick. If Busby had been a vindictive man, he might have said something along the lines of 'Every time we play you, we beat you 5–0 – that'll teach you to deny me a farewell match' but he had too many happy memories of the Anfield club, too many friends there, and too much regard for Kay, to crow and cackle.

Also he would have been well aware that, in a football season, you don't always get the last laugh.

The spanking lent urgency to Liverpool's pursuit of Albert Stubbins and the Newcastle centre-forward, signed for £12,500, proved just the catalyst they needed. Linking with Liddell and Jack Balmer, one of six regulars who had played alongside Busby before the war, he inspired an unbeaten run of 12 matches, the last three featuring Balmer hat-tricks. Now Kay's team, as well as Busby's, were among the runners in a thrilling title race.

In midwinter United's return match with Grimsby proved significant, for they travelled amid a full-back crisis exacerbated when Walton, in the course of his plumbing duties, fell off a plank, fracturing a wrist. Most squad members with full-back experience were injured, so Bert Whalley would be restored. The other position Busby decided to give to John Aston, who had been tried at inside-forward and wing-half but might, the manager thought, benefit from his habit of moving players back, making them more comfortable on the ball and increasing the team's creative potential.

Aston and Whalley, having played together in the reserves, were friends. On reaching Humberside and being told Busby was pairing them as full-backs, Whalley asked if the junior man would prefer right or left. Perhaps this was typical Whalley kindness; perhaps Busby had asked him to make discreet inquiries. Aston said he would think about it.

He then went with Whalley to a toyshop to buy furniture for a doll's house he had made for his daughter as a Christmas present. The shopkeeper, hearing their accents, assumed he was talking to United supporters and said he'd go to the match himself if it weren't for 'that bloody outside-right' of Grimsby's whose shortcomings he listed. They emerged from the shop, each with the same thought. 'Are you playing left-back then?' asked Whalley. 'I am that,' grinned Aston. He earned rave reviews and went on to become an international left-back.

At the end of a long winter of many postponements – and, away from football, much criticism of Clement Attlee's Labour government for failing to get to grips with the ice and snow – United drew vast crowds to their lodgings. They were the closest challengers to the title favourites, Wolves, when they went to Liverpool – and lost to the only goal, scored by Stubbins. Busby's team refused to give up, Rowley breaking a club record with 26 League goals, but were helpless as the race culminated in Liverpool's visit to Molineux. It was Stan Cullis's final match before retiring due to persistent concussion, and he wanted to go out with a medal.

Midway through the first half, a ball was chipped over the home defence for Stubbins, who had anticipated it and had a start on Cullis. There was only one way to stop him and, in those days, the professional foul was not an automatically dismissible offence, but Cullis couldn't bring himself to perform it. Asked why, he was always to reply: 'I didn't want to go down in history as the man who decided the destiny of a championship with a professional foul.' Instead Stubbins, having scored, got the medal.

Busby, as after leaving City, had missed out on the title by one season. Maybe he regretted tipping off George Kay about Liddell.

United finished ahead of Wolves on goal average, and to be runners-up – the club's highest position since the 1910/11 title – was highly encouraging. Less so had been a home defeat by Nottingham Forest in the Cup during which the injured Mitten's place had gone to Ted Buckle, a 22-year-old Londoner who had been spotted playing for the Navy and become the first signing of the Busby era, his November arrival preceding Delaney's by three months.

Buckle had gone on to score in wins over Charlton and Middlesbrough and was kept in the side when Mitten regained fitness. Mitten responded with a transfer request, which Busby rejected. But he continued to overlook Mitten. Repeatedly. Pointedly. For all the earnestness of Busby's utopian intentions, for all his faith that kindness in a football club would bring its own reward – the approach conspicuous by its absence from City when he had arrived in Manchester – it entailed a framework of the rigid discipline that a footballer's terms of employment then encouraged.

Nor should a director cross him lightly. Busby had, after all, come to the job with the idea of unity and, if too tactful to add that meant unity on his terms, was clear on this: he would enforce Gibson's promise of non-interference.

The first to transgress was Harold Hardman. Although a solicitor, Hardman had a football pedigree to go with his lean and hungry look. If Busby had asked to see his medals, Hardman could have flourished souvenirs of Cup finals – when a winger with Everton, he had known victory over Newcastle in 1906 and defeat by the Wednesday a year later – and, if that didn't work, flashed the Olympic gold obtained in 1908, after which he had joined United. He could have tossed in four England caps for good measure. But Busby thought Hardman's ideas hopelessly out-of-date and didn't appreciate his pithy manner.

Seated directly behind Busby during a match, Hardman had been complaining about Johnny Carey. Busby seethed but waited until half-time. He went to the gents' and, when Hardman walked in, told him: 'Never dare to say anything like that to me when other people can hear you.' When the board next met, Busby put an item on the agenda: 'Interference by Directors'. Gibson backed him. The chairman would take just a little longer to recognise that Busby's concept of managerial control applied to him as well. But eventually he, too, understood.

SOCIALISM OR WHAT?

For that exciting first season back in the Football League, Busby was awarded a bonus of £400. The players shared £220. Some might have received £15. That was the extra Murphy found in his pay packet. Tom Curry got £10. Lest this be taken to represent Busby's interpretation of socialism, it should be added that the players (if not staff) were subject to a maximum wage. Not so managers: Herbert Chapman had gone to Arsenal on £3,000 a year as far back as 1925. Busby was still on less than £1,000. But he had yet to turn United into the Arsenal of the north.

There was to be recurrent tension between Busby and his players over money. In 1946/47, most were on £10 a week basic – £2 below the maximum but still, with bonuses averaging £2–£3 a week in the season, more than twice as much as a skilled worker in the outside world. Younger ones got a little less: Crompton £8, Aston and Morris £7. Interestingly, the full £10 was paid to the old stager Billy Wrigglesworth as well as Whalley, with his additional coaching responsibilities, reflecting Busby's experience at Liverpool, where loyalty of fading players had been rewarded.

At the end of the season a pay dispute involved Henry Cockburn and Joe Walton. Both asked for transfers after being unable to agree terms with Busby and, presumably speaking in unison, informed Henry Rose of the *Daily Express*:

> We have told Mr Busby that we are prepared to give up our jobs and become full-time professionals. We were told we would not be given the maximum wage of £12 and £10 in the summer and we feel we are entitled to full pay. We feel we have been given a raw deal. Neither of us cost the club a penny. We have given our best in every match we have played.

Busby responded in the *Manchester Evening News*:

> We have offered them reasonable terms but they have asked for maximum rates for next season as full-time men. There are certain regulations about wages ... and I can state quite categorically that Cockburn and Walton have been offered maximum rates according to those.

He referred to a government stipulation that men exempted from National Service – like Cockburn and Walton – must have their cases reviewed before being allowed to turn full-time. The League supported Busby. For him it was an easy, and helpful, victory.

While Cockburn accepted the outcome, Walton remained restless. And eventually he would be let go to Preston for £10,000 because Busby had filled the full-back positions with Carey and Aston. Making full-backs of erstwhile attackers was fundamental to Busby's concept. Full-backs had to construct and not just whack the ball up the field. So Busby had done more than put his inheritance from Louis Rocca to good use. By astutely tweaking Chilton and Cockburn, and radically repositioning Carey and Aston, he had blended a potent cocktail, a new kind of team, created a form of total football that, for all the traditional English love of unceremonious defending, resonated. He told them: 'I want you to play football all the time. If you do that and lose, I won't grumble.' The public got to hear and liked the sound of it. They liked the sight of it even more and, as 1947/48 approached, the critics were ready to be wowed.

UP FOR THE CUP

Busby was playing his full part in Manchester's vibrancy. There would be Sir John Barbirolli conducting the Halle at the Free Trade Hall. L.S. Lowry painting prolifically amid spells of depression. Theatres thriving; they included the Opera House, which staged more variety than opera and whose manager, Tommy Appleby, became so friendly with the Busbys that if necessary he would delay the curtain until Matt and Jean arrived and were seated with their guests. And Busby himself, with Manchester United his canvas, creating art that appealed to critics such as Donny Davies.

H.D. Davies was known to the readers of the *Manchester Guardian* as 'An Old International' because he had played for the England amateur team. He had gone on a European tour before the First World War, in which he had become a prisoner, almost starving to death. On his return, he had played cricket for Lancashire and eventually joined the *Guardian*, where his flair for language – and not just English, for he enjoyed reading favourites such as Baudelaire, Cervantes and Heine in native editions – dovetailed beautifully with a passion for sport. Davies lived in Prestwich, not far from Louis Rocca, and hoped United might emulate the prestige of Chapman's Arsenal, but in Busby's style.

He would not have long to wait, but, for such a momentous season, 1947/48 began oddly. United went nine matches without a win and were close to the relegation zone in mid-October. That most of the players were now on the maximum wage did not prevent the slump; it could be dated from a draw with the champions at Anfield after United had led 2–0 through a restored Mitten and Pearson after 15 minutes. Among the Liverpool fans packed behind Crompton's goal were a couple of cocky Mancunians, who called out: 'We're with you, Jack!' Liverpool drew level and, during a brief pause in the excitement, a Scouser yelled: 'You're on your own, Crompton – they've gone.'

Busby wasn't as worried as chairman Gibson, who, pointing to the club's improved financial position – and in contravention of Busby's rules of engagement – wanted him to splash out in the transfer market.

Gibson, perhaps emboldened by the success of his pre-war signing Rowley, kept suggesting names to Busby and eventually protested: 'You are always telling me no.' There was a transfer-listed player at Newcastle – Len Shackleton was known to be restless there – whom Gibson wanted. 'Now,' he said, 'go and sign him!' This was a battle Busby had to win. He stood his ground, adding: 'I will remind you ... that I lived long before I ever saw you.' Gibson stormed out. But returned to say: 'I am sorry this has happened. We will carry on as we were.'

Not only did Gibson keep this promise; from then until his death, he both upheld Busby's independence and ensured every other director did so, even from the sickbed to which he took after a stroke. From time to time he would summon Busby. 'Is anyone interfering with you?' he would ask. 'If there is, he'll have to go.'

Busby could afford to joke about it now. When two of the board members argued, as they often did, about how Old Trafford should be rebuilt – architects had drawn a state-of-the-art structure accommodating up to 125,000 and William McLean, a hard-drinking doctor, was its most fierce advocate while Bill Petherbridge urged caution – he would play the boxing referee and call 'Break!' Even Hardman accepted Busby's ways with good humour, telling board meetings: 'Our manager has asked for our advice and we will give it to him ... and then he'll please his bloody self.'

Sticking to the 1945 statement of principles was brave and brilliant management. Busby didn't want a structure that, however admirable, would be temporary. Yes, it was possible to purchase success as Liverpool had with Stubbins. But Busby could point to their mixed fortunes since.

Many supporters remained anxious and one of the 50,000 at Maine Road for the visit of Sheffield United, a 17-year-old Keith Dewhurst, found himself looking up to where Busby sat at the front of the directors' box. The visitors led and, as the big and willing Ronnie Burke kept missing chances, defeat loomed. Busby was impassive. Dapper as ever, he puffed on his pipe, leaving any frantic attempts at adjustment to Murphy, of whom Bill Foulkes was later to say: 'When I first heard him coaching from the touchline, I thought there was trouble in the crowd.' The equaliser never came and Busby felt obliged to soothe the public, saying: 'It is a loss of rhythm and everything will soon come right.'

In truth Busby had been looking for a goalscorer. Not as urgently as Gibson wanted. But one day he was in Scotland watching Dundee's Ronnie Turnbull. He didn't move for the English-born striker, who went to Sunderland for £10,000 and from there to Manchester City before appearing to find his level with Swansea in the Second Division. But Busby was able to help out a friend who liked a bet. Busby tipped United for the Cup, insisting they were in a false position, and his chum obtained 25–1 from bookmakers aware of their handicap in having no true home ground; they couldn't even play at Maine Road as long as City remained in the competition and were drawn at home.

By the time the Cup came round, United had emerged from their poor run. At one stage Busby had called his players to a meeting in the dressing room. 'We can't go on like this,' he said. 'We have to sort it out.' The response came from Chilton and it might have been taken as insubordinate not only to Busby but his captain, Carey. 'You sit in the corner and be quiet,' Chilton told the manager. 'I know these better than you.' Busby would hardly have taken that from a director. But he let the big defender go on. Chilton duly made his observations, which were especially unflattering to a couple of players. 'If it were up to me,' he told them, 'I'd leave you in the bath.'

Soon the season was reborn. As Busby had promised. And to sustained dramatic effect. When United visited Wolves, the home side's 6–2 defeat was their heaviest for 13 years. Delaney, Morris, Rowley, Pearson, Mitten; what a forward line. Amid the easing of austerity people were ready for entertainment and 'Matt Busby United' – the press sobriquet captured how closely their style was identified with their manager – were only too willing to provide it. A magical Morris scored three in a 4–0 triumph at Chelsea. Portsmouth, putting the final touches to a successful team, were beaten home and away, Burnley thrashed 5–0. And so, unbeaten in 13 and up to fourth place, United turned their attentions to the Cup.

The draw had done them no favour: Aston Villa away. And before they had kicked the ball it was in Crompton's net. Carey, for some reason, smiled. Perhaps it was embarrassment. Or perhaps he had been shown the script beforehand. By half-time United led 5–1, their large contingent in the rainswept crowd euphoric. But Villa pulled one back, then two and, when a Chilton foul enabled Dickie Dorsett to make it 5–4 from the penalty spot with nine minutes left, the noise was deafening. It remained so until Pearson, from a corner, wrote the last meaningful word of perhaps the most entertaining first chapter a football story ever had.

The next round would reacquaint Busby with Paisley and Liverpool. But first there was a League match against Arsenal that attracted a Football League record 81,962 to Maine Road. A 1–1 draw emphasised the contrast in philosophies. Arsenal, now under Tom Whittaker with Joe Mercer captain, tried to stifle and yet Busby's United struck post or crossbar three times, prompting chroniclers to wish they had edged it in the cause of adventure.

Among United's admirers was Ivan Sharpe. The former amateur international had won an Olympic gold medal with Great Britain in 1912 at the end of a successful Second Division championship campaign with Steve Bloomer at Derby. He had gone on to sign for Herbert Chapman at Leeds City so he could combine his football with journalism for the *Yorkshire Evening News*. Sharpe had then succeeded Jimmy Catton, the diminutive doyen of football writers, as editor of the influential *Athletic News* and was now chairman of the new Football Writers' Association. As the season proceeded towards its climax, Sharpe declared that Busby's United were playing the finest football since the First World War.

The final component of the team had arrived by train. Five days before Christmas, the reserves had set off early for Newcastle. Among them was Johnny Anderson, a 26-year-old wing-half who had joined United ten years earlier but never played for the first team. His opportunity arose when Busby lost the services of his captain. Carey, who had temporarily reverted to right-half, reported a stomach upset hours before Middlesbrough arrived at Maine Road.

So Busby sent a telegram to Leeds station, where the reserves were due to change trains, and an announcement summoned Bill Inglis to the stationmaster's office, where he was handed the message that Anderson must return immediately to Manchester. The reason was not given; Busby appeared happy to let Anderson assume he would be twelfth man, a largely idle duty in the days before substitutes. But his boots were dug out of the skip and off he went to his debut. Maybe he had insufficient time to get nervous. At any rate, he got the better of Wilf Mannion as United, captained by Pearson, won 2–1.

Anderson kept the No.4 shirt for the next stage of the Cup odyssey. United were drawn at home, but so were City so Busby had to choose the venue for the meeting with Liverpool. He went for one a short walk from Anfield. The opposition had only to cross Stanley Park. But Busby explained to his players that Goodison's big pitch would suit United, as would ticket arrangements friendly to Everton supporters, who would in turn be friendly to the team who weren't Liverpool. A packed Goodison duly saw United dominate.

At 0–0 there was a scare when Chilton cleared off the goal-line. But, as at Villa Park, the tiger's tail was tugged. From then Mitten, Morris and Rowley interchanged bewilderingly as United struck three without reply. Paisley and Liddell, Balmer and Stubbins; all were present but barely noticed and a scoreless second half offered opportunity to shine only to the goalkeeper, Ray Minshull, of whom Donny Davies wrote in Monday's *Guardian*: 'His fingers must be tingling yet!'

The fifth round brought Charlton, the holders, and once more home comfort was denied because City needed Maine Road. Charlton wondered if United might fancy Stamford Bridge or Highbury but Busby was never going to fall for that and chose Huddersfield Town's Leeds Road. His team might have repeated their six-goal thumping of the London side earlier in the season but for a display by Sam Bartram so defiant that, after a standing ovation, the goalkeeper was shouldered by Charlton fans grateful for the modesty of a 2–0 defeat.

On the same day, City lost to Preston. So, if United were drawn at home in the quarter-finals, they could at last play at Maine Road.

As they did. Against City's conquerors, Finney and all. Preston also had Shankly, now 34. They were fourth in the League, a place above United. They had drawn with Busby's team at Maine Road and beaten them at Deepdale. But Busby had more important considerations in the build-up to this match.

Johnny Anderson was in mourning. On the way back from Sheffield United, he had been told by Busby that his wife was in hospital. When he got there, he discovered she had tuberculosis. Busby provided a car so he could visit her as often as possible. But now she had died and was to be buried the day before the quarter-final. Busby said he could play or not play. But added: 'There's nothing more you can do now.' He played.

More than 74,000 were at Maine Road and Mitten and Pearson had United two up before Willie McIntosh went past Anderson to pull one back. Pearson headed his second and United's subsequent control was barely reflected by one further goal, from Rowley. As the teams walked off, Shankly proved a generous loser. 'The way you lot are playing,' he told Mitten, with the first recorded utterance of an expression that would become familiar, 'you could win the Boat Race.'

Before the semi-final against Derby, it was rumoured the opposition had been promised an illicit £100 to win. The United players directed skipper Carey to ask Busby to match it. Busby refused. He convinced them pride was a higher reward, but it was becoming more difficult with crowds flocking to see them and ticket touts sharing liberally in the profits. The maximum wage remained £12, and there were strict limits on bonuses, which Busby was determined to observe.

Derby had won the Cup two years earlier and, according to a player with whom Carey and Crompton had a pre-match chat at Hillsborough, wore glittering mementoes; when they admired his gold watch, he said it had come from the directors.

Contrary to the belief that Busby was a laissez-faire manager, he briefed his team with care as usual, letting them know their opponents' strengths and weaknesses. That Derby had plenty of the former was obvious from a three-month unbeaten record. But, after an even half-hour, a misunderstanding between their centre-back Leon Leuty and goalkeeper Jock Wallace (father of the keeper who was to manage Rangers and Leicester) enabled Pearson to head home. Wallace was certainly the culprit when Pearson nodded another. After a Chilton error let Billy Steel reduce the deficit, Derby had the momentum and it took a counterattack plucked from the Herbert Chapman manual to swing the match back United's way. Mitten was sent clear on the left and Pearson, chasing a hat-trick, pointed to where he wanted the ball. Mitten, as so often, delivered perfection; Pearson didn't need to break stride as he drove in off the hapless Wallace.

It would be a dream final against Blackpool, who had signed the 32-year-old Stanley Matthews from Stoke. When, on a Channel ferry carrying journalists back from England's 5–2 victory over Belgium in Brussels, it had been decided to form the Football Writers' Association, the former Arsenal star Charlie Buchan had successfully proposed that members elect a Footballer of the Year. In the six weeks between the semi-finals and the final, they were to choose Matthews. So at Wembley on 24 April 1948, it would be the neutrals' favourite player against many of the same neutrals' favourite team.

During those six weeks, Busby felt the pressure associated with management down the ages. While League results were good enough to lift United into second place, the time often dragged, especially at night, when he would lose sleep fretting about form and fitness. He was confident enough that, if United were in peak condition at Wembley, they would win. But condition could be fickle. And then what if Blackpool's Stanleys – Matthews and the prolific centre-forward Mortensen – did their worst?

For all the calmness of his demeanour, and the ordered quality of his mind, those dark nights found him feeling for once helpless, the weight of the world on his shoulders.

At least the days brought the usual distractions. At United's invitation, photographers from 18 newspapers arrived at Old Trafford to snap the finalists but were kept waiting for an hour while the team had a meeting. Eventually Carey emerged and, with Busby at his side, said the players felt they should receive some payment; Busby would not have opposed that as regulations allowed 'player pools'. But the photographers picked up their cameras and left.

Although the team had come almost to pick itself, right-half still concerned Busby. While Anderson was the man in possession, Warner had greater experience. And 36-year-old legs that, on the lush Wembley turf, a more strength-sapping surface than the threadbare earth of most pitches at this stage of the season, might not stay the course. Eventually that settled the argument. Busby opted for Anderson.

On the day Arsenal clinched the title, Busby left Murphy in charge of United. They lost at home to Everton with a team weakened by the concurrent Scotland v. England match at Hampden, in which Delaney opposed Cockburn and the debutant Pearson. Ominously, Mortensen scored in England's 2–0 victory. But the break did Busby no harm; he enjoyed a Saturday night of song at the Dysart Club in Bellshill. The following weekend his Wembley team came unscathed through a 5–0 home triumph over Chelsea and so it was with relief that he started to prepare for the final.

He had one other problem to address first: Jack Crompton's back. Or rather the abscess at the base of the goalkeeper's spine, which refused to go away. Early in the week, Busby had accompanied him to Ancoats Hospital, where a specialist said he might be able to remove it – at the weekend. Crompton was aghast. Busby requested a private word with the doctor, who, when they returned, took another look. The patient was whisked away and given a local anaesthetic, the abscess cut out and a relieved Crompton, heavily bandaged and clutching a supply of painkillers, proclaimed his readiness for Wembley. It was just as well. Busby's next best goalkeeper, Berry Brown, was only 20 and too great a risk.

United travelled south in a train packed with fans, many wearing the Cup final uniform of the time – Sunday best with giant rosette – and whirling wooden rattles. When the team arrived in Weybridge, they liked their hotel. They also found a trim expanse of grass similar to Wembley's on which they could reacquaint themselves with underfoot conditions barely experienced since the onset of winter. They absorbed Busby's game plan and eventually their coach edged through the crowds towards the stadium. The players could see negotiations aplenty, for many Lancastrians, coastal and urban alike, had made the journey without tickets, which were changing hands at ten times face value.

The sunlit crowds poured down Wembley's tree-lined approach road, newly completed in readiness for the Olympic Games, passed through the turnstiles and enjoyed entertainment from the Band of the Grenadier Guards, whose repertoire featured tunes from popular musicals such as *Oklahoma!* Then there was the community singing; the choices suitably included 'She's a Lassie from Lancashire' and culminated in the Cup-final hymn, 'Abide with Me'.

Because of National Service, khaki sprinkled the terraces as the teams were led out by Busby and Joe Smith, each neatly suited, booted and trilby-hatted, with captains Carey and Harry Johnston next in line, ready to make the introductions to King George VI, who had conquered his stammer and was accompanied by his wife, the future Queen Mother, and teenage daughter Princess Margaret.

The idea that Busby had little time for tactics – 'Go out and play' – was again contradicted by his approach to the threat of Matthews. Crompton would send his clearances down United's right and they would concentrate on that side, reducing the Blackpool right-winger's supply. At least in theory. And, for when that didn't work, Mitten would funnel back to help Aston. But the other Stanley did a lot of damage.

Less than a quarter of an hour had gone when Mortensen sped clear of Chilton, who decided cynically to stop him with a sliding tackle that never had a hope of finding the ball. The referee, incorrectly deeming the foul to have taken place inside the penalty area, pointed to the spot, from which Eddie Shimwell scored. Rowley equalised, artfully touching the ball over the Blackpool goalkeeper, Joe Robinson, and rolling it into an empty net. But Mortensen was to strike before half-time – and no team had led twice in a Cup final and lost.

Busby still believed the cause was alive and during the interval, while making further adjustments, he received valuable support from Carey. Today the captain's voice was going to be the one everyone heard and Busby never forgot the leadership he showed in demanding that his team-mates keep attacking exactly as they had, promising that goals would come. Midway through the second half, it began to happen.

First Morris took a free-kick so quickly, pushing his team-mate Delaney aside, and placed it with such accuracy that Rowley was able to escape his marker and nod wide of Robinson. United, level again, were flowing. Blackpool flowed in the opposite direction. It was a wonderful match. And then, amid all the artistry, sheer grit took a hand. Jack Crompton's painkillers may also have done their bit.

Mortensen was not finished with United. He dispossessed Chilton, took a few steps and let fly to the right of Crompton. The patched-up goalkeeper had earlier made a brilliant one-handed save from Walter Rickett. This time he dived and not only stopped the ball but, ignoring any reminder of the wound on his back, held it.

He got up and found Anderson, who in turn released Pearson with a through ball. Here was another hero on a day gloriously fit for them. Pearson ran on and his low shot went in off a post.

During the ten minutes that remained, Anderson scored a fourth from long range. The drama was all but over. The celebrations could begin. Busby could quietly congratulate himself on the tactical tweak Matthews believed had changed the match – the interval instruction to harry Blackpool's wing-halves Johnston and Hugh Kelly – and wise selection at right-half. And Anderson, as he watched Crompton and Mitten hoist Carey with the trophy, pinched himself.

The final was not televised and so United and their fans had to rely on the cinema for a record of the occasion. What Anderson said when he discovered Pathé News had used up their film on the first five of the day's six goals, or maybe decided to leave Wembley early in order to beat the rush, is not known, perhaps fortunately. But newspapers assured posterity that he had shot from fully 35 yards. It was also noted that a deflection off Kelly had helped to leave Robinson stranded.

Even the King, as he handed out the medals, told Carey he had 'thoroughly enjoyed' the final. Was it the greatest any monarch had ever surveyed? It would certainly be difficult to think of a greater Cup run than United's, with the high-class opposition they faced and the attractiveness of the football repeatedly displayed. W. Capel-Kirby of the *Empire News*, who had seen every Wembley final, declared this the finest, not least because United had followed 'the pure, subtle principles outlined by their manager'.

According to Carey, the team had a motto: 'The ball should never stop.' Their game was based on first-time passes. 'If we were accurate and didn't lose the ball, it was devastating. By pushing the ball around and running into open positions we made it almost impossible for defenders to pick us up.' And thus it had been at Wembley: 'Never in the whole game did I feel we were going to be beaten.'

Busby was so grateful for Carey's half-time oratory. It was important for everyone to believe in this purist style of his, ahead of its time in the sense that five years would pass before the Hungarian national team, influenced by Jimmy Hogan, arrived at Wembley and taught England a lesson.

Among those who had listened to the final on radio, a nine-year-old subject of a kingdom divided by Raymond Glendenning's plummily urgent commentary, was a Glasgow schoolboy, Patrick Crerand, who loved Celtic but on that day was supporting United because his parents had come from Ireland and Johnny Carey was Irish. Meanwhile, in the mining community of Ashington in Northumberland, a ten-year-old Robert Charlton was with friends whose parents had a radio and every so often they broke off from their street football to pop in and ask the score and, in the way of boys, increasingly sought to replicate the drama taking place in London. When finally it was confirmed to Robert that Manchester United had won, he decided that, when he grew up and became a professional footballer, there would be nothing better than to play for them.

It was 1948 and the advertisement on the scoreboard had preached austerity, advising: 'If you don't need it, don't buy it – buy National Savings instead.' When the players got back to the surprisingly spartan Wembley dressing room, with walls of whitewashed brick and a bare lightbulb over the treatment table, bottles of champagne were produced from a plain cardboard box. There was, of course, no spraying, but plenty of sipping from glasses before they bathed and changed and went to the banquet at the Connaught Rooms.

Their followers gravitated to Piccadilly Circus. Back in Manchester, countless glasses were raised and Albert Square prepared for the victorious homecoming. This did not take place until the Monday because, after the banquet and a night's sleep, the directors, led by Harold Hardman in James Gibson's absence, took Busby and his players in the opposite direction: to Brighton, where they had lunch, a stroll and dinner at the Metropole. Then it was back to London and another overnight stay.

Their train stopped short of Manchester. They trooped off at Wilmslow and made for Gibson's home in Hale Barns, a suburb resplendent in its spring leaf. The chairman and saviour had missed Wembley on doctor's orders. But the Cup was his dream made flesh. For what had he said about a Manchester team formed of Manchester players? If you included Mitten, who had been born in Burma and raised in Scotland but lived in the city since adolescence, no fewer than 7 of the triumphant 11 – all except

Carey, Chilton, Delaney and Rowley – were from Manchester and the surrounding area.

Every player save Carey gathered on the lawn below Gibson's bedroom. Carey and Busby took the Cup upstairs and presented it to Gibson, who then appeared at the window and declared: 'I'm proud of you boys. This is a moment I have been waiting for.' The players then went up one by one to be congratulated. And the party set off for the city centre. An estimated 300,000 were in Albert Square, among them Billy Meredith, who recalled that there had been nothing like as many out to welcome the team – 'Rocca's Brigade' – back in 1909.

And eventually Carey, informed by Busby that it was his duty as captain to look after the Cup, bore the trophy to Chorlton-cum-Hardy and put it under his bed.

Two League fixtures remained and, after losing at, of all places, Blackpool, United beat already-relegated Blackburn 4–1 at Maine Road to clinch a second successive runners'-up spot. The average home attendance of around 54,000 confirmed that 'Matt Busby United' were a box-office hit.

CHAPTER SIX

THE 1948 TEAM: TOUGH AT THE TOP

THE MONEY WILL COME

Busby, even in the afterglow of Manchester United's first Cup win since 1909, was concerned about the longer term. A year earlier Jimmy Murphy had alerted him that, although the reserves had won the Central League, none could make the step up. Not to the level United wanted. So Busby had resolved to spread the net. Louis Rocca wasn't getting any younger or stronger. Sooner or later a new chief scout would have to be found to extend United's horizon beyond James Gibson's noble Mancunian vision.

Busby preferred not to buy and, in any case, booming gate receipts would be needed for ground redevelopment. Old Trafford had accommodated an all-ticket 36,000 for an English Schools Cup final replay between Salford and Leicester – but with police keeping spectators away from the bomb-damaged areas. City, meanwhile, were tiring of the rental arrangement at Maine Road. United would have to repair their home.

A further financial pressure was building in the dressing room, although this had yet to surface when Pearson, Aston and Cockburn joined England's 1948 summer tour of Italy and Switzerland. It was Cockburn's first trip abroad and he marvelled at Lake Maggiore before taking part in a 4–0 victory in Turin that would be long regarded as one of England's finest. The rest of the United squad went on a tour of Ireland, treating it as a holiday with hearty food and a relaxation of Busby's drinking rules.

There was dog racing at Shelbourne Park and a porter at the Royal Hotel in Bray had approached Mitten, whose fondness for the greyhounds was well known, with a tip. Although he had been promised the dog in question would win, the porter hastily added that it might be nice to make sure; didn't the football party have some useful potions? Mitten promised to make enquiries of Tom Curry and the physiotherapist Ted Dalton. They smiled and, with Busby's consent, concocted a placebo, which was duly administered in Dalton's hotel room. The dog did win.

It was a busy summer for Busby, who then began work with Great Britain's Olympic squad. In appointing him, Stanley Rous had explained that, although the 26 amateurs would be picked for him, he would select the team and have complete control of their preparation.

They overcame the Dutch 4–3 after extra time at Highbury and beat France 1–0 at Craven Cottage to reach the semi-finals but Busby feared Yugoslavia, fielding 'shamateurs', would be too strong, and so it proved. The tournament was won by a Swedish team featuring Gunnar Gren, Gunnar Nordahl and Nils Liedholm, who would go to Milan and win a *scudetto*. But at least Britain could be said to have emerged victorious in the shape of George Raynor, the Yorkshireman who managed Sweden both in 1948 and a decade later, when they reached the final of a World Cup held on home soil only to encounter a teenager known as Pelé.

When the United players returned for pre-season training, discontent became evident. They may or may not have known about Busby's bonus for winning the Cup – £1,750 – but must have suspected it outweighed the amount they shared. Their contracts provided £20 each, with a bit more for other achievements in the season.

While accepting that the system was stacked against players, they believed other clubs, such as Derby with their watches, found ways around it. They wanted a bigger share of United's profits and it was no longer just the likes of Morris complaining; Chilton and Delaney were angry. Even the establishment figure Carey accepted his mandate to accompany Morris on a visit to Busby. As always,

Busby reminded them of their legitimate perks – the cinema passes, the trips to Blackpool, the Davyhulme golf days – and reiterated that Manchester United would operate only within League rules.

In that case, said someone, why not be a bit more generous in interpreting the rules? Say, for example, a set of expensive golf clubs were given to each player as 'training equipment'? Busby demurred and the revolt went on. So the next day Harold Hardman came to the dressing room. He backed Busby. There would be no rule-bending.

Busby had gone into management wanting to behave decently. When Anderson needed transport to visit his wife, he had responded. He had made time to accompany Crompton to hospital. Every player was in the family.

No less the staff. Bert Whalley had been encountering eye trouble. While watching a schoolboy match, he had been hit in the face by a stray ball and, after mentioning difficulty with his vision, been taken to hospital, where he was told he might lose sight in one eye. On Christmas Eve, he was lying despondent when Busby came in and said: 'Don't worry, Bert – no matter what happens, you'll always have a job at Old Trafford.' As Whalley did, for every remaining minute of his life. 'I couldn't let the Boss down, ever,' he would say.

So few thought Busby anything but a good man. It was just that many considered him tight-fisted with club money. There was a story he told about Louis Rocca which, presumably, dated from his own playing days at Manchester City. He had planned to see his manager about a wage rise:

I remember him [Rocca] putting his hands out and saying, 'You want my advice, you want my opinion?' I wanted his opinion because I always respected him. And he said, 'You do your job and the money will come to you.'

Busby was to repeat those words to many a player as he strove to be fair within the rules. Rules which just happened to allow his earnings to take the escalator while the players' inched up the stairs.

The aftermath of the golf-clubs wrangle lingered. Two days before the opening fixture of 1948/49 – by a malicious irony it was to bring Derby with their gold timepieces to Maine Road – the players threatened a training strike. Busby persuaded them to relent but, demotivated, they lost 2–1 with no one among a crowd approaching 53,000 knowing why.

THE WALKOUT

United's form was inconsistent when Johnny Morris dropped out, initially through a knee injury. He missed the last three fixtures of 1948 and, upon returning for a home victory over Arsenal on New Year's Day, looked unfit. In the same match, Ronnie Burke scored his fourth goal in as many matches.

Burke stayed in for the Cup and got two of six goals against Bournemouth. Rumours of Morris's unrest persisted even as he appeared in the first episode of a trilogy with Bradford Park Avenue, which was eventually to see United triumph 5–0 over the Second Division side in front of a Maine Road packed even on a Monday afternoon, such was the Cup's magic in Manchester.

Morris still struggled for form and fitness and Burke, having scored twice in the conclusive match against Park Avenue, and twice more in the ensuing 8–0 victory over the Southern League club Yeovil Town, was a minor hero. Minor, inevitably, with Rowley around. For Rowley hit five against Yeovil.

When United went to Hull, champions-to-be of the Third Division (North), 15,000 travelling fans contributed to an attendance record of 55,019 that would stand until Boothferry Park closed in 2002. There was plenty to discuss on the Pennine journey, for the stories about Morris had been confirmed. He had fallen out with Busby – and been made available for transfer.

Busby could get on with most players. He could cope with quirks and would let Mitten come into the dressing room as little as half an hour before a match if the greyhound enthusiast was anxious to check the result of a race. Individualism was fine. But the banter with Morris often had an edge to it. Morris's tongue could be as harsh as his tackling, which Jimmy Murphy, who had dished out plenty in his time, deemed the fiercest he had known from any creative player.

There was a devil in him that Busby could never quite tame. He confided in one of Morris's team-mates: 'I've tried every angle. I've bullied, I've used flattery, I've tried every way, but I just cannot get through.'

That getting through meant everything to Busby was evident in a description of his tracksuit management written by Rocca for the *Evening Chronicle*:

The United manager is also a psychologist. He has imparted his football knowledge to the players by playing with them. He goes on to the field in practice games at Old Trafford on Tuesday mornings. You will, if you are lucky enough to be watching, hear his words of advice to one and all ...

Players were encouraged to express opinions and, although he might appear not to take much notice, he would come up a few days later and say: 'I've been thinking about what you said.' And then explain why he agreed or otherwise. That was what Rocca meant by psychology.

But Rocca added that, if, by any chance, the plans for the weekend match had 'not produced the desired results', the Tuesday sessions would also be used to rectify faults. And it was during one of these inquests that the incompatibility of Busby and Morris was exemplified.

United had conceded a goal from a direct free-kick, so Busby was trying to construct a more solid defensive wall. He prescribed five men instead of four and it seemed to work in rehearsal. Repeatedly. Busby expressed satisfaction and said the players could go for lunch. Morris disagreed. He argued that five men could still be beaten. 'Right,' said Busby. 'You show us.' And Morris did.

The most serious challenge to Busby's authority occurred when Morris lost his place. He protested, and Busby made equally clear that he picked the team. Morris trained with a level of enthusiasm that eventually prompted the manager, though it was his rule not to tell players off in public, to pull Morris aside and ask why he wouldn't put in a shift. Morris replied that there was no point in training for reserve football and started to walk away. It was very public now. 'If you walk off this pitch,' called Busby, 'you'll never kick a ball for this club again.' Morris kept walking.

Busby completed the session, went to his office, picked up his telephone and told the national news agency the Press Association that Morris had been transfer-listed. Later, Morris took a call. He was asked for his reaction to the news. And that was how he found out that, when Busby spoke, for all the gentleness in which his words were wrapped, a threat and a promise were the same thing.

Maybe Morris was not too bothered. The favourites to sign the widely coveted entertainer, about to be called up by England, were soon established as Derby and the lure, it was said, exceeded a gold watch; he was to get a tobacconist's shop and there was no smoke without fire as Busby saw it because, although he would let Morris continue to train with the United players, one unsettling word to the others and Morris would be reported to the League.

The first club to agree a fee were Liverpool. It was £25,000 and this would have been a new world record had Morris not declined to go to Anfield before duly joining Derby, whose bid of £24,500 still exceeded by £1,500 the sum paid by the Argentine club River Plate for Bernabé Ferreyra.

United's new No.8 had already made his debut. Even before Busby had received the Morris money, he had spent £18,000 of it on Johnny Downie, a quick and clever Scot who had impressed during United's struggles with Bradford Park Avenue. True to Busby's family ethos, Jack Crompton was taken aside by Tom Curry and asked to look after the newcomer.

Downie was absent, Cup-tied, when the semi-finals took United to Hillsborough to face Wolves, now managed by a 31-year-old Cullis. Neither side deserved to win. Chilton's pass back helped Sammy Smyth to put Wolves ahead, Mitten equalised and the rest was over-physical stalemate; at one stage, with Cockburn concussed, Johnny Anderson claimed to have tackled his colleague to prevent him from continuing to dribble towards Crompton's goal.

The replay at Goodison became, if less funny, equally tempestuous when Wolves' left-back, Terry Springthorpe, attempted to intimidate Jimmy Delaney. Busby's friendship with Cullis, so close that Cullis's children would call him 'Uncle Matt', became strained enough for them to exchange angry views. United did most of the attacking but in a late breakaway Jesse Pye sent in a cross-cum-shot that Crompton could only parry, the ball looping into the air so Smyth could head in with ease.

This broke Busby's grip on the Cup, and, while he remained silent on the subject of Morris, there were players who believed they would have retained it with the 1948 side intact. Especially as, had they ousted Wolves, only the lowly Second Division Leicester would have stood between them and the trophy. Wolves were duly to seize it on the same day as Portsmouth clinched the League.

United's part in both competitions – they were again League runners-up – was recognised by the election of Carey as Footballer of the Year. The average home League attendance was down by 6,000 but the Cup had kept profits rolling in and Busby received a salary rise to £3,250, or five times his players' earnings with bonuses included.

So he had hardly been tempted by an offer of £2,750 to manage Tottenham, who, after he had spurned them, brought his wartime assistant Arthur Rowe back to White Hart Lane. A humbler post – that of managing Carlisle in the Third Division (North) – went to Bill Shankly.

Busby reached 40 with an unshaken belief in growing from the roots. And now he had found the man to secure the best talent – Mancunian or otherwise – before rivals did. Joe Armstrong had yet to be given the title 'chief scout' but already he was doing Rocca's job of capturing the boys Busby and Murphy would turn into men. Armstrong was a charismatic little fellow, sharp and good-natured in the Mancunian way. And experienced; Busby had noted his work for Manchester City in the 1930s.

For the fans, the joy of the summer of 1949 was that they would soon be heading home to Old Trafford. Alf Clarke had written in the *Evening Chronicle* that the ground would be ready for the next season with an initial capacity of 50,000 and confirmation came in an announcement of the latest government licences. There would be a rebuilt main stand holding 3,000 and further cover for 15,500.

The builders were behind schedule when the season began with a visit to Derby, who had made Johnny Morris captain for the day. In the early summer, he had scored on a winning England debut in Norway. In France, alongside Rowley and Aston, he had scored twice. So he could look forward to the visit of the Republic of Ireland, captained by Carey. It would be Morris's first international on home soil. He had never been an international with United; the thought may have crossed his mind as he lined up against them at the Baseball Ground.

A face less familiar to the men in red was that of the 17-year-old Brian Birch, a Salford boy deputising for the injured Downie; Busby had sold Ronnie Burke to Huddersfield for £16,000. Also absent was Chilton, who had asked for a transfer; it was thought that, with his wife unwell, he might be seeking a move back to the north-east. The reserve Sammy Lynn helped to keep a clean sheet and a goal from Rowley won the match.

Then came the return to Old Trafford on the evening of 24 August 1949. The roof was still missing from the stand, with rudimentary cover available only for directors and press but, at that time of the year, the paying spectators were open-necked and bare-headed. United won 3–0 and their first defeat was in their ninth match, at Burnley a few days after Carey had skippered Ireland to a historic triumph. At Goodison Park they had become the first foreign team to beat England in England and, while Aston survived, his fellow former MUJAC did not. Morris's international career was over. It had lasted four months. He was to remain a fine club player but, unlike such former team-mates as Carey, Chilton, Pearson and Rowley, never win another medal.

A LITTLE STAR TWINKLES

Two weeks into 1950, United hit the top of the table. They had won the first Old Trafford derby since the war – Cockburn was sent off with City's Billy Linacre after they had traded blows – and also shone at home to Wolves and Arsenal, both rivals for the title. And, although the campaign eventually fell under the cloud of a home loss to the most durable contenders, Portsmouth, this had a silver lining: there were two first appearances that warm April day. One was by the 20-year-old Salfordian full-back Tommy McNulty. The promise of the other debutant testified to Joe Armstrong's effect on a revived scouting effort. The wing-half Jeff Whitefoot from suburban Cheadle was, at 16 years and 105 days, the youngest player to have represented United at the time.

Armstrong had not been the first to show interest in Whitefoot. But he'd been the best. Armstrong was shrewd and charming, a little star who twinkled, a Manchester Catholic with wavy grey hair and a near-permanent smile of unquestionable sincerity who had worked as a Post Office engineer for many years and remained only too happy to locate and knock on doors.

'I'd had telegrams from Wolves,' Whitefoot recalled, 'and Bolton, and Burnley. And Manchester City had actually offered my father a job [it was common for parents to be paid for 'scouting' as an inducement]. But Armstrong came to the house and took the trouble to convince my old man that I should go to United.' Was Whitefoot's father, a builder's labourer, also offered a 'job' by United? 'No. He didn't get anything as far as I know. And all I got was the permitted £10 signing-on fee.' He later heard that Dennis Viollet, who signed for United at around the same time, got £500. 'They were very selective,' said Whitefoot; in other words, if Busby felt he could avoid condoning anything dubious, he did.

Whitefoot started work in the office at Old Trafford where Crickmer and Les Olive were now based. 'And there was me,' said Whitefoot, 'and one other. It was only a little place and people used to come to collect their match tickets.' One day he was called to Busby's office. 'He told me I was going to be in the first team against Portsmouth. I couldn't believe it. When I went home my mother and father looked at me as if I was mad.

'The club did all they could to settle my nerves. The night before, I stayed with Jimmy Murphy and his family. He had five children – so you can imagine how peaceful it was. They tried to relax me by taking me and Dennis Viollet to the Hippodrome [a theatre in Hulme used for variety shows] but I don't think I got much sleep.' In the morning, Murphy accompanied him to Old Trafford and ushered him into a dressing room sprinkled with stars. 'They were all very kind,' said Whitefoot. Even if they may have found it odd that Busby had turned to the kid for such an important match.

United began it as League leaders with Portsmouth second. Whitefoot kept a newspaper photograph of him running out. 'I look exactly what I was – a little boy lost! It was a hot, sunny day and I was up against Len Phillips, an England international inside-left. You've got to remember that in those days a wing-half was supposed not only to look after the opposing inside-forward but to get up and support the attack and after 20 minutes I thought I was going to explode.'

The match remained scoreless until the closing stages, but McNulty's error let in Duggie Reid and Jack Froggatt got a second goal for Portsmouth, who leapfrogged United into top spot.

Whitefoot and McNulty had been brought in due to international calls. Otherwise, there had been a settled look about Busby's team. Except in goal. While Crompton was out with a wrist fracture, he had used three keepers – including the 18-year-old Ray Wood, newly arrived from Darlington – and even made one last attempt to sign Frank Swift, now 36 and retired to concentrate on journalism. City, who had retained Swift's registration, refused an offer of £5,000 and Swift remained with the *News of the World*.

After United had reached the Cup quarter-finals with a brilliant performance at Portsmouth, there was talk of the Double. But they fell behind after only six minutes at Chelsea – with Crompton culpable – and lost 2–0. They could concentrate on the League. And seemed to display a determination to retain its leadership with a 7–0 thrashing of Aston Villa in which Mitten completed a hat-trick of penalties in the very pinnacle of style.

The Villa goalkeeper, Joe Rutherford, had saved two penalties at Everton but now came up against a master. Mitten placed the ball, stepped back four paces and pinged the ball past the keeper; it struck the upper part of the stanchion to Rutherford's left and bounced out. Next time, the same. So, before the third penalty Rutherford tried a little gamesmanship.

'Where's this one going, Charlie?'

'Same place.'

And the same stanchion shuddered.

Crompton's problems, however, continued during a run of eight matches without a win that saw Busby's team slip out of title contention. They finished fourth. Portsmouth won the League, Arsenal the Cup with Joe Mercer as Footballer of the Year. Manchester City were relegated, and Tottenham promoted as champions in Arthur Rowe's first season with a style of football, known as 'push-and-run', that was very much in harmony with Busby's.

On 13 June 1950, Louis Rocca died aged 67. After a requiem mass at his old church in Ancoats, his body was taken to St Joseph's Cemetery in Moston and buried in the presence of Manchester United staff, supporters and players past – notably Billy Meredith – and present. A little square of the Old Trafford turf was laid on his coffin.

For at least 18 months Armstrong had been hard at work in Rocca's former role. United would naturally continue to apply their finest-tooth comb to the Manchester area. Two of their teenagers – Viollet, from Fallowfield, and Whitefoot – were locals and there would have been another if Busby had persuaded Brian Statham, an outside-left, to ignore his father's wish that he play cricket for Lancashire instead. But David Pegg had been born and brought up in Doncaster, Yorkshire, and Jackie Blanchflower, younger brother of the Barnsley player Danny Blanchflower, was from Belfast. And soon the net would be cast even over fields traditionally patrolled by such proud footballing institutions as Wolves and Newcastle. To great effect.

The close season saw Busby both gain and lose significant players. He ended a perennial search by paying Queens Park Rangers £11,000 – a world record for a goalkeeper – for the 31-year-old Reg Allen. But, at the end of a tour of North America, he felt impelled to part with one of his most cherished performers. After the winter of Johnny Morris's discontent, this was the summer of Charlie Mitten's flight.

CHEEKY AND CHEEKY

Charlie Mitten was one of Busby's favourite players. In him he saw every attribute a winger could want – close control, speed off the mark, pinpoint crossing – and more. Mitten could shoot well enough in open play to contribute his share of goals and was exceptional with not only penalties but free-kicks. Busby admired how he kept his dead-ball skills finely honed, dragging Crompton back out for extra practice after the rest had finished. No wonder John Arlott saw no instrument in football more precise than Mitten's left foot.

So 'Cheeky' was a serious professional – and Busby liked both sides of him. He laughed with everybody else at the stories of players arriving in the treatment room to find one of Mitten's greyhounds on the table, receiving the benefit of the sun-lamp or a massage from Tom Curry. And Busby appreciated the dog-racing tips. Nor did he mind Mitten being forever 11th out of 11 into the dressing room, as long as he was just in time. Busby, ignoring attempts at explanation, would barely look up. 'Good to see you, son,' he'd murmur.

But it was Mitten's spirit of independence that was to separate them. That and money.

There was little hint of the drama to come as the United party of Busby, Curry, 17 players and the director William McLean steamed out of Southampton on the *Queen Mary*, bound for New York. They were in tourist class and very much a tourist frame of mind despite a mini-rebellion by the players over spending money of $5 a day. The outcome was the usual. Busby said there would be no increase, and reminded them of how lucky they were to be on the trip, and the players backed down before heading to Toronto, where they beat the National League All-Stars 5–0.

Upon returning to New York they heard that an English agent, Percy Wynn, was coming on behalf of the Bogotá club Independiente Santa Fe. This was big news because the Colombian FA had been exiled from FIFA over the formation of a breakaway league in which, because no transfer fees were being paid, players could earn wages beyond the most gifted Englishman's dreams. Or hitherto beyond.

Weeks earlier the much-admired footballing defender Neil Franklin had rebuffed Stoke and a place in England's squad for the forthcoming World Cup in favour of joining Santa Fe with his clubmate George Mountford and others. And even Franklin, Saturday-matinee idol of the Victoria Ground, paled by comparison with Alfredo Di Stéfano, from Argentina, and his compatriot Héctor Rial, who had also been lured to Colombia. No wonder FIFA fretted.

When Busby heard Wynn was intent on adding United players such as Mitten, Cockburn and Aston to a Santa Fe squad now featuring Rial – Di Stéfano had joined their Bogotá rivals Millonarios – there were flutters of concern which Busby moved to calm. He said of Wynn: 'I should have no truck with him. But I could not prevent him talking to the players if he did contact them. At the same time, I have no fear of losing any of our players. My impression is that they are simply not interested in such offers.'

The offers in question were said to be of £3,500 a year but Johnny Carey, in his tour column for the *Evening Chronicle*, echoed his master's voice with an allusion to the dangers: 'None of the United players would consider such a proposition because it would mean "finis" as regards our future in the game in Britain.'

Privately they did consider it. And Busby knew. He had taken the trouble to warn them that United, as well as the FA and League, would take a dim view of deserters. He also had a cautionary word about Colombian promises. He was concerned enough to talk to the England men Cockburn and Aston – and had difficulty in dissuading Cockburn in particular. It was against this background that the United players gossiped as they toured by train and plane, going by way of St Louis to Los Angeles and back.

Carey, meanwhile, told his readers about New York – the food, the traffic and the neon lights, celebrities such as the boxer Primo Carnera, a trip to the horse-racing at Belmont Park – and dwelled on the joys of Hollywood. More celebrities at the MGM studios restaurant:

> We hardly ate anything, so engrossed were we all in 'spotting the stars'. Ricardo Montalban … spoke with us for a long while … A character actor famous for his portrayal of villainy was recognised by Allenby Chilton, who told him: 'I've hissed you many a time.' The actor shrugged and replied: 'It's a living.'

As for the impression Clark Gable made on Carey: 'Ladies, I may tell you that he looks as handsome off screen as on it – and I don't say that because he was courteous enough to come over to our table and bid us welcome.'

Something akin to a film-star way of life, meanwhile, awaited Colombia's footballing imports. The driving-force behind the rebel league had been Luis Robledo, aged 26 and the son of a cattle baron who, after education at Downside School and Cambridge University, had become a diplomat in London (and, in such spare time as polo permitted, an Arsenal supporter). He believed that a first-class football league would help to dispel a politically violent mood in his country.

Some stars came from Argentina in the wake of a players' strike that prompted President Juan Perón to have the national team disbanded ahead of the World Cup. Millonarios were leading beneficiaries of Argentina's chaos and, having engaged the intermediary services of the Scottish ex-player Jock Dodds, whom Busby knew, also landed Bobby Flavell from Hearts. Atlético Junior blended Brazilians and Hungarians; Cúcuta Deportivo specialised in Uruguayans.

On 14 June, near the end of their tour, United suffered their first defeat, in Toronto to a team of familiar faces, an 'All-England XI' sent by the FA and featuring Stanley Matthews even though he was in the World Cup squad due to assemble in Rio de Janeiro in a week's time. Matthews helped to draw the biggest crowd of the tour, 25,000. Mitten scored one of two goals to the FA XI's four. He soon bade farewell to his room-mate, Cockburn, who left with Aston for Brazil. Some observers thought Mitten unlucky not to have found favour with England, for all the class of Matthews and Finney.

Back in New York, at the Times Square Hotel, Mitten took a fateful telephone call. It was from Neil Franklin. He put Luis Robledo on the line and the Santa Fe president offered the same pay and perks as Franklin and Mountford received; would Mitten like to fly to Bogotá and have a look around?

'How do I get there?'

Robledo said there would be an air ticket waiting at the front desk in the morning. He would be picked up at Bogotá airport. Mitten felt he had to try it. In Colombia the pay would be even more than rumour had it; with the signing-on fee, he might make £10,000 by next summer. No longer would he have to coach youngsters in his spare time to provide for his wife Betty and three children. He was 29. And would he really become a footballing outlaw? He had spoken to a lawyer who begged to differ from Busby on that.

So now he had to tell Busby. There was no time to lose, for the next day United would sail for Southampton. Before the end-of-tour party at the Astor Club, he went to Busby's room and knocked on the door. Busby said he couldn't just fly away from United. Mitten, standing on ground his lawyer friend had prepared, replied that his contract had expired. It was indeed waiting to be renewed at Old Trafford. Busby scorned the notion that his future at the club was, or ever had been, in doubt. Mitten, who was not sly, changed tack, saying he just wanted more tangible reward for his talent, more comfort in his life, and mentioned how much Robledo had offered. Busby's mood seemed to lighten.

'Do they want a manager?'

Mitten reiterated that his mind was set. If he liked Colombia, he would sign. If he didn't, he would return to Manchester and ask for the United contract, and a pen.

'Okay, you'd better go,' said Busby, 'or you'll die wondering.'

That was Mitten's version of the conversation. Busby's, likewise given after the passage of many years, was that he explicitly warned Mitten of the consequences: he would have no future at Manchester United. It was as simple as that.

Later, at the Astor, some players also tried to persuade Mitten not to go. But he was a gambler.

He went back to the hotel and packed his trunk ready for collection by Stan Pearson, who had promised to make sure it got back to the Mittens' home in Davyhulme. And in the morning, with his hand baggage, he picked up the ticket to Bogotá. There, Franklin and Mountford waited with their families and Robledo, to whom Mitten took an instant liking. He trained, had a medical examination and agreed a deal encompassing not only the £10,000 but a luxurious car and a staffed house – he was even going to save the £1.50 a week married players paid United in rent.

Aston took part in England's opening World Cup match, a 2–0 victory over Chile. Jimmy Dickinson was preferred to Cockburn and Arthur Drewry – presumably after consulting Winterbottom – named the same team for the meeting with the United States four days later. This meant that Matthews, who had been left out of the Chile match after arriving in Rio only the previous day, also missed the greatest humiliation in his country's football history. The loss to the United States was followed by another in the final group match against Spain and the team came home to a modest (by later standards) inquest. Aston and Cockburn were back in Manchester not long after the *Queen Mary* and Cockburn, taking account of his mother's health, assured Busby he would be staying.

Mitten, meanwhile, had returned to Colombia with Betty and the children. They had begun the journey by rail, being waved off at Manchester by, among others, Billy Meredith, who told the *Evening News*: 'If there had been chances like this when I was playing, I'd have walked to Bogotá.' Mitten certainly exhibited no misgivings, saying he would be 'able to save more in a few days than in all my 14 years at Manchester United'. In a letter to Tom Jackson of the *Evening News*, presumably intended for publication, he even said: 'I would really enjoy playing for United again when I come home on holiday from Bogotá at the end of their season ... I shall be free November, December and January.'

There is cheeky and cheeky and Busby, when the notion was put to him, made clear that, if Mitten were to return to English football, it would be to face the rigours of its disciplinary procedures. Perhaps Mitten had misunderstood the manager's response when he had gone to Old Trafford, as promised, to impart his final decision. Busby merely wished him well with a politeness whose chill Mitten failed to notice.

Inwardly, Busby had known from the moment Mitten left his room at the Times Square Hotel that he could no more back down on this than over Johnny Morris. Even if he liked Mitten more than Morris, the issue was the same. His authority had been challenged. Wherever else Cheeky Charlie would be spending his winter break, or indeed the remainder of his career, it would not be on Manchester United's premises.

Although violence still scarred Colombia's cities from time to time, Charlie and Betty hardly lived on the streets; they mixed with the ruling classes and well-heeled expatriates. Charlie had even acquired a racehorse. Although Betty worried that she could not find an English school for the children, they seemed to be enjoying themselves. And Mitten was fitting into Latin American football. After Uruguay had won the World Cup, shocking Brazil, they were invited to Bogotá for a friendly and lost 3–1 to a Colombian team sprinkled with guests, one of Di Stéfano's two goals coming from a Mitten cross.

Franklin, however, was struggling to integrate. So much talk of riots unsettled his wife and at the end of the summer the couple went home. Stoke, pre-empting action by the FA and League, suspended Franklin indefinitely. Luis Robledo felt just as badly let down. He was not alone among Colombians and the British reputation for dependability briefly suffered. But Mountford stayed, as did Mitten, and they were popular for that.

United, meanwhile, had begun the 1950/51 season with no outside-left. Billy McGlen trotted out to face Fulham at Old Trafford with 11 on his back but, whatever else this reliable servant was, left-winger did not figure on the list. United were lucky to win 1–0. They looked jaded after the tour and carried a passenger in Eddie McIlvenny, a Scottish right-half who had played for the United States against England.

After one more match, McIlvenny gave way to the 21-year-old Mancunian debutant Don Gibson, who looked more the part. McIlvenny was to remain at Old Trafford until 1953 but never again appear in the first team.

United lay fourth when Chilton slipped away to make an England debut at 32, defending alongside Aston in a 4–1 victory in Belfast. Busby called up two more debutants. The giant teenager Mark Jones replaced Chilton and Billy Redman deputised for Aston in a 3–1 victory over Sheffield Wednesday at Old Trafford.

After the departure of Delaney, who had returned to Scotland to join Aberdeen, Busby had lost both of his Cup-winning wingers and form dipped to the extent that newspapers carried rumours he might lose his job, which he decided to deny publicly. Avoiding a choice of rival papers – always a wise move – he told the magazine *All Football*: 'I am not resigning. I am not being sacked and there is neither trouble or panic in our camp. These rumours seem to have started because we are not the glamour team we used to be. Maybe we are not. You cannot stay on top all the time.'

He even conceded: 'We had a big shock when Charlie Mitten went to Bogotá. We were not prepared for that. Who was?' And he reiterated his guiding principle: 'Some of my critics say I should have gone out and spent ... well you can call me a canny Scotsman if you like, but I don't believe you can buy success.'

After United were removed from the Cup by Birmingham of the Second Division he was accused of using 'too many kids'. The side at St Andrew's was indeed youthful, featuring the teenagers Birch and Cliff Birkett. Yet there were few complaints when, a week later, Busby used Redman and the 17-year-olds Whitefoot and Jones in a 3–1 victory at home to Arsenal and United hardly looked back, winning 14 and drawing 2 of their final 17 matches to finish behind only Spurs, champions in their first season up. Blackpool, who came third and lost the Cup final to Newcastle, had the Footballer of the Year in Harry Johnston.

Mitten, meanwhile, came to the end of his year in Colombia. Mrs Mitten had, like Mrs Franklin, become homesick and there was still no prospect of English schooling. So Mitten obtained his release and got ready to fly home. What could he expect? A guide was that Franklin, when placed by Stoke at the mercy of the football authorities, had been suspended for four months, after which he had been sold to the Second Division strugglers Hull for £22,500. Mountford was to receive similar punishment and be back in the Stoke side, albeit irregularly, from September. So Mitten knew he would face a ban. But he hankered after United and was aware he had not been adequately replaced.

His flight from Bogotá landed at Heathrow one July morning. The pilot asked all other passengers to remain in their seats while 'Mr Charles Mitten' disembarked because otherwise they would walk into a crowd of reporters. Blushing, Mitten strode down the aisle to face the issues that had been debated in the letters

columns of the Manchester papers since he left. Was he disloyal
or merely trying to better himself as any other owner of valuable
talent might? A year had not eroded his sense of entitlement. He
went to see Busby at Old Trafford. He said he was a better player
for having worked with leading South Americans and wanted to
return to United.

It was like talking to a wall.

The next stage was a joint commission of the FA and League
before which Mitten, Busby and Walter Crickmer appeared. The
accusation was that he had broken a contract. He replied with his
lawyer-inspired opinion that it had expired while he was in America
with United. In terms of football and the law, he was ahead of
his time. His arguments were waved aside. He was suspended for
six months. And fined £250 by both the commission and, later,
United, who placed him on the transfer list.

Just in case he still discerned the slightest chink of light at the
end of the tunnel, Busby responded to his offer to do a month's free
trial by telling him the terms of the punishment would be strictly
observed; he would not even be able to train with his former team-
mates while awaiting a move.

And so Mitten squirmed in idleness, broken only by a well-
publicised appearance for a pub team, as the season began with
a wage rise for those on the payroll – the maximum had been
graciously increased to £14 – and his old shirt in the possession of
Ernie Bond, a tiny 22-year-old signed in the middle of the previous
season from the Lancashire Combination club Leyland Motors for
the now-piffling sum of £300.

CHAMPIONS

As if to demonstrate why he considered the wings such a vital area
of a football team, Busby found solutions on both the right and left
during a 1951/52 season of revived glory.

Although Jack Rowley provided a flying start with 14 goals
in seven matches, just as significant was the recruitment of
Johnny Berry from Birmingham for £25,000. Here was a worthy
replacement for Delaney: a winger of exceptional courage, a
morale-booster. Yet it was not until another debut took place in
late November that United found trophy-winning form. When

Billy Redman made way for Roger Byrne at left-back, it was the start of a glorious career. One that might never have flowered but for Busby's instinct.

When the former grammar-school boy Byrne had joined United, after playing alongside Brian Statham for the Ryder Brow boys' club, he was nearly 20. He reached the reserves but, playing at left-half, was a mixture: extremely quick and adept at interception but all right foot and no great ball-winner on the ground or in the air. But Busby and his assistants saw something in that pace – an inkling, perhaps, of what was to become the overlapping full-back – and on Byrne's first appearance at Liverpool it proved the highlight of an otherwise mundane scoreless match. Also Jackie Blanchflower replaced Don Gibson as Armstrong's boys continued to make their mark.

Any remaining hope Mitten might have harboured of returning to the left wing evaporated shortly before the end of 1951, when his suspension was to expire. Busby told him he was going to Fulham. A fee of £22,000 had been agreed. While United were to spend much of the second half of the season jousting for the League title without a regular outside left, Mitten would be trying to avoid relegation. Fulham lay 21st out of 22 after a plucky 3–3 home draw with United on Boxing Day.

After suffering the shock of the Cup's third round in losing at Hull, United drew with promoted City on the Old Trafford ice and prospered through the rest of the winter. Although Busby kept tinkering, results were more consistent than his selections and at Easter an ecstatic Old Trafford saw Liverpool beaten 4–0 and Burnley 6–1, keeping United in first place, which they had occupied since overcoming Spurs at home in a late-January classic.

Busby had reacted to defeats by Portsmouth and relegation-bound Huddersfield with yet another shuffle. It sent Byrne to the left wing so Aston, who had been moved to centre-forward, could return, at least temporarily, to his international position. Against Liverpool, Byrne scored twice and was hailed as a 'revelation'. He found the net three times in two matches against Burnley. Was this stuff out of the *Boys' Own Paper*? And then he got another in a draw at Blackpool.

This left United with two more matches, both at home. The first was against Chelsea. On the same Monday evening, Arsenal visited West Bromwich and the possibility was of results conspiring to produce a winner-takes-all finale at Old Trafford in five days' time.

Pearson put a nervous United in front and then Carey came up with an example of the big-occasion class Busby so admired, flighting a left-footer from 30 yards that left the Chelsea goalkeeper Bill Robertson helpless. There were reports that Arsenal trailed at the Hawthorns and a prolonged ovation for the goal signalled the crowd's sense of history in the making. A deflected effort from Cockburn relieved the last vestiges of anxiety and, after the final whistle, a second roar greeted confirmation that Arsenal had lost. Now they would have to win 7–0 at Old Trafford on the final day to deny United the title. Captain Mercer was realistic enough to send Busby a congratulatory telegram.

The United players had a few beers and Carey walked home to Chorlton, where his wife asked him to do the washing-up while she put the kids to bed.

For the Arsenal match, Busby announced an unchanged team: Allen; McNulty, Chilton, Aston; Carey, Cockburn; Berry, Downie, Rowley, Pearson, Byrne. Rowley scored an early goal and went on, by completing a hat-trick, to 30 for the season in a 6–1 triumph over Whittaker's team, reduced to 10 men by a wrist injury that forced the defender Arthur Shaw to withdraw at half-time. United had won their first League title for 30 seasons.

The Old Trafford pitch was a sea of joyous faces and floating on it was Johnny Carey, carefully chosen symbol of Matt Busby's Manchester United. Somehow space was cleared for the Beswick Prize Band (who, according to the old Manchester joke quiz question, played for United and City on alternate weeks) and 'See, The Conqu'ring Hero Comes' entertained the hordes until the players began to force their way towards the tunnel and the tune changed to 'Auld Lang Syne'. Once in the dressing room, they made for the communal bath, into which they gleefully plunged to hold out teacups for Bill Inglis, as ever looking more a grocer than a trainer in his light cotton coat, to pour in the champagne.

If only James Gibson could have been there. He had suffered a second stroke early in the season and died a few weeks short of what would have been his 74th birthday. So Hardman was now chairman in name also. Although there would be no threat to Busby's power, Gibson had arranged for his son Alan to replace him on the board, with instructions to check the manager received the same total support as before.

Delaney, Morris and Mitten apart, familiar faces had disappeared from the playing staff. Warner had moved to Oldham as player/coach the previous summer and was heading across the moors to Rochdale to become manager. Ronnie Burke, although Huddersfield had been promoted, was staying in the Second Division with Rotherham. Brian Birch was leaving Wolves for Lincoln. Mostly, young as well as old, they were on the way down.

Among the very young, the school-leavers, was Harold Riley, the boy Busby had thanked for helping to clear glass from the Old Trafford pitch. While playing for Salford boys, Riley had been invited by Rocca to train with United but now, approaching his 17th birthday, he went to Busby with a dilemma: he had been offered a scholarship by the Slade School of Fine Art at University College, London. Busby advised him to take it.

The decision to release wing-half Riley into an artistic life in which he would become close to Lowry and paint the portraits of, among others, Nelson Mandela, John F. Kennedy, the Duke of Edinburgh, three Popes and Busby himself cannot have been too difficult. Not only had Busby won the League with fine wing-halves; Don Gibson was in reserve, Jeff Whitefoot and Jackie Blanchflower were hinting at true excellence and, having booked another Salford boy in Eddie Colman, he was on the trail of an exceptional prospect from the West Midlands called Duncan Edwards.

The club had, as Gibson envisaged, bought The Cliff and installed floodlights so the youth development programme could be conducted in all seasons. One Thursday evening in January 1951, the youngsters had been called in and confronted with not only the embryonic lighting – powerful lamps mounted on poles running the length of the pitch – but Busby and Jimmy Murphy, kitted out and booted and ready to join in a match. 'It may be regarded as the real opening of the floodlit era,' wrote George Follows in the *Daily Herald*, quoting Busby and the referee for the occasion, Gordon Gibson, on the success of the experiment.

Gibson, a headmaster who had officiated at international matches, said the concentration of light on the pitch would help both players and spectators, while the greater clarity afforded by a white ball would 'cut out many press-box inquests on "who scored?"' Busby declared: 'I think this is the way that football will be played in the future. It speeds up the game for the spectators and gives practically everyone the chance to watch midweek matches.'

Youngsters such as Dennis Viollet, Albert Scanlon and Bill Foulkes would become accustomed to floodlights, for the FA and League were to drop objections. In November 1955, Carlisle would illuminate a Cup replay against Darlington, and a week later Wembley's lights were switched on for the last 15 minutes as England, with Roger Byrne at left-back, beat Spain 4–1. And in February 1956 the League were finally to allow Portsmouth to illuminate a First Division match against Newcastle. Where would it all end? By then, of course, Busby knew.

While the youths destined to represent United in Europe worked at The Cliff, the first team continued to train around Old Trafford, with the toughening sessions 'round the back' still very much part of Busby's routine. Mollycoddling had no place in his concept of care. He thought it hardened the youngsters to be boys against men – the Cannibal Island principle of youth development – and made the seniors spend a day a week on the shale, kicking lumps out of each other and, when the ball flew on to the railway line, arguing over who should leap over the fence and retrieve it.

With the Mancunian rain soaking their woollen jerseys, the smoke and grime from Trafford Park reaching for their lungs and the smell of heavy industry lingering in their nostrils – in later life that smell would always remind them of their playing days – it was not a life of unbroken glamour.

How Mitten must have yearned for it. He had been unable, despite an explosive start against Middlesbrough and 6 goals in 16 matches, to keep Fulham in the First Division. He retained his charm and his love of the dogs – a young Johnny Haynes once went for treatment and found a greyhound on the table – while forging a notable partnership with Haynes in a decent side featuring Bobby Robson and Jimmy Hill. It was fun. But it was the Second Division.

For Neil Franklin, the Second Division was less fun, because on damaged knees he couldn't keep Hull out of the Third and he took further steps down the ladder to the Cheshire League with Macclesfield Town. George Mountford went into the Third Division with Queens Park Rangers.

As for their fellow rebels, Alfredo Di Stéfano stayed in Colombia while Héctor Rial joined Nacional of Uruguay. Both were to end up at Real Madrid, making history of a different kind.

According to Mitten, he and the two Argentines had met the former Real captain Santiago Bernabéu towards the end of

Mitten's time in Bogotá. Bernabéu had become president of Real and resolved not only to displace Atlético as the leading club in Madrid but to build the biggest club in Europe, with the biggest stadium. Would they all join him in this venture? The wages were of Colombian proportions.

Mitten later said the regret of his life was that, due to his children's education mainly – but also because the death of another dream, Luis Robledo's, was all too fresh in his mind – he said no. Within five years, Real's stadium held 125,000 spectators and the basis of a team, including Di Stéfano and Rial, that would rule Europe. Mitten was subsequently to envisage himself in Bernabéu's all-conquering side, saying of the electric left-winger Francisco Gento: 'If he got away from you, you could never catch him. I'd like to think I could have brought a little more thought to the Real left flank.' Perhaps. But the memory can play tricks. Gento was 12 years younger than Mitten. By the time Gento, with Di Stéfano and Rial, won the first of Real's five consecutive European titles, Mitten was 35 and player/manager of Mansfield Town. Di Stéfano and Rial were still in their twenties.

And Matt Busby was building a team who would challenge them.

Even while planning for the 1952/53 season, Busby was starting to build that team, with Armstrong's help securing Duncan Edwards to add to David Pegg, Jackie Blanchflower, Ronnie Cope, Geoff Bent, Viollet, Foulkes, Scanlon and the recently signed Eddie Colman in the ranks of Murphy's aspirants, wondering whether to keep Byrne in Mitten's old place on the left wing or make him Aston's successor at left-back.

Busby was not going to rest on laurels earned by his first great team. The League championship side contained five regulars from the Cup winners of 1948 – Carey, Chilton, Cockburn, Pearson and Rowley – and only Berry and Byrne from the team of the future. So the 1951/52 triumph belonged to what would be forever known as the 1948 side, even if it now faced the beginning of the end.

CHAPTER SEVEN

THE 1958 TEAM: BIRTH OF THE BABES

TO DUDLEY AND ASHINGTON

If Busby shared a suspicion that the 1950 tour had eaten too greedily into the players' summer, he didn't let it put him off another Atlantic crossing. They boarded the *Queen Elizabeth* at Southampton. At dinner, champagne arrived. A familiar face beamed from across the room. There, glass convivially raised, was Louis Edwards, a man in his late thirties with a family meat business, a friend of Busby's and fellow Manchester Catholic whom the players had seen at matches. His family connection to United was distant – one of his sisters had married Louis Rocca's cousin Joe – but his support unquestionable. If Busby didn't already have plans to draw him closer to the heart of things, he soon would.

And so to New York – no worries about the blandishments of Bogotá this time – and on to Philadelphia for the first of a dozen matches. Anyone imagining that visits by United and others had created an insatiable appetite for the game in gridiron country was hopelessly optimistic. In Montreal and Chicago, Los Angeles and Detroit, attendances strained to reach 10,000. They exceeded 20,000 only in the final two matches when Tottenham Hotspur were the opposition and United had a winning habit broken to the discordant tunes of 5–0 in Toronto one day and 7–1 in New York the next.

Spurs might have been anxious to punish United for beating them to the title. Or did these dodgy results owe something to another dispute over spending money? As Jeff Whitefoot recalled: 'We did ask for more. Chilly was the ringleader. And Busby was very disappointed. On the boat home, he walked around with Tosh Curry and never spoke to another soul.'

The players were just happy to be making the return journey with photographic mementoes of gatherings with more celebrities, such as the English-born comedian Bob Hope ('I grew up with six brothers. That's how I learned to dance ... waiting for the bathroom') and Bing Crosby. The slapstick actor Jerry Lewis, whose stage and screen partner was Dean Martin, had obliged them with suitably zany poses. In most of the photographs, Busby was next to the star.

It had been in Los Angeles, where the United party met Hope and Crosby while relaxing between stormy encounters with the Mexican club Atlas, that Roger Byrne was subjected to Busby's discipline. Of all the players who passed through Busby's hands at United, Byrne was the most difficult to control in the early stages. The bright brain that had earned him a grammar-school place, the single-minded character; they had to be tamed because he was worth taming.

Busby and the more established players knew, from having met Atlas in 1950, that the Latin American and British approaches to the game did not always mix. Sensing fists might again fly, he got Carey to tell everyone to keep calm. Byrne nevertheless reacted to a kick from one Mexican by punching another and was sent off. Busby was angry; the reputations of club and country mattered. So he ordered Byrne to apologise to Carey or pack for home. He had two hours to decide. Within 15 minutes, the apology had been received. 'Roger rose in my estimation,' Busby said later. Typically elegant.

While the tour went on, important work was continuing in Manchester: the recruitment of those who would join Byrne in Busby's next great team. One day Bert Whalley waited in the forecourt of London Road (later Piccadilly) railway station. On a train from the Midlands were two likely lads. More than likely in the case of Duncan Edwards.

At 11, Edwards had been playing alongside 15-year-olds such as his second cousin, Dennis Stevens, in the schools' select team of his native Dudley, near Wolverhampton. He could use each foot to equal effect – and already weighed 11st – by the time he became England schoolboy captain. The Midland clubs, led by Wolves, were on his trail. So were United, through Joe Armstrong's man in the Midlands, Reg Priest. But no club was trying harder to land the boy wonder, even if he could not be officially approached before leaving school at 15, than Bolton.

They had already signed Dennis Stevens. And captured Edwards's predecessor as England schoolboy captain, Ray Parry, and made him the youngest-ever First Division debutant at 15 years and 267 days. So Edwards would get his chance if he went to Bolton, where Bill Ridding was anxious to sign another England schoolboy, David Pegg. And Mr and Mrs Edwards were fully versed because Ridding's chief scout, Frank Pickford, had become a regular visitor.

Meanwhile Busby, knowing Joe Mercer had done some coaching with the England schoolboys and was from Merseyside, rang to ask about a goalscoring inside-forward from the Wirral called Alec Farrall. Forget it, said Mercer; Farrall was Everton-mad and Goodison-bound. But had Busby not seen a much better prospect, the lad Edwards? Busby replied that Priest was on the case and, because he lived in Dudley, could react quickly if anyone else made a move. But the vigil was intensified.

Busby must have gone to see Edwards play because later he wrote:

> What everyone said about him was correct. It was obvious he was going to be a player of exceptional talent. So easy on the ball, two-footed, perfect balance, legs like oak trees and a temperament to match. We had to have him, but there was one thought in the back of my mind. Would Duncan, like the Farrall lad, want to play for his local side, which was Wolverhampton Wanderers?

Someone from United then followed Bolton in breaking the rule against approaching schoolboys – perhaps Joe Armstrong decided to fight Frank Pickford's fire with fire – because, Busby continued, 'as soon as we met, he said Manchester United were the greatest team in the world and, as soon as he was old enough, he would sign for us'.

Still Pickford would not give up. One day, he drove Ray Parry to Dudley. While Parry waited in the car, a conversation with the parents took place and at the end of it Edwards strolled out, eased himself into the seat next to Parry and began: 'Sorry, Ray, but ...'

His mind was set. But, as the schools broke up in early summer, Priest heard Bolton were planning one last attempt. He rang Old Trafford and it was Bert Whalley who grabbed forms and dashed to his car, only for it to break down on the way south. He hitch-hiked back to Manchester and, with Busby in America, met Jimmy Murphy, who had spoken to an increasingly fearful Priest. Murphy never drove. He would hire a car and Whalley take the wheel. By the time they got to Dudley, it was 2am. They knocked on the door and Mr Edwards, pyjama-clad, went upstairs to waken his son. Rubbing his eyes, Duncan told Murphy and Whalley they need not have bothered. He had given his word. He would sign for United. And, there and then, he did.

Nine days later he and his goalkeeper friend Gordon Clayton went to Manchester. Edwards boarded the train at Dudley and had a waving arm outstretched when the towering Clayton appeared on the platform at Stafford. They stowed their suitcases and chattered. At Manchester, Whalley waited, wearing a blazer with a flower in the buttonhole.

He took them by taxi to Birch Avenue, Old Trafford, where they would be looked after by Mr and Mrs Watson in a pair of terraced houses that had been knocked together and converted to provide digs for lorry drivers, commercial travellers and the young footballers of Manchester United. Edwards and Clayton were introduced to older residents such as Mark Jones and Jackie Blanchflower, who greeted them with perfunctory handshakes and lukewarm shoulders.

Another of the Watsons' boys was David Pegg. He, too, had disappointed Bolton. And was likewise only months from his first-team debut, for the 1952/53 season was to be remarkable in that Busby gave first appearances to no fewer than six teenagers – Edwards (16), Pegg, John Doherty and Eddie Lewis (all 17), Johnny Scott (18) and Dennis Viollet (19) – and the 20-year-old Bill Foulkes.

Three more players in their teens – Whitefoot, Jones and Blanchflower – figured in the campaign while Byrne, who had made his debut the previous season, played throughout. That Joe Armstrong's production line had gathered momentum was emphasised by the inaugural FA Youth Cup. Right from the start, when the lights at The Cliff were switched on for the visit of the Mid-Cheshire League club Nantwich Town's youngsters. There seemed a reasonable prospect of progress. But did anyone expect 23–0? Edwards and Pegg scored five each.

One misty and freezing day towards the end of a vindictive winter – smog had claimed thousands of lives in London – Joe Armstrong picked his way across stiff ruts of mud to stand on the touchline and watch East Northumberland schoolboys play Hebburn and Jarrow. A Sunderland scout was also present and, when the final whistle sounded, made for the East Northumberland goalkeeper. Armstrong had eyes only for a team-mate. Bobby Charlton had not performed spectacularly but Armstrong approached his mother. 'I don't want to butter you up, Mrs,' he said, 'but your boy will play for England before he's 21.' He then asked Bobby if he would like to join Manchester United and the boy said yes.

A month later Charlton was in Manchester – but at Maine Road. He had come to play in a morning trial for the England schoolboys and afterwards been approached by Don Revie, whose style he admired. Revie, stressing the size of the stadium, tried to convince him City had more of a future than United, but Charlton didn't waver, especially after the schoolboys' bus had passed Old Trafford on the way to the railway station from lunch in Sale. People were pouring across Chester Road to see the debut of a centre-forward and the eagerness of the crowd was infectious.

The clubs chasing Charlton included Newcastle – whom he supported – and Sunderland. One club tendered £800. Another promised to double any offer. But Charlton's second cousin was Jackie Milburn, a centre-forward of such panache he had taken Hughie Gallacher's place in the affections of St James' Park, and he warned Bobby to be sceptical. Newcastle had asked him to convey a promise of a sports reporter's job on the local evening paper, and he did so, but Milburn was also scathing about his club's youth policy, which amounted to little more than a choice between sinking or swimming.

The boy and his mother, Cissie, had decided early on Manchester United. Was it the memory of the '48 triumph? Or the pains taken by Armstrong? Time and again he would visit the Charltons' home in the mining community of Ashington, often bringing his wife Sally. He used to tell people he was Bobby's uncle and refer to his wife as 'Auntie Sally'. Cissie often told people that part of the story. She didn't seem to mind.

When United reached the Youth Cup final, it was encouraging for Busby to see nearly 21,000 at Old Trafford for the first leg. The people were receiving his message. At the annual general meeting, shareholders had complained that his champions were ageing and fading but Busby, as if pre-empting demands to indulge in heavy spending, had assured them £200,000 worth of talent lay in the reserve and youth teams. In the months since he had provided illustrative glimpses.

Now the youths would take on Wolves, the other great nurturers, United under the command of Jimmy Murphy while Stan Cullis would personally supervise his aspirants. If an extra ingredient were needed, it would be Wolves' frustration at having seen United pinch Edwards from their doorstep.

Already blooded in Busby's first team had been Edwards, Pegg and Eddie Lewis; all the others would get there to lesser or greater effect except Bryce Fulton, a full-back. Gordon Clayton was in goal with Fulton, Ronnie Cope and Paddy Kennedy from Ireland at the back. The wing-halves were Edwards and Eddie Colman, the little sorcerer from Salford. On the wings were Noel McFarlane and the often thrilling local boy Scanlon, with Billy Whelan – known to his fellow Irish as Liam – and Pegg at inside-forward and the 13-stone Lewis spearheading the assault on a Wolves defence yet to concede a goal in the entire competition.

Whelan had just arrived from Home Farm. Bert Whalley had crossed the Irish Sea to watch another player but been more taken with Whelan and snapped him up to play in the Youth Cup final because John Doherty was injured. An amateur initially, Whelan was soon to emerge from Old Trafford with the regulation signing-on fee. Pulling the £10 note from his pocket, he told two waiting pals: 'I am a professional footballer.' And then they walked up Warwick Road to celebrate with the fish and chips served to United supporters throughout Busby's decades.

For all his sense of wonder, Whelan fitted into United's football like a finger in a glove. He scored as United romped to a 7–1 victory over Wolves' youngsters at Old Trafford, and again in a 2–2 draw at Molineux.

Among the newcomers who watched the home match was Wilf McGuinness. He had been approached by Armstrong a year earlier. 'I was 14 when Joe knocked on the door,' he recalled. 'Maybe he shouldn't have done it before I left school. But he was coming to see my parents, not me.' Of course. 'United didn't miss many good local players in those days and Joe was the first scout to get to my dad. The others came when I played for England schoolboys. From every club in Lancashire, it seemed. And Wolves and Chelsea.

'United and City being around was nice for me, having been born in Collyhurst [among the younger lads now playing on the streets of that district was Nobby Stiles, while Brian Kidd had just begun to kick a ball]. But United had the best youth policy and that's why I ended up signing for them. That and other things. But I won't go into them.' Inducements? McGuinness always seemed to be smiling and this was no exception. 'These were things my dad knew about, not me.

'When Joe spoke to me, the first thing he said was "Call me Uncle Joe." The other scouts thought I was related to him. He was a clever bugger. It was only later that I found out all the United players called him Uncle Joe. Rascal! But I was delighted to join United because they were so youth-conscious.

'You might think I was being brave going there as a wing-half because they already had Eddie Colman and Duncan Edwards, who were a year older. But I didn't look at it that way. The way I saw it, as I watched them give outstanding performances against Wolves, was that, if United could do this for them, what could they do for me? After all, I'd played for Manchester boys, Lancashire boys and England boys – and captained the lot. Later Eddie became my best pal. Him and Bobby Charlton.'

Charlton, rather than work on the ground staff – his mother envisaged more constructive use of the time that stretched to his 17th birthday and professional status – was given a place at Stretford Grammar School, near the digs in Birch Avenue. But he felt cut off from the other lads and left after a few weeks. Still his mother refused to let him clean boots and sweep terraces, so it was agreed he should work for Switchgear & Cowans at Broadheath, a few miles south of Old Trafford, to undergo some vague training as an electrical engineer. He was allowed to finish early on Tuesdays and Thursdays to join the others at The Cliff and could play at weekends.

McGuinness also got an outside job to please his mother, who worried that injury might destroy his football career. Until he became a professional, he worked at Richardson Textiles, parcelling shirts and underwear for dispatch. Edwards and a couple of others did joinery, Jones continued his training as a bricklayer. Jackie Blanchflower tried plumbing.

Albert Scanlon took the ground-staff option. On his first day, in the summer of 1952, he had reported to Bill Inglis and been told to start by having a look around Old Trafford. He met some painters working on the stands who asked him to fetch a 'sky hook'. Not wanting to appear ignorant, he went back to Inglis, who said there was no such thing as a sky hook and assigned him to a dark and stuffy gymnasium, which he had to sweep and clean daily. He also had to treat the players' boots with dubbin, a wax grease designed to keep leather as supple as possible.

Despite Busby's family ideals, there was a hierarchy and the youngsters had to be careful to knock before going into the dressing room or indeed do anything that might annoy Chilton – 'Mr Chilton', to them – or the irascible Jack Rowley, whose tongue could sting like a swipe of the captain's hand.

Reg Allen was another. He had endured severe undernourishment in a Japanese prisoner-of-war camp and didn't suffer fools gladly. Young fools especially. And so it was unwise of Eddie Lewis, for all his bulk, to take a liberty when he entered the dressing room and espied Allen's jar of Brylcreem on a shelf. It was known that, of all receptacles of hair product on the planet, none was so firmly out of bounds as this and, as Lewis advanced on it, his pals had to remind him.

'That's Reg's!' they cried.

'Fuck Reg,' he quipped, opening the jar and scooping out a generous white dollop.

When Allen found out, he went for Lewis and tried to throttle him so determinedly that, by the time Bert Whalley and Tom Curry had managed to drag them apart, the burly youngster's face was turning blue and his tongue extruding.

TIPPING A WINNER

With Jack Rowley entering the final phase of his career, Busby needed a high-class replacement up front. Eddie Lewis had a long way to go. Tommy Taylor was already there. For the 21-year-old Taylor, tipped as the great Nat Lofthouse's England successor, Busby would get out the cheque book. And open his wallet.

This was in March 1953, towards the end of a season that had not begun easily for Busby. In mid-October, his champions were second from bottom and Roger Byrne had asked for a transfer. Busby had decided that, after Byrne's heroics late in the title campaign, he should stay on the left wing. But Byrne wanted Aston's position at left-back. Busby told him he would play where he was picked or not at all and that was when Byrne sought a move. He was promptly left out of the side that lost 6–2 at Wolves.

There were some who thought Byrne had a case, others who deemed him obstinate to the point of arrogance. Carey and others warned him not to miss exciting times ahead. Wait, they said, and you'll surely get your wish. Had they been primed by Busby? It would not have been beyond him. At any rate, Byrne listened, withdrew his transfer request and was restored. At left-back. Against Preston, who were beaten 5–0.

Byrne was to be a left-back for the rest of his life. And England, as well as United, to reap their benefits of Busby's magnanimity, or manipulation, or whatever it had been.

By Christmas, United were up to ninth but hopes of a long Cup run were dashed at Everton and the fans welcomed the excitement of a rare big buy in Taylor. The British record was £34,500, which Sheffield Wednesday had paid Notts County for Jackie Sewell. Busby was only too happy to give £30,000 for the Barnsley-born Taylor, who had scored 26 goals in 44 matches for his home-town club. But Busby didn't want to burden Taylor with a '£30,000 player' tag.

So, at the end of the negotiations at Oakwell, he handed a tip to the lady who had been serving tea. Lily Wilby was delighted to receive a £1 note. Barnsley got the other £29,999. It proved a very good deal for Busby. Taylor was more than a goalscorer, devastating with his head; he was brave, intelligent, energetic and selfless. Within a couple of months England would take him on a tour of South America. In Argentina, he was handed the first of 19 caps and a week later in Chile he scored the first of 16 goals.

At United he had made an instant impact, scoring twice in a 5–2 win over Preston while young Bobby Charlton daydreamed on the train back to the north-east; Taylor was the centre-forward the crowds had flocked across Chester Road to see that day.

The season might nevertheless have petered out but for yet more youngsters. Bill Foulkes, for example. In his impressive debut at right-back there was evidence of Bert Whalley's worth, for Foulkes still worked part-time at Lea Green colliery and, because he trained only on Tuesdays and Thursdays, the painstaking Whalley would write to him every week. On a Friday morning, the letter would arrive with details of the man he would be marking for the reserves – or first team – the next day. Whalley, who never stopped helping the young players, made Foulkes feel less of an outsider.

There was no hint of insecurity in Duncan Edwards, even though he was aged only 16 years and 185 days when he wore the No.6 shirt normally taken by Cockburn – or a larger version of it – in a 4–1 home defeat by Cardiff at Easter for which Crompton's goalkeeping took the rap. The next day, Carey was quoted as calling Edwards 'the best I've seen at his age'.

Soon Dennis Viollet was making a similarly acclaimed debut, even if the romance of Les Olive's appearance somewhat overshadowed it. Walter Crickmer's assistant was in his mid-twenties and had figured in the subsidiary teams, usually in defence. At Newcastle, however, and at home to West Bromwich a week later, he played in goal because Crompton, Wood and Allen were unavailable. United won the first match and drew the second.

He was not the only unusual United goalkeeper that season, for, as if Carey needed to emphasise his versatility after representing United in eight of the ten outfield positions, Busby handed him the jersey at Sunderland when Wood was on National Service and Crompton fell ill on the morning of the match. It was a 2–2 draw and Carey, needless to say, played well.

Carey had decided to retire at the end of the season because he was feeling his 34 years and wanted to quit at the top. Busby suggested he stay at Old Trafford, bow out gradually and, starting with the youngsters, move up the coaching ladder. But there was an opportunity for Carey to do as Busby had done and go straight into management.

So, just as Busby had spurned George Kay's pleas to stay at Liverpool, Carey was to leave United. He made his final League appearance in a 5–0 defeat at Middlesbrough that saw United fall from sixth to a final position of eighth. Arsenal pipped Preston for the title and Blackpool beat Bolton 4–3 in the Cup final forever to be named after Stanley Matthews. Lofthouse succeeded Billy Wright as Footballer of the Year.

Carey had one last touch of class to display. To commemorate the impending coronation of Queen Elizabeth II, a tournament had been arranged in Glasgow – the Coronation Cup – between leading clubs from both sides of the border. United began against Rangers at Hampden Park. A ball was cleverly flighted over Carey's head towards the left-winger Johnny Hubbard and, though most defenders would have been left stranded, Carey read it, half-turned smoothly, caught it on his toe and, without letting it touch the ground, began a counterattack, to the applause of 70,000 Rangers fans.

In their next match, United were beaten by Busby's boyhood love Celtic, captained by Jock Stein, and that was the end of the thinking man's footballer. Carey was to become manager of Blackburn Rovers in the Second Division. Busby gave the captaincy to Stan Pearson, which rewarded another graceful and highly intelligent footballer of selfless character; Carey considered Pearson the finest of all he had played alongside for United.

THE ACME OF IMPUDENCE

Busby headed back to the United States, this time alone, to do some coaching at the request of friends. He was in New York to meet the England party when they landed from South America in early June to play the United States in a 'Coronation Celebration' watched by 7,271 sprinkled across Yankee Stadium. England won 6–3 without recourse to Tommy Taylor, who had proved himself in Santiago and Montevideo.

The coronation itself had taken place a few days earlier, prompting a spurt in sales of television sets. A quarter of households owned them now and the range of programmes provided by the BBC was extending, with the launch of *Panorama* and a wildlife show presented by Peter Scott, son of the late Antarctic explorer.

And football; the Matthews final had been televised live. For all the horrors of the winter that had preceded it, the British summer of 1953 was a time of celebration, with a lovely new Queen and man finally reaching, if not the Moon, the summit of Everest. There was even an announcement by the government, now led by a 78-year-old Churchill for the Conservatives, that rationing of sweets would cease.

Busby did, however, have to absorb the sad news that Alex James had died of cancer at 51. The other hero of his youth, Hughie Gallacher, remained in the north-east. Gallacher's occupations had included football writing and he must have gone about it properly because at one stage Newcastle banned him from their ground. But after Hannah's death in 1950 he had become depressed, often drunkenly, so the grapevine conveyed nothing of encouragement.

United resumed without Johnny Downie, who would spend 1953/54 with Luton in the Second Division. Busby got £10,000 of his £18,000 back and the player had a championship medal to show for three-and-a-bit seasons with the club. Even so: quick and clever on the field, cheerful and well liked off it, Downie was a bit of a mystery, even to Busby. The most plausible theory for his inability to fill the boots of Johnny Morris was that he never appreciated how talented he was.

On the face of things, Cullis had the edge over Busby now. Wolves were an outstanding team with Bert Williams in goal, Billy Wright and the gifted amateur Bill Slater, the wingers Jimmy Mullen and Johnny Hancocks at the peak of their powers, and Roy Swinbourne at centre-forward. One of the inside-forwards, Dennis Wilshaw, scored with the frequency of Pearson at his peak; the other, Peter Broadbent, proved that Cullis understood the value of craft as well as power.

But Busby had yet to show his full hand. The time was approaching and, after a dull victory over Aston Villa – the maximum wage had been raised by £1 and one observer wrote that 'you expect £15-a-week players to come up with something much better than this' – he began to reveal the next United. Under Kilmarnock's new floodlights, he used kids; they won 3–0 and the next League fixture, at Huddersfield, was to become generally regarded as the point of no return.

In truth, Busby made only one unenforced change in the friendly – Viollet replacing Rowley, who displaced the winger Harry McShane – but Cockburn sustained an injury and, with substitutes allowed in a friendly, Edwards came on. Pearson had fallen ill and would have been replaced by Blanchflower anyway. But suddenly only Chilton and Rowley were left from 1948. Even with them in the side, the average age was just under 24. The other nine averaged 21.

They did well in a scoreless but entertaining encounter with Huddersfield and the headline over Alf Clarke's report in the *Evening Chronicle* – 'Busby's Bouncing "Babes" Keep All Town Awake' – spawned a phrase that would live for ever. They then shared four goals with Arsenal at Old Trafford before stringing together a couple of pearls; the performance that brought a 6–1 victory at Cardiff was, if anything, exceeded as United took on Blackpool at Old Trafford with nearly 52,000 fortunately watching.

Blackpool possessed four of the England team due to face Hungary at Wembley on the Wednesday: the great Matthews, Harry Johnston, Ernie Taylor and Stan Mortensen, who would surely relish the opportunity to put Tommy Taylor's claims to the England No.9 shirt in their proper place.

In the event, the Cup holders chose to rest Matthews. Although United drove Blackpool back, a break saw Bill Perry put the visitors ahead. Taylor then started on a hat-trick. He equalised by heading in a cross from Rowley. Viollet edged United in front and Taylor rounded off one of many slick combinations before a shot from Johnny Berry was parried and, winning the race to the ball, he claimed his third.

Donny Davies, having savoured it all, tendered the following description to *Guardian* readers:

> Nothing amuses the ordinary citizen so easily as the spectacle of a dignified policeman trying in vain to fasten his grip on a quick-witted, eel-like ragamuffin. There was some such flavour ... when Manchester United's team of young hopefuls, steadied by one or two seniors of vast experience, ran rings round Blackpool to the tune of four splendid goals to one. It was, as one 'liter'y gent' tried to explain to an open-mouthed bus conductor later in the evening, 'the apotheosis of the upstart, my friend! The acme of impudence'.

After training on 25 November 1953, Margaret Watson's lodgers settled down to watch the second half of the international against Hungary; the first half had not been broadcast. Mark Jones was, as usual, smoking his pipe and must have nearly bitten through the stem when he saw the score. Yes, the Hungarians had not lost for three and a half years. But England had never succumbed to an overseas team at Wembley. They had lost to the Carey-captained Irish in 1949 – but that was at Goodison Park. Wembley seemed symbolic, redolent of the Empire that had lent its original name, protective of the old order. And yet it had seen Hungary outclass England.

The United lads had not witnessed how the Hungarians ran up a 4–2 lead. But, as if laying on an action replay for their benefit, the Magical Magyars added two more goals in the space of a few minutes before Alf Ramsey limply replied with a penalty.

It was Busby's kind of football, with swarms of attack and the ball being moved with just one or two deft touches to the next subtle runner. But the flexibility of it all; in the English game, you would hardly expect an outside-left to turn up on the right wing as if it were the most normal thing in the world. That was what Zoltán Czibor had done in setting up Ferenc Puskás for a dragback and blast inside the near post. The United lads would have to wait for the next edition of Pathé News to see it, because it had happened before the interval.

There were calls for an English football revolution. Some thought Busby was working along the right lines. Charlie Buchan disagreed, hailing Cullis's as the way forward and citing Wolves' victory over Spurs' push-and-run, praising their speed and directness, arguing that they were as skilful and methodical as the Hungarians.

When Sir Stanley Rous (he had been knighted in 1949) invited managers as well as club chairmen to the FA, Busby arrived by taxi with Carey. Nothing much was decided. Busby, who believed a smaller First Division would help by reducing the number of fixtures played by elite performers, was never going to make much progress there with the chairmen, concerned as they were to maintain revenue.

Back in Manchester, however, one lesson was put into practice when Busby's friend the City manager Les McDowall had his reserves adopt an aspect of the Hungarians' tactics. Their centre-forward was withdrawn, in the manner of Nándor Hidegkuti, so the inside-forwards could make surprise strikes like Puskás and Sándor Kocsis.

At the end of the season, McDowall said his first team would learn the system. The deep-lying centre-forward would be Don Revie. How appropriate, given that Jack Reynolds had fathered Total Football with Ajax in Amsterdam, that this development should take place in his home city of Manchester.

For Busby, there remained one nagging question. First Division crowds generally had peaked in 1948/49 and fallen by about 10 per cent since. United's decline in home support during that period had been much sharper: more like 27 per cent, even if a kind statistician could partly ascribe it to the reduced capacity at Old Trafford.

United finished fourth in 1953/54. Wolves took the title for the first time. The runners-up, West Bromwich, obtained consolation by winning a Cup final against Preston, whose Finney was Footballer of the Year.

So Cullis and Busby each had one League and one Cup. But they were, of course, competing on two levels and Wolves now had an opportunity to disturb United's supremacy in the Youth Cup. Once again both clubs reached the final, the first leg of which took place on the same day – 23 May – as another attempted score-settling, an international in Budapest. After the youths had drawn 4–4 at Old Trafford, nearly 29,000 turned up at Molineux to see the job's completion. But United held out and a penalty from David Pegg kept the trophy in their hands.

If only England had been as resilient in Hungary. By the time they were able to score, six Hungarian goals had flown past Gil Merrick. The leeway was reduced by Ivor Broadis but even this seemed tactically naïve when Hungary, as if irked by such temerity, responded with a seventh. At left-back was Roger Byrne, who had made his debut against Scotland a month earlier. He would play in every England match for the next three years. But this would have been a good one to miss. It was a long hot afternoon in the packed Népstadion and afterwards Broadis said: 'It's the first time I've ever come off the pitch with a sunburned tongue.'

WHATEVER NEXT?

Busby attended the 1954 World Cup in order, he said, to study training methods and match preparation and came back more enamoured of the Hungarians than ever, deeming them 'the greatest international team I have ever seen … every member of the side an artist in his own right'.

They had gone to Switzerland unbeaten in four years and followed up a 9–0 win over Turkey by beating West Germany 8–3. In the final, they met West Germany again and, after taking a two-goal lead, lost late on, becoming the first of many victims of German resilience in football tournaments. Busby called it 'a travesty of justice', arguing that the draw had given the Hungarians an inordinate workload and that injuries, to Puskás especially, and refereeing decisions, notably in the final, had gone against them.

England had been beaten 4–2 in the quarter-finals by Uruguay and, since it had been a fine match against reigning champions who had thrashed Scotland 7–0 during the group stages, this was respectability regained. Tommy Taylor played two matches and Roger Byrne in all three with Allenby Chilton also in the squad.

Chilton had been appointed United captain in succession to Pearson, now with Bury, and Byrne – in a far more significant Busby move – made vice-captain. By the time the players reported to The Firs, Billy Redman had followed Pearson to Gigg Lane and soon they would be joined by Cockburn as Busby made space for the younger men who had been taken on a post-season trip to Zurich, where they won a tournament against Swiss equivalents and learned a bit about different football styles.

After a derby defeat in their tenth match had knocked United off the top of a competitive division, they slipped to seventh. They were said to be a soft touch away from home and, as winter approached, to dislike the mud. Edwards missed a match with a boil on his ankle and Byrne sat one out with carbuncles on his neck.

Whatever next?

More changes, more debutants: Freddie Goodwin, a 21-year-old who had begun a parallel sporting career as a fast-medium bowler with Lancashire's seconds in the Minor Counties Championship, the left-winger Albert Scanlon, the full-back Geoff Bent.

The highlight of a New Year's Day victory over struggling Blackpool was Edwards's first senior goal, to which Donny Davies devoted due attention. The goalkeeper was George Farm and, for the benefit of *Guardian* readers not among a full house at Old Trafford, 'An Old International' wrote of Edwards:

Darting forward, he put every ounce of his prodigious strength into a mighty, uninhibited swipe. There was a sharp crack of boot on leather – a veritable detonation, this – and a clearing of the atmosphere by a blurred object, which first soared over Farm's upraised arms then dipped suddenly and passed in under the crossbar. A scene of great commotion followed. Spectators hugged each other, then threw their heads back and brayed their approval. Edwards leaped and gambolled like a soul possessed, until his adoring colleagues fell upon him and pinned him down with their embraces.

John Logie Baird had been lucky. If every reporter had been able to transmit a moving picture to the human brain with the skill of Donny Davies, there would hardly have been a need to invent television.

As Edwards's stock rose, the veteran Chilton's fell. He compounded the ignominy of a Cup derby defeat at Maine Road by being sent off. It was to be Jack Rowley's last match for United and Chilton didn't last much longer. He was once more tormented as City completed a hat-trick of derby wins with a dazzling display at Old Trafford. True, City were in such form there was premature speculation about the Double, but 5–0 represented humiliation.

When, later that day – much later – Edwards was spotted riding his bicycle unsteadily down the main road from central Manchester to his digs, the policeman pointed out he was using no lights. Out came the notebook and Edwards was warned to expect a fine. That didn't worry him; all he feared was that Busby would find out. The policeman reassured him. But by the next day Busby knew. There was little he didn't discover about what players got up to.

The next match was another home defeat – by Wolves on a snow-covered pitch – and Chilton knew the game was up. He had set a club record with 175 consecutive appearances but now he asked Busby for a rest and it became permanent with Mark Jones seizing the veteran's shirt.

Whelan was the last of Busby's debutants, all home-produced, that season. But it was Edwards who kept commanding attention. Television helped to make him a national figure when the cameras were at Wembley for his England debut against Scotland in early April. He was the youngest England senior for nearly three-quarters of a century (and remained the youngest until Michael Owen appeared against Chile in 1998). England won 7–2, the Scots' torment coming at the end of a week in which Busby and his wife had returned to their home in Wilbraham Road to discover they had been burgled. They called the police and reported the loss of cash and jewellery to the value of £50.

Of United's men of 1948, only Crompton now remained on the scene, occasionally displacing Ray Wood. Rowley and Chilton had become player/managers, Rowley with Plymouth of the Second Division and Chilton at Grimsby of the Third (North). John Aston had not appeared in the first team, because of age and now tuberculosis, for a year. At the end of the season he was to retire and join the coaching staff.

The squad was further trimmed by the £8,000 sale to relegated Sheffield Wednesday of Don Gibson, whom Busby had transfer-listed after he became engaged to his daughter Sheena; this, like his later decision not to give an Old Trafford apprenticeship to Sandy (a wing-half like his father), reflected footballing judgment as much as any disinclination to encourage mutters of nepotism.

United had finished fifth and halted the slide in attendances. Chelsea had taken the title. City, though two places behind United, arguably had a better season because they reached the Cup final only to be reduced to ten men by injury and lose 3–1 to Newcastle. Revie was named Footballer of the Year.

Continued dominance of the Youth Cup meant so much to Busby that he left Edwards out of the first team's concluding matches. Edwards and Shay Brennan, a cheerful Mancunian of Irish parentage, were the inside-forwards, Colman and McGuinness the wing-halves. Charlton enriched the attack and scored in a 4–1 victory over West Bromwich at Old Trafford. Upon the completion of a 7–1 aggregate, Jimmy Murphy was made assistant manager. Officially; the title seemed overdue. He and Busby attended the Zurich tournament, which had been instituted by the Blue Stars club in 1939 (and was to last the test of time, eventually being adopted by FIFA and expanded to include South American clubs). United again reached the final but lost to Genoa.

SOCCER REVOLUTION

English football was acquiring a European dimension. Old Trafford still lacked floodlights but City had installed them at Maine Road and Stan Cullis insisted on state-of-the-art pylons at Molineux, for he saw how significant night matches could be. Wolves' lights were used for friendlies against, among others, Celtic, Spartak of Moscow and the Argentine tourists Racing Club.

Cullis developed a habit of watering the already heavy Molineux pitch to the disadvantage of visiting technicians, notably a Honved featuring Puskás and five other members of the great Hungary team in December 1954. When Wolves, two down at half-time, ploughed to a famous victory for the long-ball game, some observers hailed a vindication of footballing Englishness – and Cullis was in no mood to deny it. He told his players they were the champions of the world.

Others begged to differ. The Anglophile Austrian Willy Meisl, younger brother of the *Wunderteam* manager Hugo Meisl, was in the process of writing *Soccer Revolution*, which became a perennially acclaimed book, tracing a link between a rigid WM formation and England's humblings by the Hungarians. For now, he gently pointed out that beating Honved, while admirable enough, did not make a team world champions. If it did confer such an honour, he added, Wolves would have to share it with Red Star Belgrade, the second-best team in Yugoslavia at the time, for they had just beaten Honved too. And not on a 'quagmire', as Meisl put it.

Another cautionary voice was that of Gabriel Hanot. A former full-back who had played for France, he now edited the sports daily *L'Équipe* and wrote in response to Cullis's claim:

Before we declare that Wolverhampton Wanderers are invincible, let them go to Moscow and Budapest. And there are other internationally renowned clubs, AC Milan and Real Madrid to name but two. A world club championship, or at least a European one… should be launched.

Hanot called a meeting in Paris. Fifteen clubs attended. Permission was sought from FIFA to start in the next season, 1955/56. FIFA had no objection as long as the competition was run by itself or the new Union of European Football Associations (UEFA). Things moved so quickly in those days. A consensus favoured a cup rather than the league envisaged by Hanot and by January 1955 – just weeks after the Honved match – the Spanish FA had offered support, adding that Real Madrid would be delighted to participate.

Invitations went to 18 clubs. Not necessarily champions; a letter from Hanot was received by Chelsea, England's League leaders, instead of Cullis's Wolves. Chelsea declined on the firm recommendation of the League, whose most reactionary force appeared to be its assistant secretary Alan Hardaker. The League's priorities were beginning sharply to diverge from those of the FA and the outward-looking Rous, who had always got on so well with Busby.

Hibernian were neither League leaders nor champions in Scotland but they got the invitation from Hanot and agreed to take part in the European Cup, starting in September 1955. How Busby wished his young men could be in the shoes of the Famous Five, Hibs's celebrated forward line, as they looked forward to their opening match against Rot-Weiss Essen in Germany.

WONDERLAND

To The Firs came a 14-year-old John Giles. United wanted the Dublin schoolboy to feel part of the family. They had sent his father one ticket for the ferry, so John had arrived alone. 'United were never generous,' he said. 'Anyway, at Liverpool I had to get on a bus and then a train to Manchester and that was the only time I got worried. Joe Armstrong was supposed to be waiting – what if he didn't recognise me? Where would I go next?

'But Joe Armstrong was an expert at meeting people and, of course, he knew me from my battered suitcase. He took me to Old Trafford and there I was having a cup of tea when Bill Foulkes came in, and Freddie Goodwin. I knew them all by sight. While we were waiting for the bus to take us to Fallowfield, I saw Duncan Edwards. He was sitting on top of a post-box eating an apple. He wasn't friendly and he wasn't unfriendly. Like most of the first-team players. One of the lads who made me feel at home was Shay Brennan, with his Irish background. Wilf McGuinness too. And a couple of Irish lads who used to take me to the pictures.

'I was supposed to be there for two weeks but near the end of that time I was messing around with Liam Whelan at the training ground – we were throwing water at each other – and didn't I slip, fall on a glass and cut my hand to bits? I couldn't go home then. Because my mother hadn't wanted me to come in the first place. So I asked if I could stay another two weeks, thinking it would give my hand time to heal. To me it was heaven, training for a month with young lads like Mark Pearson and Alex Dawson, who'd just come from the England schoolboys team.' As always, United had claimed a couple of those. They had also signed the Wales boys' right-winger, Kenny Morgans.

Although Busby and Jimmy Murphy had made a point of greeting Giles, there was little further contact at that stage. Giles didn't expect it. He was just happy to be in 'wonderland', training, playing and watching practice matches: 'First team against reserves and Bobby Charlton couldn't get a start, brilliant as he was.'

Reg Allen had retired but, if Eddie Lewis thought this gave him more licence to swagger around the dressing room, his own days were numbered; by mid-season he would have joined Preston, bringing another £10,000 into the Old Trafford coffers. For Busby was doing excellent business. Of the 17 players who were to make a dozen or more League appearances in the season, only three had cost fees: Wood, Berry and Taylor had together cost £1 less than £60,000. And, of that modest outlay, nearly £40,000 had been recouped in fees for home-grown players. Ted Drake had spent well over £100,000 on making Chelsea champions. And, unlike Drake's team, Busby's was getting better.

Of the 1951/52 title winners, only Berry and Byrne remained. There was fierce competition on the right side, where Berry had to fend off Colin Webster, Whelan to contend with Blanchflower and Doherty and Whitefoot to endure the rise of Colman; and the left wing, where Pegg would regain ascendancy over Scanlon. But Wood, Foulkes, Byrne, Jones, Edwards, Taylor and Viollet were regulars from the start of the 1955/56 season. The only other substantial contributor would be Ian Greaves, who was to take over from Foulkes at right-back for the last three months.

The highlight would be Taylor's partnership with Viollet. But a feeling remained that United lacked the experience to sustain a challenge for the title. The manager's response? More debutants. McGuinness was introduced at home to Wolves. A couple of weeks short of his 18th birthday, he would be up against the elegant Peter Broadbent. McGuinness never needed much winding up but, just in case, Jimmy Murphy asked what he planned to do with his win bonus. McGuinness said he'd give some to this mother. Well, said Murphy, if she didn't get that money, it would be because Broadbent, with his wiles, had stolen it. Broadbent, being as much a sportsman as a stylist, approached the youngster just before kick-off to wish him an enjoyable career. 'Keep your thieving hands out of my pockets!' screamed McGuinness.

He got his bonus. United won a thriller 4–3. Victory at Cardiff gave them the leadership and, although they temporarily lost it through defeat at Bolton, a star emerged that day. It was a bad day for Jeff Whitefoot. Or maybe his worst had come a week earlier, when Arsenal pinched an unexpected draw at Old Trafford. For it was Whitefoot's performance against Arsenal that had persuaded Busby the time was right to promote Eddie Colman.

By Whitefoot's own recollection: 'I played like a twat. I played when I shouldn't have played. I had flu. But I played. And I played like a twat. And I never played again after that.' Not in the League; he did make one further appearance in the FA Cup. It was because Edwards had an injury, and Bristol Rovers beat United 4–0.

When John Giles returned at Christmas 1955, Whitefoot had been displaced. 'I was amazed to find Eddie Colman in the first team. I thought Whitefoot was better.' Young Giles had always been football-wise beyond his years. His father had ensured it. Christy Giles had played for Bohemians and Shelbourne and managed Drumcondra. Once, John found a photograph of his dad with Stanley Matthews. 'I asked what he was like. "Oh," says my dad, "he's a lovely fella – but he knows fuck-all about football." That was my dad. He loved Matthews but would never get carried away by reputations.'

John Giles was not to know there had been tension between Whitefoot and Busby. Whitefoot was on his way out and Colman very much in.

Colman was a lovable character, a dedicated follower of fashion in clothes and music. He was about to jettison Frank Sinatra, in whose honour he had taken to wearing a pork-pie hat, in favour of Bill Haley and the Comets, Elvis Presley and the sideburns, long jacket and crêpe-soled brothel-creepers of the Teddy Boy.

THE 1958 TEAM: BIRTH OF THE BABES

What an entertainer Colman was in his own right, with his delicately incisive passing, dribbling, fondness for a dragback and a body-swerve that quickly earned him the sobriquet 'Snake Hips' (after a dance popularised before the Second World War by the black American entertainer Earl Tucker, aka 'Snakehips' or 'The Human Boa Constrictor').

To the fans, Colman was one of their own. He would walk to Old Trafford from his family's home across the Salford border in Ordsall, taking the route followed on match days by droves of his neighbours, their shoes drumming an urgent rhythm on the cobbles until they reached the swing bridge and flocked to the turnstiles.

Colman lived in Archie Street, which became the model for *Coronation Street*. When the soap opera started a few years later, some Mancunians were to deride it as a false portrayal of working-class life, but it did accurately reflect the warmth and wit of the great conurbation, as evident in the atmosphere around Colman's generation of Busby Babes as in any other workplace.

RUNYONESQUE

Matt and Jean had come to love Manchester. Although Busby had become one of its most prominent and admired citizens, he remained unpretentious – when he and Jean had moved from Wilbraham Road, it was only to a similarly routine three-bedroom property in nearby Kings Road – and liked being able to spend his off-duty hours untroubled.

He pursued his only known vice, gambling, at the various horse-racing venues within reach of Manchester or the city's dog tracks, Belle Vue and White City. He was happy to confess to a flutter, but sometimes his bets could be heavy because he trusted the guidance of the bookmaker Johnny Foy, a close friend, a gregarious type who drove a Jaguar.

Foy happened to be a Catholic, as was the champagne-drinking Louis Edwards. Willie Satinoff was a Jew who manufactured clothing and looked good in it. He owned racehorses and loved to follow Manchester United and, like Edwards, dreamed of being invited on to the board. Busby, Edwards and Satinoff were all in their late forties.

Satinoff had got to know Busby through another member of his inner circle: Tommy Appleby of the Opera House, who would introduce Matt and Jean to the stars of musicals such as *South Pacific* or variety shows. Jean delighted in this, being the more naturally extrovert of the couple. In years to come, when United were travelling, she would organise trips to the Opera House for the wives and girlfriends and Appleby would greet them with a friendly face. He, too, dressed immaculately and had a gentle charm that put people in mind of the actor David Niven.

But Busby's best friend, Jean apart, was Paddy McGrath. He was certainly the embodiment of Busby's fondness for characters who might have been plucked from the pages of Damon Runyon. The chronicler of New York's amiable roguery would surely have seized on the tall, dark and handsome McGrath as Busby had when they met in Blackpool. This was soon after the war had ended and Busby got down to work with United. They were introduced by Jock Dodds, then with Everton but later to become a Colombian intermediary.

McGrath was a Mancunian, a Collyhurst Catholic like Louis Rocca, a big man who had boxed professionally but clearly not lost too many bouts. On the outbreak of war he had moved to Blackpool to become a physical-training instructor for the RAF. Naturally, he knew Rocca and, in the United cause, to which he subscribed with the same passion, would select from his ranks the best footballers and send them to Old Trafford to supplement the club's wartime strength.

He could hardly have enjoyed a more fertile war, being both an enthusiastic bachelor in the seaside resort and an up-and-coming entrepreneur, starting in ice-cream and moving into candy-floss and lettered rock. It was inevitable that he should come into contact with the local underworld and learn – if a Collyhurst lad, handy with his fists, needed such education – how to look after himself and his businesses, which came to include gaming, in partnership with the quietly terrifying Owen Ratcliffe.

McGrath had moved back to Manchester in the early 1950s, bringing, with Ratcliffe's investment, a welcome addition to its nightlife. The Cromford Club, in an alley off Market Street, became known as the place for sportsmen and other celebrities to enjoy cabaret and surprisingly good food.

Midfield maestro: a 23-year-old Matt Busby, having successfully converted from inside-forward to wing-half, is photographed before Manchester City's match at Chelsea in December 1932. City lose 3–1 but later that season reach the FA Cup final at Wembley, only to be beaten by Everton.

In 1936, Busby moves from Manchester City to Liverpool. Here he poses with the elder of his children, Sheena.

After moving to Liverpool, Busby kept in touch with his former Manchester City clubmate Len Langford. They were so close that Busby's children called Len's wife 'Auntie Tilly'. Here Busby shows Len's son Sam how to kick a ball properly.

After the Second World War began, Busby enlisted with the King's Regiment (Liverpool), but he was soon sent to Aldershot to join the Royal Army Physical Training Corps, whose badge is seen on his beret. There he was chosen to lead a touring team of professional footballers. He is pictured below with Joe Mercer, then of Everton, and Don Welsh, of Charlton Athletic. All are wearing the stripes of a sergeant, having received this rank as physical training instructors.

Busby, though he represented his country in only one official international, often captained Scotland in wartime matches. On this day at Wembley in April 1944, he met Field Marshal Montgomery, but England, captained by his friend Stan Cullis, won 6–2.

You never lose it: Busby at Old Trafford after the installation of floodlights in 1957, has his back to the scoreboard as he demonstrates the skills that helped him to set a new style in management by training alongside his players.

With Busby and his press friends now regular European travellers, it's time to do some research on Real Madrid, who happen to be playing in Nice. Here, on the Promenade des Anglais, Busby takes a stroll with (from left) Frank Taylor, Henry Rose, George Follows and Tom Jackson.

The hat-trick: in the spring of 1957 Busby, having won his third League title in six seasons, gazes fondly at the trophy.

Tracksuit manager: Busby does a bit of modelling with perhaps the two most influential Manchester United players of the pre-Munich era, Duncan Edwards (left) and Roger Byrne. Within a matter of months of this picture being taken, Edwards and Byrne were dead.

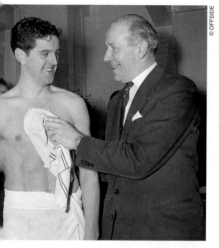

Home and dry? Not quite. It is January 1958 and United have taken a 2–1 lead over Red Star Belgrade in their European Cup first leg at Old Trafford. A smiling Busby helps Tommy Taylor as the centre-forward emerges from the shower. Three weeks later they went to Yugoslavia by way of Munich.

When Sandy Busby first saw his father lying in an oxygen tent in the Rechts der Isar Hospital, Munich, he barely recognised him. Matt seemed to have turned into a frail old man overnight.

So much to ponder: recovering in the Munich hospital, Busby was beset by many thoughts. They turned dark once he had been told the full casualty list. He despaired, lost all interest in football and even wanted to die. Jean gradually made him realise that he should not abandon his life's work.

Home at last: Busby, released from hospital and refreshed by convalescence in Jean's company at Interlaken, travelled back to Manchester overland. On crutches, and with his lower right leg still in plaster, he arrives at 214 Kings Road …

… and Sheena reintroduces the pet poodle to her parents as they turn to acknowledge the well-wishers before entering a hallway filled with flowers.

A kiss for the bride: in the summer of 1958, Sandy Busby marries Irene Stott, who proffers a cheek to her new father-in-law. Irene, who was to present Matt with four of his seven grand-daughters, kindly donated this picture.

Matt Busby, CBE, with Jean and Sandy outside Buckingham Palace. This was in July 1958, only a few weeks after Sandy and Irene's wedding. Quite a summer for the Busby family.

The 1948 team pictured with the FA Cup, obtained through a 4–2 victory over Blackpool. Secretary Walter Crickmer is standing on the left, with directors including Harold Hardman (right) also suited. The players standing are (from left) Johnny Anderson, Allenby Chilton, Jack Crompton, John Aston Sr, Henry Cockburn and reserve Jack Warner. Seated are Jimmy Delaney, Johnny Morris, Johnny Carey, Busby, Jack Rowley, Stan Pearson and Charlie Mitten.

The 1958 team lining up for their final match in Belgrade (from left): Duncan Edwards, Eddie Colman, Mark Jones, Kenny Morgans, Bobby Charlton, Dennis Viollet, Tommy Taylor, Bill Foulkes, Harry Gregg, Albert Scanlon and Roger Byrne. Morgans had just taken over from Johnny Berry on the right wing. Gregg, recently signed to replace Ray Wood in goal, would become a hero the next day.

The 1968 team with their European champions trophy. Back row (from left): Bill Foulkes, John Aston Jr, Jimmy Rimmer, Alex Stepney, Alan Gowling, David Herd. Middle row: David Sadler, Tony Dunne, Shay Brennan, Pat Crerand, George Best, Francis Burns, Jack Crompton (trainer). Front row: Jimmy Ryan, Nobby Stiles, Denis Law, Busby, Bobby Charlton, Brian Kidd, John Fitzpatrick. Law, injured, was absent from the final line-up along with Rimmer, Gowling, Herd, Burns, Ryan and Fitzpatrick.

Depending on their status, they might be met by McGrath himself – Matt and Jean Busby were the first two names on an A-list featuring friends such as Foy, Appleby, Louis and Muriel Edwards and the Satinoffs.

Journalists went to the Cromford to eat and drink and, in some cases, pick up stories. They might be greeted by McGrath's cigar-smoking assistant, Arthur Conway. He was a friend of the press who, while taking him at cheerful face value, reckoned part of his job was to discourage publicity for the gaming room (of unknown but decidedly suspect legality) at the back of the club. If true, this represented an unnecessarily belt-and-braces approach, for the best protection was surely afforded by the profession of several of the Cromford's most regular gamblers: senior police officers from Bootle Street.

At McGrath's club, or at the racing, Busby could enjoy the company of the larger-than-life. He could laugh at the stories of Blackpool and mischief. He liked the banter but would participate sparingly. As for his sometimes reluctant and invariably long-winded attempts at joke-telling, the verdict of the comedian Jimmy Tarbuck, with whom he became friendly, was that it was just as well Busby was such a good football manager.

When the Busby Babes also became known as the Red Devils, a nickname Busby much preferred despite its blatant theft from the Salford rugby-league club, it seemed to suit their precocious football but also served as a reminder that some were no angels. So Busby never minded if players took their partners to the Cromford, for they would know he might be around too. In which case, he would usually send them over a drink. As his son Sandy later said: 'He could monitor them there.'

What he didn't see he usually found out about. At one stage McGuinness, Colman and Brennan precociously toyed with the idea of investing in a nightclub. 'The opportunity cropped up' said McGuinness, 'and we thought it would be a good idea to see the place, have a look around. It was just a little place. The next morning I went in to training and Matt called me upstairs to his office.

'"What's this I hear about you buying a nightclub?"

'It was only the night before.

'"You go in enough of them without buying one."

'"Well, Boss, it was only an idea … "

'"Forget it. Have you looked in your contract?"

'"No, Boss."

'"Well, have a look."

'And, sure enough, if we wanted to do an outside job or acquire a business interest, we had to ask permission. So that idea was finished. But what amazed us was that he found out so quickly.'

As in the case of Duncan Edwards, his bicycle and the policeman on Washway Road.

Although Edwards hardly drank and Billy Whelan was an especially clean-living lad, Tommy Taylor and others were happy to quaff their share and more on a Saturday night, when the match was played and Sunday morning could be reserved for extra running to sweat those pints out.

One Saturday night, Colman and Pegg partied into the small hours with Sandy, who was around the same age and no shirker from the drink culture. When the players reported at the ground, Colman and Pegg, knowing Busby would be alert to their hungover state, sought refuge in the dressing room. Hearing his approach, they locked themselves in lavatory cubicles. He came in and chatted to Tom Curry, asking about any injuries and so on. Then he went to use one of the cubicles. Colman and Pegg held their breath. At length, he emerged. 'Tom,' he said, 'tell Colman and Pegg they can come out now.' And with that he strode off.

Mostly the younger players' nightlife revolved around dance halls such as the Plaza, where Jimmy Savile was resident DJ and assistant manager, and the Locarno in Sale. Girls were chased with a becoming shyness, according to Savile and more durably respectable witnesses, although Dennis Viollet was always something of an exception, pursuing this activity with impressive dedication and a natural talent enhanced by Italianate good looks and sharp dressing.

CHAMPIONS AGAIN

United retained the leadership despite a defeat at Preston on 21 January 1956. They won the next five matches and this was Donald Saunders's account in the *Daily Telegraph* of Busby's demeanour after one victory on a carpet of snow at Luton, where not only Colman but Edwards and Foulkes were absent playing for the British Army against their Belgian counterparts in Brussels:

As Manchester United's grip on the championship tightens week by week, Mr Matt Busby is becoming something of a rarity in the world of professional soccer. Here is a manager without, it seems, a single care hidden behind his ready smile. Mr Busby, of course, has much to make him happy. Not only do United look potential champions but they are likely to win the title by playing football of a quality guaranteed to satisfy the most demanding manager. Moreover, they appear to have an endless supply of replacements to be fitted into the machine – as were Blanchflower, Goodwin and Greaves on this occasion – without disturbing its smooth efficiency.

This was also noted by Don Revie, who, while injured, watched a Central League fixture between United and City and said of Busby:

If he isn't the happiest manager in Britain he ought to be. His first team (most in their twenties) top the First Division and are already being hailed as the team of the season. Yet his reserve team are so good that I wouldn't back the so-called first team to beat them. It's quite true. For 20 minutes I saw this reserve team roll the ball around with the slick precision passing which I thought was the copyright of the Hungarians.

By now an expanded Old Trafford had caught the mood and the hectic Easter period began with nearly 59,000 revelling in a 5–2 triumph over Newcastle. Devon Loch might have belly-flopped in the Grand National when five lengths ahead with 40 yards to go but United, as if warned by the fate of the Queen Mother's horse, just kept going until they could clinch the title by beating Blackpool at home.

And how would they prepare? With a couple of days at their favourite Lancashire resort. But for Busby's habit of taking them there, it might have been considered a little impudent.

When the gates closed 15 minutes before kick-off, a post-war ground record of nearly 63,000 had been set, leaving police to control the 10,000 who stayed outside, ears cocked for a tell-tale thunderclap. But those present did not include Busby. He had taken

Jean back to Scotland for her mother's funeral, leaving Murphy to supervise the team.

He kept in touch through an open telephone line to the press box. He would not have been too perturbed to hear Matthews was taking an early throw but, when the ball was flicked on, Dave Durie forced it past Wood. Later, Tommy Taylor and the Blackpool defender Jackie Wright were being treated after a collision of heads when John Doherty was brought down in the penalty area. With most of the crowd baying for Byrne to equalise, the captain, who had missed a couple from the spot, tossed the ball to Berry and the winger's thwack set up a thrilling finish. Ten minutes were left when a patched-up Taylor scrambled home the winner.

United, with their second title in a decade of Busby, had equalled the sum of their previous history. And Busby had neither seen it nor been able to join in the celebrations, the effects of which could be detected on the Monday when they joined him in Scotland for a friendly at Dens Park, Dundee. The home side beat a depleted United 5–1.

Byrne, Edwards and Taylor were the only United players Busby watched the following weekend, for he again missed the League fixture in favour of staying close to the family and taking in the Scotland v. England match. After the preliminary roar from nearly 133,000 had caused the visiting goalkeeper, Reg Matthews, to pass out briefly like a guardsman on a warm day, Busby saw Byrne and Taylor create a late equaliser for Johnny Haynes. And then the party crossed the border to meet Busby at Troon on the Ayrshire coast in readiness for another friendly. This, against Celtic, proved a more respectable 2–2.

The concluding First Division match, a 1–0 victory over Portsmouth, meant United remained undefeated in the League since the 21 January match at Preston. At the end, Byrne climbed the steps to the directors' box to receive the trophy before it was carried by open-top bus to a civic reception.

United flew to Dublin for a friendly against Home Farm, the club that had produced Carey and Whelan (and just sent over another prospect, the full-back Joe Carolan). And still they had another match, although no one minded making an effort for John Aston, whose testimonial drew more than 40,000, a slight increase on the number present for the trophy presentation; more cared to support an unselfish stalwart than wallow in the glory of the championship.

That side was later compared by Harold Riley with what happens when a painter chances upon a magical combination of colours. It might equally have been described as an excellent example, like Busby's 1948 team, of the energy that comes from blending, as opposed to merely assembling, capable footballers. Either way, they were a potent balance of complementary forces: at full-back the aggression of Foulkes with the lightning pace of Byrne, at wing-half the power of Edwards with the subtlety of Colman, up front the bludgeon Taylor with the rapier Viollet. Yet even that attempt at simplicity would founder in that Edwards was much more than a mere dynamo and Taylor, if an iron fist, one not only velvet-clad but containing a fairly sophisticated computer for a brain.

They had won the League by 11 points – the biggest margin since Blackburn's in 1913/14. Yet they enjoyed no monopoly on Mancunian glory, for City had finished a creditable fourth and won the Cup final against Birmingham. City also boasted successive Footballers of the Year, Don Revie having been followed by the former prisoner-of-war Bert Trautmann, a goalkeeper more than filling the massive gap left by Frank Swift's entry into journalism. Trautmann, a villain to the post-war protestors, had long since become a local hero and now, having played on in the Cup final despite a broken neck, verged on a national treasure.

While a German was honoured in Britain, a Briton was feted on Europe's mainland. Stanley Matthews picked up the inaugural Ballon d'Or – chosen by sports journalists in a poll organised by *France Football* to find the leading player in Europe – ahead of Alfredo Di Stéfano. How Busby itched to get his players into such company. How Rous shared his wish.

CHAPTER EIGHT

THE 1958 TEAM: FLOODLIT NIGHTS

THE LETTER

Around the time the youths left for Zurich in 1956, a letter from Sir Stanley Rous arrived. It was the invitation Chelsea had reluctantly rejected. Would United like to take part in the following season's *Coupe des Clubs Champions Européens* – the European Club Champions' Cup?

It would not have come as a surprise to Busby. He had been following the inaugural competition, from which Hibs had removed Rot-Weiss Essen and Djurgården of Sweden before being knocked out by Stade de Reims. The final was at the Parc des Princes in Paris, where Reims had played their previous matches. Not that this saved them from a 4–3 defeat by Real Madrid.

Before attending the first of three momentous meetings of the United board, Busby had taken soundings from the League, based at Preston. Although Alan Hardaker planned to reduce the number of League fixtures by having five 20-club divisions, he wanted to fill the gap with a second knockout competition, the Football League Cup. This would be a floodlit competition open to all 92 clubs, not just the champions or any others invited to play in Europe. So there was a clear conflict with Busby's European aspirations.

When the United board first met, he recalled, 'I was very keen on the idea.' More so than Hardman. A letter was then received from the League forbidding United to take part and now Busby proposed that, if the FA were willing to sanction participation, United should recognise their seniority and enter. Hardman and the other directors agreed to this.

Busby then travelled to London to see Rous and an FA headed by Arthur Drewry. If the League and Rous didn't quite see eye-to-eye, Drewry seemed to face both ways. A recently retired fish merchant, he represented a football club, Grimsby, that was unlikely to be invited into Europe in the foreseeable future. But he also had international ambitions. He was intent on becoming FIFA president. He had forsaken the League's blinkers for the binoculars of Rous.

Before leaving, Busby asked Rous if anything in the FA's regulations would prevent United from entering the European Cup. 'No,' said Rous, with a firmness that enabled Busby to return to Manchester sure of his power base.

He still had to satisfy his own directors on matters of detail and League officials were hopeful this would defeat him given that United still had no floodlights and would be reluctant to go cap-in-hand to City again. But Busby was able to persuade the board that, if they could just rent Maine Road once more, enough profit could be raised from a season in the European Cup to fund lights of their own. With a bit left over for the bonuses of the players, who would also benefit from the experience.

A deal was duly done with City, who would receive £300 per European match or 15 per cent of the gate, whichever were the greater (it turned out to average more than £1,000 a match). At Old Trafford, work would start on erecting the pylons and, at some stage in the season to come, United would be switched on.

IRRESISTIBLE FORCE

By now United ran five teams – in addition to the 'A' and 'B' youths, the Juniors took part in the Altrincham Junior League – and all had become accustomed to winning titles. Nor did the Youth Cup side, a selection of the club's best young players, let anyone down, beating Chesterfield in the final.

In May 1955, Edwards had been in the youth team. A year later, he was starring for England in front of 90,000 in Berlin. They beat the World Cup holders 3–1 and the opening goal came when Edwards picked up a loose ball just inside the German half, turned and, with the barely perceptible acceleration of a Rolls-Royce, split two opponents, evading a trip and then gliding past another world champion in almost the same movement as he shot, the ball smacking the net, falling and spinning as if in delight before the goalkeeper had completed an obligingly picturesque but utterly vain dive.

To watch such irresistible force was to understand a couple of stories about Edwards. One, recalled by Arthur Hopcraft in *The Football Man*, was of an inside-forward hurling himself repeatedly at Edwards, either missing or bouncing off, and on each occasion the spectator next to Hopcraft drawing in his breath, shaking his head and murmuring, 'Nay lad, not with 'im, not with 'im.' The other concerned Jimmy Murphy when in charge of Wales against England at Cardiff in 1957. In his talk before the match, he went through the strengths and especially weaknesses of every England player. Except one. The Newcastle inside-forward Reg Davies noticed the omission. 'What about Edwards?' he asked.

'Just keep out of his fucking way, son,' replied Murphy.

When United prepared for the 1956/57 season – from now this would take place on their own land at The Cliff rather than The Firs – the first-team squad was unchanged but the youth ranks had been replenished. John Giles was in Stretford with an Irish landlady, Mrs Robb. His life reflected Busby's technique for collecting young talent in bulk, often to the ire of competitors. Giles did not join the ground staff but followed Charlton to Switchgear & Cowans. 'I didn't learn anything about engineering,' he recalled, 'just helped one of the lads there as best I could.

'Busby was very clever. He signed all these young players from England, Scotland, Ireland and Wales and you have to give him credit – it's easy to copy but he led the way. His trick was to get so many of them.'

Busby denied overloading but he did use his contacts to supplement the ground staff by organising those jobs, seeing the youngsters through to their 17th birthdays when the most gifted could become professionals. Edwards had benefited from that. And now Giles, who recalled: 'They [United] were sending three quid a week home to Dublin for me. And paying my digs – another three quid. And I was getting two and a half quid from Switchgear & Cowans. That's eight and a half quid. A good wage in 1956. In fact more than I got after turning pro. Then, I was on eight quid a week and seven in the summer! My father did his best to avoid me having to take a drop – I think he went to Busby and Murphy and said "Look, can you still pay his digs?" The answer was no.'

In time, Giles would come under the rasping, often wounding but expert tutelage of Murphy. 'Jimmy would make you or break you,' said Wilf McGuinness. 'He was the best coach I ever had.' Bobby Charlton thought him 'the greatest teacher of football I would know'. It was a near-unanimous chorus. 'He taught the lads how the game should be played,' said John Doherty, adding that Murphy should be considered indivisible from Busby. 'They were the perfect complement for each other – a pipe-smoking Scot with the air of a nobleman and a cigarette-gasping Welsh dragon who would have your guts for garters.'

An example of Murphy's tough love came the day after the reserves had won 9–0 at Blackpool, where Doherty believed he had performed with – though he said it himself – especial accomplishment. After training and lunch, he was asked by Tom Curry to get back into kit and meet Murphy on the otherwise deserted pitch. He was ordered to hit a long crossfield pass. And then to run after it, bring the ball back and do it all again, repeatedly. George Follows happened to be watching and the *Daily Herald* man, bewildered, asked Murphy to explain. He was told that Doherty, amid his Blackpool masterclass, had spurned the opportunity of a simple but effective short pass in favour of a 'glory ball' across the field.

At other times Murphy could be kind. At half-time in a reserve match at Preston, he approached Scanlon and said: 'Well played, Albert.' The others could not believe their ears; to them Scanlon had been awful. In the second half he was brilliant.

I HAVE NEVER HEARD SUCH NOISE

A new topic entered pre-season conversation because the European draw had pitted United against Anderlecht. It looked a tough one, for the Brussels club, managed by the Liverpool-born Bill Gormlie, a former goalkeeper with Blackburn and Northampton, had completed a hat-trick of Belgian titles. Still, Busby's players would enjoy the voyage of discovery, even if some were as nervous about seasickness as flying.

United had a long trip to Newcastle four days before performing under the Parc Astrid lights. After a 1–1 draw at St James' Park, they nevertheless did well in Brussels, securing a 2–0 win. And less than three days later, back at Old Trafford, Busby's men sparkled, taking a three-goal lead over Sheffield Wednesday with little over half an hour gone – Berry's flying header brought the house down – and ending up 4–1 winners.

Leading the League once more, they fitted in a derby triumph at Old Trafford before Anderlecht came to Maine Road for a night that deserved a bigger attendance than 43,635. A few would have been kept away by the Mancunian monsoon, a few more by the predictable nature of the aggregate outcome. But the stadium would have been bulging had anyone suspected what fare Busby's players would serve up.

Accounts convey a sense of Anderlecht's bewilderment as pinball wizardry took place around them. The rhythm of United's passing was interrupted only by goal celebrations: of Taylor's efforts in the 9th and 21st minutes, Viollet's in the 27th, 34th and 40th – yes, a hat-trick in the space of 13 minutes – Whelan's first (64 minutes), Viollet's fourth and last (75), one for Berry (85) and another for Whelan (87) that took the score into double figures. And still United did not relent because the only forward who had not scored was David Pegg and he had been their best performer. Busby recalled with affection: 'I can still see young Eddie Colman running to collect the ball for a throw-in with only two or three minutes remaining as if we were losing and his life depended on it.' Ten men with but a single thought: to help their comrade Pegg to find the net. In this one respect, they failed.

Busby said he had never seen such teamwork. And 65 hours later all but one of the same players were trotting out at a packed Highbury, to win 2–1. Ronnie Cope made a typically assured first appearance in place of the injured Jones.

Debuts were becoming less frequent. But, with Taylor on England duty, Bobby Charlton's came five days before his 19th birthday. Because he was on National Service, he had not trained. Moreover, he had a nagging injury. But, when Busby asked how the ankle was, he sensed what the reply must be. 'Great, Boss.' Busby smiled. And Charlton played. Against Charlton Athletic. In a 4–2 home victory, he scored twice and each time there was a sweet stab of pain in his tender foot.

Taylor, Edwards and Byrne were back when United suffered their first home League defeat in 32 matches, their first League defeat anywhere in 26. It wasn't narrow either. Everton came from behind to beat them 5–2 and this time there was evidence of tiredness after Europe. And an element of complacency, small but significant? Plenty of critics thought so; Frank Taylor in the *News Chronicle* called them 'cocky'.

On the Wednesday night, they had resumed the European quest against Borussia Dortmund and this time the Maine Road turnstiles had whirred, nearly 76,000 seeing Viollet, his partnership with Taylor clicking repeatedly, score twice and Pegg force an own-goal in the first half. Yet, if the baying crowd expected another 45-minute procession, they underrated the Germans, who made it 3–2 and went close to equalising. Hence Frank Taylor's observation. Reinforced by Everton.

On Borussia's icy pitch, however, United showed they could defend if necessary. A scoreless outcome saw them through to a quarter-final against Atlético Bilbao, conquerors of a Honved suffering the after-effects of the Hungarian Uprising. They would travel first to the Basque country, to meet a club temporarily deprived of their traditional English title – Athletic – by Francisco Franco's insistence that all institutions must have Spanish names.

But that would be in January. There was one match left in November, a true test of United's ability to recover from Europe in that it was a chance for Spurs to go top in front of their own supporters. They scored twice in the opening minutes, only for United to draw. United were never to relinquish the leadership and, as the wins piled up, there was even talk of the Double. Indeed, there was speculation about a new concept – the Treble – and Busby and his players were eventually to buy into it.

Their football helped to refresh a nation dismayed by Sir Anthony Eden's doomed invasion of Egypt. As John Moynihan wrote in *Soccer Syndrome*:

> Matt Busby's new Manchester United matured about the time of the inglorious Suez Crisis ... There was rarely a dull moment watching them. They attacked without mercy and scored goals without mercy. If they were behind, they fought

back and beat the opposition by sheer exuberance ... They greeted their goals with outrageous enthusiasm, throwing up their hands and leaping with delight.

Three days after Eden resigned as Prime Minister on 9 January 1957, to be succeeded by Harold Macmillan, United played their last match before Bilbao, an obligingly one-sided 6–1 victory over Newcastle that allowed Donny Davies to give a Colman masterclass the treatment he had accorded Edwards's first goal. 'Never has this gifted young half-back,' he wrote of Colman:

> intervened more cleverly, used the ball more wisely, or sold his dummies more slyly than in this instance. He had on the other side a formidable rival ... But in comparison with Colman's joyous and effective artistry, [Jimmy] Scoular's work, though telling, seemed heavy and laboured; Colman might have been the *premier danseur* in a Footballer's Ballet and Scoular the dogged leader of a Chain Gang. One of these days, perhaps, when Colman is in the mood, we shall have the Beswick Prize Band accompanying him with snatches of reasonably tuneful ballet music, say, from *Swan Lake*. Then we shall see the little fellow at his best.

United left from Ringway airport on a frosty Monday morning and any optimism that it might be a little warmer in Spain's Basque country was dispelled by the sight of snow – and precious little else – on the ground there. The pilot, Captain Charles Riley, could see no runway and, while circling his Dakota, was indelicate enough to broadcast a request for passengers to let him know if they saw anything that might fit the description.

Eventually he discovered the airport had been closed. After urgent requests from British Consulate staff waiting to welcome United, it reopened and the plane somehow landed, much to the relief of Chairman Hardman, whose hypothermia was the worst of the discomforts encountered on the cold and bumpy ride to the Biscay coast. Edwards and Pegg suffered from acute airsickness, and, while there was much gentle ribbing, this had been a difficult journey for even the normally tranquil travellers.

Now there was steady rain in Bilbao and, come match day, a pitch boggy even by English standards. From the moment of landing, Busby had feared a postponement and consequent delay in returning to England for the weekend match at Sheffield Wednesday; he could ill afford to vindicate the Eurosceptic forces of the League. Bog or not – now with a mischievous crust of fresh snow – he deemed it playable and so did the German referee. The Basques of Bilbao too; they, it seemed, could play on anything and by half-time, with majesty befitting a team who had finished ten points ahead of Real Madrid the previous season, they led 3–0.

Both Busby and Murphy spoke during the interval and it may have been the latter's fire-and-brimstone that stimulated a revival in which Taylor and Viollet scored. Then Bilbao scored twice. But a final word came from the modest Whelan, who broke free, cut in from the left, dropped a shoulder and drove high into the net to make the score 5–3. Although a heroic effort, it owed its subsequent entry into footballing folklore to the subsequent Maine Road occasion it inspired, one that would eclipse even the visit of Anderlecht and disprove Busby's declaration on that occasion: 'I can never hope in the rest of a lifetime to see anything better than this.'

But first United had to get home. Hillsborough awaited. And, when they returned to the airport in the morning, it must have seemed to Busby that fate was conspiring with the League, for the Dakota had been left unattended. It was covered with snow and ice. Busby issued a general order to get it airworthy and, with Captain Riley directing operations, players, staff and journalists alike got to work with brushes and shovels. By lunchtime the pilot had pronounced himself satisfied and taken off – only for the Dakota to face recurrently fierce headwinds. Finally, after a stop for refuelling on Jersey, the party landed and gratefully dispersed.

The players had only the Friday to get the trip out of their legs and it proved insufficient. Upon crossing the Pennines, they incurred the club's first post-war defeat by Wednesday, for whom the exciting Albert Quixall scored a decisive second goal.

United were soon back in form. A Cup romp at Wrexham preceded a 4–2 derby win at Maine Road, where even Trautmann was left gaping by an Edwards thunderbolt. And four days after that it was back to City's ground for the visit of Bilbao. Such was the anticipation that Walter Crickmer reckoned he could have sold 400,000 tickets. Of the 70,000 printed, some went for 30 times face value.

And then Busby, who had taken his team to the Norbreck hotel to escape the madness, brought them to Maine Road. People miles away could have sworn they heard thunder. If so, it was the roar as Byrne led United out of the tunnel.

Bilbao tried to lower the volume, but Edwards rampaged and it was from one of his drives, as half-time approached, that the ball came off a defender's foot to Viollet, whose predatory art was all but defined by a neat sidestep and drive artfully slashed out of the goalkeeper's reach. At length, the outstanding Taylor brought the sides level on aggregate. Had it finished that way, the clubs would have gone to Paris for a play-off. But Taylor was not finished and with four minutes left, ignoring a host of prayers to go on and burst the net, unselfishly laid on the winner for Berry. Amid the tumult even Busby lost his composure; he and Murphy were hugging each other. While Busby broke away to do a jig, Murphy burst into tears.

And beyond the factories and suburbs, across the moors and up into the Pennine foothills, a mill villager putting his cat out for the night might have cocked an ear and cast an eye at the faint glow in the Mancunian sky and muttered: 'That's some storm.'

Afterwards Ferdinand Daučík, Bilbao's Slovak manager, said: 'In all my years in football, I have never heard such noise.' At the Midland Hotel banquet, Busby, with Jean at his side, went through the formalities, keeping his elation under decorous control, complementing the sportsmanship of the acclaimed defender Jesús Garay, who was generous in praise of Taylor. And meanwhile, behind the black glass of the *Daily Express* headquarters on the other side of Piccadilly, the presses were rolling. The headline on Henry Rose's report read: 'The Greatest Victory in Soccer History'. Meanwhile the *Herald*'s sub-editors were trying to come up with something to fit George Follows's description of 'the greatest football match I have seen ... the greatest football crowd ... and the greatest centre-forward display'.

This, of course, was before the days of hype.

Was it inevitable, after such an outpouring of adrenalin, that United should dip, as at Hillsborough, on the Saturday? Apparently not. Arsenal came to Old Trafford, doing well under the new management of Jack Crayston, and took the lead through David Herd after two minutes – and were beaten 6–2. It could have been more. This time Whelan was the star. Next, young Charlton heaped further punishment on his lowly namesakes with a hat-trick at The Valley.

That Busby had no monopoly on precocious talent was evident to Bill Shankly. Shankly had left Carlisle for Grimsby because he sensed greater potential but admitted his error and gone back to basics with a vengeance at Workington, where his multitude of tasks included answering the telephone. Tiring of this, he had gone to relegation-bound Huddersfield to look after the young reserves for Andy Beattie and these had included a pale and skinny Scot, not yet 16, called Denis Law.

Busby knew all about Law. He had watched him during a youth-team match against United and immediately offered £10,000, which Beattie had spurned with a nice-try glance. With his broad grin and blond hair, Law was to remind Busby of Tommy Steele, the Londoner about to reach teenage-idol status with 'Singing the Blues'. But for now all Busby could see was a new Peter Doherty.

United's habit of flopping in the Cup was kicked when Edwards broke Everton's resistance and they survived an even harder match at Bournemouth, giant-killing conquerors of Spurs and Wolves. They still led the League and for Busby there was the added pleasure of a successful experiment in rotation at Goodison Park, where Colman, Edwards and Berry were among six rested and one of the replacements, Colin Webster, scored both goals in a 2–1 win. In the semi-finals United would travel to Hillsborough to meet Birmingham and be clear favourites.

It was time to eye Europe. In particular, Real Madrid, with whom United had been paired in the semi-final draw. To be accurate, United would meet Real or Nice, whose second leg, the culmination of a staggered quarter-final process, would be in France on 14 March 1957. Real had taken a 3–0 lead in the Bernabéu. Busby was accompanied to the Côte d'Azur by the now-familiar squad of journalists; with the likes of Henry Rose, George Follows, Frank Taylor and the evening-paper men Alf Clarke and Tom Jackson, he strolled along the sunny Promenade des Anglais before the match, one of Alfredo Di Stéfano's many triumphs. Now 29 and at the peak of his powers, the maestro adopted the roving role that would forever be associated with his glittering gifts. He scored twice in a 3–2 win and moved Busby to proclaim: 'I have never seen a better player.' As for the winger Gento, he'd never seen quicker. Busby's players read all this and winced; was it worth even turning up in Madrid? He was merely forewarning and forearming them.

The danger of believing their own publicity was evident in a brochure, printed and produced by Follows's *Herald* and offered by the club for a little over the price of standing admission. Packed with messages from advertisers including Willie Satinoff's Alligator Rainwear and Paddy McGrath's Cromford Club – 'meet the stars of sport, screen, radio and television ...', it began with a message from the Lord Mayor, Harry Sharp, who spoke of 'a great football team, which has added lustre to British football'. Busby's chairman, Harold Hardman, conceded that, for all the wonders of 1909 – his day – 'the greatest eleven that has represented Manchester United ... is the one now captained by Roger Byrne'. Johnny Carey pronounced it superior to the 1948 team. Tom Finney said: 'It is a whole lifetime since the imagination of the sporting public was so captured by the exploits of a single team. They have done as much – if not more – than Arsenal did before the war. They have lifted English football up at a time when a lift was badly needed.' And Stanley Matthews: 'No football team has had so much publicity since the war – and no club has earned it more – than Manchester United.'

The centre spread was a three-tiered arrangement of 21 players. Busby was in the middle of the first tier, next to Byrne. On the flanks were Murphy and other staff. The headline read: 'The Team of the Century!' If Busby wanted to keep a lid on Treblemania, this was not helping. United had won nothing yet.

After his return from Nice, they scraped a draw at Wolves. Then lost at home to Bolton on the night Old Trafford's lights were finally switched on: 25 March 1957. Busby had his men kitted out in all red (one-colour strips adopted first by Don Revie at Leeds and then Shankly at Liverpool were to prove more enduring) and 60,000 turned up. But the injured Taylor was being missed. How they wanted him back for Madrid, where the first leg would be.

He returned with five days to spare, in a scoreless home match with Tottenham. That was on the Saturday, 6 April. On the Monday, they flew blazered from drizzly Ringway to a Madrid resplendent in sunshine. Busby, learning from complaints about unfamiliar dishes in Bilbao, had obtained assurances from the Hotel Fénix that his players would be served only English-style food. They attracted a lot of attention in the streets and squares and, when they went to train at the Bernabéu, by now every inch the towering football cathedral, it only added to the atmosphere of glamour.

The journalists were enchanted, Donny Davies telling *Guardian* readers:

> All were left speechless by the thrilling and exciting architecture of the vast concrete amphitheatre whose tall twin towers and hanging terraces gleam like marble in the sun ... As a spectacle it is more impressive than Hampden Park or Wembley, perhaps because its sides are elevated at a sharper angle, and the excitable Spaniards who occupy the topmost tier will have a bird's-eye view.

Busby's plan to deal with Di Stéfano was that Colman would shadow him in midfield so the defence, in which Jackie Blanchflower had established his footballing virtues after an injury to Jones, could keep as much of its shape as possible. He indulged in a little light psychological warfare by claiming: 'Real will need at least three goals to take back to Manchester.' The longer those took to come, the greater might be the anxiety among the 130,000 on the Bernabéu slopes. Apart from the five planeloads from Manchester.

Maybe he sensed a trick from the other side when, shortly before kick-off, Real officials came into the United dressing room with photographs of the 11 home players, handed them to Busby and asked him to reciprocate. Busby calmly replied that he had never heard of such a custom. When the request was repeated, he became unusually irritated – the period before a big match away from home could test any manager's equilibrium – and, having promised that Real could check United's passport photographs if they came to the Fénix afterwards, ordered the officials out.

He then stalked off with Murphy to have a look at the pitch and a final think amid the sanctuary of the centre circle.

Santiago Bernabéu's dream had come true in the form of balletic figures in brilliant white, set against a magnificent backdrop from which white roses now cascaded. In all red with their distinctive white V-necks were the embodiments of Busby's own vision. As the noise hit a blue sky – Real's stadium was not to be floodlit until later in the year – the Dutch referee Leo Horn began a first half that, one-sided but scoreless, brought frustrated whistles from the crowd, sweet music to the crafty Busby.

He had noted with approval Colman's harassment of Di Stéfano, who so maliciously lunged at Blanchflower that Horn might, on less combustible territory, have sent him off. But on the hour things began to go wrong for United. Gento, whose pace had tormented Foulkes, put a cross on Rial's head and the Bernabéu exploded in relief. Next, Di Stéfano worked himself free of a wearying Colman and chipped Ray Wood. There were 15 minutes left; the *olés* rang out.

And yet, as the young bull seemed on the verge of collapse, it rallied. From a Whelan cross, Taylor headed home. Viollet hit a post, Taylor claimed a penalty in vain. Only for Real, the more experienced side, the more sophisticated, to hurtle to the other end and, through the ecstatic local boy Enrique Mateos, make the final score 3–1.

If Busby's pre-match declaration were to be believed, Real might yet struggle in Manchester. Taylor suggested as much at the banquet, a convivial affair during which the amiable Yorkshireman mingled with defenders who had kicked him from pillar to post and Real presented each United player with a gold watch.

In the fortnight before Real came, United, who had overcome Birmingham at Hillsborough to reach the Cup final, would make sure of a second successive League title, Byrne describing it as the 'least glamorous' of their three objectives, albeit the most arduous.

They won at Burnley on Good Friday by virtue of a Whelan hat-trick before clinching it a day later at Old Trafford, where Sunderland were routed. The players could hardly celebrate amid an Easter programme that would make the Real return leg their fourth match in six days. At least, the title secured, Busby could rest players on Easter Monday when they played Burnley again, this time at Old Trafford.

He chose to leave out no fewer than nine, retaining only Wood and Foulkes, and yet avoided League disapproval because United won more comfortably than 2–0 might suggest, the first goal coming from the 17-year-old Alex Dawson on his debut.

The Real match was almost upon Busby. If he had needed a reminder, it had come when the Spaniards' bus went straight from Ringway to Old Trafford during the first half of the Burnley match. Having no doubt been impressed by Busby's reserves, they returned to their coach to face abuse from United supporters.

There was just time for Busby to take his first choices to Blackpool for fresh air and peace. They would all be ready for Thursday night: Wood, Foulkes, Byrne, Colman, Jones (restored in place of Blanchflower), Edwards, Berry, Whelan, Taylor, Charlton (often in for Viollet, who had persistent groin trouble) and Pegg.

Some accounts of the first leg had mentioned Pegg's ascendancy over the right-back José Becerril, even if Donny Davies and, privately, Busby wished it had not taken the winger until the closing stages to appreciate it. But, if Pegg had looked forward to taking full advantage, he and Busby were disappointed to find Becerril's position now filled by the quicker Manuel Torres, whom Real had hurriedly signed on loan (within the regulations) from Real Zaragoza. This took even the programme editor by surprise. There, in the *United Review*, was Becerril's name.

Not that Busby was above a ploy or two. Taking a leaf from Stan Cullis's European textbook, he had ordered the Old Trafford groundsmen to sprinkle the surface until it flooded. On match-day morning, Real officials saw photographs of the sprinklers in the *Daily Mirror* and rushed to Old Trafford to demand they be stopped; otherwise Real would fly home. Walter Crickmer rang Busby, who complied.

The 'excitable Spaniards' of Donny Davies's description found their echoes amid the Old Trafford throng of nearly 62,000 that greeted the teams, led by Byrne and Miguel Muñoz. United, again in all red, again trailed by two goals, as against Bilbao. But this time they couldn't take the encouragement of a lead. Real, commanding as the Basques never had been, impervious to the noise, scored the first goal, neatly slipped past Wood by Raymond Kopa as the United defence looked threadbare. And scored again: Rial, from Gento's cross.

At half-time Busby urged his men to keep going forward. He wanted a respectable result. An inferiority complex, even about Real Madrid, was the last thing his young men needed. They drew level on the night through Taylor and Charlton, enabling Busby to say, after the final whistle had gone on an ultimately ill-tempered match and he had pointedly tapped his watch in front of the referee Marcel Lequesne, as if a couple of more minutes would have surely produced as many United goals: 'Real Madrid beat Manchester United because a great experienced side will always beat a great inexperienced side. Their average age was 28 while ours was just 21.'

His arithmetic was creatively managerial; United averaged more than 24. But the point was made: 'I still believe my boys possess the potential to beat Real Madrid in a short time. If not next year then the one after.' Brilliant. How could their heads stay down after that? Bring on next season and another crack at the European Cup.

Di Stéfano viewed things from a different perspective. He was to recall the prelude:

> The news that had reached us from Manchester was that they [United] had created an invincible aura around themselves. They had overestimated themselves. Matt Busby, who was a great manager, had developed a team from the junior ranks and brought together some special players. But they came here [to Madrid] and found that their muscle and all their sticking their chests out was not enough.

He also noted their mood at the banquet in Manchester. When Bernabéu asked if Di Stéfano was enjoying the occasion in the Midland, he replied; 'Great, but if we had lost ...' Bernabéu seemed put out. Di Stéfano explained:

> I said that to him because of the behaviour of the English players, who had lost but were socialising and laughing with us. It showed they were really good sportsmen. But, if we had lost, we'd have almost certainly come to blows. Go dancing, fine, if you've won. But when we lost nobody partied.

How could Di Stéfano have known? Real had never attended a Champions' Cup banquet as losers.

But Busby was not merely attending to his players' psychology when he looked to a redemptive future. He believed in it. Thus, it was not temptation but politeness that caused him, upon being quietly approached by Bernabéu at the banquet and offered the Real manager's job – José Villalonga was to leave at the end of the season – to say he would think about it and then write.

It was not the first time he had been extended such an invitation; he and Jean had discussed an Italian approach in 1952, and more recently Bilbao placed lavish terms on the table. Now here was Bernabéu, according to Busby, promising him a 'heaven on earth' – only for Busby in due course to reply that he already had his heaven in Manchester.

Bernabéu might have found that amusing. Around Old Trafford the chimneys of the grimy factories belched out foul fumes that, if the wind were in the wrong direction, could seem closer to hell and no less acrid than the atmosphere that accompanied Real's reassertion of superiority. The booing had continued even as Di Stéfano and his team-mates celebrated after the final whistle and the next morning George Follows in the *Herald*, implying that it had merely stimulated Real, wrote:

> Manchester football fans helped to knock their own Red Devils out of the European Cup last night and at the same time they threw away their own good names as sportsmen with a public display of bad manners that made me ashamed to be English.

After the final, which Real had been all the more anxious to contest because it was to be in their own stadium – they duly overcame Fiorentina 2–0 – Villalonga's successor was announced as Luis Carniglia, the Argentine manager of Nice, and he would, like Villalonga, supervise the acquisition of consecutive European titles.

CUP-FINAL CALYPSO

The deferral of Busby's own European quest hardly left him idle. There was a domestic Double to be completed and that, hitherto achieved only by Preston and Aston Villa in the nineteenth century, would be some consummation.

When United completed their League programme by drawing 1–1 at home to West Bromwich on the Monday evening before the Cup final, Busby again turned to reserves, including Gordon Clayton as deputy for Ray Wood, whose fitness for Wembley was in doubt. A rise in the season's average crowd justified plans for further, and dramatic, expansion of Old Trafford, but first there would be the invasion of London, accompanied by a new sound.

New to football, anyway; the calypso had been associated with cricket since the West Indies celebrations of 1950, the songs written and recorded by exponents who had arrived amid the first boatloads of immigrants from the Caribbean. Edric Connor had left Trinidad towards the end of the war and done much to introduce England to his native culture, including steel bands. In 1955, as the Busby

Babes took flight, he had been inspired to write a calypso in praise of them. It featured the following immortal stanzas:

If ever they're playing in your town,
You must get to that football ground,
Take a look and you will see,
Football taught by Matt Busby.

Manchester,
Manchester United,
A bunch of bouncing Busby Babes,
They deserved to be knighted.

It hadn't taken off quite like 'Cricket, Lovely Cricket!', for, although parts of English conurbations – Notting Hill in London, Moss Side in Manchester – had become noticeably Afro-Caribbean, immigrant communities from the old empire tended to associate themselves with the summer game. Moss Side, where some streets formerly occupied by Irish immigrants now housed Caribbean newcomers, was hardly solid behind Manchester City, while on visits to Old Trafford the smiling black faces would be around the cricket ground.

But the beginnings of multiculturalism were embraced by Busby's United, who had printed the words of Connor's song in the programme for the title-clinching match against Sunderland. And now it became the supporters' marching song. It was played over the public-address systems at London Road and Victoria stations as they trooped on to their trains and sung all the way to Wembley Hill.

The following year, Edric Connor became the first black actor to perform with the Royal Shakespeare Company at Stratford and he went on to have parts in films. But he died unaware of just how popular his calypso would be among United followers. After 1957, it was sung in pubs now and again but only in the late 1990s, some three decades after Connor's death in London, did its strains become so evocative of the slopes of Old Trafford.

The notion that Busby's Babes, having further rested at the Norbreck, would carry too much bounce for a mid-table Aston Villa seeking their first trophy in 37 years lasted just a few minutes. And then, suddenly, they became 10 against 11. To all intents and purposes; although Ray Wood did groggily return to the field for the closing stages of the first half, and continued on the right wing for most of the second before returning to goal near the end, the final had been turned into an unfair fight by a challenge that, even at a time when goalkeepers were treated with little more humanity than the Romans had accorded gladiators, struck many of United's followers as brutal.

This was, to be fair to its perpetrator, Peter McParland, not the neutral view as expressed by the BBC television commentator Kenneth Wolstenholme – 'this booing is rather silly' – or, more pertinently, the referee, Frank Coultas, who said afterwards: 'If Wood had not gone down, I would not have given a foul.' But the winger McParland did not charge Wood shoulder-to-shoulder, as the Laws allowed. Indeed, the Northern Irishman didn't even do what some 58 years later, at the age of 81, he said he had done. 'Jackie [Sewell] played this beautiful ball as I'm coming in from the left. It was a big chance. I made contact with my head ...' All of that was true. Not so was the remainder. 'Ray Wood came off his line to cut me out. I put my shoulder into him. At the last minute he pulled out – that's why we had the collision the way we did.'

In truth, McParland's header had been gathered by Wood, who was sizing up his options for a clearance when his adversary came recklessly hurtling in, injuring not a shoulder but the poor keeper's left cheekbone, which fractured under the impact.

Tom Curry hobbled on to supply what passed for medical attention, followed by Busby in his trilby, cigarette in left hand as he crouched over the stricken Wood. As in the case of Bert Trautmann a year earlier, there could be no substitution, so the pressure on Busby was to make the customary ruthless football decision. The jersey was dragged off the dazed Wood's back and handed to Jackie Blanchflower; Edwards moved to Blanchflower's position at centre-back; and so on.

Wood went off to have a splash of water and an inhalation of smelling-salts while Bill Foulkes took charge of retribution, elbowing McParland in an aerial challenge and earning from Wolstenholme this unwitting tribute to his skill in concealment: 'Well, it's been a real chapter of accidents.' The former Arsenal and Wales full-back Walley Barnes, invited by Wolstenholme to add his view, chose silence.

United got to the interval level but emerged again a man short, Wood missing the first ten minutes of the second half. After a pain-killing injection, he had been trying to clear his head in the car park while Busby and Murphy told their men to reduce the effect of their disadvantage by playing to feet more. Indeed they had their best spell before the match swung away, McParland scoring twice in swift succession. Towards the end, with Wood shoved back between the posts, Tommy Taylor looped in a header from a corner, but the damage was done. For Wood, unlike Trautmann, there was to be no conquering-hero role.

McParland was praised for having deferred his part in the celebrations to have an apologetic word with Wood, who accepted his handshake impassively. Back in the dressing room, Busby told his men not to despair. He thanked them for all they had put into their season and assured them that, while the reward had not been all they merited, life would not always be like that. But for the most outrageous fortune, he might have been proved right.

United were far and away the best team in England. Potentially the best ever. The eight points between them and Tottenham and Preston at the end of the League season constituted a post-war winning margin exceeded only by their own eleven points the year before. And in remaining unbeaten through the final eight matches of the League campaign, even though they could have afforded to lose the odd one while Busby was making liberal use of fringe men such as Cope, McGuinness, Webster, Scanlon and the precocious Dawson, testified to an almost embarrassing strength in depth. Which could only grow, it seemed, for after the Youth Cup final had been won yet again – a side captained by Kenny Morgans and featuring Dawson and Mark Pearson beat West Ham – the kids went to Zurich and became Blue Stars champions as well. What a future lay before Busby's club.

Busby himself was the toast of sport. The Sunday newspaper the *Empire News* had serialised his life and Bloomsbury were about to publish the first of his ghosted autobiographies, *My Story*; he was working on it with an *Empire News* football writer, David R. Jack, son of the former Bolton, Arsenal and England forward. The younger Jack's previous literary collaborations had included *Clown Prince of Soccer* with Len Shackleton, famous for its chapter headed 'The Average Director's Knowledge of Football' and consisting of a single blank page.

If Busby's book contained any laughs, they were destined not to last. He, of course, exuded confidence about the future as he spoke to Jack. But his words were to become almost unbearably poignant:

Now I look forward to the 1957/58 European Cup ...
This time, everyone on the staff at old Trafford, from the
chairman down to the humblest ground staff youth, hopes
for better results. We want to play in the European Cup
Final ... and win it.

And the book's concluding sentence: 'There is no reason why
Manchester United should not remain in the forefront of English –
and European – soccer for at least another 10 years.'

Tom Finney having been voted Footballer of the Year a second
time – Duncan Edwards was runner-up – United's consolations
included a drinks party thrown by the *Evening Chronicle*. Several
of Busby's disappointed players failed to turn up. But that was not
their manager's style.

Among those he met was a young reporter, Keith Dewhurst.
This was the 17-year-old United fan who had craned his neck to
study Busby's calm demeanour at Maine Road in 1947. But now
Dewhurst had aspirations to get closer to the heart of the matter. He
wanted to write about football for a living and, on the strength of
material published by the London *Evening Standard*, had secured
a graduate traineeship on the *Evening Chronicle*.

On the final day of the League season, with his senior colleague
Eric Todd either on holiday or concentrating on Lancashire cricket,
Dewhurst had been sent to Birmingham to cover Manchester City. A
3–3 draw at St Andrew's had been his debut as a match reporter. And
it was in the afterglow that he went to the party and was introduced to
the great man. Busby smiled and shook his hand and, in due course,
moved on. It was not until about ten months later that Dewhurst
encountered Busby again and in the interim Busby had endured
terrible things, physical and mental, from which he was still suffering.
And yet Busby remembered both Dewhurst's name and what he did.
As a definition of charm it would take some beating.

MONEY MATTERS

Success was a rod for Busby's back in that his leading players became
as widely coveted as himself. Tommy Taylor above all. As soon as
the season was over, Taylor reported for England duty. He scored
his second international hat-trick in a 5–1 victory over the Republic

of Ireland at Wembley and contributed two goals to a 4–1 win over Denmark in Copenhagen, which Busby attended. After the match an agent representing an Italian club – unspecified in the account Busby gave to David R. Jack, although the agent often worked for Internazionale – offered 'big money' for Taylor.

But Busby reasoned that, if his centre-forward were allowed to go, there would be bids for Pegg, Edwards, Whelan and the rest. They were stars of the European stage now; both Viollet, with nine Champions' Cup goals, and Taylor, with eight, had outscored even the great Di Stéfano. Taylor could receive £10,000 just to sign and in such circumstances, Busby told Jack, 'it would not have taken long for my life's work to be shattered'. So the answer was a firm no.

Not firm enough. No sooner had Busby left for Zurich with the youths than Italian representatives made a further approach to Taylor. Now Busby was angry. He told Taylor he was going nowhere and declared that the player would not be sold even for £250,000.

He appeared to win the argument, too, for Taylor, and any others tempted by the 'lure of the lira' that would see Leeds's John Charles leave for Juventus and Charlton's Eddie Firmani join Sampdoria, turned their minds back to Old Trafford. And did not stray even when, in the autumn, Gigi Peronace, the go-between in the Charles deal, watched Taylor and Edwards playing for England in Wales. Busby responded to the inevitable speculation by saying he wanted nothing more than to be able to pay his players what they were worth.

Their wages were creeping up anyway – the League had increased the maximum basic to £17 – and the very concept of a pay cap was under greater challenge than ever from the players' union, now renamed the Professional Footballers' Association and chaired by the dynamic Jimmy Hill (a perfect foil for the secretary, Busby's old Liverpool clubmate Cliff Lloyd). Busby seemed to embrace the campaign wholeheartedly; with a lyricism for which David R. Jack might have deserved some credit, he had described the latest £2 increase as 'the merest nibble at the dish of discontent so indigestible to many football folk'.

More, he noted, was to come (and the League did indeed go to £20 the following summer) but Busby dismissed such increments as mere 'excuses to dodge the main issue'. What he meant was that his United were not alone in wanting the freedom to negotiate with players individually and thereby give the likes of Taylor and Edwards more; he argued that the maximum wage sacrificed enterprise on an altar of mediocrity and denied that its abolition would, as League clubs traditionally feared, concentrate power in the hands of a few clubs. He reckoned virtually the entire First Division, from Newcastle at one end of the country to Portsmouth at the other, could compete with United on equal terms. Openly too, without making the sort of illicit payments that had been in the game since Billy Meredith's day – indeed before – and for which, as recently as that very spring of 1957, Sunderland had seen their chairman, three other directors and some players suspended.

Busby might have been right in the circumstances of the time, given the relatively even distribution of revenue among clubs and his own determination, subsequently revealed, to keep wages prudent. He never envisaged paying footballers as if they were Frank Sinatra or Elvis Presley. He had other plans for the money football could generate and they appeared to crystallise after United's visit to the Bernabéu. For this one match, it was said – and Busby was close enough to Don Santiago himself to obtain the exact figure – Real Madrid had taken gate receipts of more than £50,000.

True, they could charge more for the better seats in a stadium now holding 130,000 than United could in one barely half the size. An adult supporter paid two shillings, roughly the equivalent of £5 in 2017 terms, to stand at Old Trafford then, while even those seated near the directors handed over less than the equivalent of £20. For all that was said about clubs profiteering, United were among those careful not to antagonise a largely proletarian audience; the *noblesse oblige* of the late James Gibson was not lost on Hardman's board, and came naturally to Busby.

So Busby and his board decided to build big, to bake a cake of such size that Manchester United could both dominate the domestic game and compete with Real and any other giants of Europe such as Barcelona, who were about to open Camp Nou with a capacity of 93,000, and Milan and Internazionale, already sharing the 85,000-capacity San Siro.

The new Old Trafford, it was announced, would hold 100,000. If United could fill it for just one European tie – and, on the basis of the previous season's experience, that could almost be taken for granted – they could bank enough to pay the entire squad's wages for a year. True, those wages were increasing, and would have to increase further if the Italians were to be kept at bay. But United would be ready for the challenge. The economy of the club would swell to meet it. Busby would once again be ahead of the game. Work on rebuilding Old Trafford, it was declared, would begin in the next year – 1958.

At the end of a summer in which Busby absorbed the sad news of Hughie Gallacher's suicide – finally destroyed, rejected by his two sons after an incident they had reported to police as an assault, he had died under the wheels of an express train hurtling through the outskirts of Gateshead – United returned to training, won pre-season matches in Berlin and Hanover and resumed the quest for greater glory.

Busby believed they could be champions of Europe. But domestic ambition burned just as bright. He wanted to emulate the daddy of all managers and Herbert Chapman had built, at both Huddersfield and Arsenal, teams who won the title three times consecutively.

The season began at promoted Leicester, where Johnny Morris would be joined by John Doherty as Busby accepted £6,500 for the injury-cursed inside-forward. Billy Whelan opened the scoring in the 71st minute and by the 79th had completed a hat-trick.

Busby's team could be irresistible on their day. On one such day, after Busby had spent a September morning signing copies of his book in the Sherratt & Hughes shop in St Ann's Square, they might have beaten Arsenal more comfortably than 4–2. On another, they won 2–1 at Nottingham Forest in a match Donny Davies considered the most enjoyable of his lifetime: 'A great exhibition of football in which skill was the final, the only, arbiter, and ... the splendour of the performance was enriched by the grace of sportsmanlike behaviour.' But United were inconsistent, especially in defence, and Busby resolved to find a more commanding goalkeeper than Wood.

The irony was that Wood, still only 26, had given a brilliant display of shot-stopping at Nottingham. The flaw in his game was, and always had been, a hesitance in coming for crosses. Despite a respect for everything else about his goalkeeping, his speed, agility and other qualities that had brought international status, a story was often told – perhaps unfairly, if always affectionately – about his lack of assertiveness.

Jackie Blanchflower: 'Ray – you must be the second worst goalkeeper I've ever played with.'

Wood: 'Who's the worst?'

But the confidence of most men would have been affected by what happened to Wood in the Cup final. Busby, in his book, would say: 'McParland, for some reason best known to himself ... threw himself at the goalkeeper ... so unexpected, so unnecessary ... the ball was, in cricketing parlance, "dead".' And yet when the Charity Shield match, forerunner of the Community Shield, took place in October, his natural inclination to smooth things over prevailed in an arrangement that Wood and McParland should be captains for the occasion. They duly shook hands. 'It's all part of the game,' said Wood after United had beaten Villa 4–0.

Within a couple of months Busby had made a goalkeeper his first purchase since May 1953. Four-and-a-half years after signing Tommy Taylor from Barnsley, he returned to South Yorkshire and paid a world record fee for a keeper. An assertive keeper. A keeper of the Frank Swift type, at last. Yet in one sense it was a brave move, for there was assertiveness and there was the baggage that came with Harry Gregg.

At Second Division Doncaster, under the management of Peter Doherty – Gregg's boyhood hero – he had built on a promising start with Coleraine, his home-town club. But he recalled: 'One time I got injured and, although I declared myself fit, I was sent to play for the second team at Bradford Park Avenue. Now I had a chip on my shoulder. And I was a stupid young man that day. This boy at Bradford was causing me a bit of trouble so eventually, when I put the ball down for a goal-kick and he kicked it away, I gave him a crack. And it was worse than I intended because it broke the bone near his eye. On the Monday the manager called me in and said, "This young man you've hurt is a tradesman. Until such time as he's fit to return to work, you'll pay any shortfall in his wages." Then he stood up and said, "It's time, son, that someone taught you a lesson ... " I thought he was going to hit me so I said, "Don't you start or you'll get it as well." At which point he ordered me out of his office.'

Such a reputation as Gregg must have acquired did not deter Busby, or others; Gregg had come to prominence in the Northern Ireland side who, also supervised by Doherty, had qualified for the 1958 World Cup. Competition pushed the price up to £23,500, of which Busby had raised nearly half by selling Jeff Whitefoot.

If that piece of business was characteristic of Busby, so had been, in Whitefoot's opinion, the manipulation of the surplus-to-requirements player. To dwell on Whitefoot's recollection: 'After Eddie Colman got in the side, I'd been at United another 18 months or so. I'd kept asking for a move and Busby always used to say the same thing: "Give it a couple of weeks and let's see where it goes." So eventually he said I could talk to Nottingham Forest.' This would have been a good move for Whitefoot. Forest, restored to the First Division under Billy Walker, were doing well.

Whitefoot was driven to Nottingham by his pal Dennis Viollet. 'As I'm getting out of the car, ready to go in and see Billy Walker, Dennis says, "Ask him for 500 quid." So I was in there with Billy Walker. I remember every few seconds he was clearing his throat. Then I asked for the money. He certainly cleared his throat that time. And he said, "Give me the weekend to think about it." And on the Monday there's Henry Rose in the *Daily Express*: "What does Whitefoot want? They've offered him a first-team place, found him a house, this, that and the other." He didn't say anything about the money. So of course Busby called me into his office. He told me, "The FA are looking into this." Which I didn't believe for a minute. But he did say he didn't want anything like that and added "Allenby Chilton wants to see you."'

Grimsby hardly offered as enticing a prospect as Forest. Although Chilton had overseen promotion to the Second Division, they showed no sign of further progress. 'But Busby virtually pushed me into a taxi.' Whitefoot collected his wife, Nell, and off they went to Grimsby. 'Nell cried all the way. I went in to see Chilly, signed the forms and came out again. Nell said, "You've never signed." And, when I said I had, she cried all the way back again.' They were allowed to keep their semi-detached club house in Sale, formerly Jack Rowley's, for a couple of months, until Gregg moved in. 'But Busby wasn't a great deal of help then. As he wasn't with a lot of players who left.' Whitefoot was, however, eventually to join Forest – and win a Cup final.

United were going well in Europe. Having beaten Shamrock Rovers home and away, they had removed Dukla Prague to earn a quarter-final against Red Star Belgrade, with the second leg in Yugoslavia on 5 February. But in the League they still trailed not only Wolves but West Bromwich and, on goal average, Preston. If they were to stay in the race, they could afford only wins now, and the key matches were easy to identify. Wolves at home on the Saturday after the trip to Belgrade. Then, the following month,

West Bromwich at Old Trafford. If United proved twice triumphant, Busby's dream of a third consecutive title would look less forlorn.

The Gregg era began with four goals being put past Leicester and three past Luton while the new man kept clean sheets. Early in the Leicester match, Gregg came out for a high ball and knocked Duncan Edwards over. 'Keep coming, big man,' said Roger Byrne. Busby's defenders were ready to adjust to the new way. So far, so good. But draws in a Maine Road derby, then at Leeds, would have been bad enough without errors by Gregg.

It was on a Monday morning in early January, after the survival of a Cup trip to Workington, that Busby was reminded of his place in society. Having supervised such training as was necessary and completed his office work, he went home for his evening meal. He then kissed Jean goodbye and left for the BBC Manchester studio, a converted church in Dickenson Road, Rusholme, to take part in the recording of a sports panel discussion with Claude Harrison, a horse-racing broadcaster, the cricket statistician Arthur Wrigley and Harry Sunderland, an Australian rugby-league administrator and journalist.

Almost as soon as Busby's car had left the house, another, sent by the BBC, arrived to collect Jean. Her daughter Sheena then joined the gathering along with Matt's mother – Nellie was now 73 – who had come down from Lanarkshire and stayed with her daughter-in-law amid conditions of top security. Nellie had to be kept away from her son at all costs. At one stage Busby had suggested to Jean that they drop in on Sheena – and must have been surprised by his wife's reluctance. Meanwhile, Aunt Delia had flown from Pittsburgh. Another secret visitor to Manchester was Busby's boyhood pal Frank Rodgers.

As the 'sports panel' got under way, a member of the audience asked Busby about his days in Scottish Junior football. Before he could answer, a familiar voice, a resonant Irish brogue, boomed out from behind a curtain: 'That's my question!' And on to the stage, with the famous red book that meant *This Is Your Life*, strode Eamonn Andrews, to be followed by Jean, Sheena – with her brother Sandy and husband Don Gibson – Frank Rodgers, Len Langford and Jimmy McMullan from the Manchester City days, Joe Mercer and Cliff Britton, Busby's wartime aide Arthur Rowe and a host of other football figures. They included Frank Swift. Walter Crickmer, Roger Byrne and Dennis Viollet represented United.

THEY JUST STOOD CHEERING

There was something about Busby's United that refused to accept regression. It surfaced in the home leg against Red Star, on a night of fog and rain that demanded patience because, after Lazar Tasić had chipped Gregg to put the Yugoslavs in front, Vladimir Beara repeatedly bore out his reputation as Europe's outstanding goalkeeper. Eventually Charlton equalised and, with five minutes left, Colman's second goal for United – in the 104th of 107 appearances he was to make – gave them a narrow lead to take to Belgrade.

The resurgence continued with a 7–2 defeat of Bolton at Old Trafford. Charlton scored three and Viollet two but it was the team performance that had critics drooling; one called it 'perfection'. And the next League match, after they had reached the fifth round of the Cup with a routine home win over Ipswich Town, hardly paled by comparison. Its mere prospect filled Highbury, even though Arsenal were in mid-table, and the entertainment crackled from the start.

The wingers Morgans and Scanlon, who were keeping Berry and Pegg out – other internationals forced to settle for reserve duty against Wolves the same day were Whelan, Wood and Jackie Blanchflower – soon established authority over the Arsenal full-backs Stan Charlton and Dennis Evans. Morgans had set up Edwards for the opening goal, Scanlon made a beauty for Charlton and, just before half-time, the riotous flank men combined to make a third for Taylor. Highbury was stunned. But anger can lift a crowd and, after Edwards had fouled Derek Tapscott, the fightback began. David Herd pulled one back, Jimmy Bloomfield snatched another two. The noise rolled across the stadium and, when the lights came on, seemed to intensify.

Far from collapsing, however, United redoubled their efforts. Scanlon helped Viollet to put them back in front and Morgans proved the opening for Taylor to score a goal that would have finally taken the tension from the match but for the self-perpetuating character that prompted Tapscott to ensure a nail-biting last ten minutes. Dennis Evans, though he had been tormented by Morgans, later gave a perfect description of the scenes at the end:

Everyone was cheering. Not because of Arsenal, not because of United. Just cheering because of the game itself. No one left until five minutes after the game. They just stood cheering.

The 5–4 win meant United had scored a dozen goals in two League matches. Although Wolves remained six points ahead, and had beaten Leicester 5–1 the same afternoon, Busby's players had done all they could to set up a mouth-watering occasion at Old Trafford the following Saturday. They were entitled to a little celebration before the intervening trip to Belgrade and, as they chatted and played cards on the train north, the nocturnal animals exuded eager anticipation of visits to their Manchester haunts. The reserves, several of whom would be awaiting their arrival (for this truly was a family of footballers) were happy enough too; they had beaten Wolves to take a three-point advantage at the top of the Central League and several would be going to Belgrade.

The following morning, once the likes of Taylor and Colman had sweated out their beer, there were the usual fitness checks by Tom Curry and Ted Dalton, with Byrne reporting a thigh injury from Highbury and Geoff Bent hearing he would travel as the captain's possible replacement. The thing most often said about Bent was that he would have walked into any First Division team other than United's; it was just that he had the misfortune to be a left-back. Yet so highly was he regarded – he was quick, accomplished and tough enough – that many believed Busby should try the right-footed Byrne at right-back, instead of Bill Foulkes, with Bent in the No.3 shirt.

Rival clubs, Wolves included, did try for him, but Busby refused to entertain the thought, placating the 25-year-old with a familiar refrain – 'there are no first-team players here, only first-team probables' – and a club house on Kings Road into which his wife, Marion, had brought a daughter, Karen, five months earlier.

Bent was not initially in the party for Belgrade because defensive cover would be provided by the versatile Ronnie Cope. So it may have seemed like a rare stroke of luck when Busby decided on like-for-like cover for Byrne. Cope absorbed his disappointment. Bent, in truth, had mixed feelings. He disliked flying; it gave him nosebleeds and sore ears.

He was also one of Busby's true family men. Before Christmas, while attending Eddie Colman's 21st birthday party, he had slipped away to check on Marion and Karen. Unlike Edwards, he had taken to his joinery apprenticeship and enjoyed making things for people. He had made Karen's cot. And, early on the morning of Monday, 3 February 1958, he tried not to wake her as he crept out of the house, suitcase in hand.

He smiled. There was mischief to be made, revenge to be taken on a friend who lived next door. There would be no more sleep for him. They often played practical jokes on each other and the most recent Bent had suffered had been disconcertingly noisy. So, he gave a firm and prolonged push to the neighbour's doorbell before hurrying off to Old Trafford.

One of Bent's pals, Colin Webster, would not be among his fellow reserves in Belgrade due to flu. Everyone else reported at Old Trafford for the bus to Ringway except Jimmy Murphy. This was because he and Busby had become part-time international managers.

Murphy had been the first called by his country, Wales deciding he was the man to steer them to the 1958 World Cup. Results had been respectable at home, with Czechoslovakia and East Germany beaten in Cardiff, but the Czechs qualified as winners of a three-country group and Wales, as runners-up, would have missed out had not Belgium refused to play off against Israel. Wales, next in line, readily accepted. After winning the Tel Aviv leg 2–0, Murphy's men were overwhelming favourites to reach their first tournament.

The second leg was on the same day as the Belgrade match and, although Murphy told Busby his primary duty was to United, the manager persuaded him to see the job through in Cardiff: 'If anything went wrong there, you'd never forgive yourself.' So Bert Whalley would sit next to Busby on the plane.

Busby had agreed to manage Scotland, starting with the annual collision with the English – Byrne, Edwards, Taylor and all – in April and continuing with pre-tournament friendlies against Hungary and Poland before Scotland's opening match of the World Cup, which would be against Yugoslavia in Vasteras. Who knew what lay in store for Busby and Murphy in Sweden – might they find themselves in opposition?

And then there was Peter Doherty. The dazzler who had outshone his own contribution to Manchester City – a sore point with the outwardly invulnerable Busby, according to Gregg. Might Busby at some stage be asked to outwit the Northern Ireland manager? Or risk being thwarted by his own men, Blanchflower as well as Gregg? Or come up against Byrne, Edwards and Taylor, and even Colman and Charlton too if their rich form persuaded the FA in time?

Murphy would enjoy the party in Cardiff. Israel would carry little of the threat posed by Wales's most recent visitors, England, who were unbeaten in 15 matches, Edwards and the free-scoring Taylor to the fore, and looked ready to face the best. It was when England were coasting in Cardiff that Edwards had trotted close enough to the Wales dugout to call to a glum Murphy: 'Are there no early trains to Manchester, Jim? You're wasting my time here.'

Maybe only Edwards could get away with that. Busby and Murphy delighted in his sense of fun and, because he contributed so much on and off the field, because he was not just richly gifted and titanic – 'the most complete footballer I have ever seen', said Busby – but so single-mindedly dedicated to the game and its winning, could not see the touch of arrogance others discerned. Not all others by any means: 'grand physique, modest bearing', Donny Davies had scribbled in private notes. But to Busby and Murphy – and his team-mates, and even the likes of Wilf McGuinness, whose path to the No.6 shirt his presence barred – the boy from the Black Country who called everyone 'Chief' could do no wrong.

In years to come, Busby would fondly, like a father, recall how Edwards spoke in the dressing room: 'You'd done your last few minutes talking before they went out, and big Duncan used to say "Listen, lads, we haven't come here for nothing. *We ain't here for nothing!*"' But it was the way he said 'nothing' that made Busby chuckle. 'Nuffin.' Busby spelled it out: 'N-U-F-F-I-N. That's how he said it. And that was always his famous saying before going out.' And the boss's fond eye would glisten.

ALL OVER SMILES

Duncan Edwards used to cycle to Old Trafford. Eddie Colman, as usual, walked across the bridge from Ordsall on the cold, damp and misty morning of 3 February. Of the lovable Colman, Davies had observed, in notes to be published in 1962: 'Humorous and chubby, shooting can be very dangerous from two yards, sings ballads, sentimental, likes fish and chips.' One by one they gathered, until all but Mark Jones were present. Would there be no duet on this trip? Colman might have wondered. For he and Jones loved to entertain the troops with 'Frankie and Johnny', as featured in the 1956 film *Meet Me in Las Vegas*.

Big Jones was another of the family men. He had a two-year-old son, Gary, and a wife, June, five months pregnant. They had met when he was 15 and she assumed he was just another apprentice brickie; he didn't mention football for a year. June once jocularly asked Tom Curry what the players got up to on their trips to European cities. 'If they were all like your Mark,' Curry replied, 'no one would have to worry.' Jones's idea of a drink was the odd shandy and, when it came to womanising, he represented the opposite end of the scale to Dennis Viollet.

One of his ambitions was to play in an FA Cup final, because he greatly admired the Duke of Edinburgh (so it had been a double disappointment when injury gave his place at Wembley the previous season to Blanchflower, so close a pal he had been best man at Jones's wedding). Jones certainly shared the royal fondness of a field sport. He liked to don tweeds and go shooting with his black Labrador, Rick. Sometimes he brought Rick into Old Trafford and, at the groundsman's request, blasted the pigeons from the rafters. Yet his hobby was gently to nurture birds.

He bred budgerigars and canaries. That was what had made him late. One of the budgies was ill and, after being up half the night nursing it, he had overslept. Busby wasn't too hard on him as Jones ruefully arrived, muttering, 'You should have gone without me.' He was always one of the reluctant fliers.

The genial giant – 'always ready for a talk,' noted Donny Davies – was from a Yorkshire mining background. Like Taylor and David Pegg. 'All over smiles' was Donny's description of this close pair of pals who shared lodgings in Great Stone Road, a few hundred yards from Old Trafford. 'Babyface' Taylor was 'full of fun, imitates crooners'. Pegg would probably have been even more fun this morning if he had not lost his place to Albert Scanlon, a certain starter in Belgrade after his brilliant performance against Arsenal. But Pegg was an easy-going character. He had made his England debut in Dublin only a few months earlier and such were his gifts that, at 22 (the same age as Scanlon), his resurgence seemed only a matter of time.

Pegg and Taylor were among the bachelors who enjoyed a night out. It looked as if Pegg would be the last one single now, for Taylor had got engaged, as had Eddie Colman.

Billy Whelan was a different sort of unmarried man: a devout Catholic, modest to the point of shyness off the field, still happiest when back home in Dublin with his family, although more settled in Manchester now he had moved in with an Irish family. Whelan's simple view of life came from his faith. One of his best friends was a priest and rumours that he planned to become one at the end of his playing days circulated until he told a reporter it would be impossible given his intention to marry a girl from Ireland the following June. 'Quiet but with a ready smile' was Donny Davies's description of the freckled Whelan, whose sense of fun revealed itself in the occasional nutmeg. He even promised to slip the ball between Edwards's legs when England played in Dublin – and proved as good as his word. At the cost of a clip on the ankle which, typically, he pronounced accidental on his clubmate's part.

Whelan's sense of humour was never more needed than when he drove around Manchester. His car was the most unreliable of old bangers, forever stalling or making unannounced stops. The suspicion was that, had Whelan not been a prominent United footballer, a police officer would surely have ordered it off the road. But Whelan would not have welcomed recognition, let alone privilege. So bereft of ostentation was he that, when required to wear a club blazer in public, he would often hold a raincoat over his chest so as to obscure the badge.

As a footballer he lacked nothing but half a yard of pace and, like Pegg, would always have been in contention for a shirt. But Bobby Charlton, though just 20 – two years younger than Whelan – was leaving Busby with no choice. The young Englishman was scoring abundantly, often spectacularly and from a range that reflected his burgeoning confidence as well as Murphy's advice to shoot without looking up in order to make it more difficult for the goalkeeper to read the ball's flight. So Whelan would join Pegg on the sidelines in Belgrade. As, of course, would Bent, assuming Byrne were fit.

There was never much doubt. Byrne was strong in every way. 'Morally one of the biggest men I ever met,' Harry Gregg later said of his club captain, who had 'the moral fibre to fight the club's battle with the players and the players' battle with the club'. He was the only player who would ever 'stand up to Matt'. But he would do it politely now. Sandy Busby suspected Byrne was being groomed by his father for the succession; he had often seen them talking quietly together.

Byrne certainly placed the same importance as Matt Busby on mutual loyalty and togetherness: according to his wife Joy, he would never hear a word against 'my team'. He hardly missed a match except to represent England and was not going to let a sore thigh make this an exception. Even as the bus left Old Trafford for Ringway, Geoff Bent knew Byrne, and not he, would be ploughing through the midwinter mud of the JNA Stadium in two days' time.

'Great confidence in own powers'. That was one phrase Donny Davies used about Byrne in his notes. So was 'well educated' (Byrne had not wasted his time at grammar school and was training to be a physiotherapist; he read widely and enjoyed classical as well as popular music) and 'good home'. But so, too, was 'amused twinkle', for the power of Byrne's personality did not preclude a giggle. When Gregg first came to Manchester, he had stayed with Roger and Joy in Flixton, not far from the Davyhulme golf club, and recalled an incident with their dog, a mongrel called Sandy: 'I'd always been a dog man, so this one knew he was welcome to come into my bedroom. And one day, for some reason, he pissed on the floor. And I thought they might think I'd done it. So there I was, down on my knees, desperately scrubbing at the carpet, unaware that Roger and Joy were by the door, shaking with laughter.'

Byrne's problems with his car, a Morris Minor, were less to do with the workings of the engine than the impatience of the driver, although he did claim to have been swerving to avoid an errant van when, on the way to training the previous February, he had careered into a garden of a house in Chorlton-cum-Hardy; it happened to be next door to that of his manager, who was finishing breakfast. Busby heard the noise, dashed out and, after recovering from the surprise, calmly drove his captain to work. How fond he was of these boys. How he looked forward to their next few years together.

CHAPTER NINE

MUNICH

BE LIKE THAT, DAD

The party flew to Belgrade by charter because, less than a year after the chaotic journey back from Bilbao, there had been delays in returning from Prague. There, United had conceded a first-half goal but protected the remainder of a 3–0 lead from Old Trafford. The next day, fog in England stopped flights. In little over 48 hours, United were supposed to be trotting out to face Birmingham City at St Andrew's. Eventually their plane did leave – but for Amsterdam. Crickmer, acutely aware of Busby's concern that the team got back for the League match, had arranged road and rail transport to the Hook of Holland, then a ferry to Harwich, where the weary travellers arrived in the small hours of Saturday. They were then driven the 180 miles from East Anglia to the West Midlands, where, not surprisingly, reports deemed them lucky to escape with a 3–3 draw.

They could not risk a repeat because the League, now under the firm guidance of Alan Hardaker, had stipulated that any club playing in Europe must be back 24 hours before kick-off on the Saturday. Chartering, it was reasoned, would give United more control over their movements.

It was mainly due to European football that Crickmer's job had expanded so quickly. The little Lancastrian was much liked, and respected by Busby, especially for his work in the difficult post-war years. Busby would listen to Crickmer, who shortly before the trip to Belgrade was overheard by Harry Gregg telling him, over some matter or other: 'Matt – get your feet back on the ground.' But Crickmer was having to learn things as he went along. Such as the fine detail of chartering an aircraft.

The club did, however, have a travel agent and contact had been made with British European Airways's charter department. And there, on the Ringway tarmac that misty Monday morning, sat a twin-propellor Airspeed Ambassador of the class known as Elizabethan because they had been introduced around the time of the coronation. They were comfortable, the high-wing design not only providing uninterrupted views but making the cabins less noisy than on Dakotas and others used on scheduled flights.

As the players filed on, the card school of which Harry Gregg had become a member eyed a distinctive feature of the seat arrangement: a table for six on the left side as they looked towards the cockpit. This was duly claimed by Gregg, his boyhood pal Blanchflower, Byrne, Berry, Whelan and Wood. There was a four-seater across the aisle. The rest of the seats were in pairs. Four pairs either side faced backwards from the cockpit. Six pairs either side faced forward. The tables were in the middle.

The players were welcomed by two stewardesses, Margaret Bellis and Rosemary Cheverton, and their colleague Tommy Cable, a United fan who had swapped shifts for the pleasure of serving his heroes on flight 609.

Neither Harold Hardman nor the other two remaining directors, Bill Petherbridge and Alan Gibson, boarded. During the night before the Arsenal match one of their number, George Whittaker, had died in the team hotel, the Russell in Bloomsbury; the players had worn black armbands during a minute's silence before the excitement of that great match took over. Whittaker's funeral would take place on the Wednesday, shortly before United kicked off in Belgrade, and naturally the chairman and Petherbridge would attend. Gibson was in hospital recovering from an ankle break.

Whittaker had been a man of firm opinions, one concerning Busby's friend Louis Edwards; any suggestion of his addition to the board should, Whittaker said a couple of weeks before he died, be opposed. Had Whittaker lived, given Hardman's wish for unanimity, a more plausible candidate might have been Willie

Satinoff. An ardent United supporter – he never missed a European trip – Satinoff was as close to Busby as Edwards. So Satinoff qualified on that very important count. He also had a bit more style than Edwards. He was more ambassadorial. And always ready to contribute to the cause, as indicated by the advertisement for Alligator Rainwear in the Treble brochure. Satinoff was, as usual, on the plane when it set off shortly after 8am for Belgrade via Munich, where it would refuel.

According to Martin Edwards, his father had changed his mind about going. Martin remembered Busby attending a cocktail party at the Edwards home just before Christmas and giving him a half-crown. Martin was 12 in December 1957, back from prep school for the holiday. He would, like most schoolboys, have loved the feel of a half-crown; they were substantial coins with milled edges that could purchase admission to a football match, say, with a visit to the cinema afterwards and plenty left over for sweets and comics. Not that Martin Edwards needed the price of admission to a football match. When he had seen United for the first time, at seven, it was with his parents in the directors' box. Either his father or mother, or both, took him from then on. When he was at school, they kept the programmes for him. 'I still have them from all through the 1950s.' Throughout his adult years, accusations were to be hurled at Martin Edwards, and none was to carry less weight than the taunt that his affection for United was shallow, hastily acquired when he grew up and realised the club could be worth many, many million times more than half a crown.

Martin's recollection was that his father decided to relinquish a seat on the plane after hearing Whittaker had opposed him. 'Harold Hardman, who had proposed my father, went to Whittaker afterwards and said, "I want you to think carefully. I'm going to propose it again at the next board meeting. And I'm hoping it will be unanimous."' Martin later heard from his father that Whittaker had indicated – to Louis – an intention to support him. Nevertheless: 'Father decided it would be a bit embarrassing if he went on the plane. Also, they [the Edwards meat company] were after a big contract. So he decided to stay back. But the opposition to him on the board had gone away.'

With Satinoff on the passenger list was Bela Miklos, the travel agent, accompanied by his wife Eleanor. Bato Tomašević, a 28-year-old from the Yugoslav embassy in London, was there to help smooth over any customs, visa or other problems. He had volunteered because in Belgrade he would ask for permission to marry his English girlfriend, Madge Phillips, whom he had met at Exeter University; the Cold War was at its height and he reasoned that a personal plea to the authorities might be more effective than a letter.

The press gang, as always, featured Alf Clarke and Tom Jackson, United fans all the more popular with their readers for unapologetically seeing every match through red-tinted spectacles. Of Clarke it was said that, 'if a United player got kicked, Alf limped'. The journalistic community celebrated his utterances. Such as when, phoning the office from Dortmund at the time of a beer festival, he described the scenes around him as 'fucking in the streets to music'.

There being no strict segregation between players and press, Donny Davies had clambered up the steps behind Bill Foulkes, after pausing for a group photograph. Next to Davies was Crickmer: small men with flat caps. Frank Taylor, mid-thirties, squat and dark, with a high forehead and a little moustache, represented the *News Chronicle*. For some reason, he was 'Dad' to Frank Swift, who towered over everyone. Swift lent jollity. He was there because, although the *News of the World* had wanted him to cover Wales in Cardiff, Busby had ensured his old friend's presence by offering a free trip. Archie Ledbrooke – tall, bald, slightly aloof – might also have missed out according to Peter Thomas, a former northern sports editor of the *Daily Mirror*. Thomas had given Ledbrooke an ultimatum: finish a long-awaited series on Joe Smith, Blackpool's veteran manager, or be replaced on the flight by Frank McGhee. The material had been delivered.

Eric Thompson of the *Daily Mail* was rotund, twinkling, given to mimicry. By consensus George Follows was the wittiest wordsmith, Donny Davies notwithstanding. A miner's son, fortyish, with horn-rimmed glasses, Follows had been sent to the Doncaster yearling sales and begun his *Herald* piece: 'The top-price colt … yesterday was 15,000 guineas. The top price in the horse-meat shop just down the road from the racecourse was one shilling and sixpence a pound. Seems even in the world of horses it depends who your dad was.'

Follows could have become England's answer to Damon Runyon, in Frank Taylor's opinion. But he wasn't the biggest fish in the pond. Not with Henry Rose around. Rose so warmly embraced the status of celebrity as to distribute Christmas cards with himself as Santa. Asked to admit he was an egotist, he replied: 'Why not?'

Born in 1899 to a Ukrainian Jewish couple and brought up in Cardiff, he had adopted the more personal style of sports writing that crossed the Atlantic between the wars. Not for him the pseudonym. As the *Express* smashed circulation records, his fame spread and he milked it. Brian Glanville (later to become arguably the finest of all football writers) had seen him when United opened their European campaign against Shamrock Rovers in Dublin; as locals milled around the press box, giving him 'the bird', Rose had stood and conducted them. At Liverpool, where he was ritually booed by the Kop, 'he would rise, immaculate with cigar, overcoat and brown trilby', and doff the hat to them.

His columns were peppered with unrestrained opinions and firm forecasts and, because of the huge audience he commanded, Busby indulged him. Over Tommy Taylor, for example. Rose had taken much convincing that Taylor was from the top drawer and even after his hat-trick against Denmark called for England to drop him. If Taylor were the country's best centre-forward, Rose wrote, 'I am Santa Claus'. Two months later, exulting in United's victory over Bilbao, he added a special message to the star among stars: 'Santa Claus salutes you, beard and all.' Rose, however, continued to question Taylor during a lean start to the 1957/58 season and Busby became upset.

He didn't fall out with Rose, instead made a joke of it while quietly letting Rose know of the attributes Taylor brought to the team whether scoring or not. By the time of the flight to Belgrade, Rose and Taylor had become friendly enough to sit together for a while. A photograph was taken on the Elizabethan. Taylor was politely making a point while Rose, dark moustache and temples now ever so slightly greying, listened with a respectful smile.

In the cockpit, conducting their checks, were Captains James Thain and Kenneth Rayment. The BEA pilots were close friends and neighbours in the lush Berkshire countryside near Heathrow. Thain had been put in charge of the flight but suggested Rayment, recently recovered from a hernia operation, join him as first officer. While in Belgrade, they could discuss Rayment's notion of taking up poultry farming as Thain had done.

When they had flown together before, Rayment had been in command and, on this occasion, he accepted Thain's invitation to exchange roles on the return journey. Rayment was a highly distinguished flier, decorated during the war, who had become very experienced in flying Elizabethans. Unlike Thain, who had no interest in football, he knew Busby and the rest of the United party, having taken them to and from Madrid the previous season.

The crew was completed by the radio officer, Bill Rodgers, and cabin staff including the 42-year-old Cable, whom some of the journalists greeted as Tommy; he was known from previous football trips.

Near Busby and Whalley sat Tom Curry. How the players made fun of Curry. On a Blackpool sojourn, a few, having broken Busby's 11pm curfew, had tiptoed back into the Norbreck to find old Tosher asleep in the lobby. They scribbled a note – 'Didn't want to wake you' – and placed it on his lap before creeping to their bedrooms. Curry would get his own back. He kept a cut-throat razor for shaving at Old Trafford and, if they played badly, would leave it open on the treatment table, saying: 'Help yourself, lads.' They loved him, and his fellow man of the church Whalley; if these were parts of the Manchester United furniture, which could hardly be denied, they were wonderfully comfortable. Their good nature did much to create the environment in which Busby believed.

The doors were closed and the announcements made. Seat belts clicked, cigarettes were stubbed out. Thain and Rayment expected, and were duly to deliver, a comfortable flight to Munich, where the plane refuelled and journalists could ask Busby about Byrne's chances; although he exuded optimism, they noticed the manager looked a little peaky and wondered why. A couple of weeks earlier he had undergone an operation on varicose veins, the affliction that had initially kept his father out of the First World War.

Conditions deteriorated as the plane continued east and by Belgrade were so wintry that the Elizabethan was the only plane to land at Zemun airport that day. By early evening, the party had reached the warmth of their city-centre hotel. The Majestic seemed to be reserved for important foreign visitors to Tito's bold venture into independent (of Russia) communism and, when the message was conveyed to senior staff that the players should be served food suitable for British palates, they understood. A drawback was the proliferation of well-briefed minders but some players, taking a stroll before dinner, saw enough to form the usual British opinion of life to the east of Trieste. If this was communism, thought Dennis Viollet as he contemplated ill-shod children and queues outside sparsely stocked shops, they could keep it.

The next morning United went to train at a small ground next to the JNA Stadium. The match had been switched from Red Star's then humble and dilapidated home because Partizan's JNA could hold 52,000. The intensity of interest was almost tangible. But United had become accustomed to that. For Busby, the priority was to check Byrne's fitness. After a bit of lapping – not much could be done on an ice-flecked pitch – the captain broke away, did a full-out sprint, and gave Tom Curry the thumbs up.

That night, Busby let the players out to watch a film in English – their hosts kindly cleared the first two rows of the cinema – and the morning of the match brought the usual lie-in then light meal followed by a briefing from Busby in the dining room. It came with good news: a slight rise in temperature was taking some hardness out of the pitch. United had played on worse.

Afternoon sunshine even greeted the 52,000 noisily watching from behind a chicken-wire perimeter fence. But the sun faded as their favourites fell behind after two minutes, Viollet making his customary short work of an advancing goalkeeper, and there was darker to come when Charlton's superb low drive left the great Beara helpless. Charlton scored again and now there was silence behind the chicken wire.

As United went in at half time with a 5–1 aggregate advantage, perhaps Red Star were reminded that Busby's men had lost a three-goal lead at Highbury. At any rate, the Yugoslavs emerged far more threatening. A quick goal from Bora Kostić was followed by a penalty award for a debatable foul by Foulkes on Lazar Tasić, who got up to convert. The crowd were roaring and United had Gregg to thank for there being only one more goal, from a Kostić free-kick two minutes from the end. 'I've never been more pleased to hear the final whistle,' Byrne said afterwards, as the press, and crew, joined the players in celebrating with bottles of beer the club had thoughtfully brought from England.

They were in the semi-finals for a second season in succession. And how they itched for another meeting with Real Madrid. Given a choice, Busby might have preferred a third consecutive League title. But his team – and their fans, to judge from attendances – were even more excited by Europe.

Reports did, however, testify to a culture clash at odds (and not for the first time) with the conviviality of the post-match banquets. Follows seemed inordinately vexed by the hosts and the referee, of whom he wrote: 'The Blue Danube flows grey and cold through this city tonight and, for all the players of Manchester United care, referee Karl Kainer, of Vienna, can go and jump in it – whistle and all.'

With the exception of the scrupulous Donny Davies, who reckoned Kainer's performance on the whistle had assumed the proportions of a flute obbligato 'due to the frequency with which fouls were committed by both sides', the press men appeared to approach matches as if part of Busby's family, and as if the family were under threat from an alien force rather than a variety of unconnected football teams from other countries.

In Madrid the previous season, according to Follows, Real had 'hacked, slashed, kicked and wrestled their way to victory'. The referee on that occasion, Leo Horn, had 'allowed the soccer skulduggery to continue to the truly bitter end'. After which the United players happily accepted their gold watches from Santiago Bernabéu. Now Kainer's awarding of 23 fouls against United caused Eric Thompson to say of the Austrian: 'He would have been howled off an English ground for his niggling anti-tackling phobia.' While Henry Rose quipped: 'I thought Herr Kainer would have given a free-kick against United when one of the ball-boys fell on his backside.'

The man from *Politika* saw things differently, calling Busby's team 'unsportsmanlike and often unscrupulous' and asking: 'Where was the renowned British fair play? This is only a legend. There was not a single professional trick they did not use.'

And yet the players mixed convivially at the banquet, during which Busby's men had plenty to drink with their veal ragout cream soup, turkey stuffed with pork roulade and 'omelet surprise', and Busby told the Yugoslavs the doors of Old Trafford would always be open to them.

This gave one of the Yugoslav journalists present, the giant Miro Radojcić, an idea.

After the speeches, there were songs: 'On Ilkla Moor Baht 'at', started by the Yorkshire trio of Taylor, Pegg and Jones, and 'We'll Meet Again', led by Byrne, after which, with midnight approaching, the United captain scrawled a note on a napkin to be passed to

Busby on the top table. It was a reminder that he had agreed to let the players out for a while. Busby smiled and, with Wolves on Saturday in mind, said: 'Half an hour.' Groans of dissent moved him to make this an hour.

Byrne, with Foulkes, Scanlon and a few others, went to the British embassy staff club. Gregg was among those who stayed in the hotel to play poker with amusingly vast piles of the inflated dinar. Viollet, informed of the unlikelihood of finding a nightclub with a dance floor, also stayed put, joining Frank Swift in the hotel bar. Taylor and Edwards set off through snowflakes for a local spot, recommended by the journalist Radojcić, where they socialised with the brilliant Red Star midfielder Dragoslav Šekularac. Radojcić, who had accompanied them, was mixing business with pleasure. The next day he was to write an article about United.

Some of the players observed Busby's curfew. More or less. Byrne was one who slipped into the lobby and out again, returning at 3am after more drinks with the embassy group. But after Radojcić had returned to his flat he thought he might try to take Busby up on his offer, or at least travel to Manchester with the team to lend his piece greater depth and colour. He got a little sleep, packed a bag and arrived at the airport to find a group of largely hungover players. His request to travel was accepted; the arms Busby had extended the night before remained genially open. There were other new passengers: Vera Lukić, wife of the Yugoslav air attaché in London, and her 22-month-old daughter Vesna. And then Radojcić realised he had forgotten his passport.

He had one last chance. Johnny Berry had packed away his departure visa. During the delay while the suitcase was recovered, Radojcić could grab a taxi to his flat.

As on the inward journey, conditions were worsening: in Munich rain fell on snow and forecasts offered no hint of relief. Under the pilots' arrangement, Rayment took the controls. This entailed the breaking of a BEA rule, introduced after an accident involving a different airliner some years earlier, that the commander – in this instance Thain – must occupy the left seat, even if not actually flying the aircraft. The rule was frequently ignored when pilots swapped, so the co-pilot could have better access to dials and instruments used in safety checks. So Rayment eased into what was, for him, a very familiar position on the left side of an Elizabethan cockpit.

As the passengers boarded, the card school headed for the table of six. Except for Gregg. When they had played in the hotel, said Gregg, 'I'd skinned the school.' But most of his winnings had been in dinar and the Yugoslav currency would be worthless in Manchester. So he insisted on being able to use it. Amid much catcalling, the others stipulated shillings and pounds and demanded his attendance. 'No,' he said, 'I'm having a kip.' He had never intended to rejoin the school until the second leg of the journey anyway. He'd sleep to Munich then take some British money off them.

Gregg chose a seat in the front section. The one next to it was vacant; airborne, he could stretch out. Perfect. Sitting behind were Peter Howard, the photographer, and Ted Ellyard, who had wired Howard's pictures back to the *Daily Mail*. In front of Gregg was Bill Foulkes.

As the journalists made for the back of the plane, considered the safest place because so many tail-gunners had been thrown clear of crashes during the war, Frank Swift immediately buckled in and, indicating a seat next to him, called out to Frank Taylor: 'Come on, Dad. I've kept this for you. Right back in the tail.' But Taylor, feeling a little queasy, remembered having read about an air accident in which the only survivor was in a rear-facing seat. So he made for the front. 'Be like that, Dad,' said a laughing Swift, waving him on his way.

The journalists were all looking forward to the Manchester Press Ball that evening, although Henry Rose had to complete his precious 'postbag' – a column of readers' letters to which he would reply with his usual candour – before making his grand entrance to the Plaza.

By now Berry's visa and been found and checked but it had not taken quite long enough for Miro Radojcić's driver to return him to the airport in time. As the taxi screeched to a halt, Radojcić watched the Elizabethan take off. For him there would be no special story.

If only.

WHAT THE HELL IS GOING ON?

Halfway to Munich, separated from his colleagues, Frank Taylor was bored. He looked out of the porthole and tried to identify the dark mountains below. He vainly searched his bag for reading material. His thoughts turned to work and, in particular, United's squandering of three-goal leads. He would ask Busby about that. He looked to the manager's seat but Busby, with Whalley by his side, was dozing and, again, seemed a little pallid.

So Taylor got up and walked, past Busby, and Whalley and Tom Curry with his pipe, to where the other journalists sat. There was no seat for him now, as Swift pointed out. They were having fun and teased him, ordering cigars and brandy as he stood with his slicked-back hair and little moustache. 'You shouldn't look so much like a waiter,' said Eric Thompson. Alf Clarke was snoring. 'He must have been reading one of his own stories,' said George Follows. But the time passed and, when Margaret Bellis asked everyone to fasten their seat-belts and extinguish their cigarettes, Frank Taylor returned to the front for landing at Riem airport.

On a carpet of snow, Thain and Rayment could just about make out the runway from the tracks left by other aircraft, but the Elizabethan, having made bow waves of slush, came to rest without incident.

It was 2pm, and snowing again; flakes bit into the players' faces as they skated across the tarmac, Pegg and Colman pausing only to chuck snowballs at ground crew. In the warmth of the terminal they would receive light refreshments while the plane was refuelled under the supervision of BEA's station engineer, Bill Black. Someone started singing 'Baby, It's Cold Outside'. Thain and Rayment turned on the plane's anti-icing system. They inspected the wings and, seeing water run off, decided no additional de-icing was necessary. The burly Black, meanwhile, walked across the wings without difficulty.

The pilots would confirm their assessment closer to take-off. Which it was hoped would be around 2.30pm, or 1.30 in Manchester. Where families awaited and, at the Plaza, Jimmy Savile and his staff made preparations for the Press Ball.

Tom Jackson prowled anxiously. His competitor had gone missing and that was always a good way to make a journalist nervous. 'Anyone seen Alf?' the man from the *Evening News* kept asking. Follows told him Clarke was phoning over a scoop. For a moment, Jackson believed it. Then Clarke materialised. The call came to board. Henry Rose sighed with relief and mentioned the remaining work on his postbag. Back at the *Express* headquarters in Great Ancoats Street, a colleague was about to begin work on a shadow version in case the flight encountered delays. All passengers returned to their previous seats.

The propellors roared into action. As the plane gathered speed, the waves of slush grew, but then Rayment detected an uneven note in the engines and ordered the abandonment of take-off. The brakes were applied, gently, in stages, and eventually the plane drew to a halt in the snow. It had been on the move for 40 seconds. Questions sprinkled the cabin. What? Why? Only the pilots knew they had been experiencing excessive boost pressure or 'surging' which could cause the engines to malfunction in the air.

Resolving to open the throttles more gradually, a routine remedy when the problem occurred at relatively high-altitude airports such as Riem, they told the control tower they would like to go back and try again.

The passengers trooped off and returned to the terminal, where Mark Jones bought a St Christopher medal. There was barely time before everyone was ushered back on. Again they took their seats. And again it happened. Again the take-off was aborted and this time the questions – 'What the hell is going on?' bawled the normally amiable Swift – demanded some sort of answer. It was, after all, less than a year since a crash of a BEA plane on the fringes of Manchester's own airport; fifteen passengers and five crew had died along with two occupants of the Wythenshawe house the Viscount had hit while attempting to complete its journey from Amsterdam.

Rayment announced that a technical fault would have to be fixed. But this abandonment had been on the command of Thain. He wanted to discuss the fast running of the port engine with Bill Black, who came aboard. Since more gradual opening of the throttles had not worked, the engineer said, a retuning might be advisable. But it would entail an overnight stop. Thain deemed this unnecessary because the starboard engine was performing normally and, if the worst came to the worst, one engine was enough to get an Elizabethan off the ground.

The mood lightened briefly when, after cabin staff had boarded the passengers for the third time and found themselves one short, Alf Clarke was ferried by jeep towards the plane. He expected a ragging and the players didn't let him down. Nor the press men, who pretended to be observing two minutes' silence for their missing colleague. This time Clarke had indeed been phoning a story. In addition to his earlier intimation that Duncan Edwards, despite an ankle knock, expected to be fit for the visit of Wolves, he had dictated that, because of the severe weather, United might have to stay in Munich overnight.

Now the Elizabethan had fallen near-silent. The odd joke was doom-laden. Several players changed seats this time. Bobby Charlton and Dennis Viollet moved forward and David Pegg, no longer caring for the diversion of cards with Foulkes and Kenny Morgans – a less intense school – joined Eddie Colman, Tommy Taylor, Duncan Edwards and the journalists near the back. These were significant risk reassessments.

Over the intercom had come assurances that everything was fine. And Thain and Rayment would hardly risk the safety of those on board, including themselves, would they? But the tension was there. It would hardly have eased had the whole plane heard the conversation between tower and cockpit.

At 3.02pm the controllers told Thain and Rayment: 'Your clearance void if not airborne by zero four. Time now zero two.' This – two minutes – was not an unusually severe deadline. Nor did it mean the third attempt would be the last of the day, the last before Alf Clarke's scenario unfolded and United faced the possibility of punishment by the League. But it could have been interpreted as a move in that direction.

Thain took another look at the wings and, having decided there was no need for a sweep, assisted Rayment to control the surging until, with the engines on full power, the plane reached 117 knots. That was Velocity 1, the last speed at which it was safe to abandon take-off, and Thain duly called out 'V1.' Next, he looked for an indication of more speed. Then, at 119 knots, he could call 'V2' and that was the speed required to hoist the Elizabethan into the sky.

It was never reached. Instead the needle dropped to 112, then 105. 'Christ!' said Rayment. 'We won't make it.'

Through the snow Thain could make out a house and a tree. In a desperate attempt at braking, Rayment ordered the raising of the undercarriage. Thain, having complied, saw the nose burst through the perimeter fence and braced himself for the inevitable impact. He did one last thing before it came: he tried to steer the plane away from the house.

Some passengers had peered through portholes as the speed increased, willing the wings to tilt upwards. Gregg had looked across to the six-seat table. 'Little Digger Berry was in the middle seat, between Roger Byrne and Liam Whelan. Roger had the window seat. Opposite were Woody and Jackie Blanchflower and ... well, it was usually me there. Little Digger's face was contorted. He was a bad flier. And suddenly he said, "We're all going to get killed here." And Liam Whelan – I will never, ever, forget it – said, "Well, if it happens, I'm ready." Liam was a very devout Catholic lad. He said it quite calmly.'

Two matters beset Gregg. He was of Protestant upbringing. Non-sectarian; if he couldn't find a Protestant church wherever he happened to be, he'd use a Catholic one. But he had carried into adulthood a fear of the fires of hell and on this trip had been reading a book that, he suddenly realised, might not find favour with the guardians of the Pearly Gates. (It was, Gregg said later, about as raunchy as the *Beano*, but this was a time when *Lady Chatterley's Lover* could not be published in an unexpurgated edition.) He tried to banish all thoughts of it.

Instead, he looked at the back of Bill Foulkes's head. To Gregg's right were Vera Lukić and her child. But it was Foulkes, and in particular his head, that preoccupied Gregg. Its tightly curled squareness lay directly in front of him, protruding slightly from the top of the seat. 'And me, in my stupid Irish way, my only thought was, if this thing belly-flops, the bulkhead of the plane would bash his brains out. And mine. Because my head would be higher than his – I was taller than Foulksy. So what I did was loosen my tie and the waistband of my trousers and nestle down with my legs straight out so the seat was higher than my head. I wanted something higher than my head.'

By the time the plane was approaching V1, Foulkes too had lowered himself, becoming invisible from behind the headrest. So they were almost expecting an accident? 'It came to me that we should not be attempting to take off this third time in such terrible weather,' said Foulkes. 'Yes,' said Gregg, 'but not as bad as it turned out.'

Busby recalled how time stood still at 3.04pm: 'We sped on and on and on and my thoughts sounded just like that – "on and on and on and on" – until they changed to "too long, too long, too long, too long". We were not going up. I threw out my arms in a pathetic attempt at self-protection.'

After the plane had slid across a road, its left wing struck the house and, from engine cowl to tip, was torn off, along with much of the tail section. The plane spun and the tree smashed into the cockpit on Rayment's side. The tail section careered into a fuel compound, which exploded and burned furiously, sending dense black smoke into the air. In the house, set ablaze by stray fuel, Frau Anna Winkler, whose husband was away, had three children to save. She threw two into the snow while the other crawled through a window. All were unhurt.

Thain, the radio operator Rodgers and the two stewardesses left the plane by an emergency exit. Rayment was trapped in his seat, urging the others out. Thain, who had seen fires and feared the whole plane would go up, told his friend to 'hang on' while he went for the two portable fire extinguishers. 'I saw him running around with one,' said Gregg. 'It was the sort of thing you'd have in your car now. And he was trying to put out the flames with it.' More impressive equipment was being driven from the terminal, but, in the inordinate time it seemed to take, Thain did all he could. 'And he's shouting to everybody, in his pukka English, "Run, you stupid bastards – it's going to explode!"'

Gregg never thought about running. He had taken a bang on the head and initially feared the bulkhead had done its worst but appeared intact apart from his nose, which gushed blood. He was thinking more about Jackie Blanchflower and their days with the Northern Ireland schoolboys. Gregg had emerged from darkness through a hole in the fuselage to see Bert Whalley lying still in the snow. 'Bert, lovely man, with his red hair and his eyes wide open.' Clearly dead. And then Gregg heard a child's cry. Now it was his turn to swear. 'It wasn't like me in those days. But there I was, shouting "Come back, you bastards – there's people in there." The pilot was thinking about all that fuel – I wasn't.' He went back into the plane and scooped up Vera Lukić's daughter, handing her to Bill Rodgers, who put her in the care of Margaret Bellis. Gregg, Rodgers and Ted Ellyard then found their way to Mrs Lukić herself. 'She was in a shocking state,' said Gregg. 'I had to drag and push and kick her out – and her legs were broken.' She was also pregnant. And screaming for her baby, who had been on her lap. When they were reunited, the baby seemed all right, apart from a bad cut over one eye.

And, just as Gregg's thoughts were returning to Jackie Blanchflower, he came across Busby.

'Compared to what I'd seen and was about to see,' he said, 'Matt didn't seem all that badly injured. He was propped up on his elbows and groaning "Oh, my legs, my legs."' He had, of course, undergone the varicose-veins operation. Gregg wondered why, if his legs were the problem, he was rubbing his chest. 'And then I looked down and his left foot was completely turned in the wrong direction.' The pain in his chest can have been no less severe, as it had been crushed, several ribs fracturing. 'There was a nick behind his ear as well. All I did was get a lot of old rubbish and put it behind his back to prop him up. "You're okay, Boss," I said, "you're okay." And I left him there. And I went shouting and screaming for Blanchy.

'I found him and a few others. Including Roger Byrne. Even now I regret one thing. Why didn't I close Roger's eyes? It's stayed with me. His eyes were wide open and there wasn't a mark on him. He was lying across Blanchy, who, because Roger's body was pinning him down [Blanchflower could see only the captain's limp wrist, with a watch, and the second hand still slowly revolving] was crying, "I'm paralysed, I've broken my back." I noticed his right arm was almost hanging off and removed my tie to staunch the flow of blood.'

Gregg had dragged the bodies of Charlton and Viollet clear, through the snow, and there seemed no life in them, but now, as if by a miracle, they were back at his side. And Bill Foulkes had been found by Thain, dazed, still buckled into his seat-belt, facing the great jagged hole in the fuselage around midway where the card players had sat.

Foulkes freed himself and ran, seeing bodies in the snow and the tail section, to which the journalists and eventually Pegg and Colman had gravitated, stuck like an arrow into the roaring inferno of the fuel dump.

But by now a minibus was arriving from the terminal. Ambulances would follow and, at the Rechts der Isar (right side of the Isar river) Hospital in the Munich district of Haidhausen, preparations were under way to receive casualties. Busby and Johnny Berry, who appeared even more badly off because of facial injuries that made him hard to recognise – his lower jaw had been rammed into his nostrils – were put in the back with Blanchflower, who had suffered multiple fractures and internal damage, for the five-mile drive. Ahead of them sat Gregg and Charlton. The driver beckoned Foulkes and Viollet to sit in the front and regretted it as Foulkes, dismayed by the speed with which he drove across the slippery surface, curled an arm around Viollet's shoulders and punched him on the back of the head.

Back at the crash scene, Howard, Ellyard, Rodgers and the stewardesses continued their efforts to find survivors, freeing Ray Wood and Albert Scanlon before coming across a seriously injured Frank Taylor and the youngest of the players, Kenny Morgans, unconscious but breathing. To Thain's frustration, he still could not free poor Rayment, who, with terrible injuries, had fallen into a coma. The task of untangling his legs from the crushed cockpit was eventually completed by German rescuers.

What was it Busby had said, in the context of the player exodus he feared if Taylor had been allowed to move lucratively to Italy? 'It would not have taken long for my life's work to be shattered.'

Although he did not know it, as he was stretchered into the care of the chief surgeon, Professor Georg Maurer, a team of assistants and a nursing complement largely made up of nuns, it had happened. It had taken a mere few hours of bad luck with the weather to wreak such destruction and much, much worse. By early the next evening, when the flight carrying Jean and her children, the rest of the relatives and Murphy would touch down at Riem, most of the snow would have gone.

EVEN THE SKIES WEPT

Jimmy Murphy had been on a train back from Cardiff when the news hit Manchester. It was a cold late afternoon and light snow fell. In the *Express* office, precautionary work on Henry Rose's postbag was proceeding when the flash came in: United's plane had crashed on take-off. Everyone seized on the word 'take-off' – if the plane hadn't climbed, maybe injuries were few – but not for long. Lives had been lost, and gradually the names came through. They included Henry Rose. But every name was a shock. At least Busby had a chance. And so, it was thought, did the symbolic Edwards. The journalists worked feverishly past midnight, producing exhaustive coverage, and then drank until dawn. It was a similar story in every Manchester newspaper office.

Murphy had arrived at London Road station buoyed by Wales's completion of a 4–0 aggregate victory over the Israelis and, as if that were not enough, the Belgrade triumph that had set United up so nicely for their collision with Wolves. Life was good and, when he got to Old Trafford, he offered a celebratory sherry to Busby's secretary, Alma George. What she had just discovered shook him rigid. He could never remember what he did for the next 12 hours, before finally he left his office for home. All he knew was that he had cried for a while, and that the bottle of whisky in the cupboard was empty.

Eddie Colman's father knew. Billy Whelan's widowed mother knew. She was not on the telephone but Murphy had eventually got through by way of a neighbour in the Dublin district of Cabra. Murphy had been doing his most painful duty. He had broken the news to Mrs Whelan in the dark evening, just before the Gardaí arrived. And now all the families knew.

Sandy Busby, by now a Blackburn reserve under Johnny Carey, had got back from training in Lancashire to find his mother in a trance, staring at the fire, waiting to hear if Matt was alive. When the news came, she calmed and prepared for the journey to Munich. But she also thought of others. Sandy and Sheena were asked to visit victims' families; Sheena went to Tom Curry's house first. Paddy McGrath had collected Busby's parish priest, Monsignor William Sewell, on the way over. Among the others who arrived at Kings Road were Bill Ridding, once a young clubmate of Busby's at City. He dealt with calls from the press. Carey came from Blackburn.

Frank Swift's wife Jean arrived, and Henry Rose's girlfriend Elise Nichols, and for them there was no consolation.

Paddy McGrath was to recall the mood of a stunned city: 'a kind of depression I had never seen, even during the war'. It was certainly the conurbation's most traumatic experience since 1941. And United, who had taken more than a decade to overcome the bombing of Old Trafford; how on earth, even if Busby and the young icon Edwards survived, could the club now recover from this?

The rivalry between United and City was set aside as the crash became a national event: the coronation's tragic obverse. In homes which had televisions, families settling down to watch *Children's Hour* were diverted to the BBC's news room. Others crowded around radios.

Journalists provided a hotline to the football community. Bill Shankly was in his office at Huddersfield, where he had succeeded Andy Beattie. While relieved Busby was still alive, he was aghast to hear about Curry, under whom he had trained at Carlisle. When he had visited United with Preston after the war, Shankly, who had a supplier of still-scarce eggs, would always bring a couple of dozen 'for Tommy, because he'd been so good to me when I was a boy'.

With the long-awaited Saturday match postponed, Stan Cullis and his family prayed for the lives of Busby and Duncan Edwards, and the others fighting for survival.

Around the time Murphy had reached for the Scotch, the youths were waiting for Arthur Powell to let them leave for the day. They included John Giles and his pal Nobby Stiles. Eventually Powell came in with Bill Inglis and the Scotsman gently asked them to sit down. 'Lads, I've some bad news for you.' When he said the first-team plane had crashed and there would be details later, the general assumption was of a few bumps and bruises, maybe a broken leg. Someone attempted a joke: 'Maybe we'll get a game in the "A" team now.' Stiles took two buses to Collyhurst and was walking through the terraced streets when he bought a late-edition evening paper. 'Many Dead,' said the headline.

'Press Ball Cancelled,' said the sign Jimmy Savile fixed to the doors of the Plaza. Then he locked up. 'And we sat around,' he said, 'my staff and myself, listening to reports as they came though on the radio. We had to put the radio in the middle of the floor before it would work properly – something to do with the aerial. All around there was food prepared for the guests ...' They weren't coming. 'It was hard to conceive that such a terrible thing had happened,' said Savile, who had little interest in football. 'We stayed there all night. It was one of the most shattering experiences ever to confront a city – the biggest disaster Manchester had ever known.'

Not even when he lost his father had Busby been dealt such a blow. But he slept unaware. Later, he recalled half-waking to hear a doctor pronounce a body dead and Professor Maurer hush his colleague. But Busby didn't know he would never again see three of the young men he and Murphy had nurtured, members of the first team to win the Youth Cup less than five years earlier: Eddie Colman, Billy Whelan and David Pegg. Or that Duncan Edwards would become a fourth.

When Murphy arrived from Manchester on the flight BEA had arranged for relatives, he met Gregg and Foulkes, whom the airline had put in a hotel. They were keen to get home but Murphy, persuading them to stay one more night, took them to the hospital. 'The idea,' said Foulkes, 'was to let people see we were up and about, to put on a show for those who were injured or dying, so they wouldn't feel it was too bad.'

They were greeted by Professor Maurer. 'A tubby man,' said Gregg, 'with glasses.' At first sight an unlikely hero. Yet after Dunkirk he had been awarded the Iron Cross; he had saved the lives of British as well as German soldiers. 'He was to take us round the beds. We got to Duncan, who was sitting up with his leg in an inverted V-shape, and when Jimmy went up Duncan said, "What time's the kick-off, Jimmy?" And Jimmy, realising he meant the Wolves match, managed to stammer out, "Three o'clock, son, three o'clock." And Duncan looked up at him and said, "Get stuck in!" That was the last time I saw Duncan.' As Maurer moved on, he murmured, 'Fifty–fifty.'

Eventually they went back to the hotel. 'There were press everywhere,' said Gregg, 'so instead of taking the lift I went up the stairs. And I had got part-way up when I heard this terrible crying. And I looked round the corner and there was Jimmy, crying his eyes out on the stairs.'

When Jean, Sandy and Sheena, accompanied by Don Gibson, had met Maurer, the assessment was familiar: 'Fifty–fifty.' It was so early. Only time would tell. This was before they were taken to the fourth floor, where the most serious cases were being treated, to see Busby. They were told that, when his chest had been crushed, a lung had collapsed and so he needed artificial help in breathing.

As they walked down the corridor, Sandy, anxious to see which of his player friends were in the intensive-care ward, moved faster than the others. In one bed, he saw an old man in an oxygen tent. He looked closer. It was his 48-year-old father. Busby's hair seemed to have turned grey overnight. He was still, monochrome. Sandy turned back and warned his mother and sister.

When they approached his bed, enclosed in its transparent plastic box, he was drowsy but appeared to recognise them. They let him rest. But before Jean led her children away to see what they could do for other families, they were firmly advised that, as and when Matt was able to converse normally – and it might be never because twice the last rites had been administered by a German priest – he was not to be told the truth.

This was the truth ...

Dead were Pegg, Colman and Whelan. Also Tommy Taylor and Mark Jones, whom Pegg and Colman had joined in the back of the plane, and Roger Byrne and his understudy Geoff Bent. Duncan Edwards was dying. Busby had lost not only the heart of his team but the faithful Bert Whalley and Tom Curry. And Walter Crickmer. He had lost his great friends Willie Satinoff and Frank Swift, not to mention the other journalists with whom he got on well. Eight had died, including Donny Davies, Henry Rose and Alf Clarke, each of whom had been through two wars only to die for the sake of football.

And George Follows, who had declared in 1954 that he wanted to watch United every week because 'Matt Busby's young men make a great adventure story, just as exciting as Biggles or Dan Dare and certain to get more and more astounding'; he had chosen to analogise about aviation.

Of the press gang only Frank Taylor survived, a leg and arm among his various fractures, along with the physically unscathed Peter Howard and Ted Ellyard. They were soon back in England being interviewed, smoking heavily, Howard with the lush hair and fine features of a stage poet, the square-faced Ellyard with his military moustache. Had Gregg been the hero? 'Definitely,' exhaled Ellyard. Howard nodded. They were heroes too. As was Bill Rodgers, who would receive the Queen's Commendation for Valuable Service in the Air. First, however, he would attend the funerals of fellow airline employees. The steward Tommy Cable was dead, the pilot Ken Rayment dying. The travel agent Bela Miklos was dead, survived by his wife. That made a total of 21 dead and 2 dying.

At the hospital Gregg and Foulkes, having done a tour of bedsides during which Professor Maurer, asked if Berry might live, replied 'I am not God', wondered where they should go to see other survivors. A nurse said there were none. The truth sank in. And Murphy, aware it dare not speak its name, went to see Busby, who happened to be awake. He poked his head into the oxygen tent and Busby smiled faintly. 'Keep the flag flying, Jimmy,' he said. He could not have said it to a better man.

That day – Friday, 7 February – only three members of the first-team squad came into Old Trafford. They were Wilf McGuinness,

Freddie Goodwin and Ian Greaves. All would have been disappointed not to travel to Belgrade. But Goodwin and Greaves would get a shirt soon enough; McGuinness had to recover from a knee operation. They were told to come back on the Monday.

No directors were on what the papers called the 'mercy flight'. Hardman, Petherbridge and Alan Gibson had business to conduct on the 7th. An extraordinary general meeting. At Gibson's home in Bowdon, as green and pleasant as his late father's Hale Barns, they sombrely convened – the host arrived from hospital on crutches with his ankle in plaster, peering through pebble glasses as if surprised photographers should be taking an interest – and it was resolved that Louis Edwards, of Alderley Edge, be invited to join the board. With Satinoff gone, and the question of whether Whittaker had changed his mind no longer relevant, it was a simple decision.

No one could have suspected how big a decision. But at least they could be sure Busby, were he ever to return to Old Trafford, would approve.

The next day, a minute's silence was observed on every ground in Britain, and some in Europe and farther afield. Jimmy McGuire, an emigrant Scot who had helped to forge Busby's links with football in North America, a friend close enough to have been flown over for *This Is Your Life*, was among those who arrived at his bedside and were recognised. With Wolves not playing – Cullis's players instead stood motionless at Molineux in their rivals' honour – Preston moved to within three points of the leaders by winning 2–0 at Chelsea, while West Bromwich overtook United with a 3–2 home victory over Forest. Not that Old Trafford took much notice.

Amid its agony, a huge burden fell on the 29-year-old Les Olive. With Crickmer gone, he shelved his grief and tried to help the families. Over the next few weeks, his obligations would include asking the young goalkeeper David Gaskell, who lodged with Duncan Edwards and Tommy Taylor at Mrs Dorman's in Gorse Avenue, Stretford, to convey their belongings to their families.

Edwards was to die 15 days after the crash. He and his fiancée Molly Leach would never have a house of their own.

Tommy Taylor would not marry Norma Curtis. Nor continue his rise to international stardom alongside Edwards and Roger Byrne at the World Cup.

Over were the career and carefree life of David Pegg.

The third of the Yorkshire pals, Mark Jones, would never again see his beloved June or toddler Gary. Never see or hold the daughter June would name Lynn. Never again set off across the fields with his faithful dog Rick, who would be adopted by his brother Tom but die within a year. Nor tend his birds; June advertised for new homes for them, causing a queue of children outside her house in Kings Road. Jones would never play for England, or meet the Duke of Edinburgh.

Nor would Colman get an England cap. Or walk the cobbles of Ordsall again. Or delight his fans. Or marry Marjorie English. Or fall victim to the next fashion, or eat fish and chips, or sing 'Frankie and Johnny' with Mark Jones. Colman died with Elvis on the top of the charts. Dancing to the 'Jailhouse Rock'.

With Geoff Bent's neighbour there would be no more jokes. Bent would never see Marion or Karen again.

Billy Whelan would never wed his Irish girl. He would return to Ruby McCullagh in a coffin that 20,000 saw borne from the Church of Christ the King in Cabra to Glasnevin Cemetery, resting place of O'Connell, Parnell and Collins. Ruby would mourn with Billy's sister Rita, the friend alongside whom she worked in a biscuit factory.

Roger Byrne would never complete his physiotherapy qualifications. Or become manager of Manchester United. Despite Sandy Busby's instincts, Joy never felt her husband would want to manage. 'Roger was never a footballer at home or in our circle of friends,' she said. 'To me he was always more a physiotherapist.' But many a player has, upon retirement, been unable to resist the temptation to be tested in arguably the game's hardest and most lonely job. Nor would Byrne know he was a father. Nearly nine months after he died, Joy gave birth to a boy. She named him Roger. The mongrel Sandy, like Mark Jones's Rick, seemed just to pine away.

Of all the Manchester funerals – even those of the players, at which Sandy Busby and his brother-in-law Don Gibson were pall-bearers – none was to be better attended than that of Henry Rose. His remains were placed, like Willie Satinoff's, in the Jewish section of Southern Cemetery. Every taxi driver ferried mourners without charge. The route of the procession, of course, took in Great Ancoats Street, to which the *Express* journalists – all with heads covered in respect for the Jewish tradition – returned to work afterwards. The colour piece could be written only by Desmond Hackett, who, although London-based, was a chip off the same block. Removing his trademark brown bowler hat, Hackett sat in front of his typewriter, glanced up and briefly pondered the significance of a rainy day in Manchester before beginning: 'Even the skies wept for Henry Rose ...'

KEEP THE FLAG FLYING

Harry Gregg and Bill Foulkes had travelled back to Manchester with Murphy by train and ferry. Foulkes was a tough ex-miner and yet, every time the train braked, his heart had skipped a beat. He and Gregg were needed because United would resume playing as soon as possible. As soon as the funerals were over.

At one stage ten coffins had lain in the gymnasium at Old Trafford awaiting collection. They were kept polished, never gathering a speck of dust, by Irene Ramsden – mother of Ken, later to become United's secretary – and her sister Joan Taylor. In happier times, Irene and Joan were part of the fun around Old Trafford. They ran the laundry in a windowless cellar beneath the main stand and were known as Daz and Omo after the soap powders. No one knew which was which. 'They'd answer to both or neither,' said Ken Ramsden, 'depending on who was asking.' Apart from the first team's kit, which on fine days would be strung on a line between the back of the stand and the railway fence, they might be handed a lipstick-smeared shirt which a player didn't want to take home, or Walter Crickmer's curtains: painful recollections as they dusted the coffins.

On the Mondays after Cup rounds, the players would gather in the laundry with Busby and his staff to listen to the draw, because Daz and Omo had the only radio in the stadium. Less than a fortnight earlier, perched on washing machines, the players had been pleased to hear they would face Sheffield Wednesday at home.

Murphy, anxious to get everyone away from the mourning city, now took those who remained to the Norbreck. And there pondered how to keep the flag flying.

To his own great credit, United were accustomed to reserve strength. But, of the best players outside the first 11 at the time of the crash, Pegg and Bent were dead, Blanchflower and Berry out of consideration for the foreseeable future, if not ever, Wood far from ready and McGuinness injured. Murphy needed to recruit. Fortunately, Busby had been working on that before the crash. With the help of Paddy McGrath and his Blackpool connections.

McGrath had been told by Ernie Taylor that the Bloomfield Road club would be willing to sell him for £8,000 given his age, 32. The accomplished inside-forward said he fancied going to Old Trafford as a squad player; he could help the younger ones in the reserves while being available for the first team if required. McGrath had put the idea to Busby, who liked it. But negotiations with Blackpool had stalled when they offered to swap Taylor for Colin Webster; Busby, pointing out that Blackpool had offered £12,000 for Webster, wanted a cash adjustment. Now Murphy needed to keep Webster. And bring in Ernie Taylor as well, to compensate for the lost wiles of Colman and Whelan. And so, despite reservations about McGrath's place at the high table – Murphy was not a Cromford man, much preferring a few pints at his local, the Throstles Nest – he was grateful to revive the Taylor deal, which went through at £8,000.

Murphy thought big. He even pondered recruiting three of the great Hungarian side – Ferenc Puskás, Sándor Kocsis and Zoltán Czibor – who were in limbo, serving UEFA suspensions for leaving Honved after the 1956 revolution.

Puskás had been in Italy, looking for a club, when he heard about the crash. 'The shock was tremendous,' he said.

> I liked Matt Busby a lot. He was a great football man and Manchester United were becoming a very good side. Duncan Edwards was stunning to watch, so young and yet with such power. He was a massive physical presence on the pitch, always working for the team – a great loss to the club, and the game as well.

According to Puskás, United asked FIFA if they could 'borrow' him, Kocsis and Czibor until their suspensions expired in a few months. But FIFA were reluctant. And the FA had rules against foreign players. And would the trio have accepted the maximum wage? But it did indicate the scale Busby's United had attained. Puskás ended up with Real Madrid and Kocsis and Czibor with Barcelona.

In the new press gang, replacing the local men Clarke and Jackson, were Keith Dewhurst and David Meek. They were different, younger and broader in outlook. Meek had been engaged by the *Evening News* as a leader writer in succession to Harold Evans, later to become a great campaigning editor of the *Sunday Times*. Meek's experience of football writing amounted to a spell covering York City for the *Yorkshire Post*. Now he listened to Murphy at the Norbreck: 'I'll always associate those early days with the smell of chlorine, because Jimmy used to hold his press conferences at the end of the swimming-pool.'

The first team Murphy picked would play in the Cup against Wednesday – relegation-bound despite the excellence of Quixall – at an inevitably packed and emotionally charged Old Trafford on 19 February, just short of two weeks after the crash. 'United will rise again,' declared Harold Hardman in the match programme. It was blank where United's line-up should have been. And yet, during lulls in the raging storm on the terraces, immortal names could be heard. They were yelled at the top of voices, these unanswerable summonses.

On the day of the match, Murphy had signed Stan Crowther, the tall wing-half who had shone for Aston Villa against United at Wembley nine months earlier. He cost £22,000 and took his place, like Ernie Taylor, by special FA dispensation that United could use players who had appeared for other clubs in the Cup that season.

When the team was announced, the first name was Gregg's and it received the roar of his life. Foulkes, whom Murphy had named captain, was at right-back with Ronnie Cope in the middle of the defence and Ian Greaves at left-back. Freddie Goodwin and Crowther were at wing-half and the forward line consisted of Colin Webster, Ernie Taylor and three youngsters: Alex Dawson, still not quite 18, and Mark Pearson and Shay Brennan, debutants at 18 and 20 respectively.

Wednesday might as well have played in ballet shoes, Michael Parkinson recalled, 'so careful were they not to bruise their opponents or in any way offend the anguish of the multitude'. Other forces may have been at work, for when Brennan took a corner the wind blew it into the net. Brennan, thriving on the left wing, to which Murphy had converted him, scored again in the second half and, towards the end, with the excellent Taylor and Crowther in control, Dawson made it 3–0.

Busby knew nothing of this. Nor did he yet feel guilty, or question the faith on which his life had been built – those torments were to come – because he remained too infirm to know the fate of his players and his assistants. He suspected, though. He kept asking how they were, and being fobbed off, told to concentrate on getting better. Told by Jean, as well as the doctors; there was an understanding that, when she judged the time had come, she would break the truth to him.

After four days, he had left intensive care and been moved into a two-bed room with Frank Taylor. The journalist was the perkier of the two. He looked out of the window and could see the rooftops of central Munich. His gaze turned to the wall behind Busby, which happened to be sky blue. 'City's colours,' quipped Taylor. From Busby's bed came only a groan. It may have been the pain – for Busby was to suffer for weeks, especially during bouts of coughing – or impatience with such triviality, or both. At any rate, Taylor was soon being wheeled out to share with Jackie Blanchflower instead, the medical staff explaining that Busby needed peace and solitude.

And then, early in the morning of 21 February, Duncan Edwards passed away. According to the *Evening News*, even the nurses cried. The next day, United's biggest Old Trafford crowd since 1920 saw a 1–1 draw with Nottingham Forest. Dawson equalised with a header. Many of the 66,000 wept for Edwards while at nearby 19 Gorse Avenue his landlady acceded to a newspaper photographer's request to dust mementoes he had brought her from his trips abroad.

At least Bato Tomašević, who retained the company of Scanlon and others at the Rechts der Isar, was recovering. The Yugoslav had survived because, while players were changing seats prior to the third take-off attempt, Tommy Cable had spared a thought for him. Tomašević had been sitting in the front row of the forward-facing rear section, across from Cable. 'The steward asked if I wanted to swap,' he said. 'He died. I survived.' Cable was married with a baby daughter.

Tomašević had been refused permission to marry Madge but would do so regardless when back in Devon a few weeks later, at the cost of his diplomatic career. 'He was temperamentally unsuited to it anyway,' said Madge. He was to return to Belgrade with her and make a distinguished career in journalism and broadcasting. But his work did not find favour with the nationalistic leader Slobodan

Milošević and in 1997 the couple returned hurriedly to Devon, settling there. Both wrote books on Yugoslav history and naive art and in 2008 Bato brought out an acclaimed autobiography, *Life and Death in the Balkans*.

GUILT AND TEARS

Busby had been wondering why no one ever mentioned Edwards or Roger Byrne. Now he asked a passing monk about Edwards and the secret was out. When Jean came, she looked into his eyes and knew it was time. 'I want to know the worst,' he confirmed. 'For my peace of mind.' He spoke the names and sometimes Jean just shook her head. Now he realised all he had lost and was consumed by guilt at having taken his team into Europe, and allowed their plane to take off a third time, and anger that whatever it was – the God he had always believed in? – had seen fit to take these young men before their prime had been fulfilled and their families completed. Why, when they had gone, had he been spared? How could he face the widows and orphans?

He was later to confess that he, too, wanted to die.

Jimmy Murphy, as he made the most of managing Manchester United without not just Busby but Whalley and Curry, was never to be more alone – even if Jack Crompton, who had left to become trainer at Luton in 1956, had hurried back. Even in spirit, Murphy had been parted from Busby, who now felt no interest in football, this silly thing Frank Taylor had seen fit to joke about. Busby had no desire to return to the game, indeed an aversion to the very thought. A quarter of a century later, in an interview with Ian Wooldridge, he was to reflect: 'I was very mixed up in my mind … horrible to live with.'

It was not to be for ever. Jean would see her Matt through this crisis. She would ask if he were not turning his back on those who had lost loved ones, or the memory of those who had died. By convincing him the family still needed him, she would make it feel right to go back. And the process of reunification with his life's work would begin in only a couple of weeks, when his voice came over the Old Trafford loudspeakers.

The size of United's post-Munich crowds had spoken of a desire for catharsis and this seemed to apply even when they travelled, as to West Bromwich in the Cup quarter-finals. Dewhurst and Meek were on the bus – it was the first of many trips they would jointly make as the club's guests – and when they got there the ground was full, with thousands outside.

As the players disembarked, a strange thing happened to Harry Gregg. A man was talking to Stan Crowther. A man Gregg recognised. 'Stan didn't really resemble me – he had much fairer hair – and I got off the coach and said to the man, "I think it's me you're looking for." It was my father, who had left my mother with a young family of six. And my dear mother, after all these years, she still loved him.' Harry despised him. 'He looked at me and said, "I'm glad you're okay." And just then Jimmy Murphy told me to go to the dressing room. I said it was my father and he said, "Okay, look after your father."'

West Bromwich were a fine side, a popular tip for the Cup, and yet United's disparate collection more than deserved to draw. At Old Trafford on the Wednesday, with 40,000 locked out, the replay remained scoreless until the 89th minute when a physically restored Bobby Charlton superbly beat three men and set up Colin Webster for the winner.

On the Saturday, a day after Dewhurst had observed the scattering of Alf Clarke's ashes on the Old Trafford pitch, Albion returned for the clubs' third meeting in a week. Again, it was estimated that nearly 100,000 people were in or around the ground and, as they went quiet, the public-address system began to play a recorded message from Busby.

'Ladies and gentlemen,' he said, his voice carrying a little of its old resonance, 'I am speaking from my bed in the Isar hospital in Munich, where I have been for a month since the tragic accident. You will be glad, I'm sure, that the remaining players here and myself are now considered out of danger and this can be attributed to the wonderful treatment given us by Professor Maurer and his staff, who are with you today as guests of the club. It is only in the past two or three days that I have been able to be told about football and I am delighted to hear of the success and united effort made by all at Old Trafford. Again, it is wonderful to hear that the club has reached the semi-final of the FA Cup and I extend my best wishes to everyone.'

Upon which Harold Hardman and the Lord Mayor of Manchester, Leslie Lever, emerged from the tunnel with Maurer and 30 of his doctors and nurses. They were rapturously received, Busby's adopted city reflecting his own feelings when he had realised that Germans – a people two wars had taught the British to consider enemies – had saved his life, and what was left of his team.

And then United lost for the first time since the crash. Lost heavily. Could not score and let in four, so Gregg would not have been in the best of moods as, walking out of the ground, past the gym, which was now being used as a press room, he heard a familiar voice shout his name. 'Sadly, I found I'd not got rid of my father after the Hawthorns. So I drove him to my home and introduced him to my wife Mavis and said I had to be up early to go to Old Trafford and would drop him at the station.' And there, for the time being, the matter rested.

Understandably, United were to lose more League matches that season. Indeed, of the 14 after the crash, Murphy's team were to win only one. It was at Sunderland where, as if to show that even sympathy for a stricken club was not universal, Gregg and Ian Greaves were hit by missiles hurled from the crowd.

At Burnley, Gregg clashed angrily with Alan Shackleton and the feisty young Mark Pearson was dismissed for a tackle from behind on Les Shannon. When Burnley's chairman, Bob Lord, whose bluntness often crossed the border with fatuity – after Munich, he made the point that United had entered Europe of their own volition – accused the visitors of behaving like 'a bunch of Teddy Boys', there was widespread outrage. But perhaps Busby's calming influence on United was being missed.

Among the matches from which he remained absent was a scoreless draw at home to Preston, who would have taken both points but for profligate finishing by Alec Farrall. Busby would have remembered Farrall – the Wirral boy he had asked Joe Mercer about. Farrall had made only a handful of appearances for his beloved Everton and was not to make much of an impression at Deepdale, spending the bulk of his career with Gillingham and only there, in the lower divisions, excelling. But he lived.

Although the League campaign, for what it was now worth, had faltered, the Cup quest seemed to have a life of its own. Busby and Maurer were beginning to discuss a schedule for his return to England when United met Fulham of the Second Division in the semi-finals. After drawing 2–2 they won the replay 5–3, Alex Dawson becoming United's youngest hat-trickster, and Busby's distant eye took on a gleam; he would accompany Murphy's team to Wembley.

The big occasion was six weeks off. Maurer had strongly advised convalescence, suggesting the Black Forest or Interlaken, and Matt and Jean chose the Swiss resort between the emerald lakes of Thun and Brienz. From there, refreshed by the Alpine air, they could take the Rheingold Express up through Germany to the Hook of Holland.

After the plush train and the ferry, the last leg of the journey was by road and at length a black Humber drove the couple to Chorlton-cum-Hardy, where it gently came to rest outside 214 Kings Road. Busby struggled out of the car, leant on his crutches and thanked well-wishers who had gathered outside the redbrick house with its surrounding hedges. Sheena ran out to usher her parents into a hallway lined with flowers. It was 18 April and the next day Busby heard Billy Meredith had died aged 83 in nearby Withington.

Over that weekend, Bobby Charlton fulfilled Joe Armstrong's prediction by beginning an England career at Hampden Park, where his sumptuous volley was the pick of four goals; Scotland, whom Busby had been obliged to delegate to the trainer, Dawson Walker from Clyde, had no reply.

On the Monday, when Wolves came to Old Trafford for the deferred fixture, Dennis Viollet returned, as had young Kenny Morgans. Albert Scanlon was on course to resume at the start of the following season and, while Johnny Berry and Jackie Blanchflower remained nowhere near ready even to train, at least they were home. Which meant that, of the crash survivors, only Frank Taylor remained in the Rechts der Isar.

Wolves had run away with the title and United, after applauding them on to the field, were beaten 4–0. Cullis's team were more than worthy champions and would almost certainly have been so even if the tragedy had not happened.

On the morning of 8 February, when originally due in Manchester, they led United by six points. Even if beaten at Old Trafford, they would have been four points ahead with 13 matches remaining. Four old points. In order to regard the notional Old Trafford outcome as a title decider, it would be necessary to imagine a subsequent collapse by Cullis's men. In the event, their last 14 matches produced 22 points out of 28 for a total of 64.

That would have demanded that United drop only a further two, in other words win 11 of their last 13 and draw the other 2, which would have been asking a lot – even more than in the rousing finales to the previous two seasons – especially as they also had the FA and European Cups to contend with.

Many supporters were absent, saving for Wembley, when Busby saw his first match since the crash. It was only two days after Wolves's visit and 28,000 welcomed him back to Old Trafford on 23 April. United drew 1–1 with Newcastle.

He strove to get into the old routine. One day he went to Blackpool to see Murphy and the players. The local journalists were there, of course – but not those to whom he was accustomed. Murphy beckoned David Meek and Keith Dewhurst over to say hello. For Meek, it was the first meeting and he recalled: 'Matt still looked poorly. He was grey and walked heavily on his crutches. It didn't strike me until later that it must have been an ordeal for him as well as me. The journalists who died were from the cream of the sporting press, and very close to Manchester United because of the journey into Europe. Matt must have been devastated to lose them as well as the players.

'I was to realise how close things had been when, on one of the first trips abroad, he pulled me aside. "David," he said, "you might not have been overseas much and you might not have any local currency, so here's a little bit of cash." And he handed over an envelope. Not just to me – Keith as well.' It seemed normal practice. 'I can't remember how much was in the envelope but it paid for a beer or two and the odd meal out. United also picked up our hotel bills when we accompanied them to away matches. But that day at Blackpool I could see a look on Matt's face and it said: who are these young whipper-snappers?'

After a concluding League defeat at Chelsea, where an 18-year-old Jimmy Greaves dazzled, it was time to turn all thoughts to Wembley and Bolton, who, though captained by the popular Lofthouse, knew national sentiment was against them.

Busby intended to pursue Harold Hardman's revivalist theme when he addressed the staff and players a few days before the trip to London. He came in and, although there were a lot of people around Old Trafford that day, noticed Daz and Omo modestly on the periphery. He called them over for a hug. Then he made for the gathering in the medical room. When he entered, the players noticed how old and pale he looked; Busby still spent a lot of his time at home in bed, and needed help in dressing. He started to speak but broke down and had to be helped away by Murphy and Jack Crompton.

He then went to look at the pitch. It had never seemed so empty. At that moment, unusually for Busby – 'he was always careful with his emotions,' said Paddy McGrath – he wept. And felt better for it. Another step had been taken. It would help him on the road to Wembley.

Bolton, like Wolves, shared Busby's belief in home production. Bill Ridding's friendship with Busby, as with Cullis, had withstood competition for the best youngsters. None of the players Ridding would field at Wembley had cost a transfer fee. They included Dennis Stevens and Ray Parry. More memories of Duncan Edwards for Busby.

Applauded by supporters of both sides, he was helped to the sidelines by Ted Dalton. It would suitably be Murphy, who had guided the team to the final, leading them out in the sunshine, chatting with Ridding as he walked. Lofthouse and Bill Foulkes introduced their colleagues to the Duke of Edinburgh; Ronnie Cope was the United centre-back who shook hands with Mark Jones's royal hero.

After three minutes, Lofthouse had scored and was back in the centre circle, brandishing a fist at every team-mate whose eye he could catch. United could not rise to this occasion and soon after the interval a glorious Bolton move, a thing of flicks and dummies, ended with Stevens shooting and Harry Gregg pushing the ball high into the air. As it fell, the seeds of yet another goalkeeping drama germinated.

Gregg was not badly injured, like Bert Trautmann in 1956 or Ray Wood in 1957, but United's chance of taking the trophy had sustained irreparable damage at the hands – to be more accurate, an arm, shoulder and leading thigh – of Lofthouse. Gregg, whose neck and back had taken most of the impact of a challenge that, in order to have any chance of legitimacy, was required to be shoulder-to-shoulder, lay face down behind the goal-line. The ball was in the net and Lofthouse wheeling away as the referee, Jack Sherlock, signalled a goal.

At the end, Murphy congratulated Lofthouse. He knew Bolton would probably have won anyway.

So much for a midwinter that seemed so very long ago. Another time of Treble talk. The League, given Wolves' form from start to finish, had always been a long shot. Now the FA Cup had gone. And, as for Busby's European dream, reality brought only the semi-final with Milan, delayed until five days after Wembley, or three months after Belgrade.

For the home leg, United lacked Bobby Charlton because England came first; he struck two as Portugal were overcome at Wembley. Milan scored but Dennis Viollet equalised and was fouled late on by Cesare Maldini, earning the penalty from which Ernie Taylor edged United in front. They travelled to Italy by train and ferry, Busby staying behind as the party left for Harwich early on the Sunday; the journey lasted more than 48 hours and at San Siro they lost 4–0 to a side who would push Real Madrid all the way in the Brussels final, leading twice before Di Stéfano settled matters in extra time.

During that spring, in which United's grip on the Youth Cup was finally broken by Wolves, the ethics of the youth policy became grimly topical. This was when the wills of the Munich victims were published. The Professional Footballers' Association estimated that, although the maximum was not to reach £20 until the start of the next season, a top player would have earned at least £30 with domestic, international and European bonuses. So it was no surprise that Roger Byrne, who also had a captain's column in the *Evening News* and was one of a group who endorsed Raleigh bicycles, left £9,073. But a reminder that little separated the players, financially, from the chroniclers of their exploits was provided by the estate of the journalist nearest to Byrne in terms of age: George Follows left £6,106.

And what of Duncan Edwards? Although rumours of £10,000 were rife, the truth was interesting enough. The £4,388 he passed on was modest next to his football gifts but still raised questions given that, in his four years as a professional, he would have needed to save every penny of his post-tax earnings to get much over half that figure. Yes, he had lately been endorsing Dextrosol 'energy tablets' as well as Raleigh cycles, and had a newspaper column, and a book – *Tackle Soccer This Way* – but still the implication was clear, at least to Charlie Mitten, who later declared: 'Busby's Babes were being paid more than the officially permitted maximum. I was raging when I saw it.'

When Mitten had been at United, Busby had given the players 'a two-bit tale about how he could not pay us any extra, and we'd say fair enough because he'd lose his job ... and it works out later that he's bought seven or eight youngsters and they were getting thousands in signing-on fees ... illicit payments, bungs.'

Not that such disillusion constrained Mitten from seeking Busby's advice after he had decided to leave Mansfield and applied for First Division jobs at Blackpool and Newcastle. The latter wanted him. He rang Busby, who said the advantage of Newcastle was the scale and fervour of the club's support: 'If you put 11 black-and-white dogs on the field, you'd get 30,000 coming to watch.' Mitten agreed. But on the other hand, Busby continued, there was the power struggle between the interfering boardroom factions led by William McKeag and Stan Seymour: 'They've got more managers than players at that place.' And, for that reason, if Busby himself were being asked, he'd be reluctant to take it. The 37-year-old Mitten, offered three years with a starting salary of £3,000, took it. And immediately set about improving the club's youth and scouting departments, such as they had been.

At the end of the season Busby's remuneration increased to £5,000 a year. Having been made a CBE in the Birthday Honours – those similarly recognised included the actors Jack Hawkins and Celia Johnson and playwright Terence Rattigan – he returned to Interlaken.

Serenity would have been harder to achieve had he known that, in the early stages of the World Cup, the former Arsenal defender Bernard Joy, now a journalist, had been seeking out Jimmy Murphy on behalf of his erstwhile club, who had just parted company with Jack Crayston. Or so it was thought; at any rate, Murphy, in the Wales team hotel, kept dodging Joy as his team drew with the Swedish hosts, Mexico and Hungary before overcoming the Hungarians in a play-off and narrowly losing to Brazil in the quarter-finals, a couple of days after which Crayston's successor was announced as George Swindin.

Could Murphy ever have left United? There were a few offers from home and abroad and evidence suggests he considered this one, to the extent of sounding out his former pupil John Doherty as a possible assistant. But on reflection he preferred to avoid the question because the answer would have disappointed Bernard Joy. To Murphy, loyalty was a way of life.

Northern Ireland, captained by Danny Blanchflower – Footballer of the Year while his poor brother faced career demise – also reached the last eight. Despite the 4–0 defeat then administered by France, Harry Gregg was named goalkeeper of the tournament.

Bobby Charlton was United's lone England representative. After a trying pre-tournament experience when England not only played a friendly against Yugoslavia in Belgrade's JNA Stadium but flew in and out by way of Munich – they lost 5–0 – he encountered mid-air turbulence on the way to Sweden. Bobby Robson, sitting alongside, noticed him rock and sweat and clench his palms. 'All right?' Robson sympathetically asked. 'Yeah, I'm all right,' replied Charlton. 'Just get this bloody plane down.' As with United, the crash was something silently to acknowledge, not to discuss.

England stayed only to the group stage, losing a play-off with the Soviet Union.

Scotland, under Dawson Walker, took one point from three matches, but could look forward to the benefit of Busby, who had promised he would finally guide them in the autumn, against Murphy's Wales and Doherty's Northern Ireland.

It was as well that Busby did not see letters which arrived unsigned at the various newspapers' offices, that he was spared the sneers of gossips who asked why, since he and not Captain Thain would really have been in charge of the flight, he had allowed a third take-off attempt. Or whether he had truly been in such grave condition in that German hospital, or merely been protected from serious questions by his friends in the press, even though they had lost a few of their own.

True, he had written of the late return from Bilbao the previous season and, alluding to the League, conceded: 'I could well imagine the consequences ...' But the notion that he had gambled with lives, including his own? Gregg had nothing but contempt for it, saying: 'People invented stories. There were those who suggested Matt had gone to the pilot and said we had to get back. Because of the League and all that. I can say categorically – no way. Even though I didn't always get on with Matt, it was very, very unfair and wrong for anyone to suggest that he would try to influence an experienced pilot.'

James Thain incurred more serious damage to his reputation. The initial German inquiry into the crash blamed ice on the wings and held him responsible. He was never again to take control of an aircraft and at Christmas 1960, several months after a British tribunal had confirmed the German verdict, he was informed of his dismissal by BEA, who also cited his seating arrangement with the late Ken Rayment. Thain maintained that the slush was to blame and resolved to continue the fight, however daunting, to clear his name.

CHAPTER TEN

THE LONG JOURNEY BACK

TROUBLE AHEAD

As the 1958 World Cup ended with Brazil triumphant, the draw for the preliminary round of the next European Cup took place in Cannes. UEFA, in a sympathetic gesture, included United, who were paired with Young Boys of Berne while England's champions, Wolves, received a bye. Harold Hardman's fellow League chairmen, however, spurned such generosity, insisting only champions must take part, a decision reluctantly accepted by Sir Stanley Rous and the FA. Young Boys proceeded unopposed to the first round with Wolves.

Although Hardman offended Busby's sense of diplomacy in telling the *Evening News* the League had threatened to suspend United if they accepted UEFA's invitation, manager and chairman were as one in their resentment. Even if United had lasted only one round, they could have done with the revenue. For all the virtues of Hardman and the late Crickmer, the club had taken out insufficient insurance for the trip to Belgrade and there were moral obligations to meet.

In addition, the £100,000 they would receive, spread over five years, hardly equipped Busby to act with the required robustness

in the transfer market. Yet his first signing since returning from
Munich broke the British record. Albert Quixall had become an
international at Sheffield Wednesday and, when Busby was visited
by his son-in-law Don Gibson, the word from Hillsborough always
glowed. Jimmy Murphy also liked Quixall, believing he would
quicken the movement through United's midfield, and so, although
the price was £45,000, Busby paid it.

The encouragement of Louis Edwards helped. Edwards had
gone on the pre-season tour, by boat and train. From Munich, the
party went to Hamburg and there some journalists, after late-night
drinks, decided to strike out for the Reeperbahn, where prostitutes
displayed their wares through large windows. Also wandering
around were Busby, Murphy and Louis Edwards but, when the two
groups ran into each other, only Murphy of the Catholic trio saw
the funny side of it; according to his young friend Keith Dewhurst,
he 'cackled'.

Although Murphy would invoke God's name when sending teams
into battle, he could have been no stranger to the confessional for,
profanity apart, he sometimes entertained an attractive creature of a
certain age. Always the same one; when crossing a hotel foyer on the
way to his room, she would take care to be on the arm of a complicit
Dewhurst, who was happy to be teased by players afterwards about
his apparent fondness for an older woman. As for Busby, it truly never
occurred to Dewhurst he would stray. Which made the great man's
gaze upon the hellish windows all the more amusing.

Busby started the 1958/59 season with five crash survivors.
Albert Scanlon joined Gregg, Foulkes, Charlton and Viollet in
beating Chelsea 5–2 at Old Trafford. Charlton scored a hat-trick
while the excellence of Wilf McGuinness, back after surgery, gave
Busby the opportunity to get rid of Stan Crowther. A surly and
often aggressive character, Crowther had turned a few training
sessions nasty and no one was surprised when he went to Chelsea
for half the price United had so recently paid. Colin Webster's move
to Swansea brought in £7,500 and Busby let Ernie Taylor join
Sunderland for £7,000, taking receipts from this flurry of business
to more than half of the Quixall fee.

With United nonetheless in danger of slipping into the lower
half, it was not the ideal time for Busby and Murphy to absent
themselves from a fixture at Everton. But Murphy was manager of
Wales and Busby kept his promise to Scotland. Off they went to

Cardiff, where Busby gave an international debut to Denis Law – even though he was 18 and in the lower Second Division with Shankly's Huddersfield – and made Dave Mackay captain at 23. Law opened the scoring as Scotland won 3–0.

Busby's pleasure was diluted by the news from Goodison. With Jack Crompton in charge, United had lost 3–2 to a lowly side awaiting the new management of Johnny Carey. Questions were being asked about Quixall. Yes, he looked every inch the star with his blond quiff and elegant technique. But he wasn't a showman; indeed, some critics wished he would be more selfish with the ball. Maybe even put it in the net now and again.

Busby reacted with changes restoring Kenny Morgans, but the young Welshman had not survived Munich like Scanlon, who was flying down the wing as of old, and played only twice before giving way to Warren Bradley.

Bradley's was an extraordinary story. Born in Hyde, near Manchester, he had become an amateur international with Bishop Auckland, who, after Munich, had kindly lent United three players for the reserves. Bradley, taking a teacher's job in Stretford, played part-time. But Busby saw the little winger's potential and he became a regular during such an improvement that briefly United led the League.

There had been a low point in January 1959: after two Cup finals, they suffered an instant knockout at the ground of Norwich, who, although of the Third Division, would also remove Tottenham on their way to the semi-finals. But United scored freely in the League, Charlton dazzling and Scanlon lending support along with Viollet, whom Busby was to make captain because Foulkes found the responsibility mentally taxing. They finished second, six points behind Wolves, again champions on merit even if their long-awaited European Cup debut had been something of a mockery of Cullis's claims to international supremacy: an immediate knockout at the hands of Schalke 04.

Cullis now had three League titles and one FA Cup. Once more, the rivals were on level terms. But, while Cullis knew Wolves would again be there or thereabouts the next season, Busby saw trouble ahead, sensing that the wave of emotion on which United rode – the average attendance exceeded 53,000 – would carry them only so far. What they had achieved in the 15 months since Munich, he thought, 'gave a false impression of our strength'.

He felt sufficiently time-healed to meet the bereaved. He asked June Jones to bring Gary and the baby Lynn and, almost as soon as she came into the room, put his head on her shoulder and cried. 'I've always thought it wonderful,' said June, 'that such a big man could feel so deeply.'

Busby went into hospital for further treatment – as was to prove necessary during the first few close seasons after the crash – and enjoyed 50th birthday celebrations including a holiday at the club's expense. With Busby, a board now including Edwards did not stint. Only Busby could do the job.

Realising it would consume all his time, he had relinquished the Scotland post after a 2–2 draw with Northern Ireland at Hampden. So Andy Beattie had overseen the England match at Wembley. Bobby Charlton had scored the only goal before touring with England in the company of Bradley, whose remarkable season was capped by a trip to Brazil, Peru, Mexico and the United States.

The members of the Football Writers' Association, much though they had praised Charlton's verve, chose as Footballer of the Year the long-serving Luton central defender Syd Owen, presenting the statuette two days before he led his team out at Wembley to be beaten by a Nottingham Forest featuring Jeff Whitefoot.

Busby had taken his first flight since the crash. Louis Edwards had joined him in knocking back a few stiff drinks before a trip to Rotterdam, chosen because United were to head there for an end-of-season friendly against Feyenoord. This was Foulkes's return to the air. 'You can imagine how the lads felt,' he said, 'especially those who'd been in the crash. As soon as we arrived in the hotel, I got on the phone to my wife – and she already knew. The Boss, as soon as we'd touched down, had rung Les Olive in Manchester to get him to inform all the wives and families that we'd arrived safely.'

After the match, Busby allowed the players out. Indeed he joined them for a while in a nightclub. They had drink vouchers and Gregg, sharing a room with Albert Scanlon, asked the others not to supply him. But he got hold of a few and, when Gregg got back, there he was, smoking, which Gregg had forbidden. According to legend Gregg grabbed Scanlon, turned him upside down and dangled him out of the window by the ankles.

Gregg had a different version of events. He said he was frustrated that Scanlon, recently introduced to the England Under-23s, might squander his career, and was trying to make the point outside the club. How else to do it than by suddenly inverting his errant pal and giving him a good shake? He added that Busby, who happened to be leaving the club at the time, didn't even blink as he wished them goodnight.

Either way, it said a lot about the odd couple who were Gregg and Scanlon. A dangling by the ankles was the sort of thing Gregg might do to someone he liked. And he liked Scanlon a lot.

On and off the field, Scanlon was a trier. A lovable dreamer known as 'Joe Friday' because, like Jack Webb's detective sergeant in the popular American television series *Dragnet*, he seemed to know everything that went on. Or think he did. On trips abroad, he would flick through telephone directories in the hope of finding a British name and then ring the number, explaining to his mates that this was how to glean local knowledge.

Scanlon was a bit of a lad and yet, in the first full season after Munich, only he and Freddie Goodwin had done duty in every match. There was spirit in him and Gregg fondly remembered how a cranial fracture suffered in the crash – 'Albert was sitting up in bed with a plaster-of-Paris skull' – failed to prevent him from pinching everyone else's newspapers.

Tragically, Scanlon no longer faced the graceful competition of Pegg. But nothing, it seemed, could quite defeat Busby and Murphy's education system for, although United had again fallen in the Youth Cup semi-finals to the eventual winners – Johnny Carey's Blackburn – the latest generation of United youths, including Giles and Stiles, did recover the Blue Stars trophy in Zurich; the club had naturally lacked the appetite for that tournament, so close to Busby's heart, the previous year.

Busby had been right to predict a dip. From the first ten matches of 1959/60, only three wins came and a 4–0 spanking at Preston left United seventh from bottom. It was during this period that John Giles made his debut. Because the visitors to Old Trafford were an unbeaten Tottenham, it might have been considered daunting for an Irishman still a couple of months short of his 19th birthday. Except that Giles didn't daunt easily. It took Jimmy Murphy to daunt him. But he had been doing well in the reserves. At Leeds, where they were drawing 4–4 at half-time, one of the defenders was laid into by Murphy.

'But I ...'

'Don't give me fucking buts! You get out there and do it.'

United kept a clean sheet in the second half. Giles scored a hat-trick in an 8–4 win and Murphy, upon hearing Quixall had picked up an injury, told Busby the little inside-right was ready to step up. 'That was how it was done,' said Giles. 'Matt picked the first team but Jimmy was in charge of the reserves and youths and, if he spoke, Matt listened. I got the familiar treatment. Matt would come and take you aside with Jimmy and you'd be going round the pitch, passing the ball. If he did that, you'd be playing the next day.'

Giles duly lined up alongside Charlton and Viollet, with Bradley outside him and Scanlon on the other wing. They faced a Spurs team threatening great things under Arthur Rowe's protégé Bill Nicholson and said to have the most expensive team the English game had seen at £180,000. Some £32,000 had brought Dave Mackay from Hearts to form, with Danny Blanchflower, a contrasting pair of wing-halves to compare, in some eyes, with the lamented Colman and Edwards.

With less than half an hour gone, they led by three. If Foulkes, who had been switched to central defence towards the end of the previous season, wished he could revert to escape the rampaging Bobby Smith, he would have found no solace at right-back, for Cliff Jones was terrorising Ronnie Cope. Although Giles reckoned he played quite well in the circumstances, Busby had no consoling word for him after United's 5–1 defeat. 'He never did say much.'

Busby had more to do in the transfer market and speculation about the Scotland left-back, Eric Caldow, and two young English defenders, the Blackpool right-back Jimmy Armfield and Leicester centre-back Tony Knapp, would have been read with concern by members of a much-questioned rearguard such as Carolan and Cope. Foulkes even. For Caldow, quick and accomplished enough to appear a plausible successor to Byrne, a fee of £25,000 was agreed with Rangers. But the player decided to stay in Glasgow. United's money did not speak so firmly in those days.

When Busby travelled to Madrid to ask Santiago Bernabéu if Real would play a friendly at Old Trafford, he told reporters the intention was 'to keep Manchester United in the public eye'. But Ferenc Puskás, now playing alongside Di Stéfano, recalled that it was 'to help raise money' and Busby admitted: 'I said the crash had ruined us financially as well as physically and I would be grateful if they would take this into consideration.' Real's normal fee was

£12,000 but they charged less than half, so there was a healthy profit from the crowd of 63,000 who saw Real win 6–1.

Wolves meanwhile began their European Cup campaign with a 2–1 defeat by Vorwarts in East Berlin but went through on aggregate and next faced Red Star Belgrade. A day after United had been applauded off the Bernabéu for their part in a 6–5 defeat by Real in a return friendly (to be followed by a fundraising dinner, for Don Santiago was truly fraternal to Busby and his club), Wolves drew 1–1 in the JNA Stadium and a 3–0 victory at ecstatic Molineux could hardly have set Cullis's men up better for their next task, a visit to Barcelona.

Meanwhile they had to defend their League title. Not that United were any threat. Not with Charlton out of form; he was dropped by Busby, along with Gregg and McGuinness. Not even though, after losing 2–1 at home to Burnley on Boxing Day, they stunned Turf Moor's biggest crowd for a decade by winning 4–1, making it a weekend of double celebration for Busby because he and Jean had become grandparents when Sheena gave birth to a girl, Janie.

And thus began the Sixties.

The year had hardly turned when Busby deferred, however subtly, to fashion. One of United's defensive problems was that the centre-half, whether Foulkes or Ronnie Cope, needed help. It happened in the best of circles; a year later John Giles was to hear Maurice Norman, centre-back of a Spurs team on the brink of greatness, complaining about it to Blanchflower and Mackay. The Hungarians had used a back four and the Brazilians had taken it up, and Busby moved in that direction when, after consulting Bobby Charlton, who had played with Maurice Setters in the England Under-23s, he signed the pugnacious ball-winner from West Bromwich for £30,000. The more constructive Freddie Goodwin left for Leeds, whose £10,000 offset the cost, as had £4,000 from Tranmere Rovers for Gordon Clayton and the wing-half Bobby Harrop, home-bred players never quite as close as Goodwin to the standard Busby required.

The last League match before Setters's arrival had brought a 7–3 defeat away to Charlie Mitten's adventurous Newcastle. When Setters arrived, United had been eleventh. They ended up seventh, which Busby deemed 'quite respectable'. It would have been less so but for Dennis Viollet, whose 32 goals in 36 League matches smashed Jack Rowley's record and earned an England debut in Hungary. An indication of how Viollet covered a multitude of sins was that, while United scored more than the champions, Burnley, they conceded more – despite Setters's mid-January arrival – than the bottom club, Luton.

The Cup went to Wolves and the Footballer of the Year was their captain, Bill Slater. But there had been a chastening experience for Cullis's team in Europe. Barcelona had beaten them 4–0 at Camp Nou and 5–2 at Molineux. Barcelona then fell to Real Madrid, who won their fifth consecutive European Cup with an unforgettable exhibition in the Glasgow final, overcoming Eintracht Frankfurt 7–3. Puskás scored four goals and Di Stéfano three. Each was now 33. But, as European Cup swan songs go, this was some duet.

SOME RELATION

During the summer of 1960, at the Busbys' local church of Our Lady and St John's, their friend Monsignor Sewell conducted the wedding of Sandy to Irene Stott. The couple had met four years earlier, on one of Sandy's frequent nights out. It happened to be a Sunday, when prospective entrants to a dance hall near Oldham had to be 'enrolled' in a 'club'. Irene had this duty. 'Sandy came in with some pals, acting the goat. But I let them in and Sandy came back and asked if I finished work before the place closed. I said I did so he asked if he could have a dance. But it had to be a slow one. That was Sandy. How he walked and everything.' And, like his father, told jokes. 'Always slow.'

When she finished work, they danced. 'He asked my name and I said, "Irene – what's yours?" And he said, "Sandy." I said, "*Sandy*? Your hair's dark." He explained that in Scotland, where his family came from, "Sandy" was short for "Alexander". I was still laughing when I said, "What's your last name then?" And he said, "Busby." I thought that was hilarious. *Sandy Busby!* Then he asked my last name and I said "Stott" and he said, "You should talk!" He took me home and that was how we started.

'He was supposed to be studying electrical engineering but hated it. He loved playing for Blackburn reserves, though, and I used to go and watch him. It was horrible up there. I used to take my knitting. And there'd be a couple of old men yelling at him, "You'll never be as good as your father!"

'We'd been going out a few weeks when he invited me to a match at Manchester United. My father and brother were rugby followers and weren't really interested in football – it wasn't like today, when football's everywhere and you can't get away from it – but when I told my dad we were going to United he remembered Sandy's surname. "The manager there's Busby," he said. "He must be some relation." I went to the match but didn't meet the family. The first time Sandy took me home to meet Matt and Jean I couldn't understand a word they were saying. I remember hoping I was saying yes and no in the right places. Their accents seemed so broad. But they couldn't have been nicer to me and straight away I became friendly with Jean. We'd go out for lunch now and again. Matt was just Matt, pottering about at home, being lovely.'

Never in haste? 'No. Like Sandy he never did things in a hurry.' Her daughter Alison smiled at the recollection. 'They weren't what you'd call frenetic.' There would always be a dog around. Irene and Alison remembered a liver-coloured spaniel, and a series of black poodles: Boko, Pepe and Pepe Two. And how they remembered Nellie. '*Maw!* She was the queen,' said Irene. 'She just used to sit there with Katie, the unmarried daughter who lived with her. Matt used to tell us Maw didn't believe in drink. She kept a tight lead.' As Sandy's daughters grew up, they thought of Maw as scary, but only as a private joke. Because of the bristles on her chin, they would receive the instruction 'Now go and kiss Maw' with concealed mock-dread. And not always understand what she was saying.

Quite early in Irene's relationship with Sandy, she converted to Catholicism. 'One day he asked me to go to Mass with him and I nearly dropped dead. I hadn't known he was a Catholic. I went to Mass with him and we saw Monsignor Sewell. He said there was no pressure but I could see someone if I wanted. She was Sister Marie-Louise at High Lane Convent – a lovely person, very interesting to talk to. My dad and brother were a bit ... [the Stotts were Congregationalists]. But my mother had more sympathy. When she'd been a young girl, she'd been going out with this Catholic lad and his mother had made him give her up. So she listened to my dad and brother and then told me, "If you want to do it, do it – never mind them two." So I went about a dozen times to Sister Marie-Louise and then told Monsignor Sewell I would convert.'

Sandy and Irene moved into a house next door but one to Matt and Jean on Kings Road. They were happy times, with never a mention of the tragedy.

On match days, the 'ladies', segregated, would be looked after by the chairman's wife, the aged and chain-smoking Annie Hardman. 'We had a little room and Mrs Hardman had the keys to the cocktail-cabinet. We used to sit there while she carefully opened the cabinet. "Now," she'd say, "what would you like?" Jean would be there. Wherever she was, Jean could always find a drink.' This elaborate ritual would merely have tested her patience. 'And then, after the match, I used to come back with Jean and Sheena to Kings Road – Sandy would be off somewhere with his pals – and by now Jean would be well away. She'd start telling Matt what he should be doing with the team. And why did he keep picking so-and-so? As if we knew it all and he knew nothing! Matt would just sit there and laugh.'

YOUTH AND EXPERIENCE

Although at youth level United again had to be content with the Blue Stars trophy – among English academies Ted Drake's Chelsea was the new Oxbridge – the system still produced. Nobby Stiles had earned a trip to Edinburgh for a friendly against Hibs. 'He wasn't going to play,' said Harry Gregg. 'It was more to help look after the kit. And they were having a game of cards, a few of them. And this kid Stiles was holding his cards right up to his eyes. One of the lads kept calling him Blind Pugh. So later I had a word with him and eventually he admitted that, when he was at school, he wore glasses and the other kids called him Specky so he threw them away.

'The next time I spoke to Matt – I was having treatment from Ted Dalton and he came in – I said, "Boss, did you know the boy Stiles was nearly blind?" At which point Ted starts waffling. Matt cuts him short. "Ted," he says, "get someone to bring the boy here." And the boy comes in and Matt says, "Have you got bad eyesight, son?" Nobby says, "No." But Matt knows now. This was one of the good sides of him – there were plenty of them. He told Ted to make sure Nobby got examined by an optician. And that's how Nobby came to wear contact lenses in matches.'

Stiles would soon appear in the first team, along with Jimmy Nicholson, a wing-half from Northern Ireland, and the winger Ian Moir, a happy-go-lucky Scottish sorcerer said to have prompted a Jimmy Murphy classic. In a reserve match, Moir had repeatedly run the ball over the byline. Murphy shouted to him to change positions with the centre-forward, Sammy McMillan, who afterwards asked why. Murphy replied: 'I was hoping Ian would overrun the ball into the goal.'

Nobby Lawton had made a few appearances at inside-left and seemed a promising alternative to Mark Pearson. Lawton had taken little spotting. Not only was he the pick of an outstanding school team at St Gregory's, Ardwick; the geography teacher, Ronnie Travers, was a United scout. Moreover, Jimmy Murphy had a son, Phil, at the school and would often be seen there, sometimes with Joe Armstrong or even Busby. Bernard Halford, later to become club secretary at Manchester City, was a pupil and recalled: 'Matt liked to see the lads for himself. But he had a wonderful personality and made everyone feel at ease.'

He was solicitous when Lawton, susceptible to chest infections, became laid up in bed. 'Matt went to the house to see how he was getting on,' said Halford. 'While he had a chat with Nobby in the bedroom, Mrs Lawton made the tea. Afterwards, when Matt was putting on his coat, Nobby's mum asked a favour and Matt replied, "Certainly, Mrs Lawton." And she said, "When Norbert comes back to the club and he goes training, will you make sure he keeps his vest on?"

'We pulled Nobby's leg quite a bit about that one. But it tells you a bit about what Matt was like. People felt he had time for them and would listen.'

Meanwhile, the scouts farther afield were as alert as ever: Bob Bishop in Northern Ireland was monitoring a 14-year-old called George Best, while south of the border Billy Behan had recommended the Shelbourne full-back Tony Dunne, who cost £5,000. But it was getting harder to capture the best talent. More and more clubs were trying. And the boys who cost money were becoming more expensive. In Dundee there was Peter Lorimer. With his 15th birthday approaching, United were said to have offered his parents £5,000 – and lost out to Leeds.

But Busby and his assistants' enduring touch was emphasised by the capture of Barry Fry, scorer of five goals in six matches for

England schoolboys and spoken of in some quarters as the next Jimmy Greaves.

Joe Armstrong had arrived at the family prefab in Bedford and invited Fry's parents to accompany him to Manchester for a week at the start of the long school holiday in 1960. The United youth team were playing a semi-final at Old Trafford and so, while Busby entertained his parents, Fry was put on the coach to the golf club at Davyhulme and strategically placed next to Nobby Stiles at the pre-match meal. 'Nobby sold me Manchester United. I'd had lots of offers, and my England room-mate Ron Harris wanted me to go with him to Chelsea, but Nobby had such passion for United that I was blown away.

'They made me feel like a king and the next day Matt, having assured my mum and dad I'd be looked after, had John Aston [by now the youth coach] drive us all to the digs in Sale Moor where waiting were the landlady, Mrs Moore, and Eamon Dunphy. I knew Eamon from having played against Eire schoolboys. It was arranged that I could share a room with him. So my parents were happy and I became a Manchester United apprentice.'

With how much changing hands? Fry sighed. 'I heard that. I heard it all the time. "You must have got a new house, or a new car." Well, those prefabs were supposed to have a ten-year lifespan and my dad lived in ours for forty-nine and a half years. Never moved out of it. And never had a car either.'

As Fry, Dunphy and the other ground staff set about their tasks – cleaning boots, sweeping the dressing rooms, clearing terraces – they noticed some of the seniors had mood swings. 'We didn't know why. But one day Bobby Charlton would walk in and say, "Hi, Barry – all right, lads?" and the next day he'd be head down, wouldn't say good morning, nothing. Bill Foulkes too. Harry Gregg. But Bobby in particular. And Jimmy Murphy was brilliant. He could see our faces and he'd come over and say, "Look, it's Munich. It's still affecting a lot of the players." John Aston was the same. Wilf McGuinness too. Wilf would take the trouble to explain to us, even though the people who had died were his mates and he was still a young man.' And McGuinness was trying to come to terms with the loss of his own playing career; he had been labouring under a stress fracture and suddenly, during a reserve match at Stoke, the leg had buckled under him. He now coached the reserves.

'It was an eerie time,' Fry recalled. 'There were days when Old Trafford was full of depression. It was hard for everybody. Because some of us kids, although we'd heard about Munich – it shook the whole of football – couldn't really understand the effect on those who had seen their mates die. We were too young. Only looking back did we think, "God – how were they able to get through it?" Harry and Bill and the rest. And Bobby – he was young and he'd lost Tommy Taylor and Duncan Edwards. Jimmy Murphy said Duncan Edwards was going to be the best player in the world. With Jimmy Murphy, Duncan Edwards was on the agenda every other day. Because of his *attitude*. "You've got to be like Duncan was. You've got to train all the time and want to get to the top like him."'

How, against such a background, Busby and Murphy were able to regenerate the club became a matter of wonder for Fry. 'Especially as, for a long period of time, Matt's health was touch and go. If one day he wasn't at the ground or the training ground, people would say, "The Boss has had a funny turn." Whether it was true or not, that was always the whisper.'

Yet in the summer of Fry's arrival Busby did feel fit enough to lead United back across the Atlantic. They played Hearts four times on an itinerary that took in Toronto, New York, Vancouver, Los Angeles, San Francisco and Philadelphia.

The past months had been testing for the Busby family with the break-up of Sheena's marriage. Don Gibson had been transferred from Wednesday to Leyton Orient and Sheena had accompanied him to London, little realising he was in the midst of an affair – although, given hints that he had strayed before, discovery might have been more of a shock than a surprise. Distraught, she returned to her parents. Gibson followed her north and pleaded for another chance. She declined and, when he showed every sign of staying in Manchester – he was never to play again, for Orient or anyone else – Busby decided to make sure his daughter had time and space. There were dark hints that Gibson had been warned to stay out of town but according to the family's later testimony it was done in the way of genteel society: 'Matt bought him off.'

Gibson married the other woman and, living to a great age, was occasionally seen in Blackpool, driving a hearse for part-time work. Sheena, observing the Catholic tradition, never married again.

QUESTIONS ABOUT MATT

The 1960/61 season brought another change of captain, Setters taking over from Viollet after the forward fractured his collar-bone in November, and several debuts, some more significant than others. A 20-year-old local, Harold Bratt, made a lone appearance at right-half in the new Football League Cup, from which United departed in the second round at Bradford City. Moir and especially Stiles impressed. Nicholson stayed in with Shay Brennan moving to full-back: a Busby conversion that was to continue the noble line of Carey, Aston and Byrne.

When Brennan missed a few matches, who should come in but Tony Dunne? And who, with the possible exception of Busby, could have known the names of Brennan and Dunne would acquire such joint resonance?

So much for the future. The reality of the present was painfully obvious every time Busby's youngsters looked at a First Division table. United lay third from bottom and, David Meek recalled, 'some newspapers were starting to ask questions about Matt, wondering if the club could afford to keep him if it meant going down. So I asked for an interview with Harold Hardman. I went to his offices in town with the purpose of getting him to say it was rubbish for people to doubt Matt's future. Harold responded as I thought he would. He said it was ridiculous – Matt Busby was part of Manchester United and that was how it would stay. I duly wrote the piece. But Matt didn't see it as I had.

'Sometimes, when you had done something that displeased him, it was like being a schoolboy called into the headmaster's study. He said he didn't like me going behind his back to the chairman and added, "I know what you're up to – you're trying to stir up trouble." I put my case. I thought he was being over-sensitive.' In the end, he accepted Meek's good faith. 'But he repeated that he didn't want me going behind his back. It was a point of principle, really.'

To fend off the threat of relegation, Busby needed experience and proven quality and both came in the substantial form of Noel Cantwell. The Irishman was a natural leader. He arrived from Ron Greenwood's crucible of football learning at West Ham and, although nearly 28, cost £29,500 (much recovered by the sales of Joe Carolan to Brighton and Albert Scanlon to Mitten's Newcastle).

Cantwell could play in central defence but Busby wanted him at left-back. With Cantwell there, United settled, the wisely bought blending with the young and potent.

Over Christmas, Setters took the pressure off Foulkes by policing Jimmy Greaves and United, having won 2–1 at Chelsea, thrilled Old Trafford by beating Ted Drake's side 6–0. Dawson got three goals then, and again on New Year's Eve, when Manchester City were thrashed. So much for the neighbours' adventure in paying Huddersfield £55,000 for Denis Law, breaking the record Busby had set for Quixall; at Old Trafford Law tasted defeat by 5–1.

What, for United and Busby, who had tried for Law and would not give up until he wore red, could be better? The events, perhaps, of 16 January. It was a Monday night, fog having descended on Old Trafford on the Saturday, and the floodlights shone for the visit of the League leaders, the magnificent Spurs.

In an electric atmosphere, Stiles put United ahead. Only for Gregg to suffer, before half-time, a shoulder injury and swap places with the centre-forward Dawson. Both excelled in their emergency roles, Gregg, arm in a sling, laying on the second goal for Mark Pearson with a typically audacious backheel while Dawson kept a clean sheet. The fans buzzed. United were up to eighth with seven home-produced players in the team. This was Harold Hardman's post-Munich defiance embodied.

Except that there followed the club's heaviest defeat since before the war.

Eamon Dunphy told a story about this. He said that Busby, although a gambler himself, detested card schools when the stakes got too high, believing they could affect a loser's performance. Apparently some players were late off the bus at Leicester because they wanted to finish a game. This irked him enough. The subsequent 6–0 defeat stirred in Busby a strange kind of fury. He betrayed no sign of it as, having fulfilled his duties in the Filbert Street boardroom, he returned to the bus. And as it drove away, noting that the extravagant game of brag had resumed, calmly walked to the table, picked up the cards and hurled them out of the window.

Perhaps it would have been a less dramatic day but for Gregg's absence, which would continue for most of the season. His replacement at Leicester, the 17-year-old giant Ronnie Briggs from Belfast, shared all too generously in a nightmare of a Cup replay that Sheffield Wednesday won 7–2 at Old Trafford. So the amateur international Mike Pinner was brought from Queens Park Rangers on a short-term contract. After a predictable defeat at Wolves, the team never again fell into the lower half of the table and, having completed a derby double at Maine Road with Setters taming Law, finished seventh.

This involved more good work by Murphy. For he had taken charge between February and the end of the season, after Busby returned to hospital for surgery on his back. As Busby rested and pondered the new season, such promising signs as the progress of the youngsters, above all the deceptively slight Stiles, were offset by a sharp fall in the average League crowd.

He could only salute Bill Nicholson, the first manager to build a Double team in the twentieth century. The Spurs of 1960/61 would forever be associated with the words of their captain, Danny Blanchflower: 'The game is about glory, it is about doing things in style and with a flourish, about going out and beating the other lot, not waiting for them to die of boredom.' Busby's own philosophy could not have been better put. It had been enacted in his Babes' final domestic display before Munich. And here it was in a Nicholson side who scored 115 goals in the League alone.

They won the FA Cup by beating Leicester 2–0. The only thing they didn't win was a competition Alan Hardaker took more seriously than the public: that inaugural League Cup. The two-legged final, held over to the start of the next season, would bring a second trophy in management for Joe Mercer.

After relegation with Sheffield United, Busby's chum had appeared to leap from frying pan to fire by joining Aston Villa. They too went down but Mercer brought them back as champions with a young side nicknamed – for the Busby Babes had spawned counterparts, such as the Cullis Cubs and Ted Drake's Ducklings – the Mercer Minors. And now they were to overcome Rotherham United of the Second Division in extra time at Villa Park.

There was also innovation in Europe, where Wolves took part in the first Cup-Winners' Cup. They were knocked out by Rangers. The Champions' Cup had contained a sensation when Real Madrid, drawn against Barcelona in the second round, went out on a 4–3 aggregate at Camp Nou. Busby kept United acquainted with the big-time through the relationship with Real; he partly ascribed his team's mid-season revival to the stimulus of another fine friendly between the clubs in October, even though they had lost 3–2. It was during one of these meetings that Harry Gregg learned a bit more about Di Stéfano. 'One hard player,' he recalled. 'I loved a challenge – as long as it wasn't in my back. And he hit me. I was still shaking 20 minutes after the match.'

While the transfer market still brought Busby a few frustrations, others were worse off. Including Bill Shankly, now at Liverpool in the Second Division with Bob Paisley as his assistant. It had been slow progress at Liverpool, with a bid to bring Law from his former club Huddersfield among the disappointments that caused him to consider resigning. He kept ringing Busby, who recalled with amusement: 'I'd say, "Bill, have you got a job, some place to go to?" And when he said, "No," I'd say "Don't do anything daft until you have." Well, within the next two or three months it had turned round ...'

This was after Shankly, in the early summer of 1961, had picked up the Scottish newspaper the *Sunday Post*. He never missed an issue because the football gossip was reliable (Busby was another assiduous reader of the *Post* and its sister paper the *Weekly News*, even developing a friendship with their cheery and knowledgeable English reporter Len Noad). There, Shankly learned that Ron Yeats, Dundee United's colossal centre-back, and Ian St John, the classy and crafty Motherwell centre-forward, might be available. The board loosened the purse strings. Yeats, acquired for £30,000, became the new captain of Liverpool. St John cost £37,500.

As Shankly thrived, Charlie Mitten struggled. After a couple of seasons of entertaining football and eighth place – only one point behind Busby's United – in 1959/60, results had deteriorated and Mitten's Newcastle would not be playing at the top level in 1961/62.

To the factors of which Busby had warned him had been added the unrest of his star inside-forward George Eastham, who had been refused a transfer and gone on strike in protest against the increasingly discredited 'retain-and-transfer' system, by which clubs could keep an unsettled player's registration after the expiry of his contract and therefore wage entitlement. Eastham had missed the start of the relegation season and then, when Newcastle bowed to his wish to move, been sold to Arsenal for £47,500. The irony of Mitten, the former rebel, being thus undermined was obvious. He had, however, been able to spend £18,000 of the proceeds on

Albert Scanlon because Busby had moved Bobby Charlton to the left wing; poor Joe Friday, after all he had been through, deserved better than to be dragged into the Second Division. And then to lose the support of Mitten, who was sacked a few months into the next season.

And what of Jackie Blanchflower? He was trying to run a newspaper shop. Or a pub. Or working for a bookmaker. He was to try many things and often fall into debt. Nine months after the crash, he had been told he would never play again due to kidney damage. He was 25 and his wife was pregnant and United wanted his house back. Later he recalled Louis Edwards's idea of help: a job loading vans with meat pies.

At least Johnny Berry was into his thirties when confirmation came that his career was over. Berry, his wife and son had also been obliged to move because their house was needed for Shay Brennan. Berry worked as a labourer at Trafford Park, a mere overhit cross from the field on which he had so thrillingly confounded Bilbao, before returning to his native Aldershot and going into business with a brother, selling sports clothing.

Although Berry, like Blanchflower, kept in touch with fellow former players, his wife Hilda made no secret of her loathing for United's treatment of Munich survivors other than those, such as Busby, Charlton and Foulkes, who remained fundamental to the club's revival.

Kenny Morgans was a shadow of his pre-crash self and eventually cost his home-town club, Swansea, only £3,000. Scanlon felt let down by Busby over his departure deal, Morgans was said by Gregg to have felt similarly and the atmosphere of cold betrayal was also understandably evident in Blanchflower, who had been the sunniest of characters before the crash.

Among the widows, there was less cause for bitterness. Joy Byrne was allowed to stay in her club house indefinitely, for a token rent, while June Jones would be the last to accuse Busby of insensitivity. Along with Marion Bent, who appreciated Busby visiting her and remembered, like June Jones, his temporary anguish at not having tried to dissuade the pilots from making the third take-off attempt.

In financial terms, the proceeds of an appeal by the Lord Mayor were allocated according to perceived need. Out of a total of £52,000 (the equivalent of between £2 million and £3 million in the early twenty-first century), Scanlon said he received £260.

After his career had petered out in the lower divisions, he was to find himself working in the same Trafford Park factory as Berry had, then on Salford docks. Viewed retrospectively – and for all the shock and sympathy induced by Munich – post-war society might appear to have performed with less than assiduous care and it is in this light that Busby's contribution might most fairly be judged. It was, after all, a tough time for him too.

A CHANGE OF TUNE

For those who survived intact – or, like Bobby Charlton, with only the scars of memory – there was hope of greater reward. Because the maximum wage had been abolished.

During the Eastham stand-off at Newcastle the PFA, anxious to challenge the transfer system, had issued a writ for restraint of trade. The force was with Hill and Lloyd and as 1960 ended with players' meetings all over the country even Stanley Matthews, who had argued against militancy, voted to strike. The League gave in and by the time Tottenham were doubly crowned the maximum wage had been consigned to history.

The first player to benefit dramatically was Johnny Haynes. Fulham's chairman, the comedian Tommy Trinder, had joined Busby in arguing against the maximum, hitting the headlines with a claim that Haynes was worth £100 a week. He proved as good as his word: that was what the England captain now received.

United's players wished Busby had been as consistent, according to John Giles. 'Why did Haynes get a hundred?' Giles answered his own question. 'Because they all thought it wouldn't happen. Or it happened a lot quicker than they expected. I remember being there at the time of the campaign, going to the union meetings and so on, and Matt having meetings with the players. A bit like Trinder, he's saying to us, "Listen, lads, this maximum wage is ridiculous. You should all be on a hundred quid a week." I remember him saying it – a few times. And then, when it happened, what was Matt's first offer? Twenty-five quid a week and a fiver appearance money.'

A delegation of players went to Busby and came back with £30 plus £10 per appearance, which was agreed. But what irked Giles was the discovery that Bill Shankly had made Liverpool's players the same initial offer as Busby: £25 plus £5. It wasn't so much that

Liverpool were still in the Second Division when the maximum was abolished. More that Busby and Shankly, in Giles's view, had conspired against the players. These two sons of Scotland's Labour heartlands, former miners. Or, as Giles put it, 'these two people who had gone through the mill in their own playing careers, worse than we ever did'.

Once in positions of power – and Giles had no doubt that Busby ruled United – they behaved no more generously than their own employers before the war. 'If not worse. Busby and Shankly colluded to keep wages down as much as they could.' But was there not a difference between Trinder's Fulham, anxious to keep their outstanding player by far, and United with their depth of talent? 'That's what Matt would often say when we mentioned Haynes – "He's the exception at his club."' But it was a change of tune. 'When he and Shankly had a chance to pay their players properly, they wouldn't. It was mean. I must say I always resented Busby for that. Because Shankly was a football nut. Matt wasn't. Matt was a very experienced man, a classy individual, who would have known the score.'

Still, the days of soft serfdom had gone and First Division players, whose basic wage had been chased by the national average before Munich, could look forward to a better share. There was a growing commercialism; Haynes got £1,500 for making a television advertisement. But Busby's strategy, for all his pleas for freedom to pay more, was equally governed by the underlying message of a speech by Prime Minister Macmillan: eternal vigilance must be applied to wage inflation.

Manchester United did not feel like a moneyed institution to everyone. Certainly not the recently arrived Ken Ramsden. His recollection was that the war damage and the crash had conspired in an air of austerity that Les Olive maintained as carefully as had Walter Crickmer. One of Ramsden's first tasks was to get to know Withy Grove Stores, which sold second-hand office equipment. 'Whatever we needed – a desk, chairs, typewriters – we got from Withy Grove. We didn't really get anything *new*.' But Busby's simple needs were met. 'He'd pop in at lunchtime most days, to collect his cigarettes or a bottle of whisky to take home.'

At the end of that 1960/61 season in which Mitten took Newcastle down, Johnny Carey lost his job at Everton. Carey was a disciple. He had fostered youth at Blackburn and, on Merseyside, encouraged his players, Busby-style, to enjoy their game and entertain, laying down principles such as 'only the goalkeeper stops the ball'. But his man-management was said to lack Busby's ruthless streak and so, despite Everton's fifth-place finish – two above United – they were to begin the new season under Harry Catterick, whose Sheffield Wednesday had been runners-up to the great Spurs.

Carey was to revive his career and become a serious competitor with Busby for the First Division title. He was certainly to become the most distinguished manager from Busby's 1948 team. Allenby Chilton had got Grimsby into the Second Division but the task of keeping them there defeated him. At least Mitten, like Carey, had reached the top level.

Busby, trying to get back into his old routine after Munich, leans on a stick as he chats to Bobby Charlton before the 1958 FA Cup final.

Real friends: Alfredo Di Stéfano is warmly greeted by Busby as Real Madrid arrive in Manchester in late September 1959 for one of the frequent friendlies played in the aftermath of Munich, when United were short of money.

At last! Busby watches Denis Law sign for United. It is at least Busby's fourth attempt and the left arm resting on Law's shoulder seems almost a restraint against a late change of mind. But Law was desperate to return from Italy. Also in the picture are the go-between Gigi Peronace (left), Jimmy Murphy and United secretary Les Olive.

Busby shakes hands with the Duke of Edinburgh before the 1963 FA Cup final. Captain Noel Cantwell makes the introduction, while Maurice Setters looks on. This match was to signal the beginning of the end of United's post-Munich struggles.

Albert Quixall ruffles what is left of Busby's hair as the manager carries the Cup in 1963. David Herd, who scored twice in the victory over Leicester City, has the base. Pat Crerand and Tony Dunne are in between.

Busby pours the champagne as Pat Crerand, Denis Law and David Herd prepare to toast the 1965 title triumph in the Old Trafford dressing-room. United have just beaten Arsenal and on the same night Leeds, their closest challengers, could only draw at Birmingham.

Champions once more: Busby holds the trophy aloft at Old Trafford after the final match of 1966/67, a scoreless and meaningless draw with Stoke. United had already clinched the title, and emphasised their right to it with a 6–1 triumph at West Ham.

© PRESS ASSOCIATION

© MIRRORPIX

They shared a vision: Busby with Jimmy Murphy, the loyal assistant whose teaching skills and eye for talent were fundamental in the making of football history.

Busby's mother Nellie, known to the family as 'Maw', accompanies Matt and Jean as he is granted the Freedom of Manchester in 1967.

© MIRRORPIX

Sweat-soaked satisfaction: Shay Brennan and Bobby Charlton carry the European Cup across Wembley, joined by (from left) Alex Stepney, Bill Foulkes, Tony Dunne and Pat Crerand.

The European journey ends in Albert Square. With Pat Crerand and George Best, Busby brings the Champions' Cup to Manchester Town Hall. Below, flanked by the Lord Mayor, he shows it to the crowds, but Jimmy Murphy avoids the limelight; his head can be found a few yards to the left of Busby's, a little beyond the senior policeman in the peaked cap.

Busby had a weekly column in the *Daily Express*. Once, when his usual ghost-writer, Bill Fryer, was away, the task fell to a young reporter, John Roberts, who was delighted to be sent a proportion of the fee by Busby. In 1969 the amount, £8, was substantial – more than enough to feed the Roberts family for a week – but John declined to cash the cheque, preferring to frame this memento of a hero's generosity and hang it in his home, where he kindly agreed to have it photographed for this book. 'It was most unusual,' Roberts said, 'for the interviewer to share the largesse.'

Ballon d'Or: between 1964 and 1968, three members of Busby's last great team were voted European Footballer of the Year. George Best received the trophy at Old Trafford in 1969, and here the Northern Irishman shows it to a 60-year-old Busby, who is about to retire as Manchester United manager, or thinks he is.

Cigarette in left hand, Busby extends his right arm to introduce the successor to Wilf McGuinness as United manager. Frank O'Farrell's somewhat uneasy smile may be explained by a later assertion that he never trusted Busby after being offered one basic salary by him and another by the chairman, Louis Edwards.

Solid gold: Matt and Jean clink champagne glasses in celebration of their Golden Wedding anniversary in January 1981. Less than 18 months later, Jean was diagnosed with Alzheimer's disease.

Old pals. When Busby was captain of Liverpool just before the Second World War, a young player, Bob Paisley, arrived from County Durham. Busby warmly welcomed him and their friendship endured. Before the 1983 Charity Shield match between United and Liverpool, Busby and Paisley were driven across the Wembley pitch to a joint ovation.

Just the start: it is 1991 and Alex Ferguson has brought the European Cup-Winners' Cup to Old Trafford. But Busby can still lay his hands on Europe's supreme trophy, which his United won 23 years earlier. To Ferguson, the burden of history was clear, but he willingly shouldered it and, on what would have been Sir Matt's 90th birthday, United became European champions again. Ferguson promptly became Sir Alex.

His domain: Busby in early February 1983 outside Old Trafford. Behind him are the
Munich clock – the 25th anniversary was about to be marked – and the Red Devils
Souvenir Shop, of which the Busby family were to relinquish ownership in 1987.
Today at Old Trafford there is a megastore. Next to its entrance is a statue of Busby.

CHAPTER ELEVEN

THE 1968 TEAM: LAW, BEST AND CHARLTON

GENIUS

Bob Bishop in Northern Ireland had arranged a match between the team he ran for under-19s and the Cregagh club, whom he knew would field a little skinny lad just short of 15. The lad had scored twice and outplayed brawnier opponents. Scouts for other clubs had deemed him too frail to cross the water. But for Bishop the time had come to tell Joe Armstrong about George Best.

First, aware of what Armstrong and Busby would want to know, he did a background check on the family: George's father, Dickie, worked in a Belfast shipyard and had played amateur football while his mother, Ann, had excelled at hockey. They were church-going Presbyterians who insisted on good manners. George was offered a two-week trial. With another youngster, Eric McMordie.

Armstrong sent ferry tickets and they travelled overnight to Liverpool. No one met them so they took a train to Manchester and asked a taxi-driver to drop them at Old Trafford. It was summer; he left them at the cricket ground. A short walk led to where Armstrong waited anxiously. He insisted United had sent a taxi to the port. And then took them to their digs at 9 Aycliffe Avenue, Chorlton-cum-Hardy, the home of Mrs Mary Fullaway.

And then to train with lads who, to Best and McMordie, appeared dauntingly physical.

Barry Fry had been primed by Busby. 'He told me to look after these shy Belfast boys. Make sure they weren't lonely, maybe take them to the pictures. I can't have done a very good job.' The next day McMordie suggested the first boat home and Best agreed. Armstrong arrived at Mrs Fullaway's and quickly came up with a change of plan, persuading them to attend the first-team session and be introduced to their heroic compatriot Harry Gregg. For once, Uncle Joe's magic failed to work. Best and McMordie insisted on collecting their bags.

Having found his way home to Burren Way in Cregagh, Best knocked on the door – to the surprise of his parents, who didn't have a telephone – and handed his father a piece of paper. On it was Armstrong's number. Dickie Best now used a neighbour's phone to demand an apology for how George had been treated. A call from Busby followed and soon after George had returned to Manchester – without McMordie, who would train as a plasterer before joining Middlesbrough – the manager received advice from Murphy. 'We don't coach this boy,' it concluded. 'He's a genius.'

Busby took a look at Best and, while spellbound, could hardly miss a trait he later described as 'a congenital dislike of allowing anyone else to have a kick'. He was going to mention it to the boy but Murphy shook his head and Busby understood.

Another exceptional prospect was Bobby Noble, a Mancunian full-back, tough, quick, two-footed and clever. When United were to retrieve the Youth Cup with Best in a fine side, Noble would be captain. Many believed he would become the best full-back in the club's history. Perhaps not the most gentlemanly; when Murphy half-joked to Noble that wingers 'can't play without ankles', he was preaching to the converted.

Busby meanwhile decided Alex Dawson fell below requirements and signed David Herd, son of his friend Alex and heir to one of the hardest shots in the game, from Arsenal for £37,000. Ronnie Cope went to Luton for £10,000 and Dawson to Preston for £18,000. Busby would even take his account for the 1961/62 season into healthy profit when, amid the raising of eyebrows, Viollet was sold to Stoke for £25,000. Not one of Busby's sales was to a fellow First Division manager.

It was an odd season, one in which miserable League form was alleviated by victories over Alf Ramsey's Ipswich, champions-to-be in their inaugural First Division season, runners-up Burnley and third-placed Tottenham, and a run to the semi-finals of the FA Cup. But to many nothing was stranger that the sale of Viollet, who had been comfortably outscoring Herd before he found himself at Stoke. Admittedly an exciting Stoke who, with Viollet in an attack featuring Stanley Matthews, would be champions of the Second Division the next season. Friends nevertheless felt Viollet had been shabbily treated. 'Just because he had an eye for the ladies,' said Jeff Whitefoot.

When it came to marriage vows, Viollet was indeed flexible. Genuinely fond of women – never crude or boastful – with a philosophy of living for the moment that survival at Munich could hardly have diluted. So, fine player though he remained, he had to go. 'It was terrible, awful, to do that to Dennis,' said Whitefoot. 'But that was Busby. He liked everything to be correct on the surface. And he was very tough.'

With Giles, toughness seemed necessary. Giles was a strong personality who never quite convinced Busby he was worth the indulgence shown to, say, Roger Byrne. There was always tension. 'For a start,' said Giles, 'he'd just paid a record fee for Quixall. And Quixall was an inside-right, as I was – the perception that I was a winger converted to a midfield player is false. I was never a winger. But Matt put me on the wing and I felt it was better to play there for the first team than at inside-right for the reserves. Then, in 1961/62, I played as many matches in midfield as on the wing.'

He was at inside-right throughout the Cup run. First at home to Bolton, where Herd and Nicholson struck late in the fog for a 2–1 win. A sodden Old Trafford greeted Arsenal and, after Setters headed home from a corner, United held out. The new solidity of their defence saw them past Sheffield Wednesday and Preston to a semi-final against Tottenham at Hillsborough.

Spurs, their galaxy now featuring Jimmy Greaves, were candidates for another Double, indeed the Treble because they had made majestic progress in the European Cup and hoped the White Hart Lane atmosphere would inspire them to make light of a 3–1 lead taken by the holders, Benfica, in the Lisbon leg of their semi-final.

'They were too good for us,' Giles recalled. 'Beat us 3–1 and I was terrible. And, on that day, Matt and the staff lost confidence in me. Probably thought I'd bottled it. Not that anyone spoke to me afterwards.' Quixall returned and a few matches later, at Burnley, Giles found himself back on the wing. 'That was telling me! But I couldn't do right for doing wrong. If I went on the outside, Matt thought I should have gone on the inside, or the other way round. I'd not be crossing the ball quickly enough – and then be crossing it too quick! It can happen in football that a manager takes a turn against a player. And Matt took a turn against me.'

While good players were all very well, Busby's ambitions called for great ones, in the tradition of Duncan Edwards, to compete with the Alfredo Di Stéfanos of the future. Charlton might become one. The boy genius Best would receive every encouragement. But Denis Law; bold and brave as well as brilliant, he would let nothing stop him.

The latest attempt to bring him to Old Trafford – at least the fourth, for Busby had asked Andy Beattie, then Shankly after Munich and tried to hijack the City deal – dated back to the previous November, a few months after Law had left Manchester City for Torino, where he shared a flat with the former Hibs centre-forward Joe Baker.

John Charles was happy with Juventus and Gerry Hitchens, a centre-forward from Aston Villa, thriving at Inter. But Law fell into the other category. Like Greaves, who had returned from Milan to join Spurs, Law abhorred the defender-friendly Italian game and, while taking to the people and food of Turin, admitted to a schoolboy error over the weather. 'I was quite good in a few subjects but they can't have included geography because I didn't realise Turin was so close to the Alps. And it snowed! And I'd been thinking Naples.'

Manchester, for him, would be closer to *la dolce vita*. He had missed the murky city. 'I'd liked Manchester immediately,' he recalled. 'Compared to Huddersfield, it was Las Vegas!' And so, when the Italian League picked him for their annual fixture against the Football League, he was delighted to discover it would be played at Old Trafford.

At the banquet, Busby – innocently, he insisted – asked Law how he was enjoying Italian football. Law left him in no doubt: 'Why don't you come out and buy me?' When Busby got around to

raising the subject with Hardman, the chairman said he wasn't keen
to take the club back into debt. But the entrepreneurial influence
of Louis Edwards was growing and that was to be confirmed by his
presence, with Busby and Hardman, at negotiations with Torino
the following summer.

In the meantime, Busby had made a covert approach. 'A friend
of Matt's came over to Turin to see me,' Law recalled. And in April
1962, when Law was in Glasgow for Scotland's 2–0 victory over
England, Busby was among the 132,000 in attendance. Leaving
Murphy to supervise United's 3–1 win at Burnley, he met Law
afterwards in his Edinburgh hotel.

A couple of weeks later, Busby travelled to Amsterdam and
declared his interest to the Torino president, Angelo Filippone,
on the eve of the European Cup final, in which two goals from
Eusébio, the 20-year-old sensation from Portuguese Africa, would
complete Benfica's thrilling 5–3 victory over Real Madrid. Imagine
how Busby felt on such occasions. So much was happening in
Europe without his United. And so much of it happening to Spurs;
even though in the end they had fallen short against Benfica and
settled for the FA Cup, a gulf in class yawned. Busby could address
it if only he had Law.

Filippone quoted him a telephone number. In pounds, not lire.
But Busby knew time and Law's disaffection were on his side.

The next meeting was scheduled for Lausanne, where Torino
were in a tournament, but Filippone didn't turn up and Busby turned
to Gigi Peronace, the charismatic 33-year-old who had brokered
most of the big deals between England and Italy, including those
of Law and Baker. In Peronace's opinion, it would be difficult to
prise Law from Torino. But he'd see what he could do. A few weeks
later, his smile beamed down on Law's golden head as, watched by
an equally pleased Busby, the player put pen to paper.

There had been some intervening drama: a dash by Busby,
Hardman and Edwards to Turin, where Filippone's deputy intimated
that Law was about to sign for Juventus for £200,000. Busby knew
United could not get near that. But Law was helpful to the man
who had made him an international. He broke the deadlock by
announcing that, rather than stay in Italy, he would go home to
Aberdeen. And carried out his threat. So it was from Aberdeen that
he returned to Manchester, happily accepting a sharp drop in pay,
and moved in with his old landlady in Withington. The fee had

been agreed at £115,000, a new British record, the second Busby had set since Munich.

GLORIOUS VINDICATION

While Denis Law was being recruited, Bobby Charlton went to a World Cup presided over by Sir Stanley Rous, who had succeeded Arthur Drewry at FIFA. England were knocked out, by Brazil, who went on to retain the title. Alf Ramsey was named as the next England manager – the first with full control over selection and tactics – but would have a final season with Ipswich as they plummeted from first to seventeenth yet still finished two places above Busby's United.

Yes, 1962/63 was to be another Old Trafford season of contradiction wrapped in fluctuation. This time sealed – for Busby – with glorious vindication.

Only the manager seemed to see any sense in things. His calm judgement again reached far below the surface. While seventh place in 1960/61 had, like second in 1958/59, flattered his team, now things looked worse than they were. 'Despite our poor League position,' he said, reflecting on 15th in 1961/62, the first bottom-half finish of his managerial career, 'I could see that things were beginning to take shape.' So the initial struggles of 1962/63 were, by his own admission, 'incredibly frustrating'. Even victory over Real Madrid in a Bernabéu testimonial failed to lift the gloom.

And still Busby kept his head when all around were, if not losing theirs, bickering, falling out – Harry Gregg, for example, with the clubmate he scornfully called 'Popular Bill' Foulkes – blaming others, panicking or forming cliques as never happened before Munich.

An illustration of how Busby dealt with relegation's threats concerned Crompton. He was called into the manager's office. 'Jack,' said Busby, rummaging in a cupboard, 'sit down and stop worrying. We've been together too long ... If the Good Lord agrees we go down, we go down, but we'll come back ...' At length, he discovered a bottle of whisky and two glasses. And arranged for lemonade as a mixer for Crompton, who seldom drank alcohol. And Busby went back to 1946. He said one of his first matches in charge had been at Stoke, where Bob McGrory invited him into this office for a dram afterwards and explained to the newcomer what football management could do to a man: 'It either drives you barmy or it drives you to drink.'

Busby smiled at Crompton and raised his glass. 'Now, cheers!'

Unrest over Crompton seemed to date from the arrival of Cantwell, who hardly exempted Busby or Murphy in his ridicule of United's outmoded – as viewed from West Ham – tactics and training methods. Busby also resolved this with aplomb. He held a team meeting in which Crompton went on the attack, identifying Cantwell as a disruptive influence. Gently but firmly, Busby supported Crompton. He didn't want to lose Cantwell. But he had judged him wisely; so positive was the Irishman's response that Busby made yet another change of captain, replacing Setters with Cantwell, whom he later described as 'a straight-talking intermediary between the players and me'.

Busby's most acute dilemma, according to an autobiography published by Harry Gregg some 40 years later, involved a choice between morality and the standing of Manchester United. Rumours of match-fixing had long been heard but towards the end of that 1962/63 season reality was confronted when three Sheffield Wednesday players – Peter Swan, Tony Kay and David 'Bronco' Layne – were exposed. They eventually went to prison.

Among the United players, plots had been suggested and Gregg, believing some had been enacted, went to Busby, whose response he described as a furious 'I knew it!' But Busby didn't want his club portrayed as a school for scandal. He went to the *Daily Mail*, reporters from which had raised the matter with Gregg, and somehow secured a letter of apology. Busby then gathered the players and read it to them. The message was clear to any culprits in their midst. It had to stop.

At one stage, they were at the bottom of the First Division. Busby chopped and changed but was consistent in the style of football he demanded: constructive, attractive and (the hardest part for a losing team) enjoyable. Results took a modest turn for the better, Law scoring seven goals in five matches. Three days later, he got married to Diana Thomson.

With Law, domestic bliss brought no escape from controversy. Not that he seemed in any way to blame at West Bromwich, where he accused the referee, Gilbert Pullin, of 'needling' him every time a shot went wide or pass astray. Busby reported it to the FA and

Pullin, censured, quit the game. Law, while sorry it had gone that far, felt a marked man afterwards, liable to incur heavy policing and, when found guilty, extended suspension. It was, however, part of his game – and character – to fight for the right to perform. Which could be very difficult then.

Busby, for all his principles, equipped his team for their environment. Hence Setters. And, in February 1963, the signing of Pat Crerand, whose unquestionable skills were accompanied by a readiness to scrap.

According to Busby it was the craft of Crerand's passing United needed most. Crerand played for Celtic while Rangers had the audaciously gifted Jim Baxter. Busby asked Law who would serve him better. Law thought Crerand, while not quite as skilled as Baxter (few were), would be more reliable and Crerand, when Law told him later, understood. 'Jim was a great friend of mine,' he said, 'and a great lad – but I used to bollock him all the time about his drinking. He was George Best before George Best.'

Baxter eventually moved to Sunderland for £72,500 and, although he did enough there to persuade Nottingham Forest to pay £100,000, the Bacardi had taken its toll. Once Forest returned to the dressing room and their manager, Matt Gillies, went straight for him. 'That,' he said, 'was the worst performance I've seen from a professional footballer in my life.' Baxter grinned, rose and patted Gillies's bald head. 'Aye,' he said, 'and there's a lot more to come.' Not that much. Before long he was given a free transfer and returned to Rangers.

Busby paid £55,000 for Crerand, who wanted to leave the 'shambles' his beloved Celtic had become. One Sunday evening, just back from Mass, he heard a knock on the door. There stood the portly figure of Jim Rodger, a football journalist known as 'The Jolly' and celebrated for his contacts. They extended far beyond football, as Crerand was to discover when he married Noreen Ferry soon after joining United and a certificate of blessing arrived from the Pope. 'Jim got it for me, He was fantastic, Jim.' But that evening he was on football business. 'You're going to Manchester United,' he said. When Crerand went to Celtic Park the next day, the club confirmed it.

'I was at a loss. I'd hardly been out of Glasgow except to go on holiday to Ireland. I thought England was some pagan country! But Matt, as he waited for me at Manchester airport, had Denis with him. Denis and his wife Di. I had Noreen with me. Matt was cute there, wasn't he?'

Crerand made his first appearance in a home draw with Blackpool as football emerged from the winter of 1962/63, the coldest of the twentieth century. Snow had carpeted vast areas for week after week and, although Busby had taken United to Ireland a couple of times, they had been unable to play a proper match between Boxing Day, when they won 1–0 at frostbound Fulham, and Blackpool's visit to Old Trafford on 23 February.

At first, many observers wondered if Crerand were any better than, say, Nobby Lawton, who was to join Alex Dawson at Preston for £11,500. From Crerand's first six League matches, United took two points: relegation form writ large. Enough for Harold Hardman to pay a surprise visit to Old Trafford one Sunday and tell Busby not to worry, which was appreciated.

A defeat at Liverpool exposed the team's rough edges: Law scuffled with his compatriot St John and Stiles waved two fingers at the Kop. Only the belated start of the Cup offered encouragement. Law hit a hat-trick in a 5–0 hammering of Huddersfield at Old Trafford, where Villa and Chelsea also fell before a quarter-final win away to Coventry, managed by Jimmy Hill. The semi-final, against Southampton at Villa Park, was a dour affair settled by one of Law's scruffier efforts. But United, now bearing a £312,000 price tag, were at Wembley after an absence of five years, lending flesh to Busby's dogged arguments that a pattern was emerging.

If some deemed the family not quite as happy as of old, Law shrugged. For him it had been easy to rise above the backbiting. 'I was just happy,' he said, 'to be back in British football and back in Manchester with a guy I adored. The guy who'd given me my first cap for my country.' And who remained almost parental. 'You went to him with all of your problems. Family problems. Getting a house. Getting married. Having children. Yes, even when I told him I was going to get married. Is she the one for you? Is she happy to come down from Aberdeen? He just wanted to be sure. And his wife was like a mum to a lot of the guys. It was always Matt's thing that, if your family life was not happy, you were not a happy player. So he would see that things were done.

'And on the football pitch I was thinking "This is the life." The thing about Italy was that, although I'd gone for the money, just one year there had improved me as a player. The opposition would put two men on me and two on Joe Baker. And we'd do the same to their two strikers. You had to learn how to get away and take the few chances you got. So when I got back to England the sense of freedom was unbelievable – I didn't think I was being marked by anyone!'

In the Cup final build-up, truncated by the winter's harshness to four weeks, United would play seven League matches. They won only two but preserved First Division status with a Maine Road draw secured by Law's fall and the ensuing penalty conversion by Quixall; it would be City instead who went down with Johnny Carey's Leyton Orient, whom United beat at Old Trafford before completing their programme with a defeat at Nottingham Forest notable for two occurrences.

One was a useful first United appearance by a player of mixed race. On the same day that West Ham aspirants captained by John Charles, who had a black father from Grenada and a white mother, overcame their Liverpool counterparts to win the Youth Cup, Busby chose the 18-year-old winger Dennis Walker from Northwich, Cheshire. The Forest match, sadly for Nobby Stiles, also featured the aggravation of a hamstring injury, which meant the only true Mancunian left in the side (now Cantwell had temporarily edged out Brennan) would miss the final.

This let in Giles, his future brother-in-law. Giles had returned for the semi-final. 'Quicky pulled out injured on the Friday. And we won 1–0. In the next League match we were at home to Sheffield Wednesday and I sensed it would be the usual stuff – "How do you think you played in the semi-final, son?" – but before Busby could ask me I asked him. How did he think I had played? He said I'd played reasonably well. And I said, "Well, if that's what you thought, why are you leaving me out?" He said it was a choice between me and Albert Quixall. I wouldn't let it drop. I said, "Well, Albert Quixall didn't play in the semi-final." And this was real cheek to Matt. "Anyway," he said, "that's it."'

As Busby shuffled his pack, Giles played in some League matches. But he was convinced only Stiles's misfortune let him into the Wembley team. He was on the right wing and Quixall inside-right against Leicester, who had finished fourth in the League and were favourites. Outside Old Trafford anyway. Barry Fry remembered: 'You were allowed to bet in those days and Noel Cantwell and Maurice Setters were saying, "Put your houses on us." I think even the kids put a few bob on United winning.'

The selection that might have cost United the match was at the expense of Gregg, whom Busby omitted in favour of David Gaskell. The experienced man went to Wembley knowing he would be a spectator but wondering why.

As the team bus edged through the crowds, the crafty Cantwell, anxious nothing should be left to chance, had a word with Gregg. The captains would be shaking hands with the referee, the distinguished Ken Aston. 'So Nosher [Cantwell] says to me, "Do you know the Masons' grip?" "Why?" I asked. "Because we've heard the ref's a Mason."' Gregg was unable to help and in any case the final would pass, unlike United's previous two, without controversy.

Among the 100,000 spectators was Busby's daughter-in-law, even though Irene had presented Sandy with a baby girl, Alison, a couple of days earlier. Busby had taken time out from the Wembley preparations to visit his new grand-daughter. She had been born in a nursing home whose rule, Irene recalled, was to keep mothers in for ten post-natal days. 'God knows why, but they did. And so everyone was going to the Cup final except me. Anyway, Matt came in and the next time I saw the matron she said, "Oh, isn't he a lovely man." And when she heard I wouldn't be going to Wembley she said, "Well, I'll tell you what I'll do – I'll look after the baby over the weekend and you can go down to London with the team." And she did. And I went.'

The crowd were all under cover, for Wembley had begun to prepare for the 1966 World Cup. The gate receipts, though a British record, were £89,000, or less than a pound per spectator on average; although players still considered themselves underpaid, their supporters got a fair deal. Tradition was also evident in the community singing and massed bands of the Royal Marines. A contemporary touch, however, was the hurling of toilet rolls from the United end as Busby and Matt Gillies led out the teams. On BBC television, Kenneth Wolstenholme mentioned it, icily.

United took control, calmly progressing through midfield while the defence coped with Leicester's longer game as comfortably as Gaskell permitted. The accusation often levelled at the young keeper was that he had more confidence than ability and early on, appearing to make an exhibition of a simple catch, he fumbled the ball, which bounced behind him, alarming his defenders. A sheepish grin suggested he might have learned a lesson but no; it was to United's great fortune that, at the other end, the goalkeeper

whom Alf Ramsey had just chosen to succeed England's ageing
Ron Springett, one Gordon Banks, would make an even more
significant botch of his job.

After half an hour, the increasingly authoritative Crerand burst
on to a risky throw by Banks, the midfielder's change of pace (not
usually a Crerand speciality) taking him deep into the penalty area,
where he gently squared the ball. Law let it pass between Richie
Norman and Colin Appleton and run behind him while smoothly
turning on to his right foot and then, instead of shooting where
Banks might have expected, twisted and rolled the ball back across
the helpless keeper, again bisecting Norman and Appleton, into an
inaccessible corner. An almost deafening roar saluted one of the
finest goals ever scored under the Twin Towers.

In the second half, Giles drifted in from the right and found
Charlton, whose unexceptional drive Banks spilled, handing Herd
the first of two easy goals. Ken Keyworth reduced the deficit ten
minutes from the end but Leicester's hopes of a thrilling finish were
extinguished when, after Law had played a glorious one-two with
Herd and headed against a post – an instinctive showman, he sank
to his knees and buried his face in the lush turf – Banks dropped a
Giles cross and Herd profited again with his 21st goal in 43 League
and Cup appearances. Law's was his 29th in 44: not bad for a player
who had never been, or seen himself as, a pure striker (one, indeed,
who would end his career wishing its entirety had been spent as an
all-round midfielder).

As the Queen handed Cantwell the Cup, Prince Philip beamed.
Between the royal couple the diminutive Harold Hardman stood
almost unnoticed. By now he was 81 and chairman in little more
than name. When Dr McLean had died, Hardman had tried to
bring on to the board Gordon Gibson, who, despite his surname,
had no family connection with United. Gordon Gibson was the
headmaster who had refereed United's first practice match under
floodlights. He now looked after visiting match officials.

He was deliciously described in Keith Dewhurst's memoir *When
You Put on a Red Shirt* as tall, bald, honest and convinced he knew
what was right: 'He would give Busby his forthright opinion of the
game we had just seen, and receive in return the most sympathetic
of cold shoulders.' So Busby had artfully seen Gordon Gibson off
with a quiet word in Alan Gibson's ear. 'Look, Alan,' he murmured,
'you're the senior director here, you should have the main say. You

should nominate someone.' At which point Alan Gibson chose someone of barely greater weight than himself: Bill Young, a farmer and lifelong friend who had protected him from bullies at school.

Louis Edwards had built up his shareholding, initially through an intermediary – a local councillor, Frank Farrington – and then by direct purchases at a premium price, the most significant from the widow of George Whittaker, who had opposed him before Munich. He was entitled to something of a proprietorial air as he gazed down on the Wembley pitch. Cantwell did a skip of honour. He had the Cup, while Crerand held the base. Cantwell threw the Cup into the air and, to Crerand's obvious relief, caught it.

Crowds would pack Albert Square to see Busby brandish his first trophy since Munich. It had a special meaning, too, for Charlton and Foulkes. But first were the London celebrations. 'As we arrived back at the hotel with the Cup,' said Crerand, 'I looked out of the coach. United, as usual, had taken all the players, including the youths, as well as the entire staff. And there, at a top-floor window, looking out at us, was George Best.'

No player could have less enjoyed the subsequent Savoy banquet, at which the Beverley Sisters sang, than Harry Gregg. 'I'm sitting there. Gaskell's sitting there. He's enjoying himself. All the lads were enjoying themselves. And I'm pig-sick. But I don't want to annoy them. And a teenage boy approaches me and says, "Harry, can my daddy come over and speak to you?" It was a great relief. And I said, "No, George, I'll come over and see your dad."' It was three days after Best's 17th birthday and his first-team debut was less than four months away.

So why had Gregg been left out? Why had Busby, by Gregg's account, responded to a plea from captain Cantwell to omit the younger man with a brusque 'Gaskell's playing'? Although Gregg was to appear more often than Gaskell the following season, his days were numbered and a later conversation with Brian McHugh, the Busbys' family doctor, who had also become the club doctor, led Gregg to believe his shoulder and back were not the only reasons.

Gregg had been through more than his fitness problems; Mavis had died of cancer, leaving him to look after their two daughters, and Dr McHugh had become a regular visitor to his home. One day, he took Gregg into his confidence. 'He said he'd been having a drink with Jimmy Murphy and happened to venture the opinion that the best fellows at the club were Harry Gregg and John Giles.

Jimmy had reached into a drawer. "Fucking read that," he said, handing over a letter. It was from my father. It said his son wouldn't give him tickets. The dirty bastard. I wouldn't give him anything. And Jimmy had obviously shown the letter to Holier-Than-Thou. It was wrong. Matt should have come to me. I could have told him this man left my mother with six kids. But he didn't. And years later I heard what his wife had said.' Gregg mimicked Jean's Scottish accent. '"*Dinnae mention that man's name in my house.*" Can you imagine how I felt when I heard that? After Munich, after everything. But Matt never came to me. So I sat on the bench at Wembley while David Gaskell had his nightmare.'

Giles had mixed reflections on Wembley. He felt good but knew why: 'In the weeks leading to the final, Busby's criticism had got me to the stage where I said, "Fuck him – I'll just go out and follow my instincts." So I was totally relaxed and played well and we won.' But peace was temporary. 'There was a thing at Old Trafford. Matt was God. Nobody disputed Matt's word.' Not since Johnny Morris. 'Actually there were two things. And the second was: nobody leaves Old Trafford and does well. That was written in stone. That was the gospel.' Giles was preparing to risk heresy.

'He didn't say anything to me and it was on tour in Italy – in Rome, I think – that I went to the bathroom and he's there with Jimmy Murphy. He nods in my direction and says to Jimmy, "What about this fellow in the Cup final?" As if it was a surprise! I was raging. I just turned and walked out. I'd made up my mind anyway. I couldn't go through another season of torture. Manchester United might have been a great club for Bobby Charlton and Denis Law. But it wasn't a great club for me.'

EYES LIKE DIAMONDS

Johnny Giles chuckled. 'Also, I'd had a bit of a row with Matt.' Another? 'When we were in Italy the lads were unhappy about the bonus for winning the Cup. There was no designated figure. We were on a crowd bonus at the time and, because there was such a big crowd at Wembley, we did well enough on that. But we felt we should get something for winning.' There had been talk in the papers of Leicester being on £2,000 a man. 'Matt said a winning bonus wasn't in our contracts. So we said he could put it in next year's contract [to be paid retrospectively]. He came back and said that, after due consideration, the board had decided to pay for the printing of our Wembley brochure. I think that was about £200 among the lot of us!

'The lads were also complaining about the wages. We were on 30 quid and a tenner appearance money and the senior players said they wouldn't re-sign for that. I went to Dublin for my holidays, got married, came back and by then everyone had signed because he gave them a fiver rise.

'By now I didn't care. I went to see him. I must have been the last person he wanted to see. And his eyes, when he got angry, would go hard, like diamonds. He said the club had been "very generous" in giving the £5 rise. [Busby himself had been awarded a £20-a-week increase to £6,000 a year on an extended contract.] I said, "I don't think they've been generous at all. I've played in the Irish team with lads getting twice as much as I am." Because I'd had a chat with Charlie Hurley, of Sunderland. "Well," he said, "you'll find they are the exception at their clubs." I said, "Yes, but we are Manchester United." "Anyway," he said, "I'll need you to sign so you can play." When, without signing, I left his office, his eyes were diamonds and I'm sure he wanted to give me a clip round the ear. But Matt never lost his head.' A week later, Giles did sign on the promise that Busby would review the situation later.

And suddenly the Charity Shield match was upon them. This fixture was henceforth to be associated with the phrase 'annual curtain-raiser' because it had been moved to the weekend before the start of the League. United, as Cup winners, would meet Everton, whom Harry Catterick had made champions. Everton, with home advantage, won 4–0. United, unchanged from the final, were so poor Busby dropped four players for the opening match of the 1963/64 season away to Sheffield Wednesday. Gaskell was replaced by Gregg, Quixall by Phil Chisnall and Herd by the 17-year-old David Sadler. Giles, of course, was the fourth, giving way to Ian Moir.

On the Tuesday, he put in a transfer request. On the Thursday, having been told by Busby that it would be 'put before the directors' – a managerial euphemism, in Giles's experience, for 'okay by me' – he was making for his car after training when Wilf McGuinness followed him. 'Go and see the Boss,' he implored. 'He might change his mind.' That annoyed Giles. 'I'm not changing *my* mind,' he replied. So no one could find a better life outside Old Trafford? He'd be different.

By the end of the month he was making his Second Division debut for Leeds against Bury at Elland Road. Busby had accepted £32,500 from Don Revie. Giles had correctly judged that Revie was taking Leeds in the right direction. Also their little general, Bobby Collins, was an idol to him. 'I'd sat down with my wife and, talking about Matt, said, "I'm going to haunt him." It was immature stuff. But it was a driving force. In a big way.'

One of the younger ones in the Wembley party had been Alan Wardle, a full-back who never got beyond the reserves. He remembered the night before the final: 'We had a choice between *The Sound of Music* and England versus Young England at Highbury. But we'd never been to Soho in our lives. So we go to this club and the lights go up and there's more United players than you've ever seen in your life. Then there's the match, and the train journey back to Manchester, and the coach to the Town Hall. One of the police outriders was the brother of my wife-to-be. He said it might be a good idea if I went home. Quite a few of us had been drinking on the train.

'The following morning, I'm in to see Matt. Looking for a wage increase because I'm getting married in a few weeks. I go upstairs. Well, I can see him now: pipe in his mouth, Scottish plaid wallpaper in the background.

'"Morning, Alan, what can I do for you, son?"

'"I'm getting married next month, Boss."

'"Congratulations, son."

'"Boss, I know that, not being a first-team player, I don't get a club house or anything, but we're buying this little house in Pendlebury and I was wondering about a wage increase ... "

'And he pulls on his pipe.

'"You're lucky to be retained, son."'

Wardle crept back to the staircase. 'You know, when you've had a near-miss in your car, the nerve in your knee starts ... well, I had to hold on to the bannister all the way down.' He stayed on £15 basic for what turned out to be his last year at Old Trafford. A few weeks later, he heard Noel Cantwell talking about an increase. '"I'll sort the old bugger out," he was saying, and all that kind of stuff. So I thought I'd hang around and see how he got on. When he came out, he looked worse than me!'

THE CATHOLIC MAFIA

Amid much loose talk of a 'Catholic mafia' in Manchester, Busby and Paddy McGrath loomed large. And no wonder; although United's identification with the Catholic community predated Busby and Louis Edwards, as the contribution of Louis Rocca emphasised, priests had been abundant in the scouting boom that followed Busby's appointment and their dark garb now flecked the main stand.

Not that they followed a Catholic club – chairman Hardman was a Methodist – or watched an overwhelmingly Catholic team. When United played, one Ulster Protestant, Gregg, stood shoulder to shoulder with Crerand while another, Best, strove alongside Stiles. Not that the priests ever had watched a Catholic team. Less than a year before the Munich crash a reporter for *World Sports* magazine had raised the subject with Busby and been told with a sigh: 'It's one of those stories that get around.' United had just drawn at home to Aston Villa and the manager, picking up the team-sheet, assured the reporter only three Catholics had played (two would have been Whelan and McGuinness, the other a question of guesswork). On other occasions Busby had insisted: 'The only person who has to hold a cross in my team is the goalkeeper.'

True, Busby was a Catholic and so was Jimmy Murphy but their bond with active men of other churches, the Anglican Tom Curry and Methodist lay preacher Bert Whalley, could hardly have been more intimate. Busby had been as friendly with Willie Satinoff as Louis Edwards before Munich. Busby's Catholicism, however powerful, was in the spirit instilled by his mother.

And yet the story was often told of how, in the Old Trafford boardroom, he had dropped to his knees to kiss the ring on the hand of the Bishop of Salford. A lot of stories were told. About the 'miraculous medals', for instance. Apparently, Joe Armstrong had bought quite a few of these cheap items of Catholic jewellery – officially known as Medals of the Immaculate Conception – on a trip to Rome and would give them to the families of Catholic youngsters. As any uncle might.

Busby was nevertheless an enthusiastic member of the Catenian Association, a sort of Catholic freemasonry. He and Jean did some of their abundant charity work with the Catenians and McGrath and his wife, although not a Catholic herself, often joined them. 'Matt and Paddy were bosom buddies,' said Crerand, who was to become another member of the circle. 'Paddy was a great fellow. A mad United fan, kind to a lot of the players. But you wouldn't want to cross him.'

McGrath's reputation lent the word 'mafia' an amusing edge, for Mancunians of all persuasions enjoyed the whispers of how he had seen off London gangsters. One tale had him waiting in the lounge of the Midland Hotel for a summit meeting with the Krays, who were on the train north. A waiter gestured towards a bulge in McGrath's pocket and, after being succinctly told to go away, disclosed that all those serving the guests that day, including himself, were in fact discreetly armed policemen.

Other accounts of the contemporary underworld stated that London gangs had little interest in the provinces and that Manchester was not the only city with myths of defiance. But without a spark of fire, could there have been the smoke that surrounded McGrath and Owen Ratcliffe, who were even supposed to have ventured south and invested in a club in a grimy London suburb where a man was shot dead? Perhaps; others from Manchester were said to have funded that club. Perhaps not. 'He had matured by the time I got to know him,' said Martin Edwards, 'but, when younger, Paddy had been a bit of a handful.'

The best of the stories was set in his maturity, in the Cromford Club. It was the one about *Danger Man*. The star of this television series was Britain's most popular actor of the time, the handsome – almost impossibly blue-eyed – Patrick McGoohan, who happened to be in a play in Manchester. He was staying at the Midland and, having asked the concierge to recommend a pleasant place to spend an evening off, was directed to McGrath's establishment in Cromford Court, a short cab ride away. When he arrived, he was recognised by Jean McGrath – 'a lovely woman,' said Crerand, 'a darling, very posh' – who told the head waiter: 'I'll deal with this one.'

Martin Edwards took up the story. 'So she walks him to a table and asks, "What would you like to drink, Mr McGoohan?" and he says, "If you'll join me, I'll have a bottle of champagne." So she calls over a waiter and orders a bottle and two glasses. Paddy is in the club and, after a while, sees Jean drinking with this guy. So he says to someone, "Who the hell is that with Jean?" And is told, "That's Patrick McGoohan." And Paddy says, "Who's Patrick McGoohan?"

'"Danger Man."

'"Who's Danger Man?"

'"He's a character on the TV."

'So McGoohan and Jean carry on drinking and the next thing is Jean calls over the waiter and orders a second bottle. By now Paddy's had enough. He storms over and says to Patrick McGoohan, "Are you Danger Man?" And McGoohan smiles and says, "Yes," and Paddy says, "Well, you've never been in so much fucking danger in your life."'

It would have been entirely innocent because Patrick McGoohan was not only happily married to the actress Jill Drummond for 58 years to his death in 2009 but a Catholic said to have rejected the opportunity to play James Bond on moral grounds because it entailed the sort of extramarital relations from which Danger Man, aka John Drake, always politely walked away. But Busby loved such stories. They were of his Manchester.

JUST SEVENTEEN

Whatever the remaining tensions in Busby's first team, there was as much fun as ever among Murphy's youths. Murphy had gathered quite a group. To Best could be added two more wingers: John Aston, son of the 1948 left-back now coaching the youths, and Willie Anderson from Merseyside. There was a goalkeeper from Southport, Jimmy Rimmer. John Fitzpatrick and Jimmy Ryan from Scotland in midfield. Bobby Noble at left-back.

The centre-forward David Sadler enjoyed the quickest promotion. Only the previous autumn Murphy had driven Busby through Kent hop fields to the village of Yalding, where Sadler's father ran a pub. As they walked in, word spread. 'Matt was very famous,' said Sadler. 'So there were people around as they sat in the bar with my father. I wasn't involved really. I'd been to Manchester. They wanted me. I think my father got a few quid out of it before I was called in to sign the forms.

'The idea was that I would continue to play for Maidstone United in the Isthmian League and work in a bank until my 17th birthday, when I'd go to Manchester. It was agreed. Matt and

Jimmy left the pub. But their car wouldn't start, which was a bit embarrassing. This man everyone had seen on the television – and his car wouldn't start! There were no end of helpers and eventually, after about an hour, they got off.

'At United, my aim was to get a game for the reserves. I'd had only one when the 1963/64 season started and Matt brought me in for David Herd. That was the real surprise, because Harry Gregg was a better goalkeeper than David Gaskell – there was no real comparison – and Ian Moir and Phil Chisnall had been at the club longer than me. But the three of us youngsters were to play, more or less, for the first dozen matches.'

By which time United were on top of the League and Best, also 17, had been blooded. Earlier than Busby had envisaged. When Moir pulled out of a match at Old Trafford, Best made a single appearance, to the memorable discomfort of the West Bromwich full-back Graham Williams. Sadler drove the only goal.

Sadler and Best were room-mates in Aycliffe Avenue. 'When the goalkeeper Briggs was let go,' said Sadler, 'George told me about the spare bed. Because I was on my own not far away, I jumped at the chance and went to join him with Mrs Fullaway. When you signed pro, you were given a players' booklet. A red book with pages of rules and regulations that Manchester United players were expected to live by. No smoking on match days. And, if the match was on a Saturday, you weren't allowed to go out after Wednesday, so you couldn't even go to the pictures on Thursday [Busby had arranged that the red book could be used for free cinema admission]. And of course Bestie did go out. He was better if he went out. He used to go to a bowling alley near the cricket ground where they had a VIP area. Sometimes he'd go on a Thursday or even a Friday. Matt would ask me and I'd say, "I'm sure he was in the house, Boss." But he was a good young professional, George, a phenomenal trainer. As he put on muscle, he became very strong and once he'd got back in the team, just after Christmas, he was unstoppable.'

Sadler, by contrast, was to become marginal for a couple of years, until Busby and Murphy found the position in which he would represent England. But he did share in a youth-team winter that young John Aston, for one, would always cherish.

Busby had been reluctant at first to sign Aston, telling his father he was too small. Other clubs made offers, but his father asked him to be patient. After six months he had a trial at The Cliff and Busby told his father: 'John is not good enough for us.' Then he was offered a ground-staff apprenticeship by Everton. His father went to Busby yet again and now the manager expressed surprise that Aston was still only 15. 'I thought he was 17,' said Busby, reaching for apprenticeship forms. 'I don't know if he really thought that,' said Aston. 'But that's how I ended up at United.

'It was truly amazing to be at Busby's club. But not in the way you might think. They were so tight it wasn't true. All the time I was there. Eventually, when I joined Luton, they told me to go to the boot room and choose my boots. I liked Adidas. So they gave me two pairs. I'd never had two pairs of boots!

'Not once, in ten years at United, did I train in boots. They had things called "dabs" – hockey boots that came over your ankles, with bars on the soles. Sometimes there were "flats" [plimsoles or pumps for harder surfaces]. A lot of times we trained on the Manchester Ship Canal company's pitches. They were about a mile away. And there were three ways of getting there. One was by car – head towards Sale, turn right at the lights – but only the senior players could drive and they weren't allowed to take a kid. Or you could run through the streets, but that was a roundabout route. So the best way was to climb over the fence behind the main stand and run along the railway line.

'God knows what health-and-safety would have said. Here were lads like George Best, David Sadler and me, running along the track. Every now and again you'd hear noise on the rails and someone would shout "Train!" and everybody would press themselves against the banking while it went past.

'When you trained at The Cliff, there were two dressing rooms. Both had a bath, but one didn't have tiles on the bottom. You started in that one and hoped to progress to the other in your second year. There used to be two groundsmen – Joe Royle at Old Trafford and his brother Dave at The Cliff. On a Monday morning, Dave would come in with the dabs, all tied together, all different sizes, and throw them on the ground. And he'd bring in the kit. Shirts, shorts, socks.

'The training shirts were never numbered. The club used Umbro but were so tight with money they got seconds. And, as the shirts got torn or wore out, they'd sew bits together. Without bothering about the colours. So you could get a maroon shirt with a blue sleeve for one arm and green and white for the other. But it didn't end there.

'Because there were no numbers, it was first come, best dressed. If you got there early, you could perhaps find the shirt you'd worn the previous day. But people usually ended up wearing shirts or shorts that other lads had been sweating in. The kit was washed once a week. It was fresh on Monday and by Friday it stank.

'We all suffered from what we called "sweat rash". Big red patches all over your skin. Lots of us got it on the arms. But there was a cure. There was a kind of medical bed in the dressing room. Nobody ever lay on it. Mainly it was used as a table for the tea and sandwiches on match days. But there was a large brown bottle that my dad told us about and it contained gentian violet. When you unscrewed the top, there was a little brush you could stick into the liquid and you'd lie on the bed and paint yourself with it.'

And did it make you better?

'It made you sting.'

Aston smiled. 'And *that* was Manchester United.

'But the strange thing is ...

'It was the era when the Beatles were starting and in all the game of football there wasn't a happier dressing room – I don't care how successful any of them were – than us in our communal bath. We'd sit in it after training. And somebody would start ...

'"*Well, she was just seventeen ...* "'

And all the rest would join in ...

'"*If you know what I mean*

'"*And the way she looked ...* "'

From 'I Saw Her Standing There', the lads would go through a repertoire of Beatles songs until the bath water became too cold and they dressed. Next, after lunch, would be the race to clean Denis Law's boots at Old Trafford. 'Everyone wanted to clean them,' said Jimmy Ryan. 'He'd had them specially made in Italy and they were quite something – all black. Denis was very friendly. They all were, I think, the senior players, but I especially remember Denis because he saw me having treatment once and laughed when I said I'd "*hurtit*" my ankle. He was always making fun of my accent.'

Ryan was from the west of Scotland: mining country, far from Aberdeen. He had been spotted by Busby's half-brother Jimmy Mathie. 'I remember this guy coming over and saying he was a scout from Manchester United and thinking he was pulling my leg.' But Ryan was offered a two-week trial, which Busby extended to a month after asking if he could afford the time off school; he remembered being asked twice because Busby, presumably aware from Mathie that his mother thought him university material, wanted to be sure.

While staying at Mrs Wilde's in Stretford he met Willie Anderson and a lifelong friendship began with evening strolls to a park near their digs where there was pitch-and-putt. 'And usually plenty of nice-looking girls, which turned out to be Willie's main reason for going – and became mine. There we met John Fitzpatrick, and sometimes George would come over from Chorlton and we'd go round the pitch-and-putt.' While keeping an eye on the girls. Ryan would also accompany Best on the odd night out. 'We were quite close friends. Quite similar in that we were both very, very shy and – I know it sounds strange to say this about George now – didn't drink alcohol.'

ETHICAL QUESTIONS

After the youthful promise of their start to 1963/64, United lay third when, in November, they visited Joe Mercer's relegation-fearing Aston Villa and were embarrassingly defeated. Villa already led by two when Denis Law, reacting angrily to a challenge by Alan Deakin, was sent off in the 33rd minute and it ended 4–0 with United down to sixth.

At home to Liverpool, they lost Gregg, his collar-bone fractured in a collision with the giant Ron Yeats, who went on to head the only goal past the emergency goalkeeper Herd. Bill Shankly, barely 18 months after guiding Liverpool out of the Second Division, had them vying for supremacy in the First. No sooner had Cullis been bettered – Wolves were to slip from fifth to sixteenth that season and eventually be relegated – than another friend had risen to challenge Busby. A friend, moreover, whom he had coaxed out of leaving Anfield in exasperation.

Although Law incurred a 28-day suspension, Busby was not alone in admiring his farewell performance. With four Old Trafford goals, Law departed for what was to become an annual festive trip home to Aberdeen, and even visiting Stoke players, who included Dennis Viollet, joined in the ovation. Law had 20 goals in as many matches. And this rate was to accelerate slightly.

Just as the title seemed feasible, however, United took another 4–0 battering at Everton. And, on Boxing Day, lost 6–1 at Burnley, where now Crerand was sent off. Burnley were due at Old Trafford in two days. Busby had to do something. Tighten the defence? Of course not. In came two teenage wingers and, while the 16-year-old debutant Anderson did well enough, Best thrilled the crowd, not least in coolly giving United a 3–0 interval lead.

Equally important had been Busby's switching of Charlton from the left wing to the deeper, more central, role in which he would do so much for club and country. He had become a star on the wing but never truly enjoyed the wait for the ball (Best, being Best, would wander in search of it). With their reshaped attack, United completed a 5–1 victory over the side who had humiliated them at Turf Moor.

An FA Cup trip to Southampton brought, with victory, a whiff of shame. Hurling toilet rolls at Wembley had been one thing; wreaking havoc on the fixtures and fittings of a train, as United followers did on the way back from the south coast, was quite another. Hooliganism was growing and those who detected a correlation between trouble on and off the pitch had the evidence of spectator scuffles after Law had been sent off at Villa Park. Now, just a few weeks later, the blight was to visit the Old Trafford terraces when Birmingham surprisingly won and, although no one was sent off that day, United's disciplinary record had suddenly become a threat to their manager's reputation.

In the first 15 years of Busby's career, three United players had been dismissed (Chilton, Cockburn and Mark Pearson). Now three had walked in as many months: Herd in the Cup Winners' Cup in Holland, Law and Crerand. There were circumstances to be assessed – referees appeared to become less tolerant of a raised arm, even if scattergun tackling was still allowed – and coincidence too. All three culprits were bought players, as opposed to home-reared under the Busby code of ethics. On the other hand, who had bought them?

In the bowels of Maine Road after his first derby, Crerand had decked David Wagstaffe – and offered the same to a City employee who remonstrated. At Burnley, his offence had been to elbow Ian Towers and, while Busby would never publicly have condoned such a breach of civilisation's boundaries, Crerand later confessed with a broad grin: 'By and large Matt's instruction was "Go out and play", but to me it was "Let him know you're there."' Crerand chose to interpret his instruction liberally and was to incur further dismissals in each of the next two seasons, completing the first unwelcome hat-trick in United's history.

United were fighting on the domestic and European fronts. They were League contenders – even if the smart money was on Shankly's Liverpool with their outstanding defence – and in the last eight of the Cup Winners' Cup, having easily overcome Willem II despite Herd's walk for retaliation in Tilburg and gone on to knock out the holders, a diminished Tottenham. Next they would face Sporting Lisbon.

In the FA Cup a three-match epic with Sunderland left Busby's men in the semi-finals. But at Hillsborough they were beaten 3–1 by a West Ham for whom Bobby Moore was magnificent; he was to be Footballer of the Year and lift the Cup after a final against Preston, captained by Nobby Lawton and with Alex Dawson in their side.

United flew to Lisbon with the comfort of a 4–1 lead but unprepared for the anger of Sporting, who had conceded a debatable penalty at Old Trafford, and were thrashed 5–0. Law, asked to confirm Busby's fury, replied: 'I don't know. I was under the dressing-room table.' Three days later, at Tottenham, Nobby Stiles had replaced Maurice Setters. To borrow John Giles's phrase, Busby had 'taken against' Setters, become tired of the sound of his dressing-room voice. Phil Chisnall was to play for United only once more. But whatever Busby said to the players in Lisbon must have worked because at White Hart Lane they revived title hopes with a superb 3–2 win.

Anfield was where hope died. Gregg was beaten three times and Busby's men had no reply except the petulance that got Law's name in the book. The Kop gleefully sang Beatles songs. Liverpool would be champions. If Busby wanted to regain English football's heavyweight title, he would henceforth have to take on Shankly. He would also have to deal with Don Revie's Leeds, whom Johnny Giles had helped to win the championship of the Second Division.

At least, by finishing second, United qualified for Europe; they would play in the Fairs Cup. So Law would have to wait for a stage befitting the European Footballer of the Year. *France Football*'s judges found him irresistible over the calendar year 1964, preferring him even to Luis Suárez, midfield maestro of the European champions Inter. But for injury and suspension, Law would have brought up a half-century of goals for United in 1963/64; as it was, he claimed 46 in 41 matches at home and abroad. Plus 11 in 7 for Scotland.

If Bobby Charlton continued to flourish, and young George Best to tap his limitless potential, United would have three world-class players. They could dream.

NOT A TRACE OF RANCOUR

The view that Busby didn't like his surplus players going to competitors had been challenged when Phil Chisnall was allowed to join Liverpool. This brought in £25,000. Mark Pearson had gone to Sheffield Wednesday for £20,000. To that could be added the Giles money, £10,000 from Charlton for Frank Haydock and £8,000 from Wrexham for Sammy McMillan. Dennis Walker went to York. So that was nearly £100,000 in. Expenditure crept just over £90,000 when, in readiness for the next season, Busby paid £56,000 for a key member of Burnley's title-winning team, John Connelly.

This was good news for everybody except Willie Anderson, Ian Moir or any other aspirant to the United right wing. Connelly was quick, could cross with either foot and scored a lot of goals. He was also an extremely pleasant man.

There was further reason for Busby to be cheerful in the retrieval of the Youth Cup. On 27 April 1964, at Swindon in the first leg of the final, Don Rogers put the home side ahead. Best equalised. On the 29th, in Belfast, Best made his second full international appearance as Northern Ireland beat Uruguay 3–0. On the 30th, he was back at Old Trafford with the youth team, dazzling in a 5–2 aggregate triumph in front of nearly 26,000.

David Sadler, who scored a hat-trick that evening, said: 'By then with George it was like putting a superstar in with ten-year-olds. It was ridiculous. Of my three goals, the farthest-out was from five yards because George was going past everybody and crossing or shooting and all I had to do was put my foot out.'

The team also included Rimmer, Noble, Fitzpatrick, young Aston and Albert Kinsey. All were to make the first team along with Ryan. 'It was certainly the best generation since Munich,' said Sadler. 'You can judge that from the number of appearances we made. And it could have been a lot more. But for injury, Bobby Noble would have been England's left-back for ten years. So the youth system was back in good order.'

Neither Alan Wardle nor Barry Fry made the cut that summer.
'Of course,' said Wardle, 'all the big clubs came in for me ...
Crewe, Doncaster and an Australian club! In the end I signed
for Altrincham in the Cheshire League and went into stationery
and office equipment. With Matt's blessing, I'd been learning the
business in the afternoons. With my contacts at United, like Les
Olive, I was soon able to start supplying the club.' So it rang true,
in his case, this Busby concept of football club as family? Wardle
smiled. 'More than. I was released in 1964 and, when we opened
our shop in St Peter's Square, by now it was 1977. I thought it
would be fantastic if he could perform the opening ceremony. He
was only too happy to help.'

Nor did Barry Fry leave with a trace of rancour. He explained: 'One
day, I'd gone to Old Trafford for some treatment from Ted Dalton.
Came out and stood at the bus stop. The Boss drove by, stopped,
reversed, wound the window down and said, "Where are you going,
Barry?" I said, "Manchester Racecourse." Because everyone from the
club had been invited. "So am I," he said. "Jump in."

'On the way he asked if I liked gambling. So I went, "Yeah, after
training we like to jump in someone's car and go to Haydock or
Chester races." And he went, "Oh – and what do you do then – go
home?" And I went, "Nah, I might go the White City dogs, Belle
Vue dogs, Salford dogs ... " "And then you go home?" "Well,
sometimes I go to a nightclub and play roulette ... " By now he's
nearly crashing the car. But I'm only telling the truth. First couple
of years, I'd hardly gone out of the house and done really well,
progressed to the reserves and been praised in print by Matt, who
said I could be the north's answer to Jimmy Greaves. But then I'd
got interested in other things.

'So he went on. "And what about the drink, Barry?" I said,
"I love it, Boss – brown ale, gin and tonic, rum and black ... "
And then he says, "What about the women?" And I say, "Boss, I
come from a little town called Bedford – I can't believe how many
women there are in this great big city ... " And he looked at me and
said, "Son, I'm going to give you a bit of advice now." "Yes, Boss."
And he said, "Moderation in all things." And it was the best advice
I ever had. And I took no fucking notice.

'When my contract was up, he called me in and said, "Barry,
I think you've been gambling too much, drinking too much and
chasing women too much. Consequently you've gone backwards.

But there a couple of clubs who want you and I'm going to give you a free transfer. I've arranged for you to see Bill Ridding at Bolton." I played three games on the trot there. We played in Cardiff and John Charles, one of my favourites, played centre-half to combat Wyn Davies's aerial ability – they both missed the ball and I scored. That was my only goal in League football.'

Fry then suffered from blood clotting and was playing non-League when, about five years after leaving United, he was approached by a newspaper. 'They wanted me to say Matt Busby had taken me away from home and not looked after me and that's why I'd not made it as a player. "No," I said, "that's a load of bollocks, mate. I never made it because of Barry Fry." And that's the truth.'

WINNING THE MARATHON

From Shamrock Rovers in the summer of 1964 came Pat Dunne, a 21-year-goalkeeper. He cost £10,500 and was not expected to make the first team so soon; after only five reserve matches he replaced Gaskell, who had let Johnny Haynes score a soft winner at Fulham, and he was to stay in for the rest of a momentous season.

At one stage Busby's team had taken 27 points from a possible 28. And scored 36 goals. But the key statistic was the concession of just 8 by a defence once thought vulnerable; such was the effect of Stiles at 22.

Busby had sold Setters to Stoke for £30,000 because Stiles would be his defensive wing-half, the man to help Bill Foulkes. Pat Dunne was in goal, the full-backs Brennan and Tony Dunne completing what was beginning to look like a back four. Crerand and Charlton were in midfield, Connelly and Best on the wings and Law and Herd up front. It was, more or less, the 4–2–4 system favoured by Brazil.

In discussing Alf Ramey's England in *My Life in Football*, published in 1973, Busby was to deplore the development of 4–3–3. He recalled that, when Ramsey had taken charge, he had consulted club managers, Busby included, and 'one of the things he said was that he could not find wingers to his satisfaction'. Busby hadn't liked the sound of that. To him, wingers were fundamental to good football, and United were to demonstrate this during the long season of renewed glory that was 1964/65.

Connelly came into the side like the answer to a puzzle. With him on one flank and Best on the other, lesser teams were overrun. Wolves, lying bottom a month after stunning the game by dismissing Stan Cullis – 'it has knocked me sick of human nature,' Busby wrote to him – were beaten 4–2 at Molineux and a week later Aston Villa took a 7–0 thrashing at Old Trafford. Amid the carnage of these defences Law plundered six goals.

But as the shops began to hint at Christmas it was time for Law to stray. At Blackpool, where a 19-year-old Alan Ball harassed him, he was deemed to have sworn at the referee, Peter Rhodes, and sent off. After the month's suspension the previous season, there was talk of six weeks and Busby decided to appeal.

A personal hearing was requested and Crerand went to Sheffield with Law and Busby to give evidence to the FA's disciplinary committee. Crerand laughed at the recollection of Busby driving across the Pennines. 'Matt was the worst person you could have at the wheel. How he'd passed his test I'll never know – he was a useless driver. When Denis and I got out of the car at Sheffield, we were white as sheets. Matt was to plead the case to the FA and I was to act as a witness on Denis's behalf, saying he hadn't actually sworn at the referee. Denis had called him a silly cunt and was arguing, with my support, that he'd called him a silly coot. Of course it was laughed out of court and Denis got 28 days again. And we had to face the drive home with Matt. Terrifying. We sat in the back with our eyes closed and didn't say a word all the way home.'

Although Law's Christmas breaks amused others, they cost him a lot of money because FA regulations forbade payment of suspended players. So he could have done with a win bonus before heading for Aberdeen. Instead, a sequence of eight League victories ended with defeat at home to Leeds, for whom Giles played. In an intensely competitive race with Leeds and Tommy Docherty's Chelsea, Busby's team slipped to third.

The FA Cup intrigued Old Trafford, big crowds watching wins over Stoke and Burnley. There was a more modest gathering for the Fairs Cup match against Borussia Dortmund, whose hopes had been crushed by a 6–1 defeat on their own ground, featuring a Charlton hat-trick and a Best solo, that Busby rated among his club's finest performances in Europe. United were next paired with English opposition in Everton and, after a draw at home, impressively prevailed at Goodison, Connelly making the difference.

Next, they went to Tottenham, whose new signing Alan Gilzean remembered Busby approaching him outside the ground beforehand. 'He congratulated me on my move from Dundee,' said Gilzean, 'and said he hoped I'd have many happy years in England. I've never forgotten the presence he had. I never had those vibes off anyone else in football.' Although United lost 1–0 that day, they redelivered championship credentials with a stylish 4–0 home victory over Docherty's leaders; Best began the rout with an early lob.

Stiles, meanwhile, was given an international debut against Scotland in the defensive midfield role; Alf Ramsey prickled when journalists called him a 'spoiler', though Stiles was to be called worse. However cerebral Busby and Don Revie had been as players, their teams were often up for a scrap. In their FA Cup semi-final, for example. Bobby Charlton saw his brother Jack clash with Law in a scoreless match that amazingly ended with 22 players on the field. Bremner won the replay with a header from Giles's free-kick. Giles would return to Wembley.

It was during that season that Giles learned to treat football like a battleground. His leg had been broken during his time at United. Now, when Leeds went to Chelsea, a lunge from Eddie McCreadie damaged his knee ligaments. 'I came in from the right wing and released the ball to Norman Hunter and saw him shoot before Eddie did me. I thought, "That is it. *That-is-it*."'

No more Mr Nice Guy?

'It wasn't going to work. I had to be nasty because otherwise I'd get a name as someone who would chuck it. Now, whatever anyone was going to give me, I'd give them more. Just to be able to play. I had to do it. The climate of the times was deadly and there was no protection from referees. If I wanted to use my skill, there was no option.'

When United scored against Leeds, it was at the fourth attempt. Connelly did it at Elland Road. Perhaps Revie's men had a little of the Cup final, which they would lose to Liverpool, on their minds. But this narrow defeat cost them the League. United marched on, again benefiting from Wembley's distractions when Liverpool visited Old Trafford without key men – Chisnall came into Shankly's side – and were beaten 3–0. Busby's men could clinch the title in their next match, just two days hence, at home to Arsenal.

The reception for Chisnall, incidentally, had been warm. In later years, a transfer between Manchester United and Liverpool would become politically unthinkable, but the East Lancashire Road was almost a well-worn path then. Nine players had taken it, including Allenby Chilton, whom Louis Rocca had lured from Anfield before he turned professional. Chisnall had been the second to move in the opposite direction with Busby's blessing, after Tommy McNulty in 1954.

'Back then it was just a footballer moving from one club to another,' said Chisnall, who noted the difference in the management teams; while at United it had been the reserved Busby in charge and his assistant the passionate Murphy, at Liverpool the boss Shankly was the fanatical Celt and Paisley a calming influence. Chisnall was never to live up to Shankly's hopes. He spent most of his three seasons at Anfield in the reserves before moving to Southend and ending his career at Stockport.

Only Leeds, who were at Birmingham on what proved a mercurial Monday night, could stop United now and when Revie's men went three goals down Old Trafford celebrated. Then Leeds scored three times. But United led Arsenal through an early goal from Best and that would still do the trick. The ground erupted as Law scored, and again when he responded to George Eastham's reduction of the deficit. Final score: 3–1. United had the title on goal average. Their first since Munich. Busby had his fourth. And dear Stan Cullis, on three, would never bridge the gap.

At the start of the season, when Wolves had been bottom without a point, Cullis had felt unwell. The club doctor had sent him for a few weeks by the sea at Eastbourne and, when he returned, the new chairman John Ireland said the board had lost confidence in him; would he resign on health grounds? He declined and was sacked. With Wolves at home to West Ham that night, Cullis took charge for one more match and they won 4–3. They were seldom to win again and, under Andy Beattie, go down.

Among countless letters Cullis received was Busby's, which asked: 'How could people do such a thing after you giving them your life's blood? What more success can they get than what you've given them? What loyalty have they shown you after the loyalty you have given them in every way?'

This left two of Busby's wartime pals out of work, for Villa had parted company with Joe Mercer after his recovery from a stress-related stroke. With the pressure of management taking such toll, it was all the more impressive that Busby, even after Munich, could absorb so much. This was a very strong man.

Nor were his responsibilities fulfilled for the summer. Fourteen days after United's domestic season had ended with a meaningless defeat at Villa Park, they resumed their European campaign. They were fortunate a 5–0 win in Strasbourg could be achieved at little more than testimonial pace and the return at Old Trafford, though scoreless, was just as one-sided. The semi-final against Ferencváros began on the last day of May. United won 3–2 at home, but ill temper carried over to Budapest, where Crerand and Pál Orosz fought and were sent off. Because the Hungarians won 1–0 and away goals made no difference, a third match was necessary. The toss of a coin gave Ferencváros home advantage.

Harold Hardman died before it took place on 16 June 1965. He was 83. United lost 2–1 under the new chairmanship of Louis Edwards, who, the previous season, had quietly obtained a majority of the club's shares by doing a deal with Alan Gibson. His friend Denzil Haroun had been added to the board. All to Busby's trusting approval.

This season had seen not only Setters but three others depart as Busby, reassured by the youth system, kept raising money. Albert Quixall had joined Oldham of the Third Division for £7,000, Jimmy Nicholson gone to Second Division Huddersfield for £7,500 and Ian Moir remained at the top level with Blackpool, who paid £30,000. With the Setters fee, sales added up to £74,500 and profit on the transfer account mattered because United were to develop their stadium. For Busby, knowing he need not buy for a while, the time was right, and it coincided with the choice of grounds for the World Cup.

The plan Louis Edwards presented gave Old Trafford the edge over Maine Road. He and Busby had been impressed with private boxes in the cantilever grandstand at Manchester Racecourse. So Edwards had asked the architects Mather and Nutter, who had worked on the racecourse stand as well as a variety of Catholic buildings in the Manchester area, to design a two-tier structure incorporating 34 'executive boxes' opposite the main stand. It would also be cantilevered, with no struts to interrupt the view of the spectators, up to 10,500 of whom would be seated with 10,000 standing in the paddock below. It would curve into the corners, facilitating further work at each end of the ground as and when further finance came through from Bill Burke's Manchester United Development Association, whose lottery, like several other sporting fund-raisers of the time, was doing splendid business.

First to lease on a box was Paddy McGrath. For £300 a season, he would entertain his friends. From their comfortable seats on the halfway line – the boxes nearer the corner flags cost £250 – they would gaze through picture windows as Best began his mazy runs, maybe even hear the excited growls of the masses. The stand would open early in the next season. So what if it put the club back into debt for a while? This was the way forward. This would be a bit more like the Real Madrid spectator experience.

Busby was cheered by the arrival in Manchester of Joe Mercer, who, against medical advice, had taken the City job. The Mercers, moreover, moved into a house in St Werburgh's Road, just round the corner from the Busbys; often the four of them would go out to dine on a Saturday night, for in those days there was never a problem with the managers of United and City being seen socialising, even if a little edge would soon be added to relationships between the respective supporters.

Malcolm Allison would be a factor in that. Mercer, accepting the need for a young and energetic assistant, had gone to Plymouth Argyle for Allison, whom he had met on FA coaching courses at Lilleshall and monitored at Bath City. 'Big Mal' was an extremely handsome and far from shy fellow in his late thirties whose professed boyhood affection for City must have dated from the Wembley sides for which Busby played. Now, soon after his arrival in Manchester, he found himself in the company of the great man at some delayed celebration of United's title triumph.

Busby, ever the diplomat, would never have crowed – in the season before Mercer and Allison arrived, City had finished eleventh in the Second Division – and instead told Allison: 'I believe there is room for two First Division clubs in Manchester.'

Allison, with his film-star looks, never had much difficulty in summoning dramatic force. He may have spoken *sotto voce*, or even left the words unsaid, but he remembered them as: 'Yes, baby, you're going to get another team in town – and a real one.' Later, Allison came across the equally forthright Crerand and, when teased that City would never lure more than 30,000 into Maine

Road, demanded the Scot put some money where his mouth was. And then informed Sandy Busby: 'Your father has got a 20-year start but I'll pass him in time.'

Under Mercer's guidance he was not to dally in fleshing out the boast; within a year City would be back in the First Division as champions of the Second, transformed.

CHAPTER TWELVE

THE 1968 TEAM: FULFILMENT OF A DREAM

1966 AND ALL THAT

Early in the 1965/66 season, which would culminate with a World Cup in England, Busby paid one of his frequent visits to Tommy Appleby's Opera House and, with another celebrity – Violet Carson, who played Ena Sharples in *Coronation Street* – was introduced to Marlene Dietrich. He would have welcomed the diversion of a night out with Jean in the presence of such an enduringly glamorous entertainer, for his team had taken a turn for the worse.

Law, now sharing the captaincy with Cantwell, had limped out of the Charity Shield draw with Liverpool and missed the first two of a dozen League matches from which only four wins were obtained. United lay 13th after a 5–1 defeat at Tottenham during which Jimmy Greaves slalomed through Busby's defence to score an immortal goal. Again Law had to go off; he was replaced by John Fitzpatrick, who thus became the club's first League substitute.

At least in Europe they progressed, seeing off the flimsy challenge of HJK Helsinki and beating Vorwärts both at home and in East Germany to earn an evocative quarter-final against Benfica.

Amid signs of improvement, Gregg recovered the goalkeeper's jersey from Pat Dunne, only to be sent off at Blackburn for kicking Mike England, which almost certainly cost United a point as the stand-in Herd was beaten twice late on. But by Christmas they had risen to third by reversing the Spurs result at Old Trafford. With Busby in Portugal watching Benfica, Jimmy Murphy oversaw the five goals. Law, who got two, said Murphy reminded him of Bill Shankly. 'Except that he [Murphy] was more fearsome.' Popular nonetheless. 'We sometimes played better for Jimmy than for Matt.'

On the first day of 1966 some 10,000 milled outside a bulging Anfield but, after Law had scored early, Tommy Smith equalised and Gordon Milne's late winner gave a renascent Liverpool the confidence to accelerate away with the title. Realistic supporters joined Busby in looking to the European and FA Cups.

Eusébio versus Stiles proved an entertainment in itself at Old Trafford, and for star quality Charlton matched the maestro from Mozambique who had succeeded Law as European Footballer of the Year. But United, 3–1 up with 20 minutes left, were breached by a header from the giant José Torres that many felt Gregg should have reached.

Benfica had never lost a European match in Lisbon, a city of which Busby's men had uncomfortable memories. The stage was set for Eusébio. But Best stole the leading role. He scored with a header as if Benfica had no goalkeeper, then ran through and despatched a low drive as if they had no defence, then left Connelly with little more than a tap-in. It would have been quite a night's work. Yet only 16 minutes had gone.

United did give Benfica a goal when Brennan inadvertently lobbed Gregg but Crerand and Charlton, the latter with audacious skill, made it a 5–1 rout, to be remembered as one of the great performances by a British club in Europe. In the dark and feline Best something more than a star was born; the aftermath was akin to Beatlemania.

The semi-final draw sent them back to Belgrade, where Roger Byrne had sung 'We'll Meet Again', to take on Partizan. A mundane United lost 2–0, Gregg and his defenders taking the blame. Now it was up to the attack that had dazzled all Europe. Except that Best had looked unfit; in truth he needed a knee operation which Busby had asked him to delay while United remained in Europe.

With nothing to lose in the League, Busby also left Law, Charlton and others out of the match preceding the second leg, a defeat at Sheffield United. But rest would not cure the damage Best had exacerbated in Belgrade. While he went into hospital, Willie Anderson was handed the unenviable task of filling his shirt at Old Trafford.

It was tense and noisy but goals would not come and eventually tempers were lost, Stiles punching Ljubomir Mihajlović, which began a brawl after which Crerand and Jovan Miladinović were sent off. Stiles did find the net soon afterwards but it was a gloomy Busby who joined his players in the dressing room, piercing the silence with uncharacteristic fatalism: would the European quest ever be completed? Crerand told him not to worry and they all went to the banquet. At the Midland, Crerand sought out Mihajlović, who, when angrily blamed for the Scot's dismissal, wisely hurried away. Normality was restored.

While Partizan progressed to the final, which they would lose to Real Madrid, United had a couple of days to patch themselves up for the FA Cup semi-final against Everton at Burnden Park. Once again they did plenty of attacking but the only goal came from Colin Harvey. United would win nothing.

During the remainder of the League season, there was serious crowd trouble amid a 3–2 defeat at West Ham in which Geoff Hurst, watched by Alf Ramsey, scored twice. The greatest glory of English football and the phenomenon that would bring its most profound shame were converging.

At West Bromwich, with Charlton, Stiles and Connelly on international duty – Yugoslavia became the third of seven countries to lose to England in the World Cup build-up – there was a debut on the right wing for Jimmy Ryan, who stayed in the side with John Aston on the other flank to the exclusion of Connelly, even though the senior man was a current international looking forward to the tournament of a lifetime.

'There was a lot going on in my life,' Ryan recalled. 'The Beatles and Bob Dylan were competing with football in my mind. One night I went to see the infamous Dylan concert at the Free Trade Hall when he got booed for playing the electric guitar. But I couldn't get a ticket, so I stood outside – I could just about hear the music. And then a television crew came along and started interviewing people. And this guy was saying Dylan had "sold out". And I was swearing at the guy! It was that kind of thing that stopped me from being a better player. Too often, my priorities were elsewhere.'

Two days after the Dylan concert, nonetheless, Ryan scored at home to Aston Villa. As if to dissipate the end-of-season mood that had brought a mere 23,000 to Old Trafford, United won 6–1 with a drive from Charlton, one of many that would be described as 'piledrivers', rounding things off. Charlton was honoured as Footballer of the Year, the first from United since Johnny Carey in 1949, before a superb Cup final in which Everton came from behind to beat Sheffield Wednesday 3–2.

In the next season there would be derbies against Mercer and Allison for Busby to relish but no reunion with Cullis, who, after a few months writing for the *News of the World*, had succumbed to the long-time entreaties of Birmingham City, where he would remain in the Second Division and at length retire.

A big drop in the Old Trafford average crowd seemed harsh on a team who had slipped from first to fourth but provided two cup runs. Had the fans become spoiled? The newspapers gave the question an airing. Busby and Edwards hoped it was academic because the new stand had a price tag and the FA's grant covered barely a fifth.

As Alf Ramsey took Charlton, Stiles and Connelly on tour with England, Law sensed an opportunity quietly to trouble Busby with a request for a pay rise and re-signing fee. 'I felt comfortable enough by then about asking for the money,' he said, 'but rather than face him I waited for the end of the season and wrote him a letter. Perhaps a little cowardice was involved.' Especially as he was threatening to seek a move.

He gave the letter to young Ken Ramsden, who said: 'I remember him handing it over. The envelope was blue. He asked me to give it to the Boss.' And then left for Aberdeen to await the birth of his second child. Busby must have been away too. 'A couple of weeks later,' said Ramsden, 'he sent for me. I always used to say to people that I never had to knock on his door – my knees did it for me. It wasn't so much fear, more awe. But on this occasion he was as angry as I'd ever seen him. He was thunderous. He thrust out the blue envelope. "Where did you get this from?" I said Denis had given it to me. "What did he say?" "He just said would I give it to the Boss for him?" And then Matt let it go. He realised I was just the postman.'

The same day, Busby sent a reply to Law. The club would accept no ultimatum; he was available for transfer. While the letter was in the post, Busby also told the press, so Law was surprised to encounter reporters on a Scottish golf course. At Busby's request he hurried back to Old Trafford. But not before a plot had been hatched. 'We did a dodgy thing,' said Law. 'He got an apology.' It was typed out ready to be signed when Law got to Old Trafford. 'And I quietly got my pay rise. I didn't get the signing-on fee, but I was quite content. Nobody knew. If any of the other players had known, they'd have wanted a rise too. So it was between Matt and me. All I had to do was say sorry in public. It was a game. And it made Matt look really good.'

The World Cup began with Charlton, Stiles and Connelly in the England side facing Uruguay at Wembley and Wilf McGuinness in Ramsey's coaching team. After a dull scoreless draw, Connelly was left out and, with Martin Peters introduced, the Wonders became almost Wingless. It required sheer class from Charlton to overcome Mexico: first a magnificent solo goal, a piledriver with two men in his wake, and then a fine pass to Greaves, whose shot rebounded to the predatory Roger Hunt.

England also beat France 2–0, amid strong criticism of Stiles's tackling; even the FA rebuked him for the tackle that put Jacky Simon out of the match. Argentina, whom England would meet in the quarter-finals, took note and their sense of impending grievance was only increased by the appointment of a northern European referee, Rudolf Kreitlein. After 35 minutes their captain, Antonio Rattín, was sent off. His name had gone in the book for a foul on Charlton and, when he repeated the infringement, the referee pointed to the tunnel; it seemed as if, fouls apart, Kreitlein wanted to be rid of Rattín's constant complaining. Later, Peters crossed for Hurst to head the only goal.

The semi-final reintroduced Stiles to Eusébio and, while the little man stuck fairly to his task, Charlton undid Portugal. His first goal was sidefooted from 20 yards after the goalkeeper, José Pereira, had come out to block Hunt, his second a luscious rising drive. Eusébio scored from a penalty but England were in the final against West Germany, whom they beat after extra time. Charlton cried, Stiles danced a lone jig and Connelly joined the celebrations.

Charlton was losing his hair but so quickly gaining friends that, in a vote for the world's most popular player, he would probably have come second to Pelé, above even the great Bobby Moore. For English people abroad, Charlton's name broke language barriers. Stiles would not have won too many popularity polls.

In just three weeks, when the new League season started, Charlton, Stiles and Connelly would be in the United side who beat West Bromwich as excitingly as 5–3 would suggest. The England trio were lauded and an ovation also given to Jimmy Murphy for completing 20 years with the club. Law, who had spent the afternoon of the World Cup final playing golf with a fellow Scot – anything to miss England's triumph – scored twice.

THE FIFTH TITLE

The problem with Manchester United was obvious: despite his championship medal, Pat Dunne was not reliable enough, while Gaskell had yet to mature and Gregg, at nearly 34, would never overcome his shoulder problems. Busby had identified the goalkeeper he wanted. He knew Alex Stepney, though Tommy Docherty had signed him for Chelsea from Millwall only a few months earlier, might be available because a new chairman, Charles Pratt, was refusing to let Docherty sell Peter Bonetti.

One day in the late summer of 1966, Stepney finished training and was told to go to Stamford Bridge to see Docherty. 'He ushered me into his car,' said Stepney. 'I asked where we were going and he said wait and see. He took me to the White House hotel near Euston station and after about five minutes the lobby doors opened and in walked Matt Busby and Jimmy Murphy. We shook hands. "Right," said Matt to Jimmy, "you take Alex and Tommy will come with me." And Jimmy tries to sell me Manchester United. He says I'll be playing with Bobby, Denis, George, Paddy Crerand, Nobby Stiles ... it was a dream, wasn't it? And then Matt comes back and says, "The deal's done."' For the third time Busby would pay a world record for a goalkeeper: £55,000.

'Tommy wished me all the best. Matt said he and Jimmy would be staying overnight and getting the 10am train from Euston in the morning. I was to meet them at 9.30 and we'd go to Manchester and complete the signing. I went back home to Carshalton. In the morning I had to get the tube to Euston in the rush hour and of course everyone's got the newspapers in front of their faces and I'm on the back page.

'I kept thinking to myself, "I've got three-and-a-half hours in a first-class carriage with Matt Busby and Jimmy Murphy – what am I going to talk about?" I met them. Matt asked if everything was all right and I said, "Fine." And he said, "Jimmy, go and get some newspapers to read on the train." And I thought, "That'll do." So we got in and he passed the papers round and, after about ten minutes, he suddenly handed over the *Daily Express*, pointed to the front page and asked, "What's all this about, son?"

'There's only a picture of my wife Pam and the headline "I'm Not Moving To Manchester – I Don't Want To Live In Coronation Street!" I didn't know what to say. "Don't worry," he said.'

With United short of money, Busby had needed to raise the bulk of the Stepney fee. Whether the solution was engineered or simply fell into his lap was unclear, but young John Aston told the story of how John Connelly and the club parted. 'John was the loveliest lad you could ever meet,' said Aston. Jimmy Ryan said the same: 'When I did well he congratulated me, even though I was in his place.' No one had a bad word for Connelly.

Yet his fate was settled, Aston recalled, on a Friday. Busby had ceased to be a full-time tracksuit manager soon after Munich. 'But on Fridays he was famous for appearing,' said Aston. 'Seventy per cent of the time he called you over with a curly finger and that was to drop you – "How do you think you're playing, son?" – but the rest of the time he'd just chat to Bobby or Denis or Pat Crerand.

'This was September and John Connelly had got his place back from Jimmy Ryan and was doing brilliantly so, when Busby called him over, he thought he was about to get a pat on the back. And Busby says, "I'm leaving you out." And John says, "You're joking." And he says, "I never joke, son." And John says, "Well, you can stick your club up your arse." And he walked away, got dressed, went home and told his wife he was finished with United. I'd never have believed *anyone* would talk like that to Matt Busby. Least of all John Connelly.'

Within a week Connelly was in the Second Division. Busby, believing Aston could plough his first-team furrow, had arranged a £40,000 transfer to recently relegated Blackburn and Connelly, a Lancashire lad, was philosophical. Yet he was only 28, a champion with both Burnley and United, fresh from contributing to England's glory, and he would never represent his country again, or even play in the First Division.

Stepney, by contrast, was on the way up. Just as, when acquiring Connelly two years earlier, Busby had completed a winning combination, so it was with the cheery keeper. Getting him into the side was easy. Almost immediately Pat Dunne let in five goals as United were swept out of the League Cup at Blackpool. This meant they had conceded 19 in the 8 matches shared among their three keepers (average 2.37). With Stepney between the posts the defence solidified. He made his debut in an Old Trafford derby scarred by trouble off the field, keeping a clean sheet while Law scored the only goal, and thereafter played in every League and Cup match, letting in a total of 33 goals in 37 games (average 0.89).

One day, Busby approached Stepney, who had been going to Carshalton after Saturday matches and returning to Manchester on Mondays. 'Son,' he said, 'I think you should bring your wife this Monday, and I'll get an estate agent to meet you and show you some houses. Because I think it's about time you bought a house in Manchester.' Since the abolition of the maximum wage, players had begun to buy houses rather than rent from the club. Stepney agreed. 'Good,' Busby said. 'So just let me know the time your train gets into Piccadilly and the estate agent will be there to meet you.'

'By now my wife's attitude to "Coronation Street" had mellowed,' Stepney recalled. 'The train pulled in, we got out – and there was Matt Busby. He walked straight past me with a "Hello, son", went up to Pam, gave her a kiss and said, "Welcome to Manchester." He explained that he would act as our estate agent. He showed us round six houses. That was class. That was Matt Busby. He took us round areas not too far from Old Trafford such as Sale, where Paddy Crerand and other players lived. The house we chose had been John Connelly's.'

With the 18-year-old Jimmy Rimmer coming along nicely, Gregg realised it was time to go. He joined Stoke on a free transfer in December and was to play only twice there before retiring at the end of the season. Pat Dunne went to Plymouth for £5,000 in February 1967. Gaskell claimed Busby had told him not to worry about Stepney – 'He'd signed him as a back-up and wanted me to teach him' – and then refused to let him move to Leicester or West Ham, both fellow First Division clubs. So he took a solicitor friend's advice and fulfilled the final 18 months of his contract by reporting daily to Jack Crompton. When he resumed his goalkeeping career, it was at Wrexham.

Bobby Noble came in at left-back and stayed in, to the exclusion of the classy but less ruthless Shay Brennan; Tony Dunne went to the right. Sadler sometimes found himself in central defence. He had always been a centre-forward but one summer in Zurich filled in at centre-back. 'I did quite well and it must have been noticed because Jimmy Murphy started using me there in training. It seemed easy – everything was in front of me. I was pretty good in the air, pretty athletic. And gradually I learned the other stuff. If Bill or Nobby wasn't able to play, I'd slot in.'

Best, meanwhile, switched from left to right wing – in truth, the young genius already tended to play where he fancied – to accommodate Aston, in whom Busby had enough confidence to permit the sale of Willie Anderson to Aston Villa for £20,000. United remained top at the turn of the year, marked by a scoreless but enthralling draw at home to Leeds, featuring Giles and Peter Lorimer.

Johnny Carey's Forest, unbeaten in 13, packed Old Trafford in February. Billed as a title decider, the match remained scoreless until five minutes from the end when Law rose to a corner, twisted and flashed an overhead kick past the hitherto defiant Peter Grummitt. Afterwards, there was a knock on Forest's dressing-room door and in came Busby, to congratulate Carey and his players on their contribution to a fine match and invite them to join the United directors for a drink. 'I remember shaking his hand in the boardroom,' said the highly rated winger Ian Storey-Moore. 'It wasn't something you get every day.'

The following Saturday, Busby and his players were again shocked by their 1959 conquerors, Norwich, in the fourth round of the FA Cup. Norwich, now a Second Division club, won 2–1 at Old Trafford, but elements of the home crowd spoiled the occasion by stoning several of the buses from East Anglia afterwards.

For all Busby's care with the image of Manchester United, too many of their adherents were at the forefront of malevolent fashion. When, after remaining unbeaten for a dozen matches, United took a large following to West Ham for the match in which they were to clinch the title in style, it was another day marred by violence – some of the most shocking the terraces of England had experienced.

Disorder even spread to the pitch after it had been invaded by the travelling hordes. United had been three goals up after 10 minutes, four up after 25 and it had ended 6–1 with Law, Best and Charlton among the scorers.

The trophy was presented before a scoreless and lifeless match at home to Stoke the following weekend. A lap of honour was run and the usual celebrations filled the streets. It was Busby's fifth title. His priority for the next season: 'We would obviously like to win the championship again. But we all feel that we must have a real go to win the European Cup.'

Sadly for Bobby Noble, he had suffered such injuries in a car crash in April that he never played again; Tony Dunne had reverted to left-back and Shay Brennan been recalled, completing a side ready to make history.

Busby's contract now extended to ten years at £10,000 plus bonuses running into several thousands for each trophy. He was earning it. If sections of the United support had been of the fair-weather variety identified in the media, the title success had brought them back. There was also a dividend from the glamour of Law, Best and Charlton.

First Division crowds had peaked at a total of nearly 18 million in 1948/49. They had gradually fallen and, before England won the World Cup, been under 13 million. The subsequent resurgence worked out at 12 per cent over two years. In those years, United's home attendances shot up by more than three times as much. Old Trafford's League average in 1966/67 was nearly 54,000.

Matt Busby's United were not following a trend. Matt Busby's United were defining themselves as different. Whether or not the Sixties swung, Busby's United did. And they had more to imprint upon the decade.

If they were to become champions of Europe, they would be England's first. Liverpool in 1964/65 had reached the semi-finals but lost to Inter. In 1966/67 Shankly had been given another chance only to encounter, in the second round, the great Rinus Michels and Ajax. While this was happening, Celtic under Jock Stein were completing a 6–2 aggregate victory over Nantes. In the quarter-finals a last-minute goal from the Bellshill-born Billy McNeill confounded the Yugoslavs of Vojvodina at Celtic Park. Next came Dukla Prague, conquerors of Ajax, and, after another native of Busby country, Uddingston's Jimmy Johnstone, had dazzled in a 3–1 victory, a scoreless outcome in Czechoslovakia saw Stein's team through to the final in Lisbon.

Crerand, whose mother and father-in-law were there, didn't even see the climax on television. Nor Busby. For United were touring the globe in 1967 and, while Tommy Gemmell and Steve Chalmers conclusively responded to an early penalty by Inter's Sandro Mazzola, Crerand and the rest were on a plane from Hawaii to New Zealand. 'When we got to Auckland,' he recalled, 'the game was over. So I phoned the *Manchester Evening News* and asked the girl on the switchboard what the score had been in the European Cup final the previous night. She hadn't a clue what I was talking about. She said she didn't know anything about football and hadn't taken much notice of an item that had been on the news – except that it was the first time somebody from Britain had won something. And that's how I knew Celtic had won the European Cup.' Bill Shankly had been in Lisbon to shake Stein's hand. 'John,' he said, 'you're immortal.'

So it would be Jock Stein's title Busby was endeavouring to take in the new season.

NOT FEELING TWO GRAND

United were away for seven weeks. They went from New York to Los Angeles, where Benfica beat them 3–1, and on to New Zealand before repeatedly criss-crossing Australia, ending up in Perth and arriving home with barely time to squeeze family holidays between the timezone adjustment and pre-season training. Not that the players minded the adventure. The younger ones at least. The likes of Jimmy Ryan and John Fitzpatrick.

Ever since their ground-staff days, Fitzpatrick had been of the militant tendency. While Ryan, even now, never demanded a first-team place – 'I didn't think I was good enough' – Fitzpatrick frequently stormed in the direction of Busby's office. And claimed afterwards to have made his point.

'Anyway,' said Ryan, 'we'd both played in the championship season.' Fitzpatrick had made three appearances at right-half, before a cartilage operation let Crerand back in, and Ryan four plus one as substitute. 'So off we went to travel the world. We were kitted out with new blazers, shirts, the lot. And the club put £100 extra in our pay.

'Then we heard the first-team regulars had got £2,000 each and they were winding us up about it. "Are you not feeling two grand?" That sort of thing. But I was happy enough – a hundred was a lot of money. "Did you get your bonus?" said Fitzy. "Yes," I said. "Good, eh?" "Not good compared with what the first team got." "But they're in the first team." "Listen," he said. "I was in the first team and would have stayed in if I hadn't done my cartilage. You had a few games – we should both be getting the same as them. I think we should go and see Busby."

'All the way from New York to Los Angeles, Fitzy's in my ear. He's also told some of the first-team players and they're saying, "Yeah – go and see him." So we get to the hotel and check in and Fitzy says, "Right – let's go." And, although I'm still reluctant, I reason that Fitzy goes to see him every other week so it'll do no harm just to watch. So we go to Busby's room. By now I'm shitting myself. Fitzy knocks on the door and a voice goes "Yes." "It's John Fitzpatrick and Jim Ryan, Boss – can we have a word with you?" "Just a minute, boys." He comes to the door in a dressing-gown. "Come in." And, because John's the only one who's spoken so far, speaks to him. "What is it, John?" And John sweeps an arm in my direction. And the Boss now looks at me. I hadn't thought of anything to say. I was just expecting Fitzy to tear into him as usual.

'And Matt says, "What is it, Jim?" I don't know what I said exactly. I just mumbled something about overhearing senior players say they'd got £2,000 and wondering if maybe we should get a bit more. And he goes "More?" And he's looking straight at me.

'"Now was that money mentioned in your contract?"

'"No."

'"So was it a gift? A gift from the directors?"

'"Yes."

'"So you're not happy with the gift?"

'*Fucking hell* – you could have set me on fire at that moment and I wouldn't have noticed. It was his voice, the gentleness of it. I felt worthless, as always when I disappointed him. Who was I, this ungrateful wretch, to question this great man who had been through so much, this man under whom Duncan Edwards had grown up and who was now confronted with *me*? And then he turns to Fitzy.

'"What do you think you have done to deserve this gift?"

'"Nothing, Boss."

'"And you, Jim?"

'"Nothing, Boss."

'"All right – go."

'And he pushed us out the door. I couldn't look him in the eye after that. I think I played half a game on the tour.'

And yet Ryan was given several appearances the next season, including one in the European Cup, while Fitzpatrick made 21 in all competitions. Was he right about the £2,000? Crerand doubted it. 'Two thousand was a crazy amount then. I'd only paid £3,500 for my first house not that many years before.'

ROUGH STUFF

John Fitzpatrick was a fiery performer. In time he'd join the list of players sent off under Busby. As would Brian Kidd, who, after impressing on tour, again did well in a 3–3 Charity Shield draw with Tottenham. No United player, though, had been dismissed in the previous season. Stiles had served a suspension for exceeding the limit of cautions. But Law had got through nearly three years without a dismissal. As if to celebrate the impending passage of the captaincy to Bobby Charlton, he fought with Ian Ure in the tenth match of 1967/68, at home to Arsenal, and this time his ban was to last six weeks; Ure was equally punished.

United would remain contenders until the last match of the season. They had new rivals and Malcolm Allison's presence made sure Manchester City would be the noisiest of neighbours. But United won the first derby in September. At Maine Road, Colin Bell scored early but Charlton struck twice before half-time and that was how it stayed. It was already clear, though, that City, after a season acclimatising to the First Division, were ready for anyone.

Busby, in an early conversation with Allison, had spoken of the comfort provided by such great talents as Law, Best and Charlton. He told Allison he never went into a match afraid. Now Mercer and Allison were to complete a triumvirate of their own. They already had Bell and Mike Summerbee and two weeks after the derby added Francis Lee, for a club record £60,000 paid to Bolton.

Busby had blooded two more players: the teenage Scottish full-backs Frank Kopel and Francis Burns. While Kopel's appearance as a substitute was fleeting, Burns stayed in at left-back, again with

Dunne moving over and Brennan dropping out. Sadler's conversion to central defence had been effected. 'As I became more regular there,' Sadler recalled, 'I'd get pulled by either Jimmy or the Boss. They'd ask how I was settling in and make the odd comment. Particularly Jimmy. Actually he was on at me all the time.

'I didn't know, at first, what he meant. But it gradually became clear that he saw defenders as people who dished it out. He thought that was missing from my game.'

He was always on at those who were too nice. Like Shay Brennan, who'd be told: 'You don't have to kick him. Just leave your foot there.' He took the same thinly veiled approach with Sadler: 'He never said, "I want you to go and kick them." It was always "Let them know you're there, son." Or "When you get an opportunity … " By which he meant, when the ball was played out wide near the touchline and the centre-forward was trying to turn you, you just took the lot.'

Sadler was never a natural assassin. 'So I'd constantly be getting "Watch Bill – look at how Bill does it." Bill Foulkes would win nine out of ten challenges in the air and he'd win plenty by heading the centre-forward on the back of his head.' As even the late Mark Jones, no shrinking violet, had said to Foulkes: 'I wish I could do things like you, Bill – in cold blood.'

Sadler made clear that he didn't receive the devil's advocacy from Murphy alone. 'Matt was no angel. I'd get it from him too. And I'd get it from Wilf McGuinness, who'd got it from Matt and Jimmy. It went on all the time I was with United. They were never worried about anything else.'

With good reason. Sadler was an elegant and effective footballer, still a few weeks short of his 22nd birthday when Alf Ramsey picked him to partner Bobby Moore in defence against Northern Ireland at Wembley. Also in November, a United back four of Dunne, Foulkes, Sadler and Burns helped the two-goal Best, brilliantly taking the role of the injury-cursed Law, to smash Liverpool's 100 per cent home record and put United back on top.

Busby, having defined the main theatre of activity as Europe, attempted to keep his players' minds on the domestic title when he called it 'undoubtedly' the first priority, 'the bread and butter that leads to slices of the cake'.

United's first slice of 1967/68 were Hibernians, a Maltese team coached by the 32-year-old Father Hilary Tagliaferro. They had disconcerted Busby only in the sense that he had a clash of footballing philosophy with a Catholic priest. This was when Father Hilary expressed a fear that 'harsh' tackling in English football would drive out invention. Busby, in a newspaper column, argued that Ramsey had done England a service by winning the World Cup with 'a game of strength that made us all proud of our football traditions'. Upon retirement Busby was to be singing a different tune: Father Hilary's, with hardly a change of note. But for now he could not expose himself to any accusation of disloyalty to the English game. At any rate, 4–0 on aggregate was comfortable enough.

The next assignment would have little to do with comfort. It took United to Sarajevo, which they reached by charter to Dubrovnik and a six-hour coach journey into the Bosnian mountains. To become champions of Yugoslavia, like Vojvodina the previous season, Sarajevo had needed to finish above Dinamo Zagreb as well as Belgrade's big two, so putting into practice Busby's more pragmatic approach to Europe – 'away from home we have to try to contain the opposition' – was never going to be painless. But heaven knows what Father Hilary would have made of the Bosnians' tackling.

After a scoreless match, Busby called it 'disgraceful ... worse than anything we have ever experienced in this competition', and even Foulkes winced: 'They were coming in chest-high.' They could also play a bit and United were glad to escape on level terms after Stepney had appeared – even to English journalists – to scoop Vahidin Musemić's shot back from over the line.

It took United 14 minutes to score at Old Trafford. Crerand played a one-two with Charlton and picked out Kidd drifting wide. Burns got a firm head to Kidd's cross and when the goalkeeper, Refik Muftić, could only parry Aston tapped in at the Stretford End. Soon the match cut up rough. It started when Best, claiming provocation, lashed out at Muftić. He seemed to miss but the fury of the Sarajevo players was evident when Fahrudin Prljača hacked Best to the ground and was sent off.

When the French referee, Roger Machin, pointed to the tunnel, he was under siege, as was a linesman after United extended their lead through Best, who volleyed home after Aston had hooked the ball back from a position the Bosnians furiously claimed to be over the byline. They were right according to Aston. 'Do I feel guilty about this?' He smiled. 'No, I do not. The ball bounced to me about waist-high and it wasn't just over the line – it was two feet over the line. The photographers scattered to get out of my way! And that was the goal that ended up taking us through.'

A late one from Salih Delalič was insufficient for Sarajevo and in the tunnel afterwards, as a rancorous Muftič ran towards Best, Crerand intervened with a sweet fist. Busby saw it but hurried his man away and, on this occasion, deemed no further action appropriate.

Next, United faced the Poles of Górnik Zabrze. At home Busby's men had only an own-goal to show for much attacking until, a minute from the end, Kidd's flick of a heel at a drive from Jimmy Ryan, operating on the right wing while Best again played the part of Law to near-perfection, made them favourites to go through. Sportsmanship prevailed this time and the Górnik goalkeeper, Hubert Kostka, went off to a standing ovation.

Snow failed to deter 105,000 spectators from filling the Slaski Stadium in Chorzow and, although Busby considered asking for a postponement, United conceded only once. For the fourth time in as many seasons of asking, United were in the semi-finals and around Europe, according to a poll of journalists picked up by the *Daily Mail*, a majority reckoned they had a better chance of lifting the trophy than Real Madrid.

THE NATIVES ARE RESTLESS

Busby took the first opportunity to watch Real, travelling with Murphy to Prague, where the draw would take place, to see how they protected a 3–0 lead over Slavia. Among those who accompanied the pair was Alan Thompson of the *Daily Express*, who reported their travels through the city by tram and taxi and even the 'sausage a yard and a half long' that constituted their lunch. Real under Miguel Muñoz, their former captain, went through 4–2 on aggregate. Busby did not seem unduly concerned. But after the draw had paired United with Real he did declare, through Thompson, that he would never forget how Santiago Bernabéu had helped United in their hour of need and added: 'If we lose to them, it will be like losing to a brother.'

Delayed on their journey home, Busby and Murphy arrived by train at Piccadilly barely a quarter of an hour before United were to kick off against Nottingham Forest. With taxis in short supply, they hitched a lift – how Thompson chortled at these men in their late fifties behaving like students – and saw United win 3–0.

At one stage United had been 6/1 on for the title. But Chelsea had become the first visiting side to win a League match at Old Trafford in two years and the Forest match was followed by another home defeat, all the more wounding for its infliction by City. Then Liverpool won at Old Trafford and the natives' restlessness was reflected in the media. Were United fans truly spoiled by success? There was plenty of evidence in the readers' letters columns of the *Evening News* and especially its Saturday results version, the *Sporting Pink*.

The *News* had swallowed the *Chronicle* (and David Meek lost the companionship of Keith Dewhurst, now devoting his energies to drama: four plays thus far, three of them televised, and scripts for the police series *Z Cars*). The *News* had become powerful under the editorship of Tom Henry, a United fan of imposing build and friend of Busby's whose anxiety to please oozed from a note telling David Meek he had been awarded a modest pay rise: 'I have spoken to Matt and he tells me you are doing a good job.' Henry's defining moment had come when in January 1960 the team lost 7–3 at Newcastle; upon being shown the understandably gloomy headline prepared for the front page of the *Pink*, he seized a pen and changed it to 'REDS IN TEN-GOAL THRILLER'.

But Henry did believe in giving the fans a voice. Even if he wouldn't take their side against Busby. Hence mid-April's 'Sports Soapbox', edited by Jack McNamara, a jaunty New Zealander who specialised in rugby league. Under the headline 'PROBLEMS FACING MATT – THE RANK INTOLERANCE OF SO-CALLED FANS', he wrote: 'It seems sad that a club with such an amazing record should suddenly find itself shot at from all sides.' One reader declared:

> Busby should have signed at least four players ... They need not be brilliant, just good professionals with guts and maturity like [Tony] Coleman of City ... It is maturity that wins the European Cup; it won't be won with key positions filled by young boys yet to learn their job.

In the *Daily Express*, which also had a Busby column, the manager defended himself with sarcasm. 'Dash it!' he wrote (as told to Bill Fryer),

> Why didn't I think of it before? It has dawned on me what Manchester United should have done to win every match by six clear goals. We should have bought Tom, Dick and Harry, not to mention Hamish and Andy, Dewi and Dai and Pat and Mick. Then we should have had the entire staff immunised against injury so that we should have won the League by September, be well on the way to winning the Cup and the European Cup and be favourites for the Derby.

When Fryer judged that the joke had been sufficiently milked, he made Busby's underlying point that United had been especially unlucky with injuries: to Law, Stiles, Foulkes, Dunne, Herd and Noble. It was also disclosed that an attempt to break the transfer record – there had been rumours about Geoff Hurst – had been rebuffed.

One of the moaners had been specific about a young player considered not up to a man's job. 'Aston,' it was stated, 'has not had a good match all season.' It was noticeable that Aston, after scoring at home to Sarajevo, had acknowledged the Stretford End almost joylessly. Maybe their explosion of gratitude was too much of a change from barracking. 'I'd suffered from crowd abuse for quite a while,' he said. 'There were stars – and there was me.'

Even the best, of course, had been barracked down the years. Busby would have known about Herbert Chapman's nursing of Alex James through early tribulations at Arsenal. But Aston could recall nothing similar in Busby's newspaper columns. 'Denis Law did an article saying "Leave John Aston alone – give him a chance". Not Matt. He was what I would call a sink-or-swim man.' Even in private? 'He never spoke to me about it. Except maybe for one time, when I was extremely down and asked to be dropped and he said, "I pick the team, son. [There had been an identical episode with Billy Whelan.] But that was as close as he got to an arm round the shoulder.'

The Stretford Enders themselves were not immune from criticism. It was said they now only cheered when United were winning.

Such was the troubled preamble to Real Madrid's visit to Old
Trafford. Again, Aston did well. United moved in front when he
got to the byline and pulled the ball back for Best, who let a bobble
tee it up for a sumptuous left-footed lash into the net. Real's star
man was Amancio. Although absent from the Old Trafford leg due
to suspension, he recalled having been warned about the especial
danger United carried in the last 15 minutes of a match. The advice
had come from a 24-year-old friend of Real of whom more would
be heard.

Julio Iglesias had been a goalkeeper in the Real youth system
before suffering serious injuries in a car crash. At least, during a long
rehabilitation, he had done something useful with the spare time:
he had learned to play the guitar. He had then studied English at
a language school in Cambridge. Now, around the time that his
breakthrough song *La Vida Sigue Igual* ('Life Remains the Same')
was being released, he had tipped off Amancio and company. (Even
though, in the season to date, Busby's team had scored 18 goals
out of 88 in the last 15 minutes, compared with 16 in the first 15:
hardly conclusive.) But there was no rousing finale this time, no
further scoring.

Nor was United's morale greatly boosted by yet another post-
Europe flop, a 6–3 defeat at West Bromwich that left their title
hopes at the mercy of City and Leeds. On the penultimate Saturday,
Leeds lost at home to Liverpool, leaving the title in City's gift. If
both City and United won their concluding matches, City would
be champions on goal average. They travelled to Newcastle on the
assumption that, with United at home to Sunderland, a lower-half
side, they could afford no slip. But United lost. For all the efforts
of Best, who scored his 28th League goal, they dismayed a full
stadium by going down 2–1. City took the title with a thrilling 4–3
win at Newcastle.

THE KING OF EUROPE

Busby had urgent work. He had to lift his players for Madrid four days
later. They would have to swallow every drop of disappointment,
block any notion of failure. Whatever he might have said, the
European Cup was everything now.

First, he went to the ITV studios in Manchester to congratulate Mercer on his triumphant return from Tyneside. The players also fraternised. When City got to the Cromford, many from United joined them. Two days before, Mike Summerbee had spoken to Best: 'I told him that, whatever happened on the Saturday, I'd see him at the Cabaret Club at 1am.' Best was there. 'Hard luck,' said Summerbee to his close pal. 'Well done,' said Best. And their partying began.

When, a few months later, Summerbee got married after a stag party attended by Best and others from United at the heavily player-patronised Brown Bull pub – a place whose name Busby jocularly refused to speak, referring to it as the 'Black Cow' or even 'Green Pig' – Best observed ceremonial duties. As Summerbee recalled: 'I was the only groom whose bride spent most of the day staring at the best man.'

Summerbee and Best had spent many a Saturday night out. Their habit was to start off at Arturo's, an Italian restaurant where Busby and Mercer and their wives often dined. They would let their managers see them accompany their meal with nothing stronger than Coca-Cola, then walk over to engage in small talk. And then they'd say a polite goodnight – and hit the town.

Not that Busby was ever in much doubt about Best's nocturnal habits, which, now his fame had grown, were no longer always as demure as in the days of trying to force down a small beer with Jimmy Ryan. When his excesses were reported to Busby, he would be summoned to the manager's office and, sometimes, weep.

In the *Evening News* souvenir edition marking the first leg of the Madrid tie, Best had been described as a 'boutique owner, restaurateur, leader of fashion'. There was a picture of him posing with Summerbee outside Edwardia, their city-centre clothes shop. And yet he still lodged with Mrs Fullaway.

The weekend over, he packed his bag for Madrid. Much seemed to depend on him, especially as Law, injected before the first leg, was now out of action completely; he had gone into hospital for an exploratory operation and awaited further surgery.

From the airport the United party went to a base in the mountains, half an hour's drive from the city. They wanted no distractions as Busby outlined his plans, which included a clean sheet in the first half hour and Stiles, now a defensive midfielder, sticking to Amancio like a poisonous limpet.

Meanwhile, Real used their customary city-centre hotel. Another well-wisher offered the same tip as Julio Iglesias: beware minutes 75 to 90. Amancio was to look back on that. And to add, just as ruefully: 'What nobody warned me about was Stiles.' Who, on the morning of the match, had gone to church with Crerand and pushed 400 pesetas' worth of notes into the collection box. 'Nobby!' said Crerand. 'That's bribery!' Later to be compounded by what Amancio viewed as assault and battery.

The 3,000 United followers among 125,000 in the Bernabéu watched with concern as Real took control, Amancio to the fore despite his assiduous escort. Busby's half-hour expired, but only two more minutes had elapsed when his quiet confidence was shaken. His defensive plans had included one requirement of Aston: 'It was the only time he ever instructed me to do anything like this. But Pirri was the playmaker and he operated from right-half and Busby asked me, when they had the ball, to tuck in from the left wing, in the hope that Pirri would release the ball quicker. But he actually scored their first goal while I was supposed to be marking him.' It would have taken some stopping: a near-post header from Amancio's free-kick that was past Alex Stepney before he moved.

Three minutes from the interval, Shay Brennan let a ball run under his foot and, with Gento on the end of it, there was no hope of recovery. This time the goalkeeper was left in an inelegant tangle as the ball rattled in off his shins. 'We'd fancied ourselves if we could just get to the interval level on the night,' said Stepney. Now, with thunder rolling through the Bernabéu canyon, another semi-final defeat loomed. Then Dunne lofted a hopeful ball towards Kidd in the goalmouth and, although Zoco got there first, the defender comically sliced past his own livid goalkeeper, Antonio Betancort. United were still a goal down, but level on aggregate.

Not for long. There was still time for Amancio to crack home with resonance. As the half-time whistle sounded, it felt like match point. United reached a silent dressing room.

'We were just sitting there,' said Stepney, 'wondering what Matt was going to say. And he had his trilby on, and his pipe in his mouth, and never said a thing. Don't forget it was only ten minutes in those days. Our heads, of course, had dropped. And then, just before the bell went, he stood up and started laughing at us. We were stunned. And he says, "What's going on? It's your greatest chance of reaching the European Cup final. You should be enjoying yourselves. You've attacked teams all season – why aren't you doing it tonight?"'

And then Busby invoked the name of Manchester United; he wanted it to be ringing in their ears when they went back out. '"You're letting me down, the club down, the supporters down. Go out and enjoy yourselves." And the bell went. "Oh, and by the way," he says, quite matter-of-fact, "it's 3–2 on aggregate. If you get an early goal, you'll win." Brilliant. It drew all the tension out of us. We started playing – and they couldn't believe it.'

Stiles did his bit, as Amancio recalled: 'By that stage of my career I'd got used to receiving a few kicks, but never before had I been punched when the ball was 30 metres away! In fact Gento had the ball and we were on the attack and I think Stiles just wanted to slow me down.' It was an open match by now. Only the soothsayers knew what would happen. Another high ball sailed towards Betancort and there was Sadler, whom Busby had told to look for opportunities to get forward, waving a foot as the keeper hesitated, nudging in the scruffiest of goals. Now the 3,000 from England could be heard. No one else. *'Uni-ted, Uni-ted ...'* It was the 75th minute.

La Vida Sigue Igual? Julio Iglesias must have been shaking his head. Especially after the 78th minute. Best took possession on the right, slipped past Manolo Sanchís to the byline and pulled back an inviting low ball. Team-mates' hearts sank as on to it strode Foulkes, from the other end of the pitch. But no striker could have made a better job of steering it away from Betancort and into the far corner. 'Until that moment,' said Aston, 'I don't think Bill had ever sidefooted a ball in his life.'

But what a moment: a Munich survivor had put United in the final. With another captaining the side. Charlton burst into tears and two United fans on the pitch tried, with Brian Kidd, to help him from his haunches. Busby was embraced by his players. In the dressing room, they saw him, too, cry, and understood.

A week earlier Busby had travelled to Lisbon to watch the first leg of the other European Cup semi-final. Benfica had beaten Juventus 2–0 without daunting him. 'If only we can survive in Madrid,' he had said, 'I feel we have an excellent chance of winning the European Cup.' Especially at Wembley. Now Benfica completed a 3–0 aggregate win. It would be Stiles against Eusébio yet again. An opportunity for the pride of Portugal to settle a score. Or for

Stiles and Charlton to add the greatest club prize to the greatest in the international game. But above all the minds of the people would be on Busby.

Best, meanwhile, was voted Footballer of the Year. The statuette had passed from Charlton to his big brother Jack at Leeds but there could be little argument with its returning to Old Trafford despite the claims of Colin Bell or Jeff Astle, the goalscoring hero of West Bromwich's Cup final victory over Everton. While Law had made only 27 appearances in all competitions, scoring 9 goals, Best had weighed in with 32 in 52. Best was as worthy of honour as Law was unlucky.

Kidd would continue up front in the final, to take place on his 19th birthday, 29 May 1968, and that meant Busby's team would contain only three bought players: Stepney, Dunne and Crerand, who had cost a total of £116,000. Brennan, Foulkes, Sadler, Stiles, Best, Charlton, Kidd and Aston had all come though the United system. For this team to be as home-grown as Busby's 1948 side was extraordinary.

United travelled by train. They went past Wembley on the way to a handsome country-house hotel near Windsor Great Park. Meanwhile, an estimated 80,000 got ready to follow them; only when Scotland played England would London have experienced such a football invasion. The official party included families of Munich victims and the survivors Gregg, Blanchflower, Berry and Scanlon. As if Charlton, Foulkes and the others needed reminding that they were not just playing for themselves.

Busby was at his best in the build-up: he had visited Law in hospital before leaving Manchester and now was calm, exuding just the right degree of confidence, careful not to say anything that would stimulate a Benfica smarting from the memory of those five goals in Lisbon. For Busby's players, said Aston, it was the lull before the storm: 'There was a lot of stilted conversation.'

Aston was thinking back to Los Angeles. There, when United had lost their friendly against Benfica the previous summer, he had faced a 'wiry, wily swine of a right-back called Cavém'. Domiciano Cavém had been a forward in his youth and, even in his mid-thirties, retained both the inclination and fitness to attack. 'He was setting *me* problems,' Aston recalled, 'rather than the other way round. So, when I heard this wasn't the guy I would be playing against, it was a boost.' Adolfo Calisto was eleven years younger than Cavém. 'But he couldn't be any more difficult.' Aston, with his father watching from the sidelines, looked forward to finding out.

Busby's final team talk seldom varied. The tips of two splayed fingers would rest on the table in the dressing-room and, when the words began, tap them out for emphasis. 'If you weren't good enough,' he would say, 'you wouldn't be here.' And then he would raise parallel arms, which would gently sway. 'Up together, back together. God bless.' Echoed, as Harry Gregg recalled, by Jimmy Murphy. 'Attack in strength and defend in depth. God bless.'

United wore all blue and Benfica all white as Charlton and Mário Coluna led the teams into a stadium dressed in red. It was a very hot evening for late May but Aston was less interested in the weather than Benfica's No.2. Busby, as usual, had preceded his basic message with brief observations about each player's direct opponent. 'He'd have them written on a small sheet of paper,'' said Aston, 'and, when it got to me, it might be ''Right, Johnny, you're up against So-and-so. He's as fast as anything. Don't try and go past him''. Or it might be the opposite.'

What he had said about Adolfo led Aston, as he surveyed the athletic-looking defender, to test him without delay. No sooner had Wembley's welcome subsided than the United No.11 rebuilt the wall of noise. 'I ran him – and straight away knew I'd got him. So I ran him two or three times more and he became very nervous.' If Benfica had been wary of Best on the right, they now realised an equal threat came from the left. But United could not afford to throw too much forward. Not while Eusébio could evade Stiles's lunges. Stepney gaped as Eusébio hit the crossbar. Then Sadler pulled a good chance wide. It was a cautious first half of few chances.

United resumed at a higher tempo and soon Sadler, drifting out to Aston's left flank, turned back and slanted in a cross to which Charlton applied a glance of his head so judicious that, while his comb-over reared like a cobra, the ball followed a gentle arc into the far corner. United were ahead for nearly half an hour. Until José Torres won a ball in the air and Jaime Graça flashed it across Stepney.

Then came the moment that would be remembered as vividly as any goal in the campaign. With Benfica threatening to obviate extra time and Stiles's socks round his ankles, Eusébio sprinted clear. He had only Stepney to beat and a shot like a mule's kick in his right boot. Why he took this one with his left could be pondered at leisure, of which Stepney felt he had none; once the ball had safely lodged in his arms, looking to throw it out to Tony Dunne rather than savour his relief, he seemed to be rebuffing Eusébio's attempt to congratulate him on the save.

Why? Did Stepney think his opponent was indulging in a bit of gamesmanship, trying to slow the counterattack? 'No. I was thinking more of the friendly we'd played in Los Angeles. There had been a bit of trouble because they were still angry about the 5–1 in Lisbon. Eusébio scored twice. Put two penalties past me. And he had this habit of smashing them, then running into the net to get the ball. And as he ran past you he'd ruffle your hair.' Irksome. But Stepney did also have an eye to the counterattack.

'What I can remember of the save itself was that, when the ball was played through for Eusébio, I thought it was a 60–40 for me and came out a fraction, only to realise that the Wembley turf was so lush it would slow the ball up. So I went back again. He was obviously going to whack it and, when someone does that, it can go anywhere. It went straight at me. It wasn't a great save. But I did somehow hold on to the ball and my first reaction was to throw it out to Tony. And as these thoughts were going through my mind I wasn't really aware of Eusébio. I didn't know what he'd done until after the game, when people mentioned what a gentleman he had been.'

Best stole the ball but put it into the side netting before Concetto Lo Bello's whistle signalled a 90-minute stalemate. As Busby and Murphy walked among their players, of course they could see how glad they were of respite. But they kept stressing that their opponents looked wearier. Busby, pointing to Best and Aston, told everyone else to ply them with possession. But they had to stay up the field. So Stepney, when he got the ball, opted for route one. He booted it long. The back of Kidd's head flicked it on and Best ran by. It was a 50–50 between him and Jacinto Santos. No contest. A delicate touch had Jacinto scything warm air. And suddenly the only obstacle was an advancing, scrambling goalkeeper. A gossamer thread would have given Best more trouble. In an instant he was round José Henrique and the ball rolling into the net. This was in the 92nd minute. By the 99th United were 4–1 up and the celebrations could safely begin. There were photographers in St Joseph's Hospital, Whalley Range, to capture a pyjama-clad Law joining in.

Kidd, after a game of head-tennis, had marked his birthday with a goal and then made a crisp one for Charlton at the near post. Young enough to be Bill Foulkes's son, Kidd had done more than his duty to the haunted generation. Charlton felt his eyes prickle but held back the tears. They were flowing by the time the final whistle had sounded and Busby reached him. They embraced. Crerand cajoled Busby to go up and receive the trophy, but that was Charlton's role. He showed it to the ecstatic crowd and seemed almost to collapse under its weight. This was the burden of history.

'We had never spoken about Munich,' said Stepney. 'Never, ever. Bobby never mentioned it. Bill Foulkes never mentioned it. I knew, when I arrived at the club, that it was a no-go area. You didn't have to be told. Yet when the final whistle went we all instinctively went to Bobby, Bill or Matt. We never really celebrated among ourselves. And we knew the families of the lads who passed away were in the stands.'

Foulkes told the press: 'I cannot find the words to express what this means to me.' Charlton said: 'We're all overwhelmed by it, but I think the fact that we have managed to do this for Matt at last has satisfied us most of all.' Even Eusébio said on behalf of Benfica: 'We are pleased ... especially for Matt Busby.' For Busby it was 'the proudest night of my life, and the end of an ambition I have held for 11 years'. Again, no mention of Munich. No need.

'Once we had got to the dressing room,' Stepney recalled, 'the champagne flowed and my brother Eric, who was 15 years older than me, somehow got in. I found out later that he'd jumped over the Wembley fence, crossed the dog-track and blagged his way up the tunnel. And of course Matt asked, "Who's that?" I said, "Boss, I don't know how he's got here, but he's my brother." And Matt said, "No problem," so I introduced them. Now this was Matt. In 1977 – nine years later – we won the FA Cup and there was a do at the Midland. We were invited to bring guests. So I invited my brother and his wife. And Matt comes over and says, "Hello, Eric – how are you?" My brother never forgot it.'

At the party in the Russell Hotel, Stepney raised a glass with Pam, whose birthday it was. A bespectacled Stiles amused his wife, Kay, by peering at a cigar almost his own size and most poignantly Harry Gregg, flanked by Johnny Berry and Jackie Blanchflower, put a paternal arm around the 14-year-old shoulders of Gary Jones, son of the late Mark.

Busby danced with Jean to the music of Joe Loss and His Orchestra while his mother, by now in her latter seventies, had a cup of tea with George Best. Busby lasted the pace better than most. 'It was the only time I ever saw him intoxicated,' said Crerand. 'Yet he'd hardly had a drink all night. He was just intoxicated by the whole glory of it. The last time I saw him at the party he was singing the Louis Armstrong song "What a Wonderful World". He must have sung it a million times.'

Back in Manchester the *Evening News*, seven weeks after bemoaning 'PROBLEMS FACING MATT', trumpeted: '250,000 WILL GREET KINGS OF EUROPE'. The advance guard, numbering some 10,000, met the United train at Piccadilly at 8.24pm and an open-top bus flanked by mounted police took Busby and his players through the cheering, chanting crowds to Albert Square. For the second consecutive year, a Bellshill hand was on the European Cup. Busby, at the front of the bus with Kidd and Best, seemed permanently attached to the giant bulb of metal he had coveted for so long.

Through a mass of euphoric humanity the bus edged to the Town Hall steps, where Busby raised the trophy to the people. The very next day, he became Sir Matt Busby. He was football's fourth knight, after Stanley Rous, Stanley Matthews and Alf Ramsey.

CHAPTER THIRTEEN

DECLINE AND FALL

BEYOND ONE HUMAN BEING

In the summer of Busby's visit to Buckingham Palace, there was blissful relief from wrangling over money as the players collected £1,000 each for the European triumph. Busby had adjusted to the abolition of the maximum wage, and the even more significant 1963 High Court victory by George Eastham and the PFA over a player's freedom at the end of his contract, by dealing with players individually: he might tussle with Law but Charlton, whose demands were always moderate, got what he sought. 'The key,' as Alex Stepney said, 'was that nobody knew anybody else's wage.'

Because secrecy was so important, a relatively junior appointment in the accounts department in 1966 had gone to the highest level, Ken Merrett being interviewed by Busby. Merrett remembered the imparting of a message about loyalty: 'I hope you're one of those people who stay in a job, because we don't want someone who's here today and gone tomorrow. We expect you to be here a lifetime.' Point taken by one who would, like his namesake Ramsden, stay to retirement.

'So,' said Stepney, 'I never knew what Bobby was on. Or George. We all knew the bonus – at that time £20 for a win and £10 for a draw. But we didn't talk wages because that was Matt's way.' In dealing with Stepney – and, for all the goalkeeper knew, others – he was resourceful. 'The £1,000 bonus for the European Cup was taxable at about 60 per cent, so he looked to see what else he could do. The year before, the PFA had brought out a pension scheme and I was paying in £20 a week. It was £20 a week for ten years and at the end you got £120 a week for life. And he called me in and said, "Son, I think we ought to reward you for what you've done for us. So we're going to pay your pension." And for the next nine years United took care of my contributions. He was that kind of guy.' Never a little too careful with the club's money? 'Not with me, he wasn't.'

After the European success the club upgraded Busby's car. If that was the phrase. The Jensen Interceptor could hardly have been more inappropriate: a two-door sports car with a long bonnet under which a V8 engine growled. The number was personalised and only the colour – fawn – seemed to defer to Busby's style. Or, indeed, the slow and unsure driving that had petrified Law and Crerand. Ken Ramsden grinned at the recollection. 'Whoever advised him to get it I don't know – maybe Sandy fancied borrowing it. I remember John Aston senior saying, "You won't believe this, but I went with the Boss to Liverpool today and we were trundling along the East Lancs Road at 25 miles an hour – in a Jensen Interceptor!" It was so embarrassing. He got rid of it after a year or two.'

A possible clue to his driving problems arose when Norman Davies, the kit man, was asked to clean Busby's vehicle. 'Norman did a thorough job inside and out,' said Ramsden, 'and when Matt got in he couldn't believe it – he could see through the windscreen! Because Matt would smoke a pipe constantly while driving and this caused a coating on the inside of the windows. He was in a permanent fog.'

The sun shone and Law returned for the opening match of 1968/69. On the Old Trafford forecourt could be found the origins of rampant commercialism, for amid the excitement of the previous season the board had authorised the spending of £1,000 on a wooden hut to serve as a souvenir shop. The average crowd had increased again to nearly 58,000 and more than 61,000 were there to greet the European champions. But Everton were unlucky to succumb. This was one of only four victories in United's opening 14 matches and they were further dismayed by the blight on football known as the Intercontinental Cup.

A year earlier Celtic, as European champions, had taken on their South American equivalents, Racing Club of Buenos Aires. Celtic had won their home leg 1–0 but lost 2–1 in Argentina, necessitating a play-off in Montevideo, Uruguay, during which two Racing players and four from Celtic were sent off (though amid the chaos Bertie Auld stayed on the pitch). Racing won 1–0 and Jock Stein declared he would never bring a team back to South America.

Busby, however, backed his diplomatic skills against the clash of cultures evident in Stiles versus Rattín at Wembley in 1966: the English thought the Argentines dirty, while the Argentines discerned hypocrites with stiff upper lips.

Accepting the risks, deeming them worth a tilt at the unofficial world title, Busby agreed that United would take on Estudiantes. In Buenos Aires they were soon reminded of Sir Alf Ramsey's description of Rattín and company as 'animals'. It also became clear that Stiles's reputation had followed him; Benfica's Brazilian manager, Otto Glória, had called him 'brutal', citing Eusébio's scar-covered knee. Busby, seeking to build bridges, thought it was a good idea to attend a reception at which the teams could get to know each other. Estudiantes failed to turn up and even Busby got angry about that.

As for the match, it picked up where Racing v. Celtic had left off. Estudiantes committed 36 fouls. Of United's 17, no fewer than 10 were awarded against Stiles, who had been butted by Carlos Bilardo (later to manage Argentina when they won the World Cup in 1986), suffering a cut above an eye. Eventually Stiles was sent off. The only goal came when a corner from Juan Ramón Verón, whose son Juan Sebastián would play for United, was headed past Stepney.

Before Estudiantes came to Old Trafford, Busby said: 'Our players showed great restraint in the first leg and I ask all of our supporters to follow suit.' A brick nevertheless flew through the window of an Argentine player's room in a Cheshire hotel. The match began badly, Verón extending the aggregate deficit, and amid further cynicism Best retaliated against Tato Medina and walked off. The Yugoslav referee let him go then despatched Medina too. United's equaliser on the night was too little and too late. Afterwards, Busby called for FIFA to ban Argentine teams from international competition. So much for diplomacy. But the righteous indignation that had replaced it hardly sat well alongside what Busby saw in the *Daily Mail* the next morning.

Stepney was at home when he got the call. 'It was from Matt's secretary. "The Boss wants to see you in his office at two o'clock." I knew what it was about. You have to bear in mind that Estudiantes had been absolute animals. They'd been spitting at us, which I for one had never experienced before. Bilardo was their captain and he'd been especially evil. And I've got to be honest – I lost my rag. Never done it before. But I had to have Bilardo. As the players came off, I waited for him. As he entered the tunnel, I raised an elbow and smashed him right in the face.

'After that I just wanted to get out of the way and home. But what I'd not realised was that the BBC had their television cameras mounted near the tunnel. I'd been caught. The incident had been spotted on television and written up in the *Mail*. So I drove to Old Trafford to face Matt. I felt worse when I saw all the press waiting in the forecourt. It must have got out that Matt had summoned me. So I walked in and went up the steps to his office. He was clever because his desk and chair were slightly elevated, so you were looking up at him. When he spoke, his voice was normal.

'"Right, son. What did you think you were doing?"

'There was still a bit of me fuming. "Well, Boss, they spat at us, they kicked us – Denis had six stitches down his shins. I had to retaliate."

'And at first he just looked at me. Then he spoke again. "How do you think I feel? How do you think Jimmy Murphy feels? And the directors of Manchester United. The staff. The ground staff. The laundry ladies ... "

'"Boss,' I said, "I'm sorry."

'"Right," he said. "The board have met this morning and we are fining you £50. And, if you ever step out of line again, you will never play for this club again."

'He didn't shout. He didn't even raise his voice. He said it almost casually. And I knew I would never do anything wrong again. Blimey!

'I asked if I'd have to face the reporters and he said he'd walk me to my car. So we went down the stairs and out of the door and the reporters asked him for the outcome of the meeting. "Gentlemen, gentlemen," he said, "have you met my first-team goalkeeper, Alex Stepney?" And he walked straight past them and took me to my car. That was Matt. Very considerate but, behind closed doors, a hard man.'

And if Stepney had waited 30 seconds and whacked Bilardo out of sight? Would United's goalkeeper have got away with it? 'Oh, yes. It was the image of the club he was worried about.'

The late goal the previous night had been Willie Morgan's first for United. He had come from Burnley and taken over from the unfortunate John Aston; no sooner had the Wembley hero routed his critics than a scoreless derby at Maine Road left him with a leg fracture. But Morgan might have come anyway. Busby rated him so highly he paid £117,000 for the winger, whose debut against Tottenham was among the silver linings of a cloudy season.

Even Crerand got a 'wee rest'. He felt Busby's kind arm on his shoulders. 'How do you think you're playing, son? You can do better.' 'Aye, you're right, Boss.'

Fitzpatrick took Crerand's shirt and the almost audibly creaking Foulkes gave way to another from the ranks, Steve James. Francis Burns, unlucky to have lost his place in the European Cup side to Shay Brennan, won it back temporarily before succumbing to knee trouble again. Carlo Sartori, whose parents had brought him from the mountains of northern Italy as a baby – his father had begun a knife-sharpening business around Collyhurst and Ancoats – played a dozen matches in midfield.

But in essence it was the same collection of stars who trailed far behind the likes of Revie's Leeds and Shankly's Liverpool. The game was changing and Busby, in his 60th year, knew it. He didn't like it. But he knew it well enough to plan, if not retirement – he could not envisage walking away from United – a new role.

John Aston had time to analyse the decline. He believed the 1968 triumph was 'meant to be'. The ball he had hooked back from over the line against Sarajevo; the 'last throw of the dice' in Madrid, culminating in Foulkes's sidefooter; Eusébio's vain advance on Stepney. 'Again, meant to be.' And, if Eusébio had scored, would United ever have been European champions in Busby's time? 'Let me think of the right sporting analogy ...' Aston could hardly have come up with better than: 'We were the last man to win Wimbledon with a wooden racket.' Because innovation was in the air. 'There were other teams catching up. Lesser teams. But they were getting results against United. They were better organised. And I think he [Busby] had gone past his time.'

Leeds were one team who had learned how to cope with Law, Best and Charlton though organisation, solidity and hardness. 'In the 1965 FA Cup semi-final,' said John Giles, 'we weren't in the same class as them. But we were a unit and we beat them.'

Giles didn't want to be misunderstood. 'Matt was a great manager. One of the greatest managers of all time. First of all, he'd had the courage not only to get all the young lads in but to play them. He was like an inventor. And after Munich he rebuilt. Ninety per cent of management is getting the right players in. And that includes character. A great manager creates an environment in which good lads prosper. So Busby didn't impose a style as such. Because he had players like Law, Best and Charlton, he had a great team. He told them to express themselves and went to the stand to watch. There was no shouting from the touchline. He gave them freedom.

'Don Revie was totally different. Matt couldn't have done what Don did. In Don's early days, he had players other clubs might not want. The likes of Norman Hunter, Terry Cooper, Paul Reaney and Paul Madeley. They wouldn't have got through the doors of Old Trafford. But Don created a really good environment. The players were coached, and coached well, by the likes of Syd Owen and Les Cocker. And we stuck together. Our opponents could feel it.'

United were to increase their contingent of European Footballers of the Year to three when Best edged Charlton into second place in 1968 – and yet they seldom got the better of Leeds, where Giles took over from Collins as the 'main man' in midfield, forming with Billy Bremner as respected a combination as any in the land. At the end of 1968/69, as Busby tried to bow out of management, Leeds would be crowned champions.

It was after a defeat at Leeds in January that Busby had announced he would step aside. Looking mightily relieved, he said it was time to hand the team to a younger man. 'United is no longer a football club. It is an institution.' As if preparing the ground for the man he had in mind, he added that he would help him in an administrative role: 'I feel the demands are beyond one human being.' Despite speculation involving Revie, Jock Stein and Dave Sexton, who had succeeded Tommy Docherty at Chelsea, Busby's instinct had always been to look inside the club.

Results remained poor until March, when Aston returned to action and Morgan scored a hat-trick in an 8–1 defeat of Queens

Park Rangers. Late that month, United reached 11th place, where they were to finish. In the FA Cup, they survived Exeter but needed replays to see off Watford and Birmingham before losing at home to Everton. In defence of the European title, however, United could raise their game.

Law scored seven times in the matches that produced a 10–2 aggregate against Waterford – an experience United fans found none the less enjoyable for the concurrent knockout of City, on whose behalf Allison had promised to 'terrify' all Europe, by the Turks of Fenerbahçe. Old Trafford then savoured 3–0 victories over Anderlecht and Rapid Vienna, the latter having knocked out Real Madrid. A confident 0–0 under the Prater wheel sent Busby's men through to the semi-finals, in which they would meet Milan, a formidable side featuring Giovanni Trapattoni, Karl-Heinz Schnellinger, Kurt Hamrin and Gianni Rivera.

On 9 April 1969, two weeks before United were due at San Siro, Wilf McGuinness was named chief coach. He was 31. His contract was for three years from June and, while he would pick, organise and direct the team, Busby would deal with other responsibilities, notably relations with the media, as general manager.

Busby, who had clearly designed this structure, would stay in overall charge for the rest of the season. But the mark of McGuinness was soon made, for three days after the announcement his protégé Jimmy Rimmer replaced Stepney in goal at Newcastle, to which the former Milan captain Cesare Maldini had travelled (leaving his baby son Paolo at home) to assess their forthcoming opponents for Nereo Rocco.

Did Stepney, when he got the dreaded arm round the shoulder, resent it? 'I couldn't believe it!' Even if he detected the hand of McGuinness. He was, after all, in what should have been his prime. Yet he was a reserve when United flew to Italy and 80,000 saw Angelo Sormani and Hamrin score unanswered goals with Fitzpatrick getting himself sent off for a kick at the Swedish winger.

A three-week rest before the second leg seemed to invigorate United and Old Trafford was as noisy as ever. A missile that hurtled from the Stretford End, hitting the Milan goalkeeper Fabio Cudicini (whose son Carlo would perform for Chelsea) hardly comforted Rocco's team, although they held out until 20 minutes from the end when Best played a one-two with Brian Kidd and deliciously beat three men, setting up Bobby Charlton for a drive that fulminated

into Cudicini's net. One more was needed to force a play-off and
Law claimed it as the ball was scrambled off a muddied goal-line,
but in vain; the defender Angelo Anquilletti, seeing Law's fists
raised as if histrionically demanding justice, shrugged and United
were out. Milan went on to collect their second European title with
a 4–1 win over Ajax in Madrid.

While considering the erection of safety fences to placate UEFA
after the missile incident, United completed their season with
a League match at home to Leicester, who were hoping not to
compound their disappointment of defeat by Manchester City in
the FA Cup final by being relegated. United's incentive was the
favour a draw or win would do Noel Cantwell, whose Coventry
were the other candidates for the drop, and Busby's men scraped it
by 3–2 for their old friend. The Leicester manager, Frank O'Farrell,
shook hands with Busby, who returned the crowd's applause before
disappearing from sight.

Despite a season in which only Mercer and Allison had brought
a trophy to Manchester, in which the City captain Tony Book
shared the Footballer of the Year award with another veteran, Dave
Mackay of Brian Clough's Second Division champions Derby,
attendances at Old Trafford had held up. They had averaged over
51,000 in the League, with full houses for most matches in the
cups. 'This is not the end, this is the beginning,' Busby had said
after the European triumph, and these figures were the proof, for
after he had gone United would remain such a big and emotionally
charged club that, even when they fell into the Second Division,
attendances averaged 48,000 – or 21,000 more than the First
Division average without them.

When he named a select XI from the players he had known,
it read: Stepney, Carey, Byrne, Crerand, Chilton, Edwards, Best,
Charlton, Taylor, Law and Mitten. But for his enforced retirement
at 23 that spring, Bobby Noble might have entered such company.
'He was the hardest player I ever saw,' said Stepney. 'In the
1966/67 championship season, I think three of our opponents
had cartilage operations.' And Noble played only 31 matches.
But the head and chest injuries he had suffered in the car crash
defeated him. He received £25,000 damages and started work
with a printing firm.

Shortly afterwards, Busby celebrated his 60th birthday. Other
news that day included the start of a public lie-in by John Lennon

and his wife Yoko Ono in a Montreal hotel room in aid of peace in
Vietnam and elsewhere. During the summer, Neil Armstrong and
Buzz Aldrin became the first men on the Moon and from Northern
Ireland, where violence was increasing, came Sammy McIlroy to
Manchester United.

Bobby Charlton was back for pre-season training and ready to
welcome the new intake of apprentices. 'Matt brought Bobby down
and introduced him to us,' said McIlroy. 'He was showing us what
the club was about. And Bobby said a few words and I'm thinking
"I've only just come and the first two people I meet are this great
manager and one of the greatest players in the world."

'He also mentioned homesickness and I *was* very homesick for
a time, so Matt would send me for a few days at the end of each
month. And bit by bit the homesickness went away.'

If the life and times of Matt Busby had become the subject
of a film, the script would have ended with the strains of 'What a
Wonderful World' in the wee small hours of that late-May morning
when United celebrated: Busby and Louis Edwards, the former
players in their quieter way, Jimmy Murphy, Jack Crompton and two
generations of John Astons, Les Olive with his memories of post-
Munich gloom, George Best and Pat Crerand, the unobtrusively
excellent Tony Dunne (as ever, it had gone barely noticed that the
Irishman had done just enough to shift Eusébio on to his left foot
as Alex Stepney and everyone else feared the worst), the two Kens,
Daz and Omo and a host of parents, siblings and children. The
credits would have rolled over Busby's warm brown voice: '*And I
think to myself ...*'

And eventually, in Busby's stormproof lee, Wilf McGuinness
would have proved a modern coach of such authority that the
Mercer/Allison axis would have been challenged and Leeds,
Liverpool and the growing force Everton obliged to think again.

Instead, Everton under Harry Catterick ran away with the
1969/70 title and United, though up to eighth, could not
even claim to be the leading club of their conurbation because
City were parading both the League Cup, after ousting United
in the semi-finals, and the Cup Winners' Cup, secured after
victory over Górnik in Vienna. Even the FA Cup had been
dangled teasingly under United's nose, for Old Trafford had
been the stadium chosen for a final replay in which Chelsea
overcame Leeds.

QUITE A SICK CLUB

At least the new regime had overseen a rise of three League places. And taken Leeds to a third match in the FA Cup semi-finals; under Busby in 1968/69 they had fallen a round earlier. And it was hardly Wilf McGuinness's fault United now lacked the delightful distraction of Europe. Given the limited and sporadic help he received from some of Busby's players – that was how they still saw themselves – it was always a battle. He tried not to be lonely but was to admit that the partnership with his mentor might have got off on the wrong foot.

When Busby had handed the team over, McGuinness felt 'a bit young'. But he hadn't worried too much. He chuckled in the McGuinness way. 'I was a very confident young man.' Yet he was overshadowed. 'Matt had been a great, great manager and was still a great man. He couldn't be anything else but the Boss. I should have gone to him more. But at the start it seemed he didn't want to be seen to be interfering. So I thought I'd better abide by that.'

After the 37-year-old Foulkes joined the coaching staff, McGuinness dropped Charlton and Law in favour of Aston and the young Irish centre-forward Don Givens and, while he took those decisions alone – Busby said later that Charlton and Law should not have been left out on the same day – Busby was hardly inactive in other team matters, as the acquisition of Ian Ure proclaimed. The blond Scot, who cost £80,000 from Arsenal, was rightly regarded as a Busby signing (McGuinness wanted the more expensive Colin Todd from Sunderland), another reason to wonder what 'full control' of the Manchester United team now meant.

McGuinness did, according to Busby, seek advice now. 'He came to me [after a 3–0 defeat at Everton on a Tuesday night] and said, "What team would you play on Saturday?" I gave him my team and he selected it.' Charlton and Law returned for Aston and Givens, while Ure replaced the 21-year-old Paul Edwards. United drew 0–0 at Wolverhampton and remained unbeaten in ten matches. So Ure helped to steady McGuinness's ship. But what he found at Old Trafford shocked him. 'Quite a sick club' was how he put it. And not just in the medical sense, although that was bad enough.

The deal had been done by Busby on the telephone to Bertie Mee while McGuinness listened obediently. The fee was agreed and, when Mee went to tell Ure, he was astonished. 'Little did United know, obviously, how bad my knee was. It was chronic. I'd been having operations for five years at Arsenal and was taking pills. Bad ones they were too – I later found out they were given to racehorses in America, just to get them on the track.

'I was amazed United had made no inquiries of Arsenal about my fitness. If they had, Arsenal would have had to tell them I wasn't worth signing. I certainly wouldn't have signed myself. I don't blame Arsenal for getting rid of me. I blame United for signing me. They must have been bloody blind.

'The medical was a farce. An absolute farce. In fact it wasn't a medical at all. I never saw a doctor. There was just Jack Crompton. He told me to bend each knee 90 degrees and that was no problem for me because I'd taken four or five of the pills that week!

'Apparently Busby had been impressed when I'd got sent off with Denis Law. I think the fight we had that day might have convinced him I was what they needed when Bill Foulkes finished. But almost a whole team was going over the hill at the same time. How Busby had let it slide was incredible. He was in complete charge. Wilf was the monkey – he was the organ-grinder. After the European Cup he should have got rid of not only Bill but Bobby. And Denis.' Law was a few months short of his thirtieth birthday when Ure joined United. 'But he had a knee almost as bad as mine. And there was terrible wear and tear on Nobby too. They were all past their best.

'Even George Best should have gone. It would have caused a sensation, but by the time I got there he was drinking heavily three or four nights a week. He was a great player and the nicest guy but he'd become a bad influence on the club.'

According to Ken Ramsden, when decisions upset players the temptation to say it hadn't been like this in Busby's day, or even have a moan to the 'Boss', often proved irresistible. Even Sammy McIlroy, in his youth, could sense it. 'Wilf had a really tough task. You know, telling Bobby what to do, Denis what to do, Paddy what to do, when maybe he had been a lesser player than them.'

Busby and McGuinness became as separate as Mercer and Allison were complementary. That the relationship had not been thought through was obvious from the start, said Ramsden: 'The idea was that Matt would deal with the media while Wilf took charge of team affairs. So Wilf would get a call from a journalist on a Friday asking who was fit for the next day's match and he'd say, "You have to speak to the Boss." And the journalist would then ring Matt, who would say, "I don't know – you'll have to speak to Wilf about team affairs." It was bizarre.' And can only have undermined perceptions of McGuinness.

Sammy McIlroy insisted: 'Wilf was unlucky, because he still got the team to three semi-finals – if he'd just got to Wembley and won a cup, things might have been different.'

But it wasn't just bad luck. On the afternoon of an FA Cup semi-final replay against Leeds at Villa Park, with the players supposedly sleeping in a Worcester hotel, McGuinness heard Best was with the wife of a businessman attending a conference. He went to Best's room and, McGuinness recalled, 'he told me he was just showing her his room'. The story spread quickly, unsettling – if not exactly surprising – his team-mates. By the time the match kicked off, the Leeds players knew too and they duly found Best off form, missing a clear chance to settle the tie.

Busby might have denied Ian Ure's scathing critique. He might have pointed to eighth place. And mentioned Bobby Charlton's presence at the 1970 World Cup after 57 club appearances in all competitions. Best had played almost as many and, if anyone now carried a decaying team, he did, for all his late nights. Law had endured a season of pain and degenerative arthritis in which he started thirteen matches, made a further three appearances as a substitute and ended up with three goals.

'It was probably the worst time,' he said, 'because the medical facilities were nothing like in the modern game. No comparison. The last few years of my career were not good because I wasn't fit. But I had to play on. For about a third of my career – at least – I had to have cortisone injections before practically every game. Because they didn't let you recover properly from injuries then. And I wasn't the only one. George Best, Francis Burns, John Fitzpatrick – others suffered. The game has changed drastically – and for the better. I'm not envious of the money today's players get, but I doubt if they realise how lucky they are in having the medical care that clubs have now.'

Although it would always be unfair to judge football clubs, or men, without allowance for the times in which they existed, little seemed to have changed at Busby's Manchester United between the Wembley afternoon in 1957 when smelling salts were waved under Ray Wood's cheekbone and any Saturday morning on which Law faced the syringe.

Law was in the last United team picked by Wilf McGuinness; he scored twice in a 4–4 draw with Brian Clough's Derby at the Baseball Ground on Boxing Day 1970. This left United fifth from bottom. Three days earlier McGuinness had supervised yet another semi-final defeat, by Third Division Aston Villa in the League Cup, and the overall effect was to cut what felt, to him, like an umbilical cord. Busby called him in. 'I think it hurt him to tell me,' said McGuinness. He was offered his old job back, and asked by Bolton to manage alongside Nat Lofthouse. But he'd had his fill of partnerships with club legends. Anyway, 'Bolton was too near Old Trafford – I needed to get away.' Eventually he went to Greece to manage Aris, of Thessaloniki, and what remained of his hair fell out. 'I do think it was the after-effects of United. It came out very quickly.'

Busby, of course, was picking the team again. Although Stepney returned at Jimmy Rimmer's expense, Busby showed no disinclination to use youth and Alan Gowling scored four times in a 5–1 win over Southampton. Yet the attendance of around 35,000 emphasised that Old Trafford no longer saw Busby as a messiah. It was a view he shared; he maintained the search for a successor. The manager/coach structure had served Manchester City well and was enjoying further success at Arsenal, who, with Don Howe working alongside Bertie Mee, were to do the Double. Yet Busby changed tack in the light of United's experience, seeking a figure of international repute in Jock Stein.

They met in the back of Busby's car – a Mercedes now, for the Jensen had gone – at a filling station on the East Lancashire Road. They had seen Leeds beat Liverpool in a Fairs Cup semi-final first leg at Anfield. Busby knew Stein was interested in a move to England, for Crerand had been briefed to tap him up after a Celtic match against Ajax at Parkhead. But according to Stein's son George, who accompanied him on the drive south, he had difficulty with Busby's insistence that several United staff members should be retained; Stein, just as admirably, wanted to bring his own men. He pondered this on the way back to Scotland and, after discussions with his wife, opted to stay with Celtic.

For Busby there was a bitter-sweet ending. The bitterness came first: yet more trouble involving United supporters at Blackpool, where rampages compounded the disgrace of a knife-throwing incident at the Stretford End during Newcastle's visit in February 1971. On top of a £7,000 fine, the FA ordered that Old Trafford be closed for two matches. By comparison, what happened on the pitch at Bloomfield Road – Crerand fought with John Craven and both were sent off – seemed almost an affectionate tribute from the feisty midfielder to his beloved Boss.

Nobby Stiles, not quite 29, had gone to Middlesbrough for £20,000. Crerand was 32 and, after the final match, would join Foulkes on the coaching staff. Now a more benign spirit of football could surface at Busby's final farewell to management, which fate had decreed would be at Maine Road, on 5 May 1971. It proved a suitably exhilarating match. But there was an allied event of which Busby knew nothing until just before kick-off.

Never had *This Is Your Life* honoured the same subject twice. It was discussed and, despite a worry that Busby would be wise to all the usual subterfuges – he had been instrumental in keeping Bobby Charlton unprepared for ambush 18 months earlier – the decision was taken to go ahead. The idea was to lure him by announcing the presentation of an inscribed clock on the pitch, the ceremony to be conducted by his friend Mercer. He naturally agreed to cooperate; after he had finished his final team-talk, he would meet Mercer in the tunnel.

The end-of-season pitch was as it would have been in his debut season 40 years earlier: caked mud with mere tinges of green, crying out for a summer's rest. But the surrounding atmosphere was different, Seventies edgy. Mounted policemen guarded the tunnel mouth. For every ten yards of the perimeter an officer stood facing the crowd. And suddenly their supervisors had second thoughts; fearing a pitch invasion and violence, they withdrew permission for the celebration. The producers, aghast, pleaded with Mercer to intervene and the City manager rescued the situation by promising the police he would take personal responsibility for any mishap.

He hurried off and met Busby in the tunnel. They could see the teams waiting either side of a table on the halfway line. On it were the clock, nestling in tissue paper, and a flat box. Out strode Busby with Mercer, who, after wisely reminding the crowd of the coincidence that Busby should be finishing his career where it had begun, announced that the presentation would in fact be made by 'a mutual friend of ours, Eamonn Andrews', who skipped from the tunnel, took the microphone and proclaimed: 'For the first time ever, I'm saying for the second time, this is your life ...' Busby looked bemused. Mercer, whom Andrews had surprised a year earlier, grinned broadly.

The programme was recorded later in the ballroom of the Piccadilly Hotel. Nellie, her white hair tightly permed, looking fit in her 80th and penultimate year, was shown film of her son being introduced to the future King George VI before the 1933 FA Cup final, and bowing more deeply than any other City player in the line. Andrews turned to her: 'Helen, did you notice the bow?' She smiled and replied: 'I was expecting him to do that.' Jean, immaculate, sat next to her husband, with Sandy, and Sheena, and Busby's sisters and half-brother, Mercer, Len Langford, Jimmy Murphy, players past and present, old pals from the Lanarkshire coalfield and the wartime troopships, Alfredo Di Stéfano and Santiago Bernabéu, Louis Edwards, Jimmy McGuire from America and Professor Georg Maurer from Munich.

For much of the time, Busby looked unusually nervous, rubbing his thumb and index finger together, licking his lips, but he relaxed and smiled warmly at a film of his six grand-daughters – for whom the recording was too late on a school night – singing the Clive Dunn song 'Grandad' and then waving as they chorused: 'Goodnight God bless, Matt!'

His final match had featured a George Best masterclass and seven goals, of which United scored four. They had finished eighth again. Their 24 points from 19 matches under Busby would, if projected over a season, have produced a total of 53. This would have left them third, 12 points behind Arsenal. The runners-up, Leeds, won the Fairs Cup for the second time under Don Revie, while Chelsea under Dave Sexton took the Cup Winners' Cup. Busby was also much taken with Frank O'Farrell's achievement in guiding Leicester straight back to the First Division as champions. That he was a man of obvious dignity, Irish and Catholic, hardly diminished his attraction.

SHAFTED

Frank O'Farrell received a call from Busby offering £12,000 a year and bonuses. This did not strike O'Farrell as generous but he wanted the job and so went through the obligatory melodrama: a meeting in the back of Louis Edwards's Rolls-Royce in a Leicestershire layby. As humbler vehicles swished by, Busby repeated the £12,000 offer. Edwards interjected. 'No,' he said, 'it's £15,000.' As O'Farrell said: 'It got us off on a bad note, me and Busby. He knew that I knew he wasn't playing it straight. From that moment I didn't trust him.'

When O'Farrell got to Old Trafford, he found Busby in the manager's office. McGuinness had worked from Jimmy Murphy's, but O'Farrell felt he had to insist. Busby would no longer be general manager. He had joined the board, to which a 24-year-old Martin Edwards had recently been added, and accepted a long-standing offer of 500 shares.

He had also been made a retirement gift of the souvenir shop, which had outgrown its wooden hut and been incorporated into the back of the stand facing Warwick Road. This was a sort of pension combined with a career for Sandy and Sheena, who would run it. Neither the club nor Busby made the arrangement public, or saw a need to do so. At that time, a director could not be paid by a club, so this stake in the future seemed a neat way of rewarding him for the past.

O'Farrell would supervise every aspect of team affairs – he had Busby's assurance – while his assistant, Malcolm Musgrove, ran the training sessions once conducted by Jimmy Murphy, who had been paid off with five years' salary – £20,000 – and a scouting job at £25 a week.

It was the end of an era. Never again would a youngster walk nervously into Busby's presence with hopes of progressing under Murphy. Sammy McIlroy would be the last of the Babes. And now O'Farrell gave him a League debut at 17. United were leaders – 'Frank had started like a house on fire,' said McIlroy – and stayed above Derby and City after a 3–3 draw in which McIlroy scored. 'Then we beat Southampton 5–2 down at The Dell. Besty got a hat-trick and I got one. Then I had to return to the youth team for the Youth Cup while the first team went to Jersey for a break.

'When they came back, they never won a game for two months.' In the League, it was more than three months. 'The wheels had flown off. And Frank started disappearing a lot. You never saw him around the place. Besty was having problems, going walkabout. Bobby wasn't happy. Denis was injured.'

United had slipped to ninth by the early spring, a belated pantomime season in which the principals were Brian Clough and Ian Storey-Moore, one of the most coveted attackers in the country who recalled, 'Brian told me a pack of lies'.

Three or four clubs, United and Derby among them, had agreed to pay £200,000 and Forest arranged for him to meet O'Farrell first. 'So we went to the Edwalton Hotel at West Bridgford,' said Storey-Moore, 'and O'Farrell came in. I was with Matt Gillies, the Forest manager, Bill Anderson, his assistant, and Ken Smales, the secretary – no agents. I'd spoken to some intermediary from the United end on the phone about salary and so on.' But O'Farrell looked blank. 'He said he didn't know anything about it and offered less. I was a bit disappointed and suggested we leave it there.

'I went back to the foyer and told Gillies, who put Clough on the line. He said he'd be over in half an hour. At which point Gillies, Anderson and Smales went whoosh – just left me on my own. Clough and Peter Taylor walked in, took their jackets off, sat down and blah blah blah. I actually signed forms. And I remember Clough saying to Taylor, "Right, take him back to the Midland Hotel." That was where Derby stayed before home games. About eight o'clock Clough arrives and says, "All sorted – Forest have signed the forms." And then – would you believe this? – he tells me he's been offered Gillies's job at Forest!

'At the very same time the Forest chairman, Tony Wood, was saying there was no way I was going to Derby. But the next day Clough paraded me on the pitch and it was only on the Sunday morning that I suspected Clough might not have been telling the truth.

'United must have been in contact with Forest because on the Monday I heard O'Farrell and Busby were on their way to my house. They drove me to Manchester and I remember Busby saying, "Oh, he's going to be in a lot of trouble, Brian Clough, over this. The FA are not happy with him and he's sailing close to the wind over various other things too, so you don't want to be playing for him." Anyway, I decided to go to Old Trafford. Whether it was the right decision I don't know. Great players were coming to the end, George Best was messing about – one day he was there, next day he wasn't – and on reflection I might have been better going to Derby.'

After his team had clinched the title that season, Clough taunted Busby that it served Manchester United right for choosing O'Farrell instead of him. Clough was not Busby's type. He thought him too noisy and self-centred (factors that, many years later, may have initially counted against José Mourinho when the likes of Sir Alex Ferguson and Sir Bobby Charlton pondered another succession).

Storey-Moore had made a dazzling start for United. O'Farrell had also done well to pay Aberdeen £125,000 for Martin Buchan. With McIlroy, that made three new talents of Manchester United scale. Yet the manager's problems were far from over for, when Best strayed, the dilemma arose: to whip him into line, risking worse results, or indulge him?

Best by now had moved from Mrs Fullaway's into a white-tiled modernist home in leafy Bramhall. It had become something of a tourist attraction, such was the celebrity of its owner, who was featured on *This Is Your Life* and the talk show hosted by his friend Michael Parkinson, to whom he spoke about the procession of girls: 'When they start to take their clothes off, they say things like "I'm not doing this just because you're George Best."' He had become the main client of Denis Law's agent Ken Stanley, earning an estimated £1,000 a week mostly from endorsements and such personal appearances as he fancied and remembered about. And yet he had difficulty sleeping, for which the remedy was often a few more vodkas.

In mid-season, after he had missed training for a week, O'Farrell announced that he was being fined two weeks' wages (about £400) and made to do extra training as well as move back into Mrs Fullaway's. While making the occasional overt visit to Aycliffe Avenue, however, Best remained in Bramhall. He gambled almost as excessively as he drank. And kept absenting himself from training, much to the disgust of Bobby Charlton, with whom he terminally fell out.

Meanwhile Busby, according to O'Farrell, broke his pledge of non-interference by telling the manager he had been wrong to drop Charlton, and by blaming Buchan for leaks in the defence. Harry Gregg, now manager at Shrewsbury, was getting calls; he heard O'Farrell was 'treating Denis Law like a tramp' and even hatched an audacious plot to offer £20,000 for the fading great. On the phone he sounded out Law, who asked which pub he was in.

'What do you mean?'

'Well, it's obviously the strongest beer they serve.'

Gregg got the impression Law wanted to stay for a testimonial but feared O'Farrell might not grant it. So next, said Gregg, he rang Busby. 'Tell Denis not to worry,' said Busby. 'I'll take care of it.'

Ken Merrett was around and, although he would never say a word against Busby, did wonder if loyalty to some of his players, those who had helped him to the European title, went too far. Even Busby's son Sandy recognised that. Sheena felt sorry for O'Farrell, whom she liked and respected. And she was not alone. Merrett's sympathies were with the Irishman. 'Here,' he said, 'I have to declare an interest. I really liked Frank O'Farrell. I thought he was a good man. And, when he took over as manager, he got shafted, basically. By the old guard.'

At the end of 1971/72, Best missed United's tour and flew to Marbella. He said he was retiring from football. He celebrated his 26th birthday with reporters who had dutifully followed him to the beach, and announced a 'comeback'. He was fined again and agreed to move in with Pat and Noreen Crerand and their three children in Sale. Another day, another futile plan. Before long he was back with Mrs Fullaway, this time for real – the Bramhall house was sold for £40,000 – but his career now followed a dismal destiny.

'Inside the club he is perfect,' insisted O'Farrell. Not on the night of Charlton's testimonial against Celtic, from which Best pulled out late through injury before heading for the Grapes, with its characterful horseshoe bar around which his companions would often now number Rodney Marsh of Manchester City. The Grapes now vied with the less trendy Brown Bull as Best's favourite. Not that he was the only drinker at United. But he was the worst. When reminded about Best's insomnia, Busby replied: 'I think he's given both of us a few sleepless nights.'

If United had one thing going for them, it was that Allison's ambition had forced Mercer out of Maine Road. Mercer was at Coventry and Allison, alone, lacked his senior's judgment. City had been on top of the First Division the previous spring when Allison upset their balance by spending a club record £200,000 to bring Marsh from QPR; they had ended up fourth.

In the summer John Aston went for £30,000 to Luton, joining Jimmy Ryan and Don Givens, Alan Gowling to Huddersfield for £25,000 and Francis Burns to Southampton for £50,000. But O'Farrell needed to spend much more than he could bring in.

He signed new strikers early in the next season, pairing the big centre-forward Wyn Davies, a £25,000 signing from Manchester City, with Ted MacDougall, whose predatory skills were reflected in a £200,000 fee to Bournemouth. But United were the lowest scorers in the First Division, in obvious danger of relegation as Christmas approached, when David Meek went into print on O'Farrell's behalf. And paid a price.

'Frank had had a difficult ride,' Meek said. 'He explained his ideas to me and I thought he had a point and so I wrote a piece for the *Evening News*. It appeared under the headline "Be Fair To Frank". I said they had sacked McGuinness after 18 months and O'Farrell had also been in the job 18 months – it wasn't enough.

'Well, the club didn't like it. They later accused me of trying to embarrass the club.' They? The club? 'Matt might have moved aside as manager but he was still the power behind the throne. In fact, he was the throne itself. And I think the decision to sack Frank had already been made when my piece came out. And I'm sure the club [in this context Louis Edwards as well as Busby] had a guilty conscience about letting down a fellow Catholic, as Frank was.

'So the *Evening News* received a letter, signed by Les Olive, which said I was no longer welcome to travel with the club.'

By now the editor was Brian Redhead, later to become an outstanding BBC radio presenter. 'It was Brian who showed me the letter,' Meek recalled. 'He asked, "Do you want me to write an apology – or tell them to fuck off?" You couldn't ask for better support from an editor than that. But in the end I told him to try to find some line down the middle. Anyway, I never got back on the coach. Later, much later, Matt had a habit of suddenly gripping my arm and saying, "We go back a long way together, don't we?" I often wondered if he thought he had treated me a bit harshly.'

United lay second bottom when O'Farrell became another festive sacking. It happened less than a week after Busby had made the short trip to St John's church to be invested as a Knight Commander of the Order of St Gregory the Great. Already a Knight of the Realm and Freeman of Manchester, he received the Papal honour with especial humility.

It was later awarded to Bob Hope, the Irish politician John Hume and, by way of contrast, Jimmy Savile, 'in recognition of their personal service to the Holy See and to the Roman Catholic Church, through [among other things] their excellent examples set forth in their communities and their countries'. A request for annulment of Savile's award was later lodged, in the light of further information about the nature of his community work, by the Archbishop of Westminster.

O'Farrell, whose most recent humiliations had included a meeting between Best and Busby at the former manager's house of which he knew nothing, was put out of his misery a week before Christmas, hot on the heels of a 5–0 defeat away to fellow strugglers Crystal Palace attended by Tommy Docherty, who had been watching Scotland candidates such as Law and Morgan. Docherty had returned to his native land after a peripatetic post-Chelsea career taking in Rotherham, QPR, Aston Villa and Porto. Busby had already spoken to Law and Morgan, among others, about him and at Selhurst Park quite literally guided Louis Edwards towards his next managerial appointment. He put them together in the boardroom, where Edwards asked Docherty if he would move to United. Docherty, who was a friend of O'Farrell – they had been clubmates at Preston – replied that United already had a manager. Edwards told him O'Farrell would be gone within days.

By the time O'Farrell's desk was cleared, United had approached the Scottish FA and soon Docherty was supervising a home draw with Leeds. At Derby, a 3–1 defeat should have been an especial ordeal for Storey-Moore, who was booed throughout yet played well, scoring United's goal, and appreciated being sought out by Busby afterwards. 'He shook my hand and said, "Well done today." It was nice of him.'

LOST TO LOVE

To Busby it looked like third time lucky. Old Trafford took to Tommy Docherty's style and attendances rose during the escape from the drop in 1973. The team that finished 18th showed big changes. Four Scots had come in, the most expensive being Lou Macari at £200,000 from Celtic, plus the cheaper but significant Irish pair Mick Martin and Gerry Daly from Bohemians. Bobby Charlton and Denis Law had played their last for United and George Best was nearing the end. The Doc was performing radical surgery.

By the start of the 1973/74 season, Law had gone back to Manchester City on a free transfer (he would return only for the testimonial that had been duly granted) and Charlton was manager of a Preston heading for relegation to the Third Division. Tony Dunne had joined Bolton. Carlo Sartori raised £50,000 from Bologna, Paul Edwards £15,000 from Oldham. The right-back Tommy O'Neil, the last Busby debutant, had gone to Southport and John Fitzpatrick retired though injury.

Also destined to make way for a new guard was David Sadler. He was only 27. 'But pretty well everyone from the '68 team was getting the old heave-ho and I was basically told I'd be going. Also I was getting the treatment – you know, come back in the afternoon and train with the kids. I remember once there was a trip to Rome and an audience with the Pope. I'd have liked to meet the Pope but, along with two or three others, was instead picked to play in a testimonial match against one of the non-League clubs around Manchester.

'But I had to admit that Tommy and his assistant Tommy Cavanagh – despicable man – weren't doing a bad job, and I accepted their right to an opinion of me as a player, even if I didn't agree with it. So it became a question of my testimonial – I'd been at the club for more than ten years and that was the accepted qualification.'

It was then that Sadler lost a little of his respect for Busby. He went to Docherty, who said flatly that there would be no more testimonials. 'That was it – end of story. No discussion.' Tony Dunne would be the last. Dunne had been a model professional. Hardly ever injured. Did everything Busby required. One day he was lying on the treatment table. 'How is he?' Busby asked Ted Dalton. 'He's got no chance, Boss. He'll never be fit in time.' Busby walked over to the table, laid a hand on Dunne's leg and said: 'I know you won't let me down, son.' Dunne played. He had been granted a testimonial and, although Manchester City had provided the opposition at Old Trafford, fewer than 18,000 had turned up. With Docherty adamant, Sadler pondered his next move.

He spoke to a couple of clubmates. 'They said, "Matt's your man. You've got to see Matt." So I went to him and he said, "I can't interfere, son." I said, "What do you mean, interfere?" He said there had been talk about his influence at the club and he'd agreed not to interfere in any aspect of the running of the football side. I was really disappointed. Something had been said after '68 on the lines of "You'll always be okay here" and, while I accepted that there was an atmosphere of euphoria after '68, I was just so disappointed he didn't feel strong enough to stand up to this mouthy manager. I carried that with me for a while. It upset me more than anything else in my career.'

There was also a harsh postscript to O'Farrell. If Busby had, as Meek suspected, encountered a conscientious discomfort over the sacking, it was given a further twist by the club's refusal to buy out the three-and-a-half years remaining on the Irishman's contract. O'Farrell was made to wait nine months in the unemployment queue – at one stage, literally – before, on the eve of a court judgement, settlement was made. Some of the responsibility for that could be laid at Busby's door. It was he, after all, who recruited the managers.

After Bobby Charlton signed Sadler for Preston for £25,000 in November 1973, only Stepney, Kidd and Best remained of the Wembley heroes of 1968, and only Stepney was to be at Old Trafford at the end of the season, when Law's almost reluctant backheel in a derby made sure United were relegated. They went down without Best. His final appearance had been in a 3–0 defeat at Queens Park Rangers on New Year's Day.

A couple of months later his youth-team pal Barry Fry became the 29-year-old manager of the perennially unsuccessful Southern League club Dunstable Town, and had an idea. He went to Manchester and visited Best's nightclub, Slack Alice.

'"Hi, Baz," said George, "What are you doing here?" I told him I'd come to ponce a favour – I wanted him to guest for me in pre-season friendlies. "Fine," he said. "Which club are you with? "Dunstable," I said. "There might be a problem," he said. I said I thought there might.

' "No,' he said, "I'd like to play. It's just that Tommy Doc has still got my registration." So I went to The Cliff next morning. Paddy Crerand took me up to Tommy's office and I asked for permission to use George. "What's your club, son?" I told him. "*Dunstabubble*!" he said. "Do you think you can get him to play for Dunstabubble when I can't get him to play for Manchester United?" Paddy said, well, they were kids together. So Tommy says I'm welcome to go and ask him. Well, of course I already had, so I went to a café for a couple of hours before telling Tommy he'd agreed to play. "Who are your opponents, son?" I said I didn't have any yet. And Tommy brought down a Manchester United XI.

'We had 10,000 in the ground. Can you imagine? George Best against Manchester United. We were on the *News at Ten*. And Dunstable Town had arrived!'

Not for long. Fry got them into the Premier Division but within a year or two the club folded, to be replaced by Dunstable FC. Much, much later Fry found himself on a television programme with Best. 'We were talking in the green room beforehand. "George, I still can't believe you came and played for me at Dunstable." "Barry," he said, "I'd never forget you. You used to give me the only money I ever had."'

'I knew exactly what he meant. When we were kids, George used to send all his wages to his mum and dad. I was going out with a girl whose dad and his mates were United-daft. So I used to organise their tickets. We got two tickets each for first-team matches but never used them because we were playing for the "A" or "B" team. They were comps, of course, but I sold them and went back to the other lads with the money. I never realised how much it meant to George. And he didn't forget.'

The joys of Best's nature conspired – with his phenomenal talent – in Busby's indulgence. 'Matt was very good to Bestie,' said Fry. 'He treated him like a son. He couldn't have done any more for George – and George would tell you that if he were here. He bent over backwards. At the end of the day, George was ill – he couldn't control it.'

And by the time of Manchester United's relegation he was one problem less. Docherty had reshaped the squad. 'His personality was like a breath of fresh air,' said McIlroy. 'He was jovial and things kicked off.' Jimmy Murphy, who now shared an office with Joe Armstrong, was used more and a little of the colour returned to his cheeks. When the teenage centre-back Arnie Sidebottom (later to bowl for Yorkshire and England, and to father a son Ryan, who would do likewise) became a fleeting first-team presence, his mane was fashionably shaggy. Murphy eyed him, thrust a fiver into his hand and said: 'For Christ's sake, Arnie, get your hair cut.'

In the ensuing season the Second Division championship was won by a United who needed only a couple of wingers to become a force in the First. 'It was an electrifying team to play in,' said McIlroy, 'and it had all the hallmarks of a Busby side – wingers, tempo, goals. If they scored two we scored three – that was the attitude. And the fans loved it.'

Sadly, Ian Storey-Moore had been left behind. 'When I got to United,' he said, 'it was a privilege to be among great players, and they were fine with me, but there was too much muttering – "Matt wouldn't have done this, Matt wouldn't have done that" – and Docherty did the right thing in clearing them out. My regret was that I only played a few games for him before I got this bad ankle injury at The Cliff. It was a very hard surface and, when I came down after challenging for a ball, the ankle just gave way. All the ligaments snapped.

'The medical treatment was abysmal. They didn't have a clue. They even – and Matt must have been involved in this – sent me to a faith healer. This guy put his hands on my ankle and started murmuring things. So for months I kept trying to play then breaking down. Eventually I went to someone who said I needed an operation. But by then it was too late – they couldn't stitch it together.' The thought of legal action never occurred to him.

It was three months into the 1975/76 season when United filled his No.11 shirt. Docherty paid Millwall £80,000 for Gordon Hill, a boyish entertainer with a goalscoring rate many a striker would envy. During the previous season Docherty had found his other winger by picking up Steve Coppell from Tranmere for £60,000 to take the place of Willie Morgan, who had been returned to Burnley for £35,000. This was the manager's reward for bringing Jimmy Murphy out of mothballs; Busby's old assistant had identified both Coppell and Hill, as Docherty generously acknowledged: 'I was happy to take his advice because I never doubted him ... Jimmy didn't get the credit he deserved. In my opinion he was as great as Busby.'

Some said Murphy was undervalued because he shunned the limelight, as when the club had marked his first 20 years; rather than receive his silver salver in front of the crowd, he had asked for a simple ceremony in the boardroom. Others hinted at a degree of neglect by Busby, especially towards the end of their partnership. This was an account by Harry Gregg:

Jimmy did so much for United it was untrue. And one day I got a call to see him. And I found myself caught in the middle between two fantastic people – in different ways.

He meant Busby and Murphy.

I went to Jimmy's house and every time he left the room his wife would tell me about things Matt had done. And sometimes Jimmy would tell me things. And eventually he said, 'Son, Steve Richards [a sports writer held in high esteem by Murphy] wants to help me write a book – would you consider being co-writer?' I was manager of Crewe at the time and, when I got home, I discussed it with my wife [his second wife, Carolyn] and realised it was because he wanted me to write the bits about Matt. He didn't want to criticise Matt.

Docherty had built a team to compete with England's best. Stepney remained in goal; Brian Greenhoff had come through the ranks to partner Buchan in central defence with Alex Forsyth and Stewart Houston, another astute signing at £55,000 from Brentford, at full-back; Gerry Daly and Sammy McIlroy were in midfield; and between the wingers lurked Macari and the £170,000 striker Stuart Pearson from Hull City (Kidd had gone to Arsenal for £110,000, to be followed by the £40,000 Rimmer). After reaching the FA Cup final, which they were to lose to Southampton of the Second Division, they finished third in the League with an average crowd of 54,000. Liverpool, the champions, had the second highest with 41,000.

What could possibly go wrong?

For a year, nothing. United slipped to sixth but returned to Wembley in May 1977 and this time won the FA Cup, beating Liverpool, denying the Treble to the team Bill Shankly had passed to Bob Paisley. Yet only a matter of weeks after Docherty's United had celebrated the club's first major trophy in nine years another manager had left Old Trafford, and in circumstances that pained Busby more than most.

Docherty had fallen in love with someone other than Agnes, his wife of 27 years. And Mary Brown was the wife of the club physiotherapist, Laurie Brown. 'No one was more surprised than the players,' McIlroy recalled. 'Laurie, Tommy Cavanagh and the Doc – everything seemed all right there.' In hotel lobbies they would chat over a pot of tea or a bottle of champagne, depending on the time of day. 'And the team was flying. If we could have added a couple more players that summer, we could have pushed Liverpool for the title. We were looking forward to that.'

Busby had become more evident than at any time since he ceased to manage, travelling to away matches with the other directors on the coach, having a friendly word with the players. 'He was never the type of man to walk past and say nothing,' said McIlroy. But there had been no mellowing of his attitude to scandal and this proved fatal to Docherty's hopes of weathering the inevitable storm. Busby knew about the affair. His circle of friends still included Crerand, who had become manager of Northampton after exclusion from Docherty's coaching hierarchy.

The news broke in the village of Mottram in Longdendale, where Cheshire meets the Peaks. Docherty, aged 49, and Mrs Brown, 31, were to make their home there and at first it seemed he would remain United's manager. 'The board want me to stay,' he told reporters, 'and that's terrific.' It was also a testament to the strength of his relationship with Louis Edwards; a jocular deference had always struck the right tone with the chairman, facilitating their friendship at a time when Louis and Busby were drifting apart, the latter coming sadly to accept that only one of their sons was ever going to be a United director.

But Louis still listened to Busby and gradually the reality of how the club looked to the outside world began to dawn. Docherty had sold his love story to a Sunday newspaper – and Laurie Brown intimated that offers were being considered for his side of it. And there was, of course, the question of right and wrong from his point of view. Later Docherty was to assert that Jean Busby influenced her husband's stance. Jean remained very much part of the Old Trafford scene, especially in helping to entertain visiting directors and their wives on match days. At any rate, it was largely due to Busby that the board's decision was reversed. Docherty would go. Brown would not only stay but receive a substantial pay rise.

This would not, however, be the last controversy involving Docherty. He was to sue Willie Morgan for libel after the player told a television audience he was 'about the worst manager there had ever been'. Alex Stepney and Paddy Crerand were due to join Morgan in giving evidence, but the trial collapsed, leaving Docherty to pay costs estimated at £60,000 and face a perjury charge, of which he was acquitted. Neither Stepney nor Crerand was called, although there was time for Barry Fry to testify to the handing of a £1,000 bung to Docherty in return for his kindness in sending a United team to Dunstable.

CHAPTER FOURTEEN

FAMILY FORTUNES

BUTCHERED

When Dave Sexton replaced Tommy Docherty, it was yet another change of tack by Busby. After the restrained O'Farrell had come the wisecracking extrovert Docherty and now here was a gentleman and scholar, an admirer of the Jesuit philosopher Pierre Teilhard de Chardin who would rather countenance poetry than an admiring horde.

For all Sexton's reticence he was popular in the game, admired for his coaching. As a manager he had followed up his early success at Chelsea by guiding QPR to their highest-ever League finish – just a point below champions Liverpool – in 1975/76. Sexton was, moreover, a Catholic whom Busby could trust with the good name of his club.

If only Busby felt the same about Louis Edwards. In the retrospective view of Martin, the elder Edwards was miscast in Eamon Dunphy's book. 'Dunphy made out that Father was a bit of a puppet to Matt,' said Martin. 'That wasn't the case at all. It was a common goal they shared.' By 1976, certainly, Louis had cut any strings. And moved the goalposts. He saw Manchester United as a way of increasing his family's fortune, and his methods dismayed Busby.

Louis Edwards had seldom let scruples get in the way of business. He had inherited butchers' shops and a sausage factory and energetically expanded, notably in supplying local authorities with school meals. During profoundly corrupt times in local politics he gave officials and councillors free meat (of a distinctly higher standard than the children were being served, it later transpired) and, when necessary, straight cash bribes.

Busby had heard the rumours. But they didn't directly affect United. Not while the Edwards business was thriving. Which it ceased to do during the 1970s, as local authorities became more careful about their practices. Louis concentrated on United and among those he consulted was Roland Smith, professor of marketing at the University of Manchester Institute of Science and Technology and 'man of a thousand boardrooms', who suggested a rights issue of club shares, by which existing shareholders could buy more in proportion to their holdings.

In 1976 Smith accompanied Edwards and two other United directors – Busby and Alan Gibson – to the London offices of the merchant bankers Kleinwort Benson. A plan was devised. Shareholders could purchase 208 for every one share held, at £1 each, which would offer every opportunity for big profits.

While the scheme was kept private – this was legal at the time – the Edwards family set about increasing their holding, buying out survivors of Harold Hardman and the Munich victim Walter Crickmer. Martin paid nearly £200,000 for a block owned by Gibson. When the intention to proceed with the rights issue was revealed at a board meeting in autumn 1978, Busby strongly opposed it. But he was the only one. Gibson, with misgivings, complied, as did Bill Young. Louis and Martin Edwards were, of course, in favour, along with Denzil Haroun.

Friends persuaded Busby not to resign. He had been made an interesting offer three years earlier by Eric Alexander, a Manchester City director, son of the former chairman Albert Alexander: why not quit and join the board of his former club? 'Now that's a thought,' said Busby, politely. But he was already disillusioned with the Edwards family over the question of Sandy joining Martin on the United board. Indeed, having proposed Sandy only to have the matter deferred, then deferred again, Busby had declared: 'I do not think that to carry on with it would be good for the club's image and that matters to me more than anything.'

Les Olive had profound concerns about the rights issue and courageously made them clear in letters to the chairman. First, he said, United had no pressing need to raise money. Then he made personal appeals to Louis Edwards and his son, pointing out that the expected opposition of small shareholders might raise awkward questions. Someone might ask, for example, from whom the club bought their meat. Answer: Louis C. Edwards and Sons (Manchester) Limited. Or into whose pockets the profits of the souvenir shop went. Answer, according to some misguided cynics who were about to get a surprise: Louis C. Edwards and his sons.

Olive also gave warning of an irate reaction if 'your family' – or anyone else in the future, he added – drew lavish dividends 'against the interests of the club'. Among those with similar suspicions, when the plan became public, was the steel millionaire John Fletcher, who unsuccessfully challenged it in court. At an extraordinary general meeting shortly before Christmas, the rights issue was approved. Martin Edwards took especial advantage, incurring further debt of £400,000 but promptly clawing about a third back with the sale of a mere 14,000 of his hundreds of thousands of £1 shares to Mike Edelson, a Prestwich-raised clothes retailer.

But Roland Smith was not the Edwards family's only angel. Louis had also been introduced to the Scottish food baronet James Gulliver, who bought effective control of his failing meat company for £100,000 (and was to transform it into the dramatically successful Argyll Foods). Gulliver also took a substantial stake in Manchester United and, in the summer of 1979, was co-opted on to the board.

FLABBERGASTED

United had nearly won the FA Cup in 1979, when Alan Sunderland snatched it for Arsenal in a thrilling climax, and they were to finish runners-up to Liverpool in the League the following season, but generally the Sexton era was one of diminishing excitement. Early on there had been the arrivals of Joe Jordan and Gordon McQueen as, for £850,000, Leeds were stripped of their Scottish backbone. Gordon Hill, symbol of the carefree Docherty days, gave way to Mickey Thomas and Alex Stepney lost his place for the last time, moving to America after the emergence of Gary Bailey. Although the staff had a familiar look, Sexton retaining not only Laurie Brown but Tommy Cavanagh as his assistant, the style of football gradually changed, becoming less attractive.

Sexton broke the British record in paying Chelsea £825,000 for Ray Wilkins, who recalled his early struggles in 1979: 'It was a nightmare. And one Friday I was in the Grill Room at Old Trafford, sitting with my head down. I felt this hand on my shoulder and heard this gruff Scottish voice. I looked up and there was Sir Matt. "Don't worry," he said. "You're a good player." That was all. And from that moment my form returned. I began to play better and better.' The Busby aura still worked. Even if the football he watched became inimical to his legacy.

The rumours of Louis Edwards's ethical shortcomings had, meanwhile, become rife and at the annual general meeting, held at the Lancashire cricket ground, one of the most persistent small shareholders, Frank Holt, rose to ask why the souvenir shop did not figure in the club accounts. He thought he knew and, when the chairman started waffling, took that as vindication. 'Louis puffed and blew,' he recalled, 'as he tried to quell me. But I'd the overwhelming support of the audience, so I got up again.' Eventually Busby intervened. 'The great man stood up and said, "It's mine." I was flabbergasted. If I'd thought the shop was Sir Matt's, I'd never have asked.'

Holt had suspected – and he wasn't alone – that Edwards had an interest in the shop. 'When I found out the truth, I was mortified. I loved Matt. After what he had done for United, he could have had anything. And I had embarrassed him in front of all those people. Also my dad loved Matt and I was going to have to tell my dad what I had done. I was dreading that.'

Afterwards there was a lunch for the shareholders at the football ground. 'When I got there I was still in a state. I bumped into Les Olive and told him how sorry I was. He asked me to follow him into the gents and, when we went through the door, there was Sir Matt. I began to apologise but he cut me short. He was wonderful. "Don't worry about it, son," he said. "Sometimes these things are better out in the open." So I could go home and face my dad after all.

'When we went back into the room, he and his wife had a photograph taken with me and he invited me to go and see him at the shop some time. I went with my dad but Sir Matt wasn't there. I saw Sandy, though, and he told us to come back the next day. When we did, he put us in his car and took us to see Sir Matt at the house in Kings Road. I wrote to Sir Matt from time to time afterwards and he never, ever, failed to respond. Even when Lady Jean had a stroke. He wrote back to say that she had gone into a nursing home.'

Busby told the journalist Stan Liversedge he had assumed people knew he owned the shop. 'There was no secrecy,' he said. 'Neither did I feel I had to advertise it to the world.' He added that the idea had been his; he had thought about it privately, then laid it before the board when he approached retirement. Early in the 1968/69 season the arrangement had been made to sell the Red Devils Souvenir Shop to Busby for £2,000 on a 21-year lease at a rent of £250 a year. It had been doing 'only fair business' at the time, Busby told Liversedge, so there had been a gamble. But it came to thrive, drawing long queues on match days, and Busby voluntarily increased the rent, which by now was into the thousands.

On the way back from one of United's three FA Cup finals in the late 1970s, Louis Edwards asked if he could sit next to Sandy's wife Irene. She winced at the recollection of his questioning: 'You know – "How's the shop going?" and so on. And "Would you like to give it up now?" I was so stupid that it wasn't until afterwards that I realised he had been pumping me for information.'

But, as it turned out, there were others on the case of Louis Edwards himself: investigators for Granada's *World in Action*. Edwards had been aware and, through United, attempted legal restraint. In vain.

Towards the end of January 1980, 'The Man Who Bought United' was broadcast. It detailed the bribes and how Edwards had prepared for the rights issue. But by implication it also damaged Busby to the extent that the club was said to have operated a 'slush fund' from which parents of promising boys were paid. Although the timescale was vague, it cast doubt on Busby's claims – on which he was never to waver – to have stuck scrupulously to football's rules.

A month later, Louis Edwards died in his bath of a heart attack and Martin accused Granada of killing him. There had, he said, been 'a complete character assassination'.

Martin was 34. He had been on the board for ten years but fellow directors thought him too young to succeed his father as chairman. They did not consider a 71-year-old too old. 'They wanted Matt,' said Edwards, 'but I said I didn't necessarily think that was the right decision because, although young, I had experience in business.' This was true to the extent that he had done the rounds of the family firm, graduating from relatively humble tasks, and been kept on by Gulliver. 'So I told the directors I wasn't happy with their choice.' And they looked at the mountain of shares on which he sat. 'They reconvened and came back with the idea to make me chairman and Matt president.' Busby remained on the board.

United finished second in the 1979/80 season in front of healthy crowds but Martin's first full season was to see a decline more typical of the Sexton era during which Docherty's verdict on his successor – 'Dave's not a coach, he's a hearse' – was often quoted along with a one-liner attributed to Mike Dempsey of the *Daily Express*. 'Dave's idea of adventure,' it was said, 'is to have an After Eight Mint at 7.45.' The travails of Garry Birtles, for whom Sexton had paid Nottingham Forest £1.25 million, kept up the supply of black comedy: hostages, released after prolonged incarceration, were said to have asked, 'Has he scored yet?'

Back trouble, meanwhile, had contributed to the failure of Nikki Jovanović, United's first foreign signing (Carlo Sartori, although born in Italy, had been a fairly typical Mancunian) and within the club the atmosphere had soured. One day, according to Harry Gregg, who had been restored to Old Trafford by Sexton as goalkeeper coach after his managerial stints at Shrewsbury, Swansea and Crewe, the team bus was about to leave Old Trafford when Busby drove by and saw his old keeper.

'Hello, son.'

'Good morning, Boss.'

'See you around.'

As Busby drove off, Tommy Cavanagh turned to Gregg.

'He's not the fucking boss here.'

'Well, he was my boss.'

'And then,' said Gregg, 'I started getting calls from Paddy McGrath. "Son," he'd tell me, "the Boss is saying for God's sake do something – the club's falling apart."'

There was, however, a structure, with Martin Edwards central to it. When, with crowds dwindling, he resolved that Sexton would go at the end of the 1980/81 season, the only director in opposition was Busby, who argued that Sexton deserved one season more. But he still took part in the search for a replacement according to Lawrie McMenemy.

McMenemy was the Southampton manager whose side had beaten United in the 1976 Cup final. He had since guided them into the top division and brought off the remarkable coup of signing Kevin Keegan. McMenemy was big and had charisma. So it was not unnatural that United should be drawn to him, even if a code of conduct among chairmen dictated that no approach should be made to anyone until the season was over.

In his book *A Lifetime's Obsession*, McMenemy recalled:

> I was invited by Sir Matt to go to a dinner. I thought it was innocent. I met a lot of United people and was totally unaware of what it was about but then I said to my wife, Anne, 'We're going back to the hotel room – this is an interview.' I'd worked it out.
>
> Sir Matt took me to the lift and offered me a wad of money. He said it was for expenses but I said, 'No chance.' Looking back, all these things were tests. He wanted to see if I would take the money.

Rumours of managers taking 'bungs' were rife and the memory of the Dunstable allegations against Docherty fresh in United minds. 'I think I must have passed them [the tests] because some time later they came back for me.' And offered the Old Trafford job. 'Looking back I should have taken it but I felt I owed Southampton something.' He was settled in Hampshire and also had a suspicion of the troublesome politics around Old Trafford and so United had to look elsewhere.

They tried Bobby Robson, the highly successful manager of Ipswich, and Ron Saunders, under whom Aston Villa had become champions, but both shied from what was now seen as a hazardous job. The next man on the list was Ron Atkinson, who embraced the scale and glamour of the club as Docherty had done and possessed an even sharper wit. There was never much doubt that Atkinson would take the job and yet, while negotiating terms, he tried his sense of fun on Edwards. When the talk turned to the company car, the chairman mentioned Sexton's Rover and Atkinson replied that he needed a car, not a dog. He got a Mercedes.

SNUBBED

With Ron Atkinson, life wasn't all about quips. His football, too, could put smiles on faces. At West Bromwich he had prospered with an entertaining style, memorably demonstrated in a 5–3 win at Old Trafford towards the end of 1978. He was quickly and shamelessly to plunder his former club, buying for midfield first the minder Remi Moses for £500,000 and then the brilliant all-rounder Bryan Robson for £1.5 million.

Sexton had gone close to the British record in signing Garry Birtles for a little less than Wolves had paid Villa for Andy Gray. Now Atkinson had broken it. Busby had done the same when bringing Denis Law back from Italy, but between 1962 and 1981 prices had increased more than tenfold and, according to Martin Edwards, this was too much for a septuagenarian. 'He couldn't accept that we should pay such a fee for Bryan,' said Edwards. 'He thought it was ridiculous money and, because he opposed the deal, he resigned from the board.'

In a statement, Busby, who remained club president, cited 'personal and domestic reasons' and the health of Jean, which was deteriorating, certainly constituted those. But Edwards insisted the Robson fee had prompted him. 'I think he found it difficult to cope with the numbers.' It was just as well, Edwards added, that he had become chairman when everyone else wanted Busby. 'If Matt had been in the chair when Ron wanted Robson, he'd have clashed with the manager.' And United might have missed out on an outstanding midfielder.

But there were other reasons for Busby's discomfort. One was that Martin, like his father, thought Sandy a nice fellow unsuited to directorship. Another was the co-option of James Gulliver, of whom Busby claimed not to have heard. Now came what Busby might have thought an indecently hasty move to add Martin's friend Mike Edelson. While consenting to the introduction of Martin's younger brother Roger in the summer, Busby had successfully opposed Edelson. But, when Busby vacated his seat, there were no prizes for guessing who would be ushered into it.

Nor had there been much doubting who would be United's paid director. Edwards had resigned from Argyll Foods upon taking the chairmanship and now saw Manchester United as the career with prospects. He began on £30,000 a year, which was not much less than the manager and leading players, and this was to rise to £40,000 the next year as United took a suitably generous share of the sponsorship revenue coming into football. Budgets were introduced, departments separated. United started to become businesslike. Although not everyone thought it was the best business practice for Edwards to draw, as Les Olive had foreseen, dividends comparable with his burgeoning salary.

Busby withdrew to his office and settled for his own business. In his world, the likes of Frank Holt would receive a handwritten reply.

Although his day-to-day influence was waning, Busby hardly spent every moment in despair. Far from it. For one thing, he enjoyed United's more vibrant football; in Atkinson's first season, they finished third and in 1982/83 they matched that while winning the FA Cup, Robson scoring twice in a replayed final against Brighton. Young players came through the ranks to gladden Busby's heart – Norman Whiteside, an exciting partner for Frank Stapleton at the front, Mick Duxbury, Arthur Albiston, Kevin Moran – and the elegant Arnold Mühren emphasised the benefits of looking overseas (although the Dutchman had come by way of Ipswich).

There were blessings to count. Certainly by comparison with those granted Bill Shankly, who had died of a heart attack in September 1981 after a short and largely joyless retirement. Shankly had such respect for Busby that once, although a non-drinker, he had forced down a sherry because it had been proffered by his friend. On another occasion he had rung Busby's home, where one of the grand-daughters took the call but ran off and forgot to tell Matt or Jean. About 15 minutes later, she remembered – and Matt found Shankly still on the line. Shankly was just 68 when he died, after being denied a directorship at Liverpool and even spurned by his old sidekick Paisley, who had found him a distracting presence at the training ground. Given that Shankly had been a great builder, Liverpool's answer to Busby, and that Jock Stein had been virtually excluded from Celtic, there had been much for Busby to ponder in his later years.

His pal Paddy McGrath was still going strong, even if the Cromford Club had disappeared under the giant Arndale Centre, completed in 1979. Before the reconstruction of Market Street had begun several years earlier, McGrath had welcomed interest in the club from Hugh Hefner's Playboy organisation in the United States. Hefner had flown over and, after documents were signed, champagne corks popped. McGrath now asked Hefner what the club would become and Hefner replied: 'A Playboy Casino.' In that case, asked McGrath, why had he not bought the gaming licence? Hefner said he had. McGrath suggested he check; it had been deliberately withheld from the deal because McGrath himself planned to open another casino. Hefner, having looked sharply at his lawyers, renegotiated. So the story went.

There were always stories when McGrath and Busby met. Busby also had plenty of time for his beloved golf, and horse-racing with friends such as Johnny Foy. In his company the bookie and the priest still happily mixed, for another keen golfer and racegoer was Father Patrick McMahon.

A lifelong United fan, McMahon had arrived in Manchester from Ireland shortly after the European Cup triumph and become a season-ticket holder. He had befriended Paddy Crerand and others, Busby included, in his parish of St Alphonsus, near the former Busby home, a semi-detached in Coleridge Road. Sheena and Sandy had been baptised at St Alphonsus by the previous priest, the stern Joe O'Donnell; a story was told that young Sandy, given half a crown by his mother and told to light some candles for the team, was falsely suspected of having neglected to slip the coin into the box and endured an excruciating wait before the priest found a single half-crown among the donations.

The Busbys later worshipped at Our Lady and St John's and Matt became close to Monsignor Sewell, whom McMahon was to succeed. 'Matt was truly devout,' said McMahon. 'I think his faith was the primary thing in his life. He loved to come in for a chat with Monsignor Sewell after Mass.'

McMahon and Busby began to socialise through a mutual friend, Tim Kilroe, a force in the local construction industry who also owned the Four Seasons Hotel. 'Matt had been made a director of the Kilroe company. Just for the name, you know. I already knew Matt well. Sometimes, when I had a round of golf with Sandy, he would play too. And we were both great men for the horses.

'About every month or two I'd join Matt and Jean for a meal with the Kilroes. Matt would have his party-piece and usually it would get to a stage where we said, "Go on, fella – sing us a song." And he'd always come up with the same one. The one about the gooseberry tree. He'd put his own Scottish lilt to it.'

This is the version Busby sang, its final ten lines to the tune of 'In the Shade of the Old Apple Tree ...'

An Irishman, a Scotsman and a Hebrew
Were sentenced to be hanged down Texas way.
The judge he said he'd grant them one last favour
They could pick the tree on which they wished to die.

The Scotsman picked a pear tree and died happy
The Irishman said any tree would do
Then the judge he turned upon the Hebrew
And these words were uttered by the Jew

'Please hang me on a gooseberry tree
My favourite tree, don't you see?
It's the tree I love best
It's my dying request
To be hanged on a gooseberry tree.'
The judge he said 'Really you know
That the gooseberry tree is too low.'
'That's all right,' says Mose,
'I can wait 'til it grows
If you hang me on a gooseberry tree.'

Since retiring from management, Busby had kept in touch with football luminaries through the League management committee. His contribution was 'quiet' according to the football historian Simon Inglis, although, after the incident in the 1980 FA Cup final in which Arsenal's Willie Young brought down West Ham's goalbound Paul Allen but was not sent off, Busby did take part, with Bobby Charlton, in the deliberations of the sub-committee led by Jimmy Hill that prompted the automatic dismissal of a player denying an opponent an obvious goalscoring opportunity.

He spent more time in the sun. He took a share in an apartment on Tenerife and went golfing there. According to his friend Jimmy Tarbuck, he would fare somewhat better on the fairways than the greens. He did, however, play off 12 at one stage and performed a hole in one at Mere, south of Manchester. With Jean he had loved to stay at the Beach Plaza Hotel in Monte Carlo. Until the curse that kept revisiting their joint lives – in the guise of miscarriage and of the crash – came back to stay.

During the summer of 1982, after two strokes from which she had appeared to recover, Jean was diagnosed with Alzheimer's disease. There had been signs. 'She'd hide money,' her granddaughter Alison recalled. 'You'd go into the washing-basket at the house in Kings Road and find small amounts she'd saved from the housekeeping. Or discover little rolls of notes in her shoes.'

It got worse. That was when she first went into a nearby nursing home. But Matt didn't like their being apart. And found the house big and empty. So he took an apartment in Cedar Court on Wilbraham Road and they stayed there together for a while, with a part-time nurse. It was hopeless. Her deterioration continued and the nursing home became the only practical answer. He went every day and held her hand and soon understood that Jean could give nothing back. But he never stopped going. He would stay for hours.

At least Jean had been able to enjoy a party on their 50th wedding anniversary in January 1981. 'All the lads from United went,' said Sandy's wife Irene, 'and Harold Riley did a booklet.' But the family's most memorable moment came when they found out Jean had been adopted in infancy. 'Would you believe it had never been mentioned?' said Irene.

Matt's habit was to see Jean after his daily visits to Old Trafford, where he would answer his correspondence with the help of Lyn Laffin (later to become Alex Ferguson's secretary) and have lunch with the two Kens in the Grill Room. 'It was a bit like a Berni Inn,' Ken Merrett recalled, 'with booths and red upholstery. We'd talk football and have a laugh. He was very loyal to his players. And he'd never accept that stuff about backhanders to young players. Never. Even the stuff about washing-machines for the parents and so on. He'd never accept that. But he did get them jobs with his friends.'

Match days remained special, none more so than in 1983, when two Charity Shield goals from Robson overcame Liverpool, by now the most consistently dominant force in the modern history of the English game, indeed arguably the leading club in Europe. Since United's most recent League triumph under Busby in 1967, Liverpool under Shankly and then Paisley had secured no fewer than seven titles (and more were to come). Since Busby's United had won the European Cup in 1968, Paisley's Liverpool had won it three times (and the Anfield club were to win it again in the coming season). Paisley had just handed the team over to Joe Fagan when he and Busby were reunited at Wembley, driven out together in an open-top vehicle to receive the plaudits of the crowd. It was 38 years after Busby, as Liverpool captain, had welcomed a young Paisley to Merseyside and their friendship glowed on a warm afternoon, each grinning broadly as they raised an arm together, fingers entwined, as if embodying a precious age.

Although United slipped to fourth in the League that season, Busby enjoyed their run to the semi-finals of the Cup Winners' Cup. The highlight drew nearly 59,000 to Old Trafford: a second leg against Barcelona, who led 2–0 and boasted Diego Maradona and yet were knocked out 3–2 on aggregate. It was like the good days – 'the best atmosphere I have ever known at Old Trafford,' said Robson, who scored twice and was carried from the field on the shoulders of exultant fans.

During this season Jimmy Ryan made a return visit. 'After Luton,' he recalled, 'I went to play in America. I stayed for eight years and, when I came back, arranged to take my son Neil to a match at Old Trafford. I went down with him to the ticket office and there were the same people I used to chat to in my playing days – the likes of Ken Ramsden and Ken Merrett – and they were so friendly to me and my lad.

'Suddenly the door opens and Busby's there. And he goes "Jimmy Ryan!" Just like that. No hesitation. And I can't tell you how pleased I was. I'd been away a long time. I never dreamed he would remember my name just like that. So I introduce him to my son and he says, "Right – let's go." He takes us round the whole stadium. At the tearoom we stopped and sat talking, the three of us, having tea and biscuits, looking down on the pitch and talking football. My lad was over the Moon. He's in his forties now [Neil Ryan followed in the footsteps of his father, who was on Ferguson's staff until retirement, by becoming a youth coach at United] and it's fresh in his mind. He still talks about it.

'When people ask me what sort of a person Matt Busby was, I tell them about that day.'

Meanwhile Martin Edwards paid a further visit to Kleinwort Benson. He had seen another way of exploiting United's value. Tottenham Hotspur had floated on the stock exchange, much to the benefit of his counterpart Irving Scholar, and Edwards wondered how United might fare in the market. He was told a flotation might raise £8 million, enabling him to make around £500,000 while retaining control.

No sooner had Edwards begun to ponder this than Robert Maxwell attempted a takeover. Things were moving fast. There were hints of £10 million. But, whatever price Edwards had in mind when, with Roland Smith acting as intermediary, he talked to the supposedly super-wealthy publisher and *Mirror* proprietor, it was not reached and the plan foundered. Maxwell instead bought Derby County. Edwards contented himself with dividends. He continued to tailor the board, persuading Alan Gibson and Bill Young to stand down in favour of his solicitor, Maurice Watkins, who had been advising the club on legal matters since the difficulty with Tommy Docherty and Laurie Brown, and Bobby Charlton.

The Charlton move was one of Edwards's smartest. Although Charlton's attempt to build a managerial career had foundered at Preston, he had obtained experience of football directorship at Wigan and performed promisingly in the travel business while building up his 'soccer schools'. And he was certainly to be an asset to the United board, a key figure in the club's best decision since Louis Rocca introduced Busby to James Gibson in 1945.

While effecting much change off the field, Edwards kept Atkinson supplied with transfer funds. In the summer of 1984, the manager bought two wide men: Gordon Strachan from Alex Ferguson's Aberdeen and the equally diminutive Dane Jesper Olsen. Again, United finished fourth but they regained the FA Cup with a sumptuous Whiteside goal against Everton at Wembley. Tragically, 39 mainly Italian supporters of Juventus died as a result of attacks by Liverpool counterparts at the subsequent European Cup final at the Heysel Stadium in Brussels, which Liverpool, so far as it mattered, lost 1–0 to Juventus. A minor consequence was that, with all English clubs banned from European competition, United could not have another go at the Cup-Winners' Cup in 1985/86.

United began the season in rampant form, winning their first ten League matches, and remained top a month into the new year. But Liverpool, under the player/management of Kenny Dalglish, proved irresistible in completing their first Double and Atkinson's team were again fourth. While there were excuses – the injury-prone Robson missed as many matches as he played – the club seemed as far as ever from the supremacy the Busby era had taught the support to crave. Atkinson even offered to go amid speculation that the board might try to tempt Terry Venables back from Barcelona, or even take a gamble on the most able Scottish manager since Jock Stein, Aberdeen's Ferguson.

Stein had died the previous autumn. He had been badly injured in a car crash in 1975 and, although initially successful on his return, seemed a faded force to the Celtic directors. They let him choose his successor – Billy McNeill – but instead of taking Stein on to the board, as he had expected, asked him to manage their fund-raising pool. Having taken this insult as a signal to leave, he spent just 44 days as manager at Leeds before coming back to Scotland to look after the national team. He made Ferguson his part-time assistant and they sat together on the bench during the 1986 World Cup qualifying match against Wales in Cardiff.

Towards the end, shortly after a Davie Cooper penalty had given the Scots the draw required to secure a play-off against Australia, Stein had collapsed and died of a heart attack. So, Australia having been despatched, Ferguson would spend the ensuing summer in charge of the campaign in Mexico. Bobby Charlton was at the tournament working as an analyst for the BBC and the United full-back Arthur Albiston remembered him taking a keen interest in Ferguson's work with Scotland. 'I never thought much about it at the time,' said Albiston, 'but Bobby kept asking what the training was like and so on.' Charlton also turned up at the camp at least once – and, after being welcomed by Ferguson, told him that, if he ever fancied a move south, a call would be appreciated.

Five months later, a draw with Coventry at Old Trafford left United in 19th place. Atkinson took his dispirited men to Southampton for a League Cup replay on 4 November and they lost 4–1. On the flight home, Martin Edwards had a discussion with Mike Edelson and it was resolved to replace the manager with Ferguson.

The next day, the board gathered. Edwards and Edelson apart, there were only Charlton and Maurice Watkins – Roger Edwards had resigned to live in Majorca, Gulliver also left and Haroun died – and the view was unanimous. Edelson picked up a phone, rang Aberdeen's number and, faking a Scottish accent, pretended to be Gordon Strachan's agent in order to get through to Ferguson. He put Edwards on the line and the chairman gave Ferguson a Manchester number. When Ferguson dialled it, Edwards asked for a meeting that night, somewhere discreet in Scotland. Did Ferguson know such a place? He did.

He spoke to his wife Cathy and consulted Jim Rodger, the all-seeing journalist who had told Paddy Crerand he was going to United, about how to handle media interest. And then told Edwards to be at Hamilton service station on the M74 south of Glasgow at 7pm. There and then, Edwards got out of his car and into Ferguson's, leaving Edelson and Charlton to follow them to the home of Ferguson's sister-in-law in Bishopbriggs. The offer was less than Ferguson might make in a successful year at Aberdeen – but he was in no mood to argue.

When he asked if United would buy his house near Aberdeen, he took no for an answer. He was warned not to expect too generous a transfer budget. Only when he asked if there was a drinking culture among the United players did there come a resounding yes, and Ferguson had expected that, because he had kept in touch with Strachan and been innocently informed of the pubbing habits most energetically followed by Robson, Norman Whiteside and Paul McGrath.

Hands were shaken and the next day Edwards and Watkins flew to Aberdeen to agree compensation for the loss of Ferguson and his assistant, Archie Knox. Atkinson was sacked with the distinction of being, thus far, United's longest-serving manager since Busby.

He was also the last to have required Busby's imprimatur. Busby played no part in the recruitment of Ferguson according to Edwards, who said: 'He was just a figurehead by then.' The prime mover had been Bobby Charlton. Hailing from so close to the border, Charlton had followed the Scottish game and understood what it had taken for Aberdeen to eclipse both Rangers and Celtic. Martin Edwards, for his part, had been impressed by how Ferguson conducted negotiations over the sale of Gordon Strachan to United – and by his tearing into his players on television after they won the Scottish Cup final in 1983. Ferguson had apologised for that but Edwards said: 'His fury showed the sort of standards he set. Just to win was not good enough. He wanted to win in style.'

There were further echoes of Busby's philosophy in his accent on youth. In his first couple of years he appointed Brian Kidd youth development officer and replaced Atkinson's chief scout, Tony Collins, with Les Kershaw at Charlton's suggestion. He also spent much more liberally than had been agreed at his interview, concentrating on strong and aggressive players, rectifying a flaw in his inheritance from Atkinson. Yet no improvement in the club's health was obvious to the public. Even in 1987/88, when United rose to second place, home attendances often fell below 40,000 and towards the end of the following season, when they returned to mid-table, matches against Wimbledon and Everton didn't even half-fill a 56,000-capacity stadium.

As Ferguson began to question himself, Busby offered consolation. 'I was very lucky,' Ferguson said, 'that Matt was still at the club.' Very wise, too, to embrace his presence. At least once during the hard times Ferguson took Busby with the players on golf trips – bonding exercises, essentially – and, amid the depths of despair over Paul McGrath's drinking problems, he encouraged the player to meet Busby, only to reflect that 'even the warmth and wisdom of that great man' had no effect (as in the case of George Best, although McGrath was to prolong his career, quite splendidly, after being transferred to Aston Villa).

Ferguson, although most of his work was at The Cliff, also had an office at Old Trafford. 'I used to love going in,' he recalled, 'and, as soon as I walked through the door, I'd know if Matt was around because I could smell the pipe smoke. It was amazing – the smell got all over the building. And I'd go in and see him for half an hour, sometimes more. He was wonderful with me. As was Bobby Charlton. They were a great support system.'

It was during this period that Busby sat for Harold Riley. For 20 years the artist had been concentrating on his native Salford, reflecting on the city's life. His friend Lowry, though a City supporter, had sometimes consented to accompany him to Old Trafford, before Lowry became too old and died in 1976. After Riley had done his preliminary sketches of Busby, he published them with an account of their conversations, during which he told Busby: 'After Munich it was very curious because everyone I spoke to in artistic circles would say "Where do you come from?" and I would say Manchester and they would say "Manchester United, Matt Busby." They would not say Sir John Barbirolli or the Halle Orchestra and they wouldn't say L.S. Lowry.' He asked if Busby thought the crash had 'contributed unduly to the legend of Manchester United' and Busby, in words whose blandness may have betrayed discomfort, conceded as much.

Neither his close friend Paddy McGrath, nor even his son Sandy, ever heard him talk privately about the crash. 'But it was always there in his eyes,' said McGrath. 'Always.' All he needed to say had been in his acknowledgement of the 25th anniversary in 1983: 'I've never come to terms with what happened. I never will. Time isn't the great healer.'

CHAPTER FIFTEEN

THE FINAL YEARS

LOVABLE. FUNNY. CARING

If the Busbys' worst news since Munich had been the Alzheimer's diagnosis, Matt now suffered the inevitable loss. Six days before Christmas 1988, Jean slipped away. Asked to find words to describe her mother-in-law, Irene said: 'Lovable. Funny. Caring.' In the third context, she mentioned Jean's care for the other wives after the crash. And added: 'She did everything for Matt. She even cleaned his shoes.'

Although Jean had been the love of his life, there was an element of relief at her passing. Matt certainly appeared less hard hit than his son. 'Sandy was in a terrible state,' said Irene. 'Much worse than Matt. Absolutely heartbroken. Even though she had been ill for so long. In fact, for two years we were worried about Sandy.' Turning to her daughter Alison, she said: 'I don't think Matt knew, did he? I don't think Sandy showed it to Matt, did he? But this was a real depression. We'd given up the souvenir shop by then. So he had nowhere to go with his grief. Nowhere to lose himself.'

The shop had ceased to be a Busby interest in 1987. In the years after Louis Edwards's death, Martin had left Sandy and Irene in little doubt the club would be happy to take it back. 'There had been the conversation with Louis on the coach back from Wembley,' said Irene, 'and then Martin took over. It started when, instead of

Sandy and me seeing the reps and doing the ordering in the usual way, these men began coming into the shop and saying they'd got this and that for us. They'd been ordering stock for us. We knew it was a takeover. But they never actually discussed it with us.'

Until finally, with two years left on the lease, Sandy agreed to take £200,000 for the shop: less than it might have seemed because the deal included £100,000 worth of stock. 'It seemed a good price at the time,' Irene reflected. Although gross profits of £100,000 had been reported the previous year, it was a buyer's market now. Matt Busby's payoff had paid its last and would henceforth be part of a rapidly growing Manchester United empire.

After Jean's death, Matt continued to live with Sheena at 6 Harboro Road, Sale, and, instead of visiting his wife every afternoon, went to her grave in Southern Cemetery. When family members accompanied him, he seemed in a trance. Nowhere near as stricken as Sandy, yet enough for Sheena to have a word with him about it, after which he reduced his visits to two or three a week.

HE'LL DO THE BUSINESS

A visitor to Old Trafford was greeted by the familiar face of Kath Phipps on reception. She rang Busby in his small office on the first floor: 'Shall I send him up, love?' The visitor found an impressive octogenarian, handshake firm, dress sense intact: light brown suit, white shirt, rust tie. 'Just a little deliberate in gait.' This was Eamon Dunphy's impression when he came to research *A Strange Kind of Glory.*

It was a strange kind of season, 1989/90. One at which a man of any age might have reeled. It began with the surreal sight of a stocky middle-aged man in club kit walking to the centre-spot. From there he trotted, juggling a ball on his head, towards the Stretford End goal, into which he resoundingly whacked it, demonstrating skills that had earned an apprenticeship with Coventry City. Michael Knighton waved to the crowd as he walked off and settled down to watch a 4–1 victory over Arsenal from the directors' box.

Neil Webb, who scored on his United debut that day, recalled: 'This chap had come into the dressing room before the game, introduced himself as the new owner and asked for kit.' Knighton was nearly right about his proprietorship of United, for once again Martin Edwards had been on the point of selling: he and Knighton had agreed a price for his 50.6 per cent of the shares. But Knighton's fellow investors were to withdraw. He settled for a seat on the board, which he occupied for three years before instead buying Carlisle United and, at one stage, becoming that club's manager, shortly before it went into administration.

Knighton later concentrated on exploring his talents for art and poetry. He reflected on his time with United: 'I got on especially well with Martin, Maurice Watkins and the lovely Les Olive.' And added: 'The great Sir Matt Busby was another wonderful colleague with whom I would spend many an hour. Sir Matt would often take me to one side to have a lovely, warm chat. Here, Matt would proffer his amazing football wisdom on all things to do with the game.' His wisdom on the subject of Michael Knighton had been forthright: 'Recent events have demonstrated all too clearly the problems that can arise from private ownership'. Though this, of course, was a dig as much at Martin Edwards as Knighton.

As for the manager, Knighton declared: 'My relationship with Alex Ferguson too was an excellent one as far as it went.' Ferguson might have been less cordial had he known what Graeme Souness would disclose in an interview with the *Daily Mail*'s Ian Ladyman many years later. Souness recalled that, when manager of Rangers, he had been secretly offered Ferguson's job by Knighton. 'Fergie was having a difficult time,' said Souness, 'and the banners were up in the Stretford End.' Souness added: 'I am not sure how well I would have been received [as a former Liverpool player] and I'm sure United supporters will look upon that as a lucky escape now! But I would have taken it.'

Ferguson, meanwhile, gazed at the banners and wondered if a farewell was indeed in order. United lay 15th when they went to Nottingham Forest in the third round of the FA Cup and Mark Hughes's artful cross spun up off the caked mud for Mark Robins to head the goal that began so much. A few months later, Lee Martin settled a replayed final against Crystal Palace and, while it would not quite be true to say United never looked back, they proceeded to win the Cup-Winners' Cup and League Cup prior to the signing that was radically to change Ferguson's fortunes.

Busby had never doubted Ferguson according to the club's security chief, Michael Kelly. 'Ned' Kelly had met Sheena when she took her father to matches and, being a neighbour in Sale, was sometimes invited to join them for bacon sandwiches on a Sunday morning. Kelly remained sceptical that Ferguson carried the weight of his precursor but, when in Busby's presence he wondered if the title would ever come back to Old Trafford, the old man would smile and wave a knowing finger. 'Ned,' he would say, 'Alex Ferguson will take us back to the top. He doesn't know any other way. He's single-minded for the team. He'll do the business, mark my words.'

Nor did Martin Edwards visibly flinch as he went about his own business, supervising the flotation that by the end of the decade, when BSkyB made a takeover bid that fell foul of the Monopolies and Mergers Commission, would see the club's value rise to more than £620 million. Such was to be the effect of not only satellite television but Ferguson's management, especially after a deal done in December 1992.

Ferguson, having been tipped off by the then France manager Gérard Houllier, signed Eric Cantona from Leeds for £1 million. Before Cantona arrived, United were averaging one goal a match. After, the scoring rate doubled. At the end of the season, United were champions for the first time in 26 years and Ferguson saw the joy in Busby's eyes: 'He joined us in the dressing room after the last home game against Blackburn Rovers and all the lads had their photograph taken with him … He enjoyed the occasion as much as they did.'

Busby was approaching his 84th birthday and Paddy Crerand, who had stood near him in the directors' box as the inaugural Premier League trophy was presented jointly to Bryan Robson, the club captain, and Steve Bruce, who had led the side in Robson's frequent absences, was irked by a missed opportunity. 'I was saying to myself, "Why don't they give Matt the trophy to hand over?" This was one of the great moments of his life, United getting the title back. What a moment it could have been. How small-minded can people be?'

But this was a time to nurse not a grievance but a drink. 'It was the first time I had ever been in the directors' room,' said Crerand, 'and I thought – why not? So I ordered a vodka and took it. I looked round and saw Matt. He was right there next to me. And I thought to myself "Oh no!" And when was it – 1993? I was 54 years of age and standing there and worrying because Matt shouldn't be seeing me with a drink in my hand! Many years later I saw David Beckham on television talking about his relationship with Alex Ferguson and something he said took me back to that day with Matt.'

Not that this effect of Busby's presence was confined to former players. Once there was a function in one of the big Manchester hotels. A famous entertainer, whom Busby knew, came in with a woman who was not his wife. He strolled around with her unconcerned, beaming, wisecracking. And then Busby came into the room. And one of Britain's most prominent performers went deathly pale, froze, and left.

LIKE A STATE OCCASION

Busby had been diagnosed with cancer of the lower lip – where his pipe had rested – and given up smoking. But the disease had entered his blood around 1989. He could no longer drive and so, on the three or four days a week when he visited the club, Ken Merrett would arrange a taxi to bring him to and from Old Trafford. Even on walks, which he always began with relish, he sometimes got lost in the relatively unfamiliar territory of Sale. But there were still laughs over lunch in the Grill Room and, when Ferguson popped in, he and Busby would gang up to tease Merrett for his supposed anti-Scottishness. When anyone asked Busby about his health, he would reply: 'Still battling along.' It became the catchphrase of his dotage.

Some days Sandy would collect him from Sheena's and take him out. On Thursday nights, father and son would dine at Chez Nous in Sale and often they would lunch at a place in Rochdale. 'Whenever he went into a restaurant,' Irene recalled, 'everybody would be looking. And he'd say hello to every table. "Hello, son – I know who you are." Still like that. He had a fantastic memory for faces as well. Right to the end.'

Martin Edwards saw him at Old Trafford a week before he died. 'Still battling along.' He had been in hospital for an operation on a blood clot in a leg before Christmas but felt well enough to receive Willie Morgan at home at Sheena's on New Year's Day. Morgan recalled arriving with a bottle of whisky from which they took a few nips while pondering when they would next make a golfing trip to Tenerife. Yet soon Busby was back in the Alexandra Hospital in Cheadle and on 20 January 1994 he passed peacefully away in his sleep, surrounded by the family.

'We were all there,' said Alison. 'His son and daughter. All the grandchildren.' Seven now, all girls. 'And the doctor cried,' Irene recalled. 'She was only a young woman.' Sandy and Sheena saw the tears welling in her eyes as, having written the death certificate, she turned and said: 'I'm sorry. It's just that he really was such a lovely man.'

To Sandy and Sheena, he had always been 'Matt'. Even to the grandchildren, and even in their youth; they had called him 'Grandad' only when they sang the Clive Dunn song for him, first at Christmas in 1970, when it was about to reach No.1 in the UK charts, and then on *This Is Your Life* a few months later. The tradition had started, said Irene, when the first of the grand-daughters, Sheena's Janie, tried to say 'Grandad' and failed. 'Matt' was easier and it just stuck. Sandy wanted to follow suit and so all the kids called him 'Sandy', not 'Daddy'. 'When Alison was about two and in her pushchair, I took her into a shop and Matt must have had one of his books out at the time because there was a big poster of him on the wall. Suddenly she pointed and cried out, "Look – there's Matt!" and everyone in the shop turned round and looked at this toddler. How did she know his name?'

So now both Naṇa and Matt were gone. Matt would never again sing the gooseberry-tree song; like 'Father Paddy' McMahon, who had become part of the family, they all remembered it so fondly, delighting in his Scottish elongation of vowels, as in 'the judge he turned upon the *Heeebrooo* ...'

Matt was to be buried alongside Jean in Southern Cemetery. But first Manchester had to wake up to the news of his death. From the early morning, flowers and other tokens began arriving at Old Trafford. By noon many had come from Liverpool. On the Saturday, the 22nd, the visitors to the stadium would be Everton and the occasion would pass with an unforgettable dignity. Would it have been different if fate had sent arch rivals, even though Busby had played for City and Liverpool? 'We were worried,' Ken Merrett conceded. 'But there's an underlying decency in football supporters. We have experienced it when there are Munich anniversaries and families are on the pitch. Visiting supporters see them as people, not representatives of United.'

The soul of Busby's United became evident. From somewhere Ken Ramsden got the idea of having a lone bagpiper lead the teams out. 'It helped to make the day,' said Merrett. As did Ryan Giggs by scoring the only goal of a suitably entertaining match: a latter-day

Babe, heir to the tradition of Scanlon and Pegg, Charlton and Best, won the points that kept United on top of the League.

Merrett and Ramsden were invited by the family to see Busby's body at the undertaker's. 'It was such an honour,' said Merrett, 'that they wanted us to share in their grief.'

The funeral was on the 27th, a Thursday. The night before, United had flown back from Portsmouth after winning a League Cup replay 1–0. Meanwhile the old players converged, early Babes such as Jeff Whitefoot, survivors of Munich, the likes of Sammy McIlroy who had spanned eras. Best, Law, Charlton and Crerand mingled with Giggs, Robson, Bruce and Peter Schmeichel. At first it seemed that, to paraphrase Desmond Hackett on the occasion of Henry Rose's funeral, even the Mancunian skies would weep for Matt Busby. But the rain had stopped and the skies cleared by the time the cortège left Sheena's apartment in Harboro Road.

At times the streets were lined 12 or 15 deep as the crowds flocked to pay their respects. 'It was like a state occasion,' said Ned Kelly. Outside Old Trafford the cortège stopped while a silent tribute was paid by thousands on the forecourt bordered by the former Warwick Road, now Sir Matt Busby Way. Opposite the hearse was the clock inscribed: 'Feb 6, 1958. Munich.' Older supporters remembered the Busby Babes. Those of all ages understood the magnitude of the human being about to be laid to rest.

The cortège moved on to Our Lady and St John's, a distance of little more than a mile, where the church overflowed. Several hundred, including many priests, heard eulogies from Harold Riley and the Right Reverend Patrick Kelly, Bishop of Salford (soon to become Archbishop of Liverpool), who declared that the firmness of Busby's beliefs had helped him so magnificently to overcome adversity.

Not surprisingly, Father Patrick McMahon agreed with this. But at a distance of more than 30 years McMahon, who knew Busby intimately, went into detail. 'Munich could have broken Matt,' he said; Busby himself had admitted his faith might have become a casualty of the crash. 'But he felt he was blessed. And I think it may have spiralled back into the players afterwards, some of the euphoria. They saw how he had survived, this solid man of faith. There is a message in unflinching goodness. And Matt inspired many people. I don't want to be a Bible-basher but that's what faith can do. For many of us – myself included, sometimes – it's

346 SIR MATT BUSBY – THE MAN WHO MADE A FOOTBALL CLUB

up here in the head. But when it's deep down at the roots nothing can faze you. And his faith was so deep that nothing could get him down. The biggest setback would have been Lady Jean's illness. Yet he went to the nursing-home every day to see her. A lot of people might have said, "Oh, she doesn't know whether I'm there or not," but he went every day and that inspired many who worked in the nursing home.'

Busby had always 'shared himself with the people', said Father McMahon, and 'never allowed himself to be carried away by the excitement and the glory'. His idea of the fruits of celebrity, even in his prime, was to be 'happy to be seen walking around Chorlton'. Not for him the celebrity culture to come: as McMahon put it, 'the guys wanting all the cameras around them and then putting on sunglasses as if they want to hide from it … that would have been anathema to Matt'.

In his will he left £224,982, which was around five times the average UK house price but nowhere near the riches amassed by the family he helped to give control of Manchester United. As John Giles observed: 'Matt encouraged Louis to buy shares. His mistake was not to buy shares himself.' A sense of betrayal, briefly evident in sharp looks from some family members when Martin Edwards turned up at the funeral, was undeniable and long-lasting. Father McMahon, asked if there were nothing in Matt Busby's life that could have saddened him to the end, replied with care: 'He was a very loyal man. And maybe the thing that would have hurt him most would have been if his bosses were not as loyal … that's all I would say.'

Sandy's wife Irene was later to say that neither Louis nor Martin Edwards would have been chairman but for Matt. And yet Martin had said it was his father's influence that got Matt on the board. 'Ooh – they make you laugh, don't they?' But did they really behave so badly towards the Busbys? 'Of course they did.' Yet Sandy had appeared remarkably forgiving, never going to the newspapers with a tale of broken promises. 'No – he didn't want to mess his name up with the club.' The old family trait of tact and diplomacy? Irene's thoughts went back to Louis Edwards's funeral in 1980. 'You know when the club came and asked Matt to speak and he did? I said I didn't know how he could. But that was Matt. Forgive and forget and don't, you know …'

Make waves, rock the boat.

EDUCATION

Sandy and Irene Busby's four girls, and Sheena and Don Gibson's three, were educated at their grandfather's expense. 'When the children began to come along,' Alison Busby recalled, 'Matt said to Sandy and Sheena that he could either set up trust funds or pay for us to have private education. He put us all through private schools because he believed in the value of a good education.' Matt's mother, who made such sacrifices for Matt's own schooling, would have approved. And both Nellie and Matt would have been proud to hear what Alan Gowling said about him many years later.

Gowling, having been sold to Huddersfield by Frank O'Farrell, gave excellent service to Newcastle and Bolton. He was always grateful to Busby for both his start in football and the business career that followed. The difference between Gowling and other graduate footballers such as Liverpool's Steve Heighway and Brian Hall, he said, 'was that I was able to do both at the same time – and Matt made that possible'.

At 16, Gowling had played for Cheshire schoolboys at Old Trafford. 'Afterwards, Joe Armstrong came into the dressing-room and asked me to go with him to see Matt Busby. So I followed Joe upstairs and there was Matt. He wanted me to join Manchester United. I said that was fine but my mum and dad wanted me to stay on at school. "Son," he said, "I know that because they're in the room next door and we've had a good chat about it." And he made the promise that I could stay on at Stockport School. He'd let me play for the school on a Saturday morning then whichever youth team was at home at The Cliff in the afternoon. I made my way through the ranks and started scoring goals for the reserves.

'When I qualified for university, he arranged for me to train at The Cliff from about 7.30 – only the groundsman and his assistant would be there – and get to my first lecture for 10. Eventually I did my masters and, when I finished football, it got me on the first rung of the ladder in industry. I worked 19 years for a chemical manufacturing company in Buxton, becoming general manager, and retired after 13 years with a company that owns 17 car dealerships. I owe that to Matt. So much in my life I owe to him.'

POLITICS AND PHILOSOPHY

Busby told Eamon Dunphy his political views were strong but private. Unlike Ferguson, who proclaimed his solidarity with New Labour and even rang Tony Blair on a victorious election night, or Jock Stein, who overtly supported striking miners, he never went public with his convictions, although the assumption was that a tribal allegiance to the Labour Party developed during a formative period encompassing the General Strike. Even if the depth of his declared sympathy for the players' union was questioned by John Giles and others.

He was, incidentally, to admit having underestimated both the maturity and fortitude of Giles. And Giles appreciated that. 'Because he never said he made a mistake over anyone else.'

Busby was careful with his words. Almost to a fault according to Keith Dewhurst, who mischievously called him 'boring' in that so often he delivered bland or frustratingly restrained views. Dewhurst also considered his praise of Jimmy Murphy and others damnably, almost cynically, faint. But the ability to keep his emotions concealed was undoubtedly a source of power and David Meek, when asked to compare his relationships with Busby and Ferguson, replied: 'I know what Keith meant about Matt's unwillingness to wear his heart on his sleeve. Alex was less guarded [in private and public], more informal.' Asked which man he preferred, as a man, Meek hesitated, interminably.

Busby, in terms of the philosophy that guided his stewardship of Manchester United, differed significantly from Ferguson. True, each wanted to entertain on a broad front, and to encourage youngsters, and they shared countless other principles, but Busby would not have adopted the mentality that fuelled the fire of the Ferguson era. In the very late twentieth century, the age of the gated community as a symbol of privilege, Ferguson captured its mood by making a stockade of Old Trafford. Busby would not have liked that.

Busby wanted United to be prosperous so they could entertain the world, not face it with the odd mixture of arrogance and pique that had been more appropriate to Ferguson's unequal battle with the Old Firm in Scotland. Busby described Real Madrid as 'a brother' and not 'that mob' – Ferguson may have had an unusual loss of historical footing there – and the internationalism Busby had so productively shared with Sir Stanley Rous would not have permitted a phrase such as 'typical Germans' (after a Ferguson player had been sent off in the Champions League) or the joke that, when told by an Italian that a dish was of pasta, he always looked under the sauce to be sure.

No wonder David Meek found Ferguson the more engaging company. But in his internationalist outlook Busby was anything but tribal. In this he exhibited an old-fashioned socialism verging on idealism. His politics could be seen as indivisible from, or at least coincident with, his faith.

MANNERS

Arthur Hopcraft, in *The Football Man*, called Busby 'not an easy-going man', mentioning his impatience with the 'the flabby question'. He was certainly never one for banal chit-chat and Hugh McIlvanney, on Busby's 1969 retirement, wrote memorably of how he was aware of being wise: 'The chin goes back towards the Adam's apple and the words are released roundly, always well in the wake of his thoughts.'

Minor pomposity he could treat with an amused tolerance, as described by his friend Eric Alexander, whose brief chairmanship of City was in succession to his father Albert and whose grandfather, also Albert, had been a director when the teenage Busby arrived at Maine Road. Busby and Louis Edwards travelled with Alexander to London for a League meeting and, in the hotel, encountered Doug Ellis, chairman of Aston Villa, then in the Second Division. Alexander recalled: 'Doug was full of ideas, which he insisted on telling us about, concluding with the words, "When I get back in the First Division, Matt, just watch me go."'

As they went into the meeting, Busby nudged Alexander and murmured: 'Our Mr Ellis is going to be a very busy man, eh, Eric?'

Although his toughness, when at the peak of his powers, had earned almost dictatorial status, beginning with his subjugations of chairmen, the staff at Old Trafford found him the most benevolent of the breed, perennially kind to all regardless of rank, if wily. In this respect Ken Merrett rated him above even Ferguson and didn't mind that Busby, like his maker, worked in mysterious, or at least subtle, ways, as in 1966: 'We expect you to be here a lifetime.'

Merrett was to retire in 2007 after 41 years. Ramsden did 50 years. Other long servants engaged in the Busby era were to range from Les Olive – 46 years as office boy, occasional player, secretary and director – and the groundsman brothers Royle to Kath Phipps, a famously friendly receptionist first at Old Trafford and then The Cliff's successor as training ground, Carrington. Busby so firmly established loyalty that the Old Trafford family long remained intact, surviving the loss of its head. But back in 1966, the point of his remark to young Merrett was to prevent any leakage to players from the payslip department, and that was also achieved.

Right to the end, said Ken Ramsden, any of the club's employees would have done anything for Busby, and he always asked nicely, for all he had been through, not only at Munich but during the lingering emptiness of Jean's last few years. It was around the time of Ramsden's retirement in 2010 that Sheena Busby approached.

'Do you know, Ken,' she said, 'we could never get over the way you looked after my dad?'

'What do you mean?'

'Well, even after he retired, if I was short of tickets and there were none left, I'd go to him and he'd say, "Ask Ken, he'll sort you out." And you always did.'

'Sheena,' said Ramsden, 'I didn't know I had a choice.'

Wilf McGuinness's wife Beryl never went to matches: 'Just to the nice functions after they had won cups and so on. And it was astonishing how he always remembered your name. And you always felt he was talking to you and no one else. A nice man.' Ian and Carol Storey-Moore had a shorter acquaintance with Busby, but that he charmed the wives was a point she, too, wanted to make. 'I liked him very much,' she said, recalling a party at the Mottram Hall Hotel after relegation had been avoided under Tommy Docherty. 'He'd put an arm round you like a father. You felt part of his family.' Nell Whitefoot added: 'We'd go to parties at his friends' houses, or to theatres.' Even her husband Jeff conceded: 'We did have a very good social life.'

THANK YOU, SIR MATT

Although Busby saw the regaining of the League title, he died a few months before United held it in 1994, completing the Double that

Peter McParland's assault on Ray Wood had denied the Babes. At least the Freeman of Manchester was spared the shock of Munich: Saturday, 15 June 1996.

In the afternoon, at Wembley, England would beat Scotland 2–0 in the European Championship with Paul Gascoigne scoring a memorable goal. But at 9.20am the centre of Manchester was quiet. It was a little early for German supporters already in the city for the match against Russia at Old Trafford the next day. But agents of the Provisional IRA were up and about in a van, which contained a huge bomb.

They parked in Corporation Street, left the scene and at 9.45 sent a coded message of warning to Granada TV. It left insufficient time to defuse the device and, although most people had been evacuated from the area, 212 were injured by flying glass. The Arndale Centre had to be rebuilt. Under the debris was the ghost of Paddy McGrath's Cromford Club, where the Busbys had spent so many happy hours.

McGrath was still around when another of Busby's dreams for the Babes – the Treble – was made flesh by Ferguson and his home-grown sprinkling in 1999. The European title was secured on what Gary Neville called a 'supernatural' night in Barcelona, United scoring twice through the substitutes Teddy Sheringham and Ole Gunnar Solskjaer to defeat Bayern Munich in stoppage time. The date – 26 May – was not lost on Ferguson. As the jubilant United party boarded the coach outside Camp Nou, he turned to the security man Ned Kelly and said: 'Isn't it amazing that it would have been Sir Matt's 90th birthday today and we won the European Cup by scoring in the 90th minute?'

As Kelly nodded – for it was more or less true, even though the second goal might have been strictly timed at 92 or 93 – Ferguson looked upwards and said: 'Thank you, Sir Matt.' Before long, he was Sir Alex. Martin Edwards was asked whether he would have a role at Old Trafford after he eventually relinquished management and the chairman's reply – 'Well, we don't want a Matt Busby situation ...' – displeased Ferguson, though he rendered the question academic by staying to provide more and more success at home and abroad until a retirement of his own choosing in 2013. Furthermore he left David Moyes a healthier situation than McGuinness had faced in 1969.

Had Busby lived to see the concluding drama of 1998/99, he might have encountered mixed feelings, for this European glory was what his lost boys had been brought up for. While sitting for Harold Riley in 1987, he had been asked many questions on a wide range of subjects, the last being: 'Is there anything you regret?'

He replied: 'Harold, I wish I had seen these boys become men and go on to be a mature team. Just that. Nothing else.'

Busby had become a European champion with another team, and three years afterwards, been asked by Eamonn Andrews to tell the nation how it felt when the final whistle had blown at Wembley ten years after Munich. On this occasion he was unequivocal. 'I never felt better in my life, Eamonn,' he said. 'I'd been searching for this. This was the ambition and, when it arrived, I thought, well ...' If the words that came into his mind at that point were '... I can die happy now', he thought again and, with characteristic precision, opted for '... this ... is ... the thing I wanted all my life.'

At that time of ultimate fulfilment when Busby sang the Louis Armstrong classic, it was not such a wonderful world for James Thain. Nor had the intervening decade been kind to the surviving Munich pilot. For Thain, there remained little sign of partial redemption, let alone the glorious vindication Busby had earned.

After losing his job, Thain had pushed on with the poultry farming but found it less than profitable. Instead of joining him in the venture, his wife had been obliged to remain a teacher in order to balance the family books. Yet he had fought on to clear his name, refusing to accept that ice on the wings had caused the accident. Only to encounter more setbacks. Even after an American investigation into a near-crash which identified the decelerating effects of slush, even after British officials had conducted similar tests with an Elizabethan and found the same, the Germans upheld their earlier verdict.

Because the airport director at Riem had been alerted that one of the flights that day might carry the Chancellor, Konrad Adenauer, precautions had been taken, including two inspections of the slush by an airport vehicle. But slush was not considered a big problem then; the BEA manual didn't say much about it. One factor may have been that it was more disturbed on the first two-thirds of the runway, which had taken most of the traffic, while at the far end, where the United plane lost speed and crashed, it lay under pristine snow.

But what more could Thain do? With the help of the British Airline Pilots' Association, he made one last tilt at justice and this time it would succeed. In June 1969, it was announced in the House of Commons that he had been cleared of responsibility. But his flying licence had long expired. His struggling business had been sold and he was dabbling in property development when he died of a heart attack in August 1975.

Shortly before this, interviewed by the author John Roberts, he was able to put his courageous campaign in context. 'If I had died at Munich,' he said, 'there is no doubt in my mind that it would have been accepted that the crash had been caused by ice on the wings and the dangers of the slush hazard would not have been realised so soon. How many more people might have lost their lives if I had not been able to battle on?'

Thain was only 54. Busby's life was to run, by his own acceptance, its full course. By 1994, a lot of his old football friends had died or faded away. Although he had not visited Jimmy Murphy in hospital before the Welshman's end came in 1989, it was only a year since he had lost Jean; perhaps he would have felt unwelcome, perhaps he lacked the strength or perhaps a bit of both constrained him. In 1990, Joe Mercer had died of Alzheimer's, the early stages of which had caused the 1992 retirement from the Liverpool board of Bob Paisley, who was to die in 1996 (Paisley, unlike Shankly, had been deemed suitable for directorial duty when he stepped out of management). At least Stan Cullis was to last until 2001.

Soon after Busby, the Munich survivor Johnny Berry had gone. Jackie Blanchflower died in poverty in 1998. To the great credit of Alex Ferguson, the manager represented United at his funeral. But it took place only a couple of weeks after a strangely half-baked and certainly belated match in aid of the Munich survivors that, because it was also billed as Eric Cantona's farewell to Old Trafford, raised £47,000 for each family. Cantona received £90,000, plus expenses for his extensive entourage. Dennis Viollet, too ill to attend, died in 1999 (after Merrett and Ramsden had somehow found club money to send to Florida to help his second wife, Helen, with expensive treatment for his brain tumour), Ray Wood in 2002, Albert Scanlon in 2009, Kenny Morgans in 2012 and Bill Foulkes in 2013.

In 2014, Sandy Busby died of a heart attack. He had been receiving treatment for prostate cancer but remained president of Northenden Golf Club, where his father had started playing when with City. A painting of them together was later unveiled in the bar. Sandy was laid to rest alongside his parents in Southern Cemetery, after a Requiem Mass conducted by Father McMahon at Our Lady and St John's. In 2015, Sheena's coffin made the same short journey.

Also that year, 214 Kings Road was for sale at 'offers in the region of £375,000'.

Bobby Charlton had been knighted a few months after Busby's death. By early 2017, when Wayne Rooney broke his club scoring record with a 250th goal, only Charlton, still a regular attender at Old Trafford with his wife Norma, and the hero Harry Gregg survived of the Munich players. The stewardess Rosemary Cheverton lived on, under her married name Blakeney, in Florida. Bato Tomašević, though not in the best of health, was still with his beloved Madge in the West Country.

Around Bellshill, the landscape had changed, but the boy born to Alex and Nellie Busby more than a century earlier was commemorated by Busby Road. Nearby was the golf club where he had caddied, its 17th hole named Babylon after the bridge, still standing. In the town centre, the Sir Matt Busby Sports Complex offered swimming, a gym and a 3G football pitch. There was an Orbiston Road but no Orbiston as the Busbys knew it. Some locals reckoned the rows into which Matt was born had been where the Orb pub stood. Others pointed half a mile to the south.

The mining industry had gone and the Dalzell steel works, the last in Scotland, been mothballed in 2015. But there was a country park and the Dalzell estate accommodated an RSPB nature reserve. Still thriving were the Catholic churches in which Busby's parents and later Matt and Jean had been married. The Church of Scotland had opened the Orbiston Neighbourhood Centre in 1995 'to bring together the people of Orbiston and Bellshill to combat poverty, isolation and intolerance'. The Central Lanarkshire Mosque in Mossend had been similarly pledged, since 2005, to cater for Muslims and non-Muslims alike.

The richness of the football tradition established by Alex James, Hughie Gallacher and Busby had been maintained by Jock Stein and the Arsenal manager George Graham, each born within a few miles of Bellshill, by Billy McNeill and John Clark of Celtic and Ally McCoist of Rangers, by Brian McClair both at Celtic and Manchester United, where he encountered Busby, and a host of others including Malky Mackay and Alex Neil. Not to mention the Labour politician John Reid, who had served as chairman of Celtic.

The area had even produced an England cricket captain in Mike Denness, and the singers Sharleen Spiteri, of the band Texas, and Sheena Easton. But Busby had his own road. And a file in the local library. Nor did he ever forget where he came from. But nowhere was he better commemorated than in the great conurbation to which he went, initially at the behest of Manchester City. There was no plaque attached to 214 Kings Road, Chorlton-cum-Hardy, or any of his other addresses. Although at Old Trafford there was a statue facing Sir Matt Busby Way, some believed his memory should have been honoured more fully by the renaming of the stadium. It was the voice of the Manchester United crowd that proclaimed his immortality. By singing the calypso their parents had carried to Wembley in the 1950s ...

> *Take a lesson you will see*
> *Football taught by Matt Busby.*

Not only that. Of United's 20 League titles, 13 were won under Alex Ferguson and the chant – '*Every one of us loves Alex Ferguson, loves Alex Ferguson, loves Alex Ferguson*' left no room for doubt. And yet ...

> *Twenty times twenty times Man United*
> *Twenty times twenty times I say*
> *Twenty times twenty times Man United*
> *Playing football the Matt Busby way!*

And ...

> *For ever and ever*
> *We'll follow the boys*
> *Of Man United*
> *The Busby Babes*

Nearly 60 years after Munich, with José Mourinho the ninth manager since Busby, his name still described the club's soul as no other. Paul Scholes, one of United's most revered players of the Ferguson era, was 19 when Busby died. But had clearly got to know the old man and understood the permanence of his idea of football. For Scholes, one March evening in 2016, was working as a television analyst at Anfield, where a shambolic United display seemed to encapsulate the partial paralysis that was often their style of play in the time of Louis van Gaal, and Scholes seethed and seethed until finally he exclaimed: '*Just go out and play!*' The legacy of Busby would never die.

BIBLIOGRAPHY

Adamson, R., *Bogotá Bandit: The Outlaw Life of Charlie Mitten* (Mainstream, 2005)

Alexander, E., *Please May I Have My Football Back?* (Know the Score, 2009)

Arthur, M., *The Busby Babes* (Mainstream, 1998)

Barclay, P., *Football – Bloody Hell!* (Yellow Jersey, 2010)

Barclay, P., *The Life and Times of Herbert Chapman* (Weidenfeld & Nicolson, 2013)

Brown, J., *The Matt Busby Chronicles* (Desert Island Football Histories, 2004)

Busby, M., *My Story* (Souvenir, 1957)

Busby, M., *Soccer at the Top* (Weidenfeld & Nicolson, 1973)

Cavanagh, R., *The Unfulfilled Dream* (CreateSpace Independent Publishing Platform, 2014)

Charlton, Sir B., *My Manchester United Years* (Headline, 2008)

Connor, J., *The Lost Babes* (Harper, 2010)

Crick, M. and Smith, D., *Betrayal of a Legend* (Pan, 1990)

Crooks, R., *Grandad – What Was Football Like in the 1960s?* (DB Publishing, 2015)

Davies, C., *United in Europe* (Pitch, 2015)

Devine, T.M., *The Scottish Nation* (Penguin, 2012)

Dewhurst, K., *When You Put on a Red Shirt* (Yellow Jersey, 2010)

Doherty, J. with Ponting, I., *The Insider's Guide to Manchester United* (Empire, 2005)

Dunphy, E., *Only a Game?* (Penguin, 1987)

Dunphy, E., *A Strange Kind of Glory* (Aurum, 2007)

Dykes, G., *The United Alphabet* (ACL and Polar Publishing, 1994)

Ferguson, A., *Managing My Life* (Hodder & Stoughton, 1999)

Ferguson, A., *My Autobiography* (Hodder & Stoughton, 2013)

Ferguson, A. with Moritz, M., *Leading* (Hodder & Stoughton, 2015)

Fisher, J., *Old Bellshill* (Motherwell Leisure, 1995)

Frank, S., *Standing on the Shoulders of Giants* (Bloomsbury, 2013)

From Malta to Wembley (Manchester United Supporters' Club Malta, 2014)

Giles, J., *John Giles: A Football Man* (Hachette, 2010)

Glanvill, R., *Sir Matt Busby, A Tribute* (Virgin, 1994)

Glanville, B., *Football Memories* (Virgin, 1999)

Goldblatt, D., *The Ball Is Round* (Viking, 2006)

Gregg, H., *Harry's Game* (Mainstream, 2002)

Hall, D., *Manchester's Finest* (Corgi, 2008)

Hamilton, D., *Immortal* (Century, 2013)

Harding, J., *For the Good of the Game* (Robson, 1991)

Hawkey, I., *Di Stefano* (Ebury, 2016)

Henderson, J., *The Wizard* (Yellow Jersey, 2014)

Holden, J., *Stan Cullis* (Breedon Books, 2005)

Hopcraft, A., *The Football Man* (Sportspages, 1988)

Inglis, S., *The Football Grounds of Great Britain* (Willow, 1987)

Inglis, S., *League Football and the Men Who Made It* (Collins Willow, 1988)

Izbicki, J., *Life Between the Lines* (Umbria Press, 2012)

Jackson, P., *Triumph and Tragedy* (Mainstream, 1912)

Kelly, N., *Manchester United: The Untold Story* (Michael O'Mara, 2003)

Lamming, D., *An English Football Internationalists' Who's Who* (Hutton Press, 1990)

Law, D., *Denis Law: An Autobiography* (Queen Anne, 1979)

Liversedge, S., *Busby: Epitaph to a Legend* (Soccer Book Publishing, 1994)

Liversedge, S. and Paisley, B., *Liverpool: The Official Centenary History* (Hamlyn, 1991)

Ludden, J., *A Tale of Two Cities* (Empire, 2012)

Lyttleton, B., *Match of My Life: European Cup Finals* (Know the Score, 2006)

McCartney, I., *Building the Dynasty* (Pitch, 2015)

McCartney, I. and Cavanagh, R., *Duncan Edwards* (Temple Nostalgia Press, 1988)

McIlvanney, H., *McIlvanney on Football* (Mainstream, 1999)

McMenemy, L., *A Lifetime's Obsession* (Trinity Mirror Sport Media, 2013)

Meek, D., *Manchester United Greats* (Sportsprint, 1989)

Meek, D., *Red Devils in Europe* (Hutchinson Radius, 1988)

Midwinter, E., *Parish to Planet* (Know the Score, 2007)

Miller, D., *Father of Football* (Pavilion, 1994)

Miller, D., *Stanley Matthews* (Pavilion, 1989)

Morrin, S.R., *The Munich Disaster* (Gill and Macmillan, 2007)

Morse, G., *Walter Winterbottom* (John Blake Publishing, 2013)

Moynihan, J., *The Soccer Syndrome: English Football's Golden Age* (Floodlit Dreams Ltd, 2015)

Murphy, J., *Matt, United and Me* (Souvenir, 1968)

O'Farrell, F., *All Change at Old Trafford* (Backpass, 2011)

Oliver, G., *The Guinness Book of World Soccer* (Guinness, 1995)

Parkinson, M., *Michael Parkinson on Football* (Hodder Paperbacks, 2002)

Pawson, T., *The Football Managers* (Eyre Methuen, 1973)

Powley, A. and Gillan, R., *Shankly's Village* (Pitch, 2015)

Quelch, D., *Never Had It So Good* (Pitch, 2009)

Roberts, J., *Sod This, I'm Off to Marbella* (Sport Media, 2010)

Roberts, J., *The Team that Wouldn't Die* (Aurum, 2008)

Robson, B., *Farewell But Not Goodbye* (Hodder & Stoughton, 2005)

Rogan, J., *The Football Managers* (Macdonald Queen Anne, 1989)

Rollin, J., *Soccer in the 1930s* (Soccer Data, 2015)

Rowlands, A., *Trautmann: The Biography* (DB Publishing, 2012)

Rowlinson, J., *Boys of 66* (Virgin, 2016)

Shaw, P. *The Book of Football Quotations* (Ebury, 2014)

Shindler, C., *George Best and 21 Others* (Headline, 2004)

Skinner, R., *The Busby Babes* (Urbane, 2016)

Smout, T.C., *A Century of the Scottish People* (Fontana, 2010)

Taylor, F., *The Day a Team Died* (Souvenir, 2012)

Taylor, R. and Jamrich, K. (eds), *Puskas on Puskas* (Robson Books, 1997)

Walsh, P., *Gang War* (Milo Books, 2005)

Whelan, T., *The Birth of the Babes* (Empire, 2005)

White, J., *Manchester United: The Biography* (Sphere, 2008)

Wilson, J., *Angels with Dirty Faces* (Orion, 2016)

Wilson, J., *Inverting the Pyramid* (Orion, 2014)

Young, P.M., *Manchester United* (Sportsmans Book Club, 1962)

ACKNOWLEDGEMENTS

Thanks are due, for their help, enlightenment and good company, to Ray Adler, Arthur Albiston, Eric Alexander, John Aston, Jan and James Barkatullah, Terry Beckett, Richard Bott, Alison Busby, Irene Busby and Mike Bones, Katy Buchan, Cliff Butler, Sir Bobby Charlton and James Lawton, Patrick Collins, Andrew Crabtree, Paddy Crerand, Harry Curran, Keith Dewhurst, Martin Edwards, Sir Alex Ferguson (for an interview given some months before Sir Matt's death), Barry Fry, John Giles, Alan Gilzean, Alan Gowling, Harry Gregg, Bernard Halford, Ian Hawkey, Barry Hayes, Jim and Kit Holden, Frank Holt, Denis Law, Angus Loughran, Wilf and Beryl McGuinness, Sammy McIlroy, Hugh McIlvanney, Father Patrick McMahon, Stuart Mathieson, David Meek, Ken Merrett, Oliver Norgrove, David Pleat, Ian Preece, Ken Ramsden and Joan Taylor, Harold Riley, John Roberts, Tony Rocca, Jimmy Ryan, David Sadler, Phil Shaw, Alex Stepney, Ian and Carol Storey-Moore, Gordon Taylor, Bato and Madge Tomašević, Phil Townsend, Ian Ure, Alan Wardle, Jeff and Nell Whitefoot and Ray Wilkins.

Inspiration came from the Mancunian Artist, whose work adorns the Circus Tavern in Portland Street, Manchester, and from the authors of so many excellent books pertaining to the life of Sir Matt; it was an especial joy to revisit the works of Eamon Dunphy, John Roberts, Keith Dewhurst, Michael Crick and the late Donny Davies. I am grateful, as ever, to David Luxton, Rebecca Winfield and Nick Walters, of David Luxton Associates, for support and friendship. And, by no means least, to Andrew Goodfellow and Laura Horsley, of Ebury Press, for so expertly and sensitively helping to shape the book, and Howard Watson, for his admirably detailed editing of a labour of love.

Patrick Barclay
London
August 2017

INDEX